Official Catholic Teachings

love & sexuality

love & sexuality

Odile M. Liebard

A Consortium Book

from McGrath Publishing Company
Wilmington, North Carolina 1978

Library of Congress Card Catalog Number: 78-53843
ISBN: 0-8434-0713-1
ISBN: 0-8434-07190-0 paper

The publisher gratefully acknowledges permission to quote from the
following copyrighted publications.

AMERICAN PRESS
   *GAUDIUM ET SPES; SECOND VATICAN COUNCIL MESSAGE
   TO WOMEN*, "Documents of Vatican II" ©1966.

AMERICAN CATHOLIC QUARTERLY REVIEW
   ARCANUM DIVINAE SAPIENTIAE, © 1880 Burns and Oates, Ltd.
   *PAPAL COMMISSION ON BIRTH CONTROL: PASTORAL AP-
   PROACHES*, "On Human Life", ©1968.

DAUGHTERS OF SAINT PAUL
   *ADDRESS OF POPE PIUS XII TO ITALIAN MEDICAL-BIOLOGI-
   CAL UNION OF ST. LUKE*, "The Human Body", © 1960.
   ADDRESS OF POPE PIUS XII TO MIDWIVES, "The Human Body",
   © 1960.
   *ADDRESS OF POPE PIUS XII TO THE ASSOCIATION OF LARGE
   FAMILIES*, "Matrimony", ©1963.
   *ADDRESS OF POPE PIUS XII TO THE DELEGATES AT THE
   FOURTH INTERNATIONAL CONGRESS OF CATHOLIC
   DOCTORS*, "The Human Body", ©1960.
   *ADDRESS OF POPE PIUS XII TO THE XXVI CONGRESS OF
   UROLOGY*, "Matrimony", ©1963.
   *THE ORDER OF THE PURPOSES OF MATRIMONY: EXTRACTS
   FROM A SENTENCE OF THE HOLY ROMAN ROTA*, "Matri-
   mony", ©1963.

L'OSSERVATORE ROMANO
   DECLARATION OF THE BELGIAN BISHOPS ON ABORTION:
   English edition   June 14, 1973 as quoted in "Yes to Life",
   Daughters of St. Paul.

OUR SUNDAY VISITOR
   *ADDRESS OF POPE JOHN XXIII TO SEVERAL ITALIAN WOM-
   EN'S ASSOCIATIONS*, "The Pope Speaks", Volume 7, Number
   4, ©1961.
   *ADDRESS OF POPE JOHN XXIII TO THE ITALIAN CENTER
   FOR WOMEN*, "The Pope Speaks," Volume 7, Number 2,
   © 1961.

ADDRESS OF POPE JOHN XXIII TO THE SACRED ROMAN ROTA, "The Pope Speaks", Volume 6, Number 4, © 1960.

ADDRESS OF POPE PAUL VI TO A GENERAL AUDIENCE, JULY 31, 1968, "The Pope Speaks", Volume 13, Number 3, © 1968.

ADDRESS OF POPE PAUL VI TO PARTICIPANTS IN THE 13TH NATIONAL CONGRESS OF THE ITALIAN WOMEN'S CENTER, "The Pope Speaks", Volume 11, Number 1, © 1966.

ADDRESS OF POPE PAUL VI TO THE COMMITTEE FOR THE INTERNATIONAL WOMEN'S YEAR, "The Pope Speaks", Volume 20, Number 1, © 1975.

ADDRESS OF POPE PAUL VI TO THE CONGRESS OF THE ITALIAN WOMENS CENTER, "The Pope Speaks" Volume 22, Number 1, © 1977.

ADDRESS OF POPE PAUL VI TO THE CONVENTION OF THE UNION OF ITALIAN CATHOLIC JURISTS, "The Pope Speaks", Volume 19, Number 4, © 1975.

ADDRESS OF POPE PAUL VI TO THE SACRED ROMAN ROTA, "The Pope Speaks", Volume 21, Number 2, ©1976.

ADDRESS OF POPE PAUL VI TO THE SOCIETY OF ITALIAN CATHOLIC JURISTS, "The Pope Speaks", Volume 17, Number 4, ©1973.

ADDRESS OF POPE PAUL VI TO THE SPECIAL PAPAL COMMISSION EXAMINING THE PROBLEMS OF POPULATION GROWTH, FAMILY PLANNING, AND BIRTH REGULATION, "The Pope Speaks", Volume 10, Number 3, ©1965.

ADDRESS OF POPE PAUL VI TO THE STUDY COMMISSION ON WOMEN, "The Pope Speaks", Volume 21, Number 2, © 1976.

ADDRESS OF POPE PAUL VI TO THE TEAMS OF OUR LADY, "The Pope Speaks", Volume 15, Number 2, © 1970.

ADDRESS OF POPE PIUS XII TO A GROUP OF CATHOLIC OBSTETRICIANS AND GYNECOLOGISTS, "The Pope Speaks", Volume 3, Number 1, © 1956.

ADDRESS OF POPE PIUS XII TO A PILGRIMAGE SPONSORED BY THE FEDERATION OF ITALIAN WOMEN, "The Pope Speaks", Volume 3, Number 4, ©1956.

ADDRESS OF POPE PIUS XII TO THE DIRECTORS OF THE ASSOCIATION FOR LARGE FAMILIES OF ROME AND ITALY, "The Pope Speaks", Volume 4, Number 4, ©1958.

ADDRESS OF POPE PIUS XII TO THE 14TH CONGRESS OF THE WORLD UNION OF CATHOLIC WOMEN'S ORGANIZATIONS, "The Pope Speaks", Volume 4, Number 4, ©1958.

ADDRESS OF POPE PIUS XII TO MEMBERS OF THE YOUNG WOMEN'S SECTION OF ITALIAN CATHOLIC ACTION, "The Pope Speaks", Volume 5, Number 1, ©1958.

ADDRESS OF POPE PIUS XII TO THE SECOND WORLD CONGRESS ON FERTILITY AND STERILITY, "The Pope Speaks", Volume 3, Number 2, ©1956.

*ADDRESS OF POPE PIUS XII TO THE SEVENTH INTERNA-
TIONAL HEMATOLOGICAL CONGRESS IN ROME*, "The Pope
Speaks", Volume 6, Number 4, ©1960.

*ADDRESS OF POPE PIUS XII TO THE WORLD UNION OF FAM-
ILY ORGANIZATIONS*, "The Pope Speaks", Volume 4, Number
3, ©1958.

*DECLARATION ON ABORTION ISSUED BY THE SACRED CON-
GREGATION FOR THE DOCTRINE OF THE FAITH*, "The
Pope Speaks", Volume 19, Number 3, ©1975.

EXPLOSION OR BACKFIRE? "Pastoral Letter of the American
Hierarchy", ©1971.

NATIONAL CATHOLIC REPORTER

*THE THEOLOGICAL REPORT OF THE PAPAL COMMISSION
ON BIRTH CONTROL* as reprinted in "Our Human Life",
Burns and Oates, ©1968.

UNITED STATES CATHOLIC CONFERENCE

CASTI CONNUBII, ©1931; *DECLARATION ON CERTAIN QUES-
TIONS CONCERNING SEXUAL ETHICS ISSUED BY THE
SACRED CONGREGATION FOR THE DOCTRINE OF THE
FAITH*, 1975, *HUMAN LIFE IN OUR DAY*, ©1968; *HUMANE
VITAE*, 1968; *SACRA VIRGINITIS*, 1954; *SACERDOTALIS
CAELIBATUS*, 1967; *TO LIVE IN CHRIST JESUS*, ©1976.

Table of Contents

Introduction

Sexuality — A Contemporary Question

Contemporary man may suitably be described as a being-in-turmoil. The child of two devastating world wars, which revealed the capacity of the human to set aside all morality and to pull down centuries—old structures which appeared to be eternal and unshakeable, he roams through the latter third of the twentieth century wondering who he is, and why. He is no longer certain of himself and does what any uncertain child will do—simply shouts that he is free, that he can do as he pleases, that he is avant garde, that he has rights. Hidden somewhere in the child is a lonesomeness, a sense of alienation, and often a timid hope that someone will come to show a way into human maturity.

Sexuality, as a theme, brings out this contemporary mood, perhaps more adequately than most themes.

Modern Western society, most notably since the end of World War II, has oriented an incredible amount of its human energy to the quest for sexual maturity. Sexual freedom has become a commonplace term. Exactly what it means is not clear but it is often indicative of the user's need to justify, rationalize or explain whatever he wants to do. Traditional modes of sexual relationships have been publicly challenged. Homosexuality, through the organization of the gay rights movement, has been presented as an authentic life style. Literature once automatically banned as pornographic is now readily available at newsstands. Theatre, cinema, and art have all turned their attention to the questions of human sexuality.

Somewhere in this process the illusion has developed that contemporary man finally is sexually free, has at last overcome the taboos and fears that for centuries surrounded the realm of sexuality. An illusion, because at the same time it is impossible for a reflective person not to notice the sexual ignorance and sexual immaturity that, as a fact, dominates our present society. The incapacity to enter or to sustain long term relationships, the tendency to identify sexuality with the simple act of sex, the naive assumption that simply because one is a man or a woman one knows all about sex are strong indicators of the present level of ignorance and immaturity.

The child that is contemporary man still has much growing to do before achieving sexual maturity. Here we can only suggest several of the elements which are essential to achieving such maturity.

A society's capacity for sexual maturity is proportionate to, guided by and controlled by the society's view of the nature of the human condition. An impoverished view necessarily produces a sexually poor people. Thus, if the human is looked upon as a machine or a thing, it is inevitable that sexuality will be identified with physical activity, that woman will end up as the plaything of man, that sex will be a means to get what one wants. Again, if the human is seen as predominantly spirit, sexuality will be treated as a human weakness, a source of evil, an obstacle to true human freedom. In neither instance can sexuality contribute to human enrichment, simply because the grounding view of the human is already a poor one.

Sexuality, like the human in which it is grounded, must be viewed as process. To consider it as static, as a mere fact of existence, is to render it sterile. A magnificent manifestation of the human condition, it must be allowed the maximum amount of freedom and flexibility in its development. That it is a way of becoming human must be emphasized over and over.

A mature understanding of sexuality can be developed only in an atmosphere of true dialogue, an atmosphere that actually grants all expressions of sexuality a thorough hearing without any prejudgment as to good or bad, right or wrong. If a given expression is judged in advance of a full explanation and hearing, neither speaker nor listener can adequately grasp the dimensions of sexuality. As a result, the human growth process will be hampered.

A contemporary theory of sexuality must be sophisticated enough to meet the demands of life in the actual world. The pressures of cosmopolitan and international life styles have shaped a human being unknown to earlier centuries. Sciences such as psychology and sociology have developed insights on the human that have yet to be considered in developing a theory of sexuality. Questions such as environment, inflation, nuclear power, communications, industry, education, employment, equality of sex and race all have an impact on sexuality. It is no longer possible to develop a statement on human sexuality in the abstract.

Role of the Christian Tradition

Christianity has always recognized the integral role that the theme of sexuality plays in human history and more specifically in salvation history. In its effort to serve mankind, it is committed to developing a theory of sexuality, that will both support and guide the Christian in time.

For the past hundred years, members of Roman Catholicism have been directed, in their search for an understanding of sexuality, mainly by papal encyclicals and speeches.

There is no doubt that at present the best known papal document on sexuality is that of Pope Paul VI, *Humanae Vitae*. Exactly what effects the document has had in shaping the lives of millions of Catholics throughout the world will never really be known. It clearly split Catholics into groups either for or against the teaching of the document. Questions far beyond that of sex were raised for the Catholic World: Is there and/or can there be a single contemporary Catholic position on sexuality? What is the role of authority (papal, conciliar, episcopal) in matters that really concern the everyday life of the millions of believers whose world seems so distant to that of popes and bishops? Must the Catholic teachings on family, love, prayer, obedience, tradition undergo yet another revolution? What is required of the Catholic Church in order to remain or become radically relevant to the twentieth century? What is the Catholic view of the human condition and how good a view is it?

These questions demand the serious reflection and response of the entire Christian community, Catholic included. And should anyone assume that the answers have already been worked out and need merely be applied, the end result will be a double condemnation—of irrelevance for the institution and its leaders, of more lonesomeness and alienation coupled with less hope for the children of God.

Purpose of Present Volume

Recognizing the immensity of the task at hand, I and several other interested Christians, saw the importance of developing adequate tools for the undertaking. This particular volume has gathered together all of the significant papal documentation on the theme of sexuality from the reign of Pope Leo XIII to that of Pope Paul VI. It is intended to be an instrument at the disposal of the English reading world as it carries out its share of the task of constructing an effective, mature, suitable, contemporary view of sexuality.

There is a total of 42 documents, drawn from the writings of five popes, the second Vatican Council, the Roman Rota, the Sacred Congregation for the Doctrine of Faith, the American hierarchy and the Belgian hierarchy. Twenty-two of the documents predate Vatican II's *Gaudium et Spes*, the Pastoral Constitution on the Church in the Modern World. Nineteen documents cover the period from *Gaudium et Spes* in 1965 to 1976.

As might be expected, the documents offer a Catholic teaching on sexuality in general as well as a position on specific questions.

More often than not, the popes developed their encyclicals and addresses in response to the problems of their times. The fact that their reflection and theologizing was provoked and stimulated by what they interpreted as the moral breakdown of a society, infidelity between husbands and wives, or insufficient dedication to the celibate life of chastity necessarily colors their handling of the theme of human sexuality. When negation and apprehension are the point of departure, the end result will be somewhat less than enriching. This fact must be kept in view when studying the documents in this volume. Otherwise, one could draw the conclusion that Catholic teaching is, of itself, negative and limiting, or that the authors of the documents were far removed from everyday reality while doing their writing. Either conclusion could be overly harsh.

Pope Leo XIII wrote *Arcanum divinae sapientiae* in 1880. In many ways, it set the tone for papal teaching on sexuality which continues through to Pope Paul VI's *Humanae Vitae* in 1968. Pope Leo's encyclical is on Christian marriage.

The traditional Christian interpretation of marriage is integral to the document. The true origin of marriage of God's creation of man and woman, the basic properties established for marriage by God are unity and indissolubility, Christ declared and openly confirmed this doctrine. Furthermore, Christ, who restored human dignity and perfected Mosaic law, ennobled the institution of marriage by his presence at the wedding in Cana and conferred a new holiness on marriage. By condemning the customs of the Jews in their abuse of the plurality of wives and of the power of giving bills of divorce, as well as by commanding that no one should dare to dissolve a union established by God, he brought back matrimony to the nobility of its primeval origin. He raised marriage to the dignity of a sacrament, holy, pure, and to be reverenced as a type and symbol of most high mysteries. Its new purpose is to bring forth children for the Church.

Though present, the positive statement on matrimony does not dominate the encyclical. Rather it gives precedence to the problematic and negative. Leo wrote in response to what were clearly major breakdowns in the society of his time. The right to legislate concerning marriage and even to perform the marriage ceremony was claimed for and by civil authorities. Divorce as a resolution of marital problems was becoming more and more common. The concepts of submission and obedience were no longer respected.

Ever faithful to his role as teacher and pastor, Leo set out to expose the breakdown, to re-educate Christians to the true nature of marriage, to guide families back to original commitments, and to denounce the causes of the problems confronting the Christian. To do this, he used a terminology that is competitive, critical and condemnatory. In the context of the times this is understandable. The enemy heathen is seen as bringing about an age of corruption and shameful lust. Christianity is locked into a struggle with the modern age. Much of the evils of the time are due to the encroaching civil order, which allows civil marriage and divorce.

Obviously, if this is the basic interpretation of the world in which the Christian dwells, the concerned teacher and pastor must expose the hidden enemy and warn his flock against all the pitfalls and dangers that await it. This calls for a clarification of purpose and a reminder of rights and duties. Thus, after reviewing the primary and secondary purposes of marriage, the pontiff reminds husband/father, wife/mother, and children of their respective rights and duties. This, coupled with the tension between the civil and ecclesial orders, fosters a terminology that is legal, minimal, and negative in tone.

The average Christian is not going to orient the time and energy toward study and reflection that is required to develop a theory of marriage. Nor will he be prepared to critique the social processes of his times and evaluate the strengths and weaknesses of what are presented as modern ideas. It is only natural to look to leaders for guidance and insight. What the leaders have to say will eventually set the pace and become the structure within which the Christian community will try to live out its life. The encyclical *Arcanum divinae sapientiae* offered many fine insights into the Christian mystery of marriage, but it laid the foundations for a structure that is predominantly legalistic and negative.

The refinement in the twentieth century of the nature of matrimony and of any other area of human sexuality was carried out within this structure. Matrimony became an area of concern for the canon lawyer. Moral theology tended to treat marriage and sexuality within the confines of "thou shalt not commit adultery." The Christian faithful became a people burdened with the evils of a carefree and reckless modern world and tried to resist by living up to what God demanded of them and revealed to them through legislation and discipline. The beauty, the joy, the spontaneity, the creative mystery that is human sexuality seemed to recede into the background. The fulfillment of duty became the order of the day.

Between Pope Leo's encyclical of 1880 and Pope Pius XI's encyclical, *Casti Connubii* in 1930, the world experienced its greatest and most violent upheaval to date, the first World War. As early as 1922, the first year of his pontificate, Pius XI voiced his distress at how the war poisoned the very roots of human society, had eroded the family structure, by taking fathers and sons away from their homes. The war destroyed respect for paternal authority, set masters and servants against one another as adversaries, encouraged violation of the conjugal bond.

Pius XI wrote *Casti Connubii* on the fiftieth anniversary of Leo's *Arcanum*. The world picture had gotten worse. Saddened by what he saw, "many unmindful of this divine work of renewal, who are totally ignorant of the sanctity of marriage, who impudently deny it, who even allow themselves to be led by the principles of a modern and perverse ethical doctrine to repudiate it with scorn," Pius endorsed and confirmed the teaching of his predecessor. He gives fuller treatment to the positive aspects of marriage than did Leo and then attacks the errors and sins contrary to matrimony. Contending that the nature and laws of matrimony are totally the work of God, he declares erroneous the theory that would attribute the institution to man. Thus he condemns the use of the power of generation outside of wedlock, temporary marriage, experimental marriage, and companionate marriage as "abominable corruptions which would result even in civilized nations adopting the barbarous customs of certain savage tribes." Contraception and abortion, though the terms are not used, are condemned as very serious crimes. The modern emancipation of woman is rejected. Divorce is seen as the major obstacle to the renovation and rehabilitation of marriage.

The encyclicals of Leo XIII and Pius XI established the framework and point of reference for future discussion of the theme of sexuality. Marriage is the key word. A person either is married or is not married. Only the married person has any right to a sex life. Any sexual activity outside the marriage bond (premarital and extramarital) and even some within is automatically sinful. The sole option for the single person is chastity which, given the narrowness of the framework, becomes basically a negative virtue, the avoidance of unlawful sexual activity.

Actually the richness of the theme of human sexuality was never adequately addressed in these two encyclicals. It is because of this absence of thematic development that marriage and sexuality became almost synonymous, with the resultant impoverishment of both. Catholic thought in this area was not prepared to cope with the rapid social changes of the 1940's, 1950's and 1960's. With each decade, the Catholic viewpoint moved further away from dialogue with the contemporary world. The already difficult task of fidelity on the part of the Catholic individual became an impossible one. Sex was looked upon as a vast, consuming problem, rather than as a vehicle for expressing the mystery of the human person. When issues were raised, such as the population explosion, women's liberation, adolescent liberation, contemporary psychological studies of human stress and emotion, scientific research concerning human life, expansion of the labor market to include large numbers of women, increased world travel, and leisure, they were responded to in relation to marriage. More often than not, the response was negative and unrealistic. It was inevitable that communication between church leaders and the average Catholic (the adolescent, the young single man or

woman, the married couple, the divorcee, the widow or wid-
ower, etc.) broke down.

The Second Vatican Council relieved the tension. Pope John
XXIII was one of the few people in Christendom who sensed
the depths of human frustration underlying the contemporary
world. Realizing the terrible dimensions of the task of restoring world views, he nevertheless called together the religious
leaders of the world and asked them to join him in leading
mankind toward a new day. The historical process of Vatican
II and the documents produced by the Council offer hope for
the Christian who wants the freedom to remove the obstacles
to human growth and to build a new, richer and more positive
view of the human person.

Gaudium et Spes, the Council's Pastoral Constitution on
the Church in the modern world, carries a tone quite different
from the encyclicals already discussed. It reveals a sensitivity
for "the joys and the hopes, the griefs and the anxieties of
the men of this age." For once, change is looked upon with
respect, as integral to the human condition and worthy of
profound dialogue, not as a problem. It suggests that many
human questions have not yet been answered and may never
be. It provides a statement on the human person that could be
a rich starting point for a new understanding of sexuality. Its
insight on man's incarnate condition recognizes the whole-
someness of matter which is the foundation for sexuality. The
document is positive and encouraging. The problematic approach is secondary.

Obviously the atmosphere and mentality of a century cannot be set aside in a day, nor can the documents of a Council
turn thought patterns around in a few years time. The task
of developing a radically positive and flexible theology of human sexuality has hardly begun. The Second Vatican Council
could do no more than open possible directions. Pope Paul VI,
with the encyclical *Humanae Vitae,* dealt a severe blow to the
hopes and expectations of millions of Catholics. This was due
mainly to the fact that he himself was and remained a child
of the spirit that dominated Christianity before the Council.
It is unfortunate that he was not more fully attuned to the

human condition and its needs, as reflected through the report of the Commission on birth control. There are other documents, however, originating in National Councils of bishops, which indicate that many church leaders really are in contact with their people and are struggling to incorporate the needs of their followers into their thinking.

Since the concept of teaching authority is expanding to involve more naturally not only popes, bishops and sacred congregations, but theological thinkers as well, there is reason to look toward the future optimistically. The Common Catechism is one good example of the direction that Church thought patterns are taking. With dedicated research, open and sincere dialogue, and creative use of insight based on both Church traditions and contemporary sciences, the Christian can realistically assume that a full, thorough, mature theology of sexuality will soon be available.

The documents contained in this volume have a key role to play. Several can serve as guides for the direction that our thinking can and should take. Others will serve as reminders of what happens when a mystery as profound as human sexuality is treated as a problem and is limited in scope to the legal aspects of marriage. In the role of reminder, they will carry out a kind of negative function, i.e., tell us what not to do. Properly studied and reflected upon, these documents can make an invaluable contribution to Christianity's process of realizing herself under the theme of human sexuality.

Subject Index

ABORTION 89–93, 348, 831, 991, 1078, 1099, 1121, 1328–1330, 1374–1384, 1395, 1397–1454, 1493, 1648–1650

ADOPTION 796–798, 813, 1409, 1557

ADULTERY 5, 58, 62, 67, 71, 99, 113–114, 423, 772, 776, 978, 1562

ARTIFICIAL INSEMINATION 246–257, 317–318, 507–508, 772–777

ASCETICISM 1206, 1552

BIRTH CONTROL 288, 354, 684, 687, 705, 826–838, 1113–1114, 1166, 1174, 1192–1201, 1212

CELIBACY 378, 392–393, 402, 409–410, 1129–1160, 1308, 1562

CHARITY 6, 56, 241, 390, 488, 642–643, 648, 1026, 1488, 1560–1561

CHASTITY 48–49, 56, 63, 82, 87, 104, 371, 445, 1031, 1056, 1063, 1145–1146, 1207, 1538, 1549–1550, 1552–1553, 1562–1565, 1569–1570

CHILDBIRTH 41, 238, 258–338, 348–352

CHILDBIRTH, PAINLESS 446–491

ARCANUM DIVINAE SAPIENTIAE
Encyclical Letter of Pope Leo XIII
on Christian Marriage
February 10, 1880

The hidden counsel of divine wisdom, which Jesus Christ, the Saviour of men, was to accomplish on earth, had for its purpose that He, through Himself and in Himself, should divinely restore the world which, so to speak, had grown old with age and decay. This much is expressed in that grand saying of St. Paul to the Ephesians, "The mystery of his will . . . to re-establish all things in Christ that are in heaven and on earth." And truly when Christ Our Lord set about fulfilling the commandment given Him by His Father, He forthwith imparted to all things a new form and beauty, banishing every trace of age and decay. For the wounds which the sin of our first parent had inflicted on human nature He himself healed; He brought back all men, by nature children of wrath, into favor with God; He led into the light of truth those who were wearied with long wanderings; He renewed to every virtue those who were worn out by every kind of impurity, and, restoring them to the inheritance of everlasting blessedness, he gave them a certain hope that their very body, mortal and frail as it was, should one day be partaker of immortality and heavenly glory. And that such wonderful blessings might endure on earth as long as men existed, He constituted the Church to carry on His work, and, looking forward to the future, commanded it to set in order whatever in human society might have become confused, and to restore whatever might have fallen to ruin.

2   But although this divine restoration, of which we have spoken, mainly and directly concerns men who are in the supernatural order of grace, nevertheless its precious and saving fruits have largely flowed into the natural order also; the result of which, not only to individuals, but to human society in general, has been no scanty measure of perfection in all respects. For the Christian order being once established, it became the happy lot of every man to learn and accustom himself to rest in the fatherly providence of God, and to cherish that hope of heavenly help which does not bring to confusion, from which follow fortitude, moderation, constancy, the equability of a mind at peace, and many great virtues and noble deeds. And to domestic and civil society also there has come a wonderful accession of dignity, stability, and honor. The authority of rulers has been made more just and more holy; the obedience of peoples readier and more easy, the tie between citizens closer; the rights of property more secure. The Christian religion has attended to and provided for everything of acknowledged utility in a state, so that, according to St. Augustine, it could not have contributed more to the welfare and happiness of existence if the good and advantage of our mortal life had been the sole end for which it came into being. We do not intend to enumerate all the instances of this; but we desire to speak of domestic life, of which the source and the foundation are in *matrimony*.

3   The origin of marriage, Venerable Brethren, is well known among all. For, although the revilers of the Christian faith are loath to acknowledge the constant teaching of the Church on this subject, and have been long endeavoring to obliterate the record of all nations and all ages, they have been unable to extinguish or weaken the strength and light of truth. We are speaking of what is known to all and doubtful to none. When on the sixth day of creation God formed man out of the slime of the earth, and breathed into his face the breath of life, it was His will to give him a companion, whom He brought forth wonderfully from the side of the man himself as he slept. And in this the design of God's providence was that this married pair should be the natural source of all mankind, and that from them the human race should be propa-

gated, and, by uninterrupted course of procreation, be preserved to all time. And the union of the man and the woman, in order more perfectly to correspond to the wise counsels of God, bore upon its face two especial properties, noble above all, and, as it were, deeply impressed and engraved, namely, unity and perpetuity. And we see this announced and openly confirmed in the Gospel by the divine authority of Jesus Christ, who declared to the Jews and to the Apostles that marriage from its very institution was to be between two only, the husband and the wife, that of two there was to be as it were one flesh; and that the nuptial bond was by the will of God so closely and strongly woven that it cannot be unloosed or broken by any among men. A man "shall cleave to his wife; and the two shall be in one flesh. Therefore now they are not two, but one flesh. What therefore God has joined together let no man put asunder." (Matt. xix 5, 6).

But this form of marriage, so excellent and admirable, began   4
by degrees to be corrupted and to die out among the heathen nations; and it seemed to be overclouded and darkened even in the Hebrew race. For among the latter common usage had sanctioned the possession by each man of more than one wife, and afterwards, when the indulgence of Moses had conceded "to the hardness of their hearts" (Matt. xix, 8) the power of repudiation, a door was opened to divorce. As to pagan society it is scarcely credible how marriage became corrupted and disfigured, exposed as it was to the flood of each people's errors and most shameful desires. Every nation, more or less, seems to have lost the idea and forgotten the true origin of marriage, and consequently laws were in many places enacted which seemed useful to the state rather than conformable to the requirements of nature. Solemn ceremonies, invented at the will of legislators, were the cause of the honorable name of wife, or the disgraceful name of concubine, being given to women; and the authority of the rulers of the state even took upon itself to decide who were and who were not to be allowed to marry, the laws being, to a great extent, contrary to equity, and resulting often in the commission of injustice. Moreover polygamy, polyandry, and divorce were the cause of a great relaxation of the nuptial tie. There was also a great

disturbance of the mutual rights and duties of married persons when the husband acquired dominion over the wife, and commanded her, often without just cause, to go her way, while he assumed to himself, in his propensity to unbridled and untamed lust, the license to "roam with impunity amongst women of servile condition or infamous life, as if the guilt of sin depended on rank and not on the will." (Hieronymi Ep. ad Oceanum. Oper., tom. i, col. 459). With this prevailing licentiousness on the part of husbands, nothing could be more wretched than the wife, who was reduced to such an abject condition that she was considered a mere instrument provided for the purpose of satisfying the passions or producing offspring. Nor was it thought shameful. to buy and sell marriageable girls like chattels (Arnob. *adv. gent.* 4); the power of inflicting capital punishment on the wife being sometimes given to the parent and the husband. The families which owed their existence to such marriages as these were necessarily either the property of the state or owned as slaves by the father of the family, to whom the laws gave the right, not only to conclude and dissolve their marriages at his will, but even to exercise over them the monstrous power of life and death.

5   But at length a relief and remedy were divinely provided for all the ignominious evils with which marriages had been defiled, for Jesus Christ, the restorer of human dignity, and the perfecter of the Mosaic laws, did not make the subject of matrimony His least or last care. He ennobled the nuptials of Cana of Galilee by His presence, and made them memorable by the performance of the first of His miracles; so that from that day dates the beginning of the new holiness which descended upon human marriage. Then He recalled matrimony to the nobility of its primeval origin, both by reproving the abuses introduced by the Jews as to both the plurality of wives and the privilege of repudiation, and by teaching them above all that no one might put asunder that which God had bound together by the chain of perpetual union. Therefore, after solving the difficulties adduced from the Mosaic institutes, assuming the part of a supreme lawgiver, He pronounced this decision in reference to married persons: "And

I say to you, that whosoever shall put away his wife, except
it be for fornication, and shall marry another, committeth
adultery; and he that shall marry her that is put away committeth adultery." (Matt. xix. 9).

But the Apostles, heralds of God's legislation, have more   6
fully and in greater detail delivered to memory and to writing
those things which have been decreed and established by
divine authority in regard to marriage. For to no other teaching
than of the Apostles must be referred what "our holy Fathers,
the Councils, and the tradition of the Universal Church have
always taught" (Trid. sess. xxiv., in pr.), namely, that Christ
Our Lord raised matrimony to the dignity of a sacrament;
that He at the same time ordained that married people,
guarded and protected by the celestial grace provided by His
merits, should derive holiness from marriage itself; and in it,
in a manner wonderfully resembling the mystical union
between Him and His Church, He perfected the love which
accords with nature (Trid. sess. xxiv., cap. 1, *de reform.
matr.*) and cemented the natural union of the man and woman
more firmly in the bonds of divine charity. "Husbands"
Paul says to the Ephesians, "love your wives as Christ also
loved the Church, and delivered Himself up for it, that He
might sanctify it . . . So also ought men to love their wives
as their own bodies, . . . for no man ever hated his own
flesh; but nourisheth and cherisheth it as also Christ does the
Church, because we are members of His body, of His flesh,
and of His bones. For this cause shall a man leave his father
and mother; and shall cleave to his wife, and they shall be
two in one flesh. This is a great sacrament, but I speak in
Christ and in the Church." (Ad. Ephes. v. 25 *et seq.*) And
in the same manner we learn from the teaching of the Apostles that Christ commanded that the union and perpetual
constancy which was required from the first commencement
of marriages should be held sacred and should not at any
time be violated. The same Paul says: "But to them that are
married, not I, but the Lord commandeth that the wife
depart not from her husband. And if she depart, that she
remain unmarried or be reconciled to her husband." (I Cor.
vii, 10, 11). And again: "A woman is bound by the law as

long as her husband liveth, but if her husband die she is at liberty." (Ibid. v. 39). For these causes, therefore, matrimony has been made "a great sacrament" (Ad Eph. v. 32), "honorable in all" (Ad Hebr. xiii, 4), pious, chaste, and venerable as representing and signifying the most exalted mysteries. Nor is its Christian perfection and completeness confined to those things which have been mentioned. For in the first place something more exalted and noble has been given to the conjugal union than it had before, inasmuch as it was bid to look not merely to the propagation of the human race but to the procreation of offspring to the Church, "fellow-citizens with the saints and the domestics of God" (Ad Eph. ii. 19), "that a people may be begotten and trained to religion and to the worship of the true God and of Our Saviour Jesus Christ" (Catech. Rom. cap. viii.). In the second place the duties of both parties in marriage are defined and their rights fully laid down. It is incumbent upon them to bear in mind and understand that each owes to the other the greatest love, a constant fidelity, and careful and assiduous support. The man is the chief of the family, and the head of the woman, who nevertheless, inasmuch as she is flesh of his flesh, and bone of his bone, should be subject to and obey the man, not as a servant, but as a companion; and so neither honor nor dignity is lost by the rendering of obedience. But let divine charity ever regulate duty both in him who commands and in her who obeys, since both are images, the one of Christ, the other of His Church. For "the husband is the head of the wife, as Christ is the head of the Church . . . But as the Church is subject to Christ so also let wives be to their husbands in all things." (Ad Eph. v. 23, 24). As regards to children, they are bound to obey and be subject to their parents, and to do them honor for conscience sake; and, on the other hand, every care and forethought should be vigilantly exercised by parents to protect their children and above all to train them to virtue: "Fathers bring them" (your children) "up in the discipline and the correction of the Lord." (Ad Eph. vi. 4). Whence it may be understood that the duties of married people are neither few nor light; yet to those who are virtuous they become, by the grace imparted through the

Sacrament, not only easy to bear, but even a source of happiness.

Therefore Christ, having renewed matrimony to such and 7 so great an excellence, intrusted and commended its entire discipline to the Church. And she has exercised authority over the marriages of Christians at every time and in every place, and has so exercised it as to show that it was her own inherent right, not obtained by the concession of men, but divinely bestowed by the will of her Author. How many and how vigilant were the pains which she took to retain the sanctity of marriages, in order that their inviolability might be preserved to them, is so well known that it need not be pointed out. And we know that loose and free love was forbidden by the sentence of the Council of Jerusalem (Act xv. 29), that the Corinthian citizen was condemned for incest by the authority of St. Paul (I Cor. v. 5), and that the attempts of very many persons who attacked Christian marriage, to wit, Gnostics, Manichaeans, Montanists, in the very beginning of Christianity, and within our memory Mormons, St. Simonians, Phalansterians, and Communists, have been opposed and rejected with the same vigor. In like manner the rights of marriage have been made equal among all persons and the same for all, the ancient distinction between slaves and the freeborn being put an end to (cap. *de conjug. serv.*), the rights of husband and wife have been equalized; for, as Jerome said (Oper., tom. i., col. 455), "among us what is not lawful for women is equally unlawful for men, and the same obligation results from equal servitude," and those **same** rights, tending to promote mutual good-will and reciprocal kindness, have been firmly established; the dignity of woman has been asserted and vindicated; it has been forbidden to a husband to inflict capital punishment on an adulteress (Can. *Interfectores, et* Can. *Admonere*, quaest, 2), or with a wanton unchastity to violate his own plighted faith. And it is also very important that the Church, as far as is right, has limited the power of fathers of families, so that their sons and daughters when desirous of marriage should not have their just liberty diminished (cap. 30, quaest. 3; cap. 3, *de cognatspirit.*); that she has decreed that there could be no marriages between relations and kindred within certain degrees (cap. 8, *de consang. et affin.*; cap. I, *de cognat legati.*), so that the supernatural love of married persons might diffuse itself over a wider field; that she has taken care that marriages should, as far as possible, be guarded against error, force and fraud (cap. 26, *de sponsal.*: capp. 13, 15, 29, *de sponsal. et matrim..*; et alibi). That she has willed the holiness of the marriage-bed, the security of persons (cap. I. *de convers. infid.;* capp. 5, 6, *de eo qui duxit in matr.*), the decorum of marriages (capp. 3, 5, 8, *de sponsal. et matr.* Trid. sess. xxiv. cap. 3, *de reform. matr.*), the inviolability of religion (cap. 7, *de divort,*), to be placed upon proper safeguard. In fine, she has fortified that divine institution so strongly and with such prudent laws, that no one can be a just judge of things who does not understand that even with regard to the subject of marriages the Church is the best guardian and protector of the human race; and that her wisdom has victoriously survived both the flight of time, the injuries of men, and the innumerable vicissitudes of states.

8   But, by the efforts of the enemy of the human race, there are not wanting those who, as the ungratefully repudiate the other benefits of redemption, in the same way either despise or altogether ignore the restitution and perfection of marriage. Is is the disgrace of certain of the ancients that they were hostile to marriage in some respects; but much more perniciously do those in our own time err who would entirely pervert its nature now that it has been made perfect and complete in all its elements and parts. Of which the cause is chiefly to be found in this, that the minds of many, being imbued with the opinions of a false philosophy and a corrupt habit of mind, bear nothing so ill as to submit and obey, and they labor with the greatest bitterness in order that not only individuals, but families, and indeed the whole human race, may proudly despise the authority of God. But since the fount and origin of the family, and all human society, consists in marriage, they will in no way allow it to be under the jurisdiction of the Church; nay, they endeavor to cast it down from all sanctity, and to drive it into the narrow circle of those things which have been instituted by human authors,

and are regulated and administered by the civil law of nations. Whence it necessarily followed that they have attributed to the rulers of the state all jurisdiction over marriage, and granted none to the Church; and if she at any time exercised power of that kind they affirm that this was done by the indulgence of rulers, or unjustly. But now they say it is time that those who rule the state should bravely vindicate their rights, and should determine to direct according to their own will all matters relating to marriage. Hence have arisen what are called *civil marriages*; hence laws enacted concerning the causes which constitute an impediment to marriage; hence judicial sentences on conjugal contracts, as to whether they have been entered upon rightly or wrongly. Lastly we see every possible power of legislating and judging on this subject taken away from the Church with so much determination that no account is any longer taken either of her divine power or the provident laws under which all the nations, to whom Christian wisdom brought the light of civilization, lived so many years.

But the naturalists and all those who, specially professing to worship the deity of the state, are striving to disturb entire commonwealths with these doctrines, cannot avoid the reproach of falsehood. For since marriage has God for its author, and since it has been even from the beginning a shadowing forth of the incarnation of the Word of God, therefore there is in it something sacred and religious, not adventitious but innate, not received from men but implanted by nature. Wherefore Innocent III. (cap. 8, *de divort.*) and Honorious III. (cap. II, *de transact.*), our predecessors, were enabled to say, not unjustly nor rashly, that the sacrament of marriage exists both among the faithful and among infidels. We call to witness also the monuments of antiquity, and, the customs and institutions of those nations which were the most cultivated and excelled in a more refined knowledge of right and equity, in all of whose minds it was a settled and foregone conclusion that the idea of marriage was connected with religion and sanctity. For this reason marriages amongst them were frequently accustomed to be performed with religious ceremonies, with the authority of the pontiffs, with the ministry of priests, so great an influence even on minds ignorant of Divine Revelation had the nature of things, the memory of their origin, the conscienceof the human race!

10   Wherefore marriage, being by its own nature and meaning sacred, it is consistent that it should be regulated and governed, not by the command of rulers, but by the divine authority of the Church, which alone possesses authority in sacred things. Then we must consider the dignity of the sacrament, by the addition of which the marriages of Christians have become in the highest degree ennobled. And, by the will of Christ, the Church alone can and ought to legislate and decide concerning sacraments, so that it is out of the question to attempt to transfer any, even the smallest part, of her power to the governors of the state. Finally, there is great weight, great force in history, by which we are clearly taught that the legislative and judicial power of which we speak was wont to be freely and continually exercised by the Church, even in those times when it is vainly and foolishly pretended that the chiefs of the state were consenting and conniving thereto. For how incredible and absurd it is to suppose that Christ Our Lord condemned the deep-rooted custom of polygamy and of repudiation by a power delegated to Him by the governor of the province or by the ruler of the Jews; or, in like manner, that the Apostle Paul declared divorces and incestuous marriages to be unlawful with the consent or by the tacit authority of Tiberius, of Caligula, or of Nero! Nor can any sane man be persuaded that so many laws were enacted by the Church regarding the sanctity and stability of marriage (Can. Apost., 16, 17, 18), and regarding marriages between slaves and free women (Philosophum, Oxon., 1851), by authority derived from the Roman emperors, the deadliest enemies of the Christian name, who desired nothing more earnestly than to extirpate by violence and blood the growing religion of Christ; more especially as the law which proceeded from the Church differed so widely from the civil law that Ignatius the Martyr (Epist. ad Polycarp. cap. 5), Justin (Apolog. mai., n. 15), Athenagoras (Legat. pro Christian., nn. 32, 33), and Tertullian (De coron. milit., cap. 13) publicly denounced as immoral, and even adulterous,

marriages which, nevertheless, the imperial laws allowed. But when all power came into the hands of the Christian emperors, the Supreme Pontiffs and the bishops, assembled in council, continued always, with the same liberty and the same knowledge of their own right, to command and to forbid in matrimonial affairs as seemed to them to be useful and in conformity with the requirements of the times, no matter how inconsistent it might be with the civil institutions of the day. No one is ignorant that many rules were made on the subject of impediments arising from obligations, vows, disparity of worship, consanguinity, crime, or public decency by the prelates of the Church at the Councils of Elvira (De Aguirre, Conc. Hispan, tom. i., can. 13, 15, 16, 17), Arles (Harduin., Act. Council., tom. i., can. II), Chalcedon (Harduin., Act. Concil., tom. i, can. 16), Milevis (Harduin., Act. Concil., tom. i., can. 17), and other councils, which frequently are far different from the decrees sanctioned by the imperial law. And so far were princes from claiming any power for themselves in the matter of Christian marriages, that they declared and acknowledged that power, in all its plenitude, was vested in the Church. In fact, Honorius, Theodosius the Younger, and Justinian (Novel. 137) did not hesitate to admit that in matters which concerned marriage they had no right to do anything except as the guardians and defenders of the sacred canons. And if they made any decrees regarding impediments to marriage, they of their own accord explained the reason to be that they had taken this upon themselves by the permission and authority of the Church (Fejer, *Matrim. ex. instit. Christ;* Pesth. 1835), whose decision they were accustomed to ask for and reverently to receive in disputes concerning the legitimacy of children (cap. 3, *de ordin. cognit.*), concerning divorces (cap. 3, *de divort.*), and, in fine, all matters having any kind of relation to the matrimonial bond (cap. 13, *qui filii sint legit).* Wherefore it was most justly decreed by the Council of Trent that the Church has power "to define the impediments which make matrimony void, and that matrimonial causes, belong to the jurisdiction of ecclesiastical judges." (Trid., sess. xxiv., can. 4).

11   Nor let anyone be led astray by that distinction so sedu-
lously urged by regalists, according to which they separate
the nuptial contract from the sacrament, in order that, while
judgment respecting the sacraments is reserved to the Church,
they may give over the contract to the authority and decision
of the civil power. For a distinction, or rather a disjunction,
of this nature cannot be established; inasmuch as it is manifest
that in Christian matrimony it is not possible to separate the
contract from the sacrament, and, therefore, that there
cannot be a true and legitimate contract without its being, on
that very account, a sacrament. For Christ Our Lord raised
matrimony to the dignity of a sacrament; and matrimony is
the contract itself, provided only that it be lawfully made.
In addition to which, matrimony is a sacrament for this
reason, that it is a sacred sign conveying grace, and presenting
an image of the mystic nuptials of Christ with the Church.
But the form and figure of these is expressed by that bond of
perfect unity by which man and wife are joined together, and
which is nothing else but matrimony itself. Therefore it is
evident that every lawful marriage between Christians is in
and by itself a sacrament; and nothing can be more opposed
to truth than that the sacrament is but an ornamental addition, or a character imparted from without, which may be
separated and disjoined from the contract at will. Wherefore
it is neither established by reasoning nor proved by historical
evidence that authority over Christian marriage is rightly
given to the state. And if in this matter the right of others has
been violated, no one can say that it has been violated by the
Church.

12   And would that the teachings of the naturalists, so full of
falsehood and injustice, were not equally fruitful in mischiefs
and calamities. But it is easy to perceive what evil the pro-
faning of marriages brings about, and how much it is likely to
inflict upon the whole of human society. For in the beginning
it was divinely ordained that we should find those things
instituted by God and by nature more useful and more salutary in porportion as they remain whole and immutable in
their original condition; since God the Creator of all things
well knew what was expedient for the establishment and

perservation of each, and so ordained all by His will and judgment that each should have its appropriate development. But
if the temerity or the wickedness of men seek to change and
to disturb the order of providence, then indeed even things
which have been most wisely and most advantageously instituted begin to be injurious, or cease to be beneficial, either
because by change they have lost the power of doing good,
or because it is the will of God to punish in this manner the
pride and audacity of men. They who deny the sanctity of
marriage, and cast it, stripped of all sanctity, into the order
of profane things, pervert the fundamental principles of nature,
and, while they fight against the counsels of divine providence, at the same time to the extent of their power destroy
its work. Wherefore it is not wonderful that from such insane
and impious attempts there springs a crop of evils than which
nothing can be more pernicious to the salvation of souls and
the safety of the state.

If it be considered to what the divine institution of marriage   13
tends, it will be very evident that it was the will of God to
comprise in it the most abundant sources of public happiness
and security. And plainly, marriages, besides that they are
intended for the propagation of the human race, tend to
make the life of married people more virtuous and more
happy; and this in several ways, as, by mutual assistance to
relieve necessities, by constant and faithful love, by the
community of all possessions, and by the celestial grace that
goes forth from the sacrament. And the same causes are most
powerful in promoting the welfare of families; for marriages,
as long as they are in accordance with nature and fitly
correspond with the designs of God, possess a power to confirm a spirit of concord among parents, to promote the good
education of children, to temper paternal power by proposing
the example of the power of God, to make sons obedient to
their parents, servants to their masters. From such marriages
states may justly expect a progeny of citizens who will be
animated with virtuous sentiments, imbued with the love and
fear of God, and will deem it their duty to obey just and
legitimate authority, to love all, to injure none.

14   These fruits, so many and so great, holy matrimony produced so long as it retained the attirbutes of sanctity, of
unity, and of perpetuity, from which it derived all its fertile
and salutary force; nor can it be doubted that it would still
have produced similar and equal results if at all times and
in all places it had been in the power and care of the Church,
which is at all times the most faithful guardian and vindicator
of those attributes. But because, ere long, in various places
the law of men was made to take the place of the divine and
natural law, not only did that most exalted form and conception of marriage which nature had impressed, and, as it were,
engraved, on the minds of men, begin to be obliterated, but
even in Christian marriages its power, the source of such great
blessings, was, through the wickedness of men, greatly
weakened. For what benefit can nuptial unions confer from
which the Christian religion, which is the parent of all good,
and which fosters the greatest virtues, exciting and urging
to everything which adorns a generous and exalted soul, is
banished? When it is put aside and rejected marriage must
needs be made a slave to the corrupt nature of man and the
passions, which are the worst of rulers, protected only by the
weak defence of natural virtue. Manifold evil, derived from
this source, has resulted not only to private families, but to
nations also. For when the salutary fear of God is removed,
and when that alleviation of troubles which is to be found
nowhere more effectual than in the Christian religion is
taken away, it often and naturally happens that the duties
and obligations of marriage appear almost intolerable; and
many inordinately desire the loosening of the bond, which
they imagine to have been tied by human law and choice, if
difference of disposition, or quarrels, or infidelity on the part
of one or the other, or mutual consent, or any other cause
make them think it expedient. And if the law denies satisfaction to the wantonness of their desires, they exclaim that the
laws are unjust, inhuman, and opposed to the rights of free
citizens, and that some provision must be made for their
abolition and the introduction of milder laws to facilitate
divorce.

But the legislators of our times, while they profess them-   15
selves tenacious and studious of the same principles of right,
cannot even, though they desire it ever so much, guard themselves from that wickedness of men of which we spoke,
wherefore the times must be yielded to, and the faculty of
divorce granted. History herself declares the same thing. For,
to pass by other instances, towards the end of the last century, in that conflagration rather than disturbance of France,
when all society was profaned and God was set aside, it was
decided that the severance of married couples should be
ratified by the laws. And many with those same laws to be
revived at this time, because they would have God and the
Church driven from our midst, and removed from intercourse with human society, foolishly supposing that the last
remedy for the great increse of corruption in morals is to be
sought in laws of this description.

It is scarcely necessary to say of how much evil divorce is   16
productive. It is the fruitful cause of mutable marriage
compacts; it diminishes mutual affection; it supplies a pernicious stimulus to unfaithfulness; it is injurious to the care
and education of children; it gives occasion to the breaking
up of domestic society; it scatters the seed of discord among
families; it lessens and degrades the dignity of women, who
incur the danger of being abandoned when they shall have
subserved the lust of their husbands. And since nothing tends
so effectually as the corruption of morals to ruin families and
undermine the strength of kingdoms, it may easily be perceived that divorce is especially hostile to the prosperity of
families and states; for divorce springs from the corrupt
morals of nations, and, as experience teaches, opens the way
and the door to more vicious habits of private and public
life. And these evils will appear to be all the more serious if
we consider that no restraint will be strong enough to confine
the faculty of divorce, when once conceded, within fixed and
foreseen limits. The force of example is very great, and greater
still that of lust. From these exciting causes it must result
that the desire of divorce, daily creeping on further, will
invade the minds of a large number of persons, like a malady

spread by contagion, or a flood of water that has burst its barriers.

17   These things surely are clear of themselves, but they become clearer by recalling past events. As soon as the way for divorce began to be rendered safe by law, dissensions, jealousies, separations enormously increased, and so shameful a manner of living was arrived at that those very persons who had been the defenders of such separations repented of what they had done, and unless they had in time sought a remedy in laws of a contrary character there would have been cause for fear lest the commonwealth itself should rush headlong to destruction. The ancient Romans are said to have looked with horror on the first example of divorce; but ere long the sense of honesty began to be blunted in their minds, modesty with its controlling power to die out, and nuptial fidelity to be violated with so great license that what we read in some writers seems to have a striking semblance of truth, namely, that women had become accustomed to count years, not by the change of consuls, but by the change of husbands. In like manner among Protestants, at first, indeed, the laws had sanctioned divorce for certain causes, and those, to say the truth, not many in number; but it has been found that these causes have, through the near connection of things resembling one another, increased to such an extent among the Germans, Americans, and others, that they whose understandings were not blunted considered the boundless depravation of morals and the insufferable rashness of the laws as deeply to be lamented. Nor was it otherwise in states called Catholic, in which, if at any time the severance of marriage ties was admitted, the multitude of inconveniences which ensued far exceeded the expectations of legislators. For the wickedness of very many persons led them to turn their minds to all sorts of malice and fraud, and by means of cruelty, by injuries, by adulteries, to invent causes for dissolving with impunity that bond of matrimonial union of which they were tried; and this with so great detriment to public honesty that all judged it necessary that the laws should as soon as possible be amended. And who will doubt that the laws favoring divorce will be followed by wretched and calamitous results

wherever they may happen to be received in our own age? Certainly the contrivances or decrees of men have not the power to change the natural character and conformation of things; wherefore they bring a small amount of wisdom to bear on the public welfare who think that the genuine theory of marriage can be perverted with impunity, and, setting aside all sanctity of religion and of sacrament, seem to wish to disfigure and deform matrimony more shamefully than even the institutions of the heathen were wont to do. And, therefore, unless their counsels change, families and society will constantly have to fear for themselves lest they be hurled most miserably into that universal strife and conflict which has long since been proposed by the flagitious bands of socialists and communists. Hence it is clear how unsuitable and absurd it is to expect public welfare from divorce, which will issue rather in the certain dissolution of society.

It must, therefore, be confessed that the Catholic Church 18 has consulted best for the common good of all people in guarding with constant attention the sanctity and perpetuity of marriage. Nor is little gratitude due to her for having openly demonstrated against the civil laws that for a hundred years past have been sinning in this particular (Pius VI., epist. ad episc. Lucion., 28 Maii, 1793; Pious VII., litter. encycl. die 17 Febr. 1809, et Const. dat. die 19 Jul. 1817; Pius VIII,. litt. encycl. die 29 Maii, 1829; Gregorius XVI., Const. dat. die 15 Augusti, 1832; Pius IX., alloc. habit. die 22 Sept. 1852); for having smitten with anathema the pernicious heresy of Protestants concerning divorce and repudiation (Trid., sess., xxiv., can. 5, 7), for having in many ways condemned the dissolution of marriages practiced by the Greeks (Concil. Floren., et. Instr. Eug. IV. ad Armenos; Bened. XIV., Const. *Etsi pastoralis,* 6 Maii, 1742); for having decreed those nuptials to be null and void which were contracted under the condition that they might at some time or other be dissolved (cap. 7, *de condit. appos.*); lastly, for having even from the earliest ages repudiated the imperial laws which perniciously favored divorce and the breaking off of the marriage contract (Hieron., epist. 79 ad Ocean; Ambros., lib. viii., in cap. 16 Lucae, n. 5; August., de nuptiis, cap. 10). In truth, whenever the Supreme pontiffs resisted most powerful princes demanding with threats to have divorces granted by themselves ratified by the Church, they are to be regarded as having combated not only for the integrity of religion but also for the security of the human race. On which account all posterity admires the proofs of an invincible mind afforded by Nicholas I. in conflict with Lothaife; by Urban II. and Paschal II. struggling against Philip I., King of France; by Celestine III. and Innocent III. against Alfonso of Leon and Philip II. of France; by Clement VII. and Paul III. against Henry VIII., and lastly by the holy and brave Pontiff, Pius VII., against Napoleon I., uplifted by prosperity and the greatness of his empire.

19   This being the case, all rulers and administrators of public affairs, if they wished to follow reason and wisdom and to be really useful to the people, ought to have preferred to let the. sacred laws of matrimony remain intact, and to apply the proffered assistance of the Church to the guardianship of morals and the prosperity of families, rather than to cast upon the Church itself the suspicion of hostility, and charge it falsely and unjustly with the violation of civil rights.

20   And that all the more, because, as the Catholic Church can in no respect depart from religious duty and defence of its rights, so is it habitually inclined to kindness and indulgence in all things which can be made to consist with the integrity of its rights and the sanctity of its duties. For which reason it has never determined anything respecting matrimony without having due regard to the state of the community and to the condition of populations; nor has it on one occasion only, mitigated, as far as it could, the prescriptions of its own laws when there were just and grave causes for such a modification. The Church itself likewise does not ignore or deny that the sacrament of marriage, since it is directed towards the preservation and increase of human society, has a relationship and intimacy with human matters, which are consequences, indeed, of matrimony, but belong to the civil order; and the rulers of the state rightly take cognizance and judge of these. But no one doubts that Jesus Christ, the Founder of the Church, willed the sacred power to be distinct from the civil

power, and each power to be free and unhampered in the conduct of its own affairs; yet with this addition, which is expedient for each and for the interests of all men, namely, that there should be a union and concord between them, and that in those things which are, though in different ways, matters of common right and judgment, the one to which human affairs are committed should depend suitably and fittingly on the other, to which are intrusted the things of Heaven. But in an agreement, or harmony, as it were, of this description is contained not only the best mode of operation of each of the two powers, but also the most opportune and efficacious means of helping the human race in what appertains to the conduct of human life and the hope of everlasting salvation. For, as we showed in former Encyclical Letters, the intelligence of men, if it agrees with Christian faith, is much ennobled and comes forth much better armed for the avoidance and repulsion of error, and faith in its turn borrows no small assistance from intelligence; so, in like manner, if the civil authority agrees amicably with the sacred power of the Church, a great increase of usefulness accures of necessity to both. For the dignity of the one is amplified, and under the guidance of religion the government will never be unjust; while to the other are supplied protection and defense for the public good of the faithful. Therefore, moved by the consideration of these things, as we have at other times earnestly, so now again at the present time we urgently exhort princes and men in authority to concord and friendship; and we are the first to extend to them, as it were, our right hand with paternal benevolence, offering the assistance of our supreme power, which is the more necessary at this time in proportion as the right of sovereign rule is, in the opinion of men, weakened, as if it had received a wound. For the minds of multitudes being inflamed with riotous liberty, and casting off with nefarious boldness every restraint of government, even the most legitimate, public safety requires that men should associate to prevent the injury of both powers, injury which impends not merely over the Church, but also over civil society itself.

21   But while we strongly advise a friendly union of wills and dispositions, and pray God, the Prince of Peace, that He would infuse the love of concord into the minds of all men, we cannot refrain, Venerable Brethren, from exhorting yourselves more and more to use your diligence, your zeal and vigilance, which we know to be very great. As far as you can attain it by efforts and by your authority, strive with diligence that among the people intrusted to your fidelity the entire and uncorrupted doctrine be retained which Christ the Lord and the apostolic interpreters of the heavenly will have delivered, and which the Catholic Church herself has religiously preserved and commanded the faithful in Christ to preserve through all ages.

22   Take especial care of this, that the people abound in precepts of Christian wisdom, and always retain in memory that marriage was instituted in the beginning, not by the will of man, but by the authority and command of God, and was sanctioned entirely under this law, that it should be of one to one; and that Christ, the author of the new covenant, translated that alliance into a sacrament, and, as far as regards the bond, ascribed to His Church the lawgiving and judicial authority. In which matter the greatest care must be taken lest the mind be led into error by the fallacious conclusions of adversaries, who would take away this power from the Church. In like manner it ought to be recognized by all, that if any union of man and woman among the faithful of Christ be contracted without the sacrament it is wanting in the force and character of a true marriage; and although it be effected in agreement with the civil laws, yet it can have no greater value than that of a rite or custom introduced by the civil law; but it must also be remembered that such things only can be ordered and administered by the civil law which are the consequences of marriage in the civil order, and which it is evident cannot be produced except a true and legitimate cause may be alleged, wish to entangle themselves in a new matrimonial bond before the first is broken by death. fully understand and recognize the truth of these things; which ought indeed to be accepted and understood, so that they may in this matter comply with the laws; for the Church

does not refuse, but on the contrary wills and hopes that the due effects of marriage should be preserved intact in all respects, and that no detriment may be entailed on the offspring. In such confusion of opinions, however, which daily advance, this also is necessary to be known, that it is not in the power of any one to dissolve the bond of a marriage solemnized and consummated among Christians; and that they are guilty of a crime who, being man and wife, whatever cause may be alleged, wish to entangle themselves in a new matrimonial bond before the first is broken by death. But if things have gone so far that living together seems to be insupportable any longer, then indeed the Church allows one to live apart from the other, and all care being taken and remedies applied to the condition of the married couple, she studies how she may mitigate the inconveniences of separation, nor does she ever cease to labor for the re-establishment of concord, or despair of bringing it about. But these are extremities to which it would be easy not to descend if married persons were not actuated by lust, but, having duly considered both the duties and the elevated motives of matrimony, came to it with proper dispositions, and wedlock were not preceded by a continuous series of offences displeasuring to God. To sum up all in a few words, marriages will be blessed with peaceful and quiet constancy if the wedded pair draw their breath and life from the power of religion, of whose gift it comes that the mind is strong and unconquerable, and by whose existence personal faults, if such exist, discrepancy of habits and dispositions, the weight of maternal cares, the toil and anxiety about the education of children, the attendant labors of existence, and adverse circumstances may be borne, not only with moderation, but even willingly and gladly.

Care ought also to be taken lest alliances be lightly sought   23
with those who are strangers to the Catholic name and faith, for it can scarcely be hoped that minds which are at variance in respect of religious doctrine should be in accord on other matters. Indeed it is most evident that marriages of this kind should be avoided from the fact of their giving occasion to forbidden communion in sacred things; they create danger to

the religion of a Catholic spouse, they are a hindrance to the good education of the children, and very frequently they dispose the mind to become accustomed to take equal account of all religions, and to lose sight of the distinction between true and false. In the last place, since we thoroughly understand that no one ought to be an alien from our charity, we commend those, Venerable Brethren, to your authority, faith, and piety, who, being indeed extremely wretched, are carried away by the tide of their lusts, and, being altogether unmindful of their own salvation, live contrary to law and right not united in a bond of lawful wedlock. Let your skill and diligence be employed in recalling such to their duty; and do you in every way strive, both by yourselves and with the interposition of good men, that they may perceive that they have acted wickedly, that they may do penance for their sin, and may turn their minds seriously towards proper nuptials celebrated with Catholic rites.

24   You easily perceive, Venerable Brethren, that these instructions and percepts respecting Christian marriage, which we have resolved to communicate to you, pertain strictly no less to the preservation of civil society than to the everlasting salvation of men. May God grant, therefore, that the more weight and importance these instructions have, the more they may find everywhere minds docile and prompt to obey. On this account let us all alike, with suppliant and humble prayer, implore the aid of the Blessed and Immaculate Virgin Mary, that, by exciting minds to the obedience of faith, she may show herself to men as their mother and helper. Nor let us implore with less earnestness Peter and Paul, the princes of the Apostles, the conquerors of superstition the sowers of the seed of truth, that they may preserve the human race from the deluge of returning errors by their most powerful patronage.

25   Meanwhile, as pledge of heavenly gifts and witnesses of Our singular good-will, We from the heart impart to you all, Venerable Brethren, and to the people intrusted to your vigilance, Our apostolic benediction.

26   Given at Rome, at St. Peter's, on the tenth day of February, in the year 1880, the second year of Our Pontificate.

CASTI CONNUBII
Encyclical Letter of Pope Pius XI
On Christian Marriage
December 31, 1930

How great is the dignity of chaste wedlock, Venerable
Brethren, may be judged best from this that Christ
Our Lord, Son of the Eternal Father, having assumed
the nature of fallen man, not only, with His loving desire of
compassing the redemption of our race, ordained it in an
especial manner as the principle and foundation of domestic
society and therefore of all human intercourse, but also
raised it to the rank of a truly and great sacrament of the
New Law, restored it to the original purity of its divine
institution, and accordingly entrusted all its discipline and
care to His spouse the Church.

In order, however, that amongst men of every nation and   28
every age the desired fruits may be obtained from this
renewal of matrimony, it is necessary, first of all, that men's
minds be illuminated with the true doctrine of Christ regarding it; and secondly, that Christian spouses, the weakness
of their wills strengthened by the internal grace of God,
shape all their ways of thinking and of acting in conformity
with that pure law of Christ so as to obtain true peace and
happiness for themselves and for their families.

Yet not only do We, looking with paternal eye on the   29
universal world from this Apostolic See as from a watch-
tower, but you, also, Venerable Brethren, see, and seeing
deeply grieve with Us that a great number of men, forgetful
of that divine work of redemption, either entirely ignore or

shamelessly deny the great sanctity of Christian wedlock, or relying on the false principles of a new and utterly perverse morality, too often trample it under foot. And since these most pernicious errors and depraved morals have begun to spread even amongst the faithful and are gradually gaining ground, in Our office as Christ's Vicar upon earth and Supreme Shepherd and Teacher We consider it Our duty to raise Our voice to keep the flock committed to Our care from poisoned pastures and, as far as in Us lies, to preserve it from harm.

30   We have decided therefore to speak to you, Venerable Brethren, and through you to the whole Church of Christ and indeed to the whole human race, on the nature and dignity of Christian marriage, on the advantages and benefits which accrue from it to the family and to human society itself, on the errors contrary to this most important point of the Gospel teaching, on the vices opposed to conjugal union, and lastly on the principal remedies to be applied. In so doing We follow the footsteps of Our predecessor, Leo XIII, of happy memory, whose Encyclical *Arcanum*.[1] published fifty years ago, We hereby confirm and make Our own, and while We wish to expound more fully certain points called for by the circumstances of our times, nevertheless We declare that, far from being obsolete, it retains its full force at the present day.

31   And to begin with that same Encyclical, which is wholly concerned in vindicating the divine institution of matrimony, its sacramental dignity, and its perpetual stability, let it be repeated as an immutable and inviolable fundamental doctrine that matrimony was not instituted or restored by man but by God; not by man were the laws made to strengthen and confirm and elevate it but by God, the Author of nature, and by Christ Our Lord by Whom nature was redeemed, and hence these laws cannot be subject to any human decrees or to any contrary pact even of the spouses themselves. This is the doctrine of Holy Scripture;[2] this is the constant tradition of the Universal Church; this the solemn definition of the sacred Council of Trent, which declares and establishes from the words of Holy Writ itself that God is the Author of the per-

petual stability of the marriage bond, its unity and its firmness.[3]

Yet although matrimony is of its very nature of divine in-   32
stitution, the human will, too, enters into it and performs a
most noble part. For each individual marriage, inasmuch as it
is a conjugal union of a particular man and woman, arises
only from the free consent of each of the spouses; and this
free act of the will, by which each party hands over and accepts those rights proper to the state of marriage,[4] is so
necessary to constitute true marriage that it cannot be supplied by any human power.[5] This freedom, however, regards
only the question whether the contracting parties really wish
to enter upon matrimony or to marry this particular person;
but the nature of matrimony is entirely independent of the
free will of man, so that if one has once contracted matrimony he is thereby subject to its divinely made laws and its
essential properties. For the Angelic Doctor, writing on conjugal honour and on the offspring which is the fruit of marriage, says: "These things are so contained in matrimony by
the marriage pact itself that, if anything to the contrary were
expressed in the consent which makes the marriage, it would
not be a true marriage."[6]

By matrimony, therefore, the souls of the contracting   33
parties are joined and knit together more directly and more
intimately than are their bodies, and that not by any passing
affection of sense or spirit, but by a deliberate and firm act
of the will; and from this union of souls by God's decree, a
sacred and inviolable bond arises. Hence the nature of this
contract, which is proper and peculiar to it alone, makes it
entirely different both from the union of animals entered
into by the blind instinct of nature alone in which neither
reason nor free will plays a part, and also from the haphazard
unions of men, which are far removed from all true and
honourable unions of will and enjoy none of the rights of
family life.

From this it is clear that legitimately constituted authority   34
has the right and therefore the duty to restrict, to prevent,
and to punish those base unions which are opposed to reason
and to nature; but since it is a matter which flows from human

nature itself, no less certain is the teaching of Our predecessor, Leo XIII of happy memory:[7] "In choosing a state of
life there is no doubt but that it is in the power and discretion
of each one to prefer one or the other: either to embrace the
counsel of virginity given by Jesus Christ, or to bind himself
in the bonds of matrimony. To take away from man the natural and primeval right of marriage, to circumscribe in any
way the principal ends of marriage laid down in the beginning
by God Himself in the words 'Increase and multiply,'[8] is
beyond the power of any human law."

35   Therefore the sacred partnership of true marriage is constituted both by the will of God and the will of man. From God
comes the very institution of marriage, the ends for which it
was instituted, the laws that govern it, the blessings that flow
from it; while man, through generous surrender of his own
person made to another for the whole span of life, becomes,
with the help and cooperation of God, the author of each
particular marriage, with the duties and blessings annexed
thereto from divine institution.

I.

36   Now when We come to explain, Venerable Brethren, what
are the blessings that God has attached to true matrimony,
and how great they are, there occur to Us the words of that
illustrious Doctore of the Church whom We commemorated
recently in Our Encyclical *Ad salutem* on the occasion of the
fifteenth centenary of his death:[9] "These," says St. Augustine,
"are all the blessings of matrimony on account of which
matrimony itself is a blessing; offspring, conjugal faith and
the sacrament."[10] And how under these three heads is
contained a splendid summary of the whole doctrine of
Christian marriage, the holy Doctor himself expressly declares
when he said: "By conjugal faith it is provided that there
should be no carnal intercourse outside the marriage bond
with another man or woman; with regard to offspring, that
children should be begotten of love, tenderly cared for and
educated in a religious atmosphere; finally, in its sacramental
aspect that the marriage bond should not be broken and that

a husband or wife, if separated, should not be joined to another even for the sake of offspring. This we regard as the law of marriage by which the fruitfulness of nature is adorned and the evil of incontinence is restrained."[11]

Thus amongst the blessings of marriage, the child holds the first place. And indeed the Creator of the human race Himself, Who in His goodness wished to use men as His helpers in the propagation of life, taught this when, instituting marriage in Paradise, He said to our first parents, and through them to all future spouses: "Increase and multiply, and fill the earth."[12] As St. Augustine admirably deduces from the words of the holy Apostle Saint Paul to Timothy[13] when he says: "The Apostle himself is therefore a witness that marriages is for the sake of generation: 'I wish,' he says, 'young girls to marry.' And, as if someone said to him, 'Why?,' he immediately adds: 'To bear children, to be mothers of families.' "[14]   37·

How great a boon of God this is, and how great a blessing of matrimony is clear from a consideration of man's dignity and of his sublime end. For man surpasses all other visible creatures by the superiority of his rational nature alone. Besides, God wishes men to be born not only that they should live and fill the earth, but much more that they may be worshippers of God, that they may know Him and love Him and finally enjoy Him for ever in heaven; and this end, since man is raised by God in a marvellous way to the supernatural order, surpasses all that eye hath seen, and ear heard, and all that hath entered into the heart of man.[15] From which it is easily seen how great a gift of divine goodness and how remarkable a fruit of marriage are children born by the omnipotent power of God through the cooperation of those bound in wedlock.   38

But Christian parents must also understand that they are destined not only to propagate and preserve the human race on earth, indeed not only to educate any kind of worshippers of the true God, but children who are to become members of the Church of Christ, to raise up fellow-citizens of the Saints, and members of God's household,[18] that the worshippers of God and Our Saviour may daily increase.   39

40   For although Christian spouses even if sanctified themselves cannot transmit sanctification to their progeny, nay, although the very natural process of generating life has become the way of death by which original sin is passed onto posterity, nevertheless, they share to some extent in the blessings of that primeval marriage of Paradise, since it is theirs to offer their offspring to the Church in order that by this most fruitful Mother of the children of God they may be regenerated through the laver of Baptism unto supernatural justice and finally be made living members of Christ, partakers of immortal life, and heirs of that eternal glory to which we all aspire from our inmost heart.

41   If a true Christian mother weigh well these things, she will indeed understand with a sense of deep consolation that of her the words of Our saviour were spoken: "A woman . . . when she hath brought forth the child remembereth no more the anguish, for joy that a man is born into the world";[17] and proving herself superior to all the pains and cares and solicitudes of her maternal office with a more just and holy joy than that of the Roman matron, the mother of the Gracchi, she will rejoice in the Lord crowned as it were with the glory of her offspring. Both husband and wife, however, receiving these children with joy and gratitude from the hand of God, will regard them as a talent committed to their charge by God, not only to be employed for their own advantage or for that of an earthly commonwealth, but to be restored to God with interest on the day of reckoning.

42   The blessing of offspring, however, is not completed by the mere begetting of them, but something else must be added, namely the proper education of the offspring. For the most wise God would have failed to make sufficient provision for children that had been born, and so for the whole human race, if He had not given to those to whom He had entrusted the power and right to beget them, the power also and the right to educate them. For no one can fail to see that children are incapable of providing wholly for themselves, even in matters pertaining to their natural life, and much less in those pertaining to the supernatural, but require for many years to be helped, instructed, and educated by others. Now it is

certain that both by the law of nature and of God this right
and duty of educating their offspring belongs in the first
place to those who began the work of nature by giving them
birth, and they are indeed forbidden to leave unfinished this
work and so expose it to certain ruin. But in matrimony
provision has been made in the best possible way for this
education of children that is so necessary, for, since the
parents are bound together by an indissoluble bond, the care
and mutual help of each is always at hand.

Since, however, We have spoken fully elsewhere on the   43
Christian education of youth,[18] let Us sum it all up by quoting once more the words of St. Augustine: "As regards the
offspring it is provided that they should be begotten lovingly
and educated religiously,"[19]—and this is also expressed
succinctly in the Code of Canon Law—"The primary end of
marriage is the procreation and the education of children."[20]

Nor must We omit to remark, in fine, that since the duty   44
entrusted to parents for the good of their children is of such
high dignity and of such great importance, every use of the
faculty given by God for the procreation of new life is the
right and the privilege of the married state alone, by the law
of God and of nature, and must be confined absolutely within
the sacred limits of that state.

The second blessing of matrimony which We said was men-   45
tioned by St. Augustine, is the blessing of conjugal honour
which consists in the mutual fidelity of the spouses in fulfilling the marriage contract, so that what belongs to one of
the parties by reason of this contract sanctioned by divine
law, may not be denied to him or permitted to any third
person; nor may there be conceded to one of the parties
anything which, being contrary to the rights and laws of God
and entirely opposed to matrimonial faith, can never be
conceded.

Wherefore, conjugal faith, or honour, demands in the   46
first place the complete unity of matrimony which the
Creator Himself laid down in the beginning when He wished
it to be not otherwise than between one man and one woman.
And although afterwards this primeval law was relaxed to
some extent by God, the Supreme Legislator, there is no

doubt that the law of the Gospel fully restored that original and perfect unity, and abrogated all dispensations as the words of Christ and the constant teaching and action of the Church show plainly. With reason, therefore, does the Sacred Council of Trent solemnly declare; "Christ Our Lord very clearly taught that in this bond two persons only are to be united and joined together when He said: 'Therefore thay are no longer two, but one flesh.' "[21]

47   Nor did Christ Our Lord wish only to condemn any form of polygamy or polyandry, as they are called, whether successive or simultaneous, and every other external dishonourable act, but, in order that the sacred bonds of marriage may be guarded absolutely inviolate, He forbade also even wilful thoughts and desires of such like things: "But I say to you, that whosoever shall look on a woman to lust after her hath already committed adultery with her in his heart."[22] Which words of Christ Our Lord cannot be annulled even by the consent of one of the partners of marriage for they express a law of God and of nature which no will of man can break or bend.[23]

48   Nay, that mutual familiar intercourse between the spouses themselves, if the blessing of conjugal faith is to shine with becoming splendour, must be distinguished by chastity so that husband and wife bear themselves in all things with the law of God and of nature, and endeavour always to follow the will of their most wise and holy Creator with the greatest reverence toward the work of God.

49   This conjugal faith, however, which is most aptly called by St. Augustine the "faith of chastity" blooms more freely, more beautifully and more nobly, when it is rooted in that more excellent soil, the love of husband and wife which pervades all the duties of married life and holds pride of place in Christian marriage. For matrimonial faith demands that husband and wife be joined in an especially holy and pure love, not as adulterers love each other, but as Christ loved the Church. This precept the Apostle laid down when he said: "Husbands, love your wives as Christ also loved the Church,"[24] that Church which of a truth He embraced with a boundless love not for the sake of His own advantage, but seeking

only the good of His Spouse.[25] The love, then, of which We are speaking is not that based on the passing lust of the moment nor does it consist in pleasing words only, but in the deep attachment of the heart which is expressed in action, since love is proved by deeds.[26] This outward expression of love in the home demands not only mutual help but must go further; must have as its primary purpose that man and wife help each other day by day in forming and perfecting themselves in the interior life, so that through their partnership in life they may advance ever more and more in virtue, and above all that they may grow in true love toward God and their neighbour, on which indeed "dependeth the whole Law and Prophets."[27] For all men of every condition, in whatever honorable walk of life they may be, can and ought to imitate the most perfect example of holiness placed before man by God, namely Christ Our Lord, and by God's grace to arrive at the summit of perfection, as is proved by the example set us of many saints.

This mutual inward moulding of husband and wife; this   50
determined effort to perfect each other, can in a very real sense, as the Roman Catechism teaches, be said to be the chief reason and purpose of matrimony, provided matrimony be looked at not in the restricted sense as instituted for the proper conception and education of the child, but more widely as the blending of life as a whole and the mutual interchange and sharing thereof.

By this same love it is necessary that all the other rights   51
and duties of the marriage state be regulated as the words of the Apostle: "Let the husband render the debt to the wife, and the wife also in like manner to the husband,"[28] express not only a law of justice but of charity.

Domestic society being confirmed, therefore, by this bond   52
of love, there should flourish in it that "order of love," as St. Augustine calls it. This order includes both the primacy of the husband with regard to the wife and children, the ready subjection of the wife and her willing obedience, which the Apostle commends in these words: "Let women be subject to their husbands as to the Lord, because the husband is the head of the wife, as Christ is the head of the Church."[29]

53 This subjection, however, does not deny or take away the liberty which fully belongs to the woman both in view of her dignity as a human person, and in view of her most noble office as wife and mother and companion; nor does it bid her obey her husband's every request if not in harmony with right reason or with the dignity due to wife; nor, in fine, does it imply that the wife should be put on a level with those persons who in law are called minors, to whom it is not customary to allow free exercise of their rights on account of their lack of mature judgment, or of their ignorance of human affairs. But it forbids that exaggerated liberty which cares not for the good of the family; it forbids that in this body which is the family, the heart be separated from the head to the great detriment of the whole body and the proximate danger of ruin. For if the man is the head, the woman is the heart, and as he occupies the chief place in ruling, so she may and ought to claim for herself the chief place in love.

54 Again, this subjection of wife to husband in its degree and manner may vary according to the different conditions of persons, place and time. In fact, if the husband neglect his duty, it falls to the wife to take his place in directing the family. But the structure of the family and its fundamental law, established and confirmed by God, must always and everywhere be maintained intact.

55 With great wisdom Our predecessor Leo XIII, of happy memory, in the Encyclical on Christian marriage which We have already mentioned, speaking of this order to be maintained between man and wife, teaches: "The man is the ruler of the family, and the head of the woman; but because she is flesh of his flesh and bone of his bone, let her be subject and obedient to the man, not as a servant but as a companion, so that nothing be lacking of honour or of dignity in the obedience which she pays. Let divine charity be the constant guide of their mutual relations, both in him who rules and in her who obeys, since each bears the image, the one of Christ, the other of the Church."[30]

56 These, then, are the elements which compose the blessing of conjugal faith: unity, chastity, charity, honourable noble obedience, which are at the same time an enumeration of the

benefits which are bestowed on husband and wife in their married state, benefits by which the peace, the dignity and the happiness of matrimony are securely preserved and fostered. Wherefore it is not suprising that this conjugal faith has always been counted amongst the most priceless and special blessings of matrimony.

But this accumulation of benefits is completed and, as it were, crowned by that blessing of Christian marriage which in the words of St. Augustine we have called the sacrament, by which is denoted both the indissolubility of the bond and the raising and hallowing of the contract by Christ Himself, whereby He made it an efficacious sign of grace.   57

In the first place Christ Himself lays stress on the indissolubility and firmness of the marriage bond when He says: "What God hath joined together let no man put asunder,"[31] and: "Everyone that putteth away his wife and marrieth another committeth adultery, and he that marrieth her that is put away from her husband committeth adultery."[32]   58

And St. Augustine clearly places what he calls the blessing of matrimony in this indissolubility when he says: "In the sacrament it is provided that the marriage bond should not be broken, and that a husband or wife, if separated, should not be joined to another even for the sake of offspring."[33]   59

And this inviolable stability, although not in the same perfect measure in every case, belongs to every true marriage, for the word of the Lord: "What God hath joined together let no man put asunder," must of necessity include all true marriages without exception, since it was spoken of the marriage of our first parents, the prototype of every future marriage. Therefore although before Christ the sublimeness and the severity of the primeval law was so tempered that Moses permitted to the chosen people of God on account of the hardness of their hearts that a bill of divorce might be given in certain circumstances, nevertheless, Christ, by virtue of His supreme legislative power, recalled this concession of greater liberty and restored the primeval law in its integrity by those words which must never be forgotten, "What God hath joined together let no man put asunder." Wherefore, Our predecessor Pius VI of happy memory, writing to the Bishop of Agria,   60 most wisely said: "Hence it is clear that marriage even in the state of nature, and certainly long before it was raised to the dignity of a sacrament, was divinely instituted in such a way that it should carry with it a perpetual and indissoluble bond which cannot therefore be dissolved by any civil law. Therefore although the sacramental element may be absent from a marriage as is the case among unbelievers, still in such a marriage, inasmuch as it is a true marriage there must remain and indeed there does remain that perpetual bond which by divine right is so bound up with matrimony from its first institution that it is not subject to any civil power. And so, whatever marriage is said to be contracted, either it is so contracted that it is really a true marriage, in which case it carries with it that enduring bond which by divine right is inherent in every true marriage; or it is thought to be contracted without that perpetual bond, and in that case there is no marriage, but an illicit union opposed of its very nature to the divine law, which therefore cannot be entered into or maintained."[34]

61   And if this stability seems to be opened to exception, however rare the exception may be, as in the case of certain natural marriages between unbelievers, or amongst Christians in the case of those marriages which though valid have not been consummated, that exception does not depend on the will of men nor on that of any merely human power, but on divine law, of which the only guardian and interpreter is the Church of Christ. However, not even this power can ever affect for any cause whatsoever a Christian marriage which is valid and has been consummated, for as it is plain that here the marriage contract has its full completion, so, by the will of God, there is also the greatest firmness and indissolubility which may not be destroyed by any human authority.

62   If we wish with all reverence to inquire into the intimate reason of this divine decree, Venerable Brethren, we shall easily see it in the mystical signification of Christian marriage which is fully and perfectly verified in consummated marriage between Christians. For, as the Apostle says in his Epistle to the Ephesians,[35] the marriage of Christians recalls that most perfect union which exists between Christ and the

Church: "Sacramentum hoc magnum est, ego autem dico, in Christo et in ecclesia;" which union, as long as Christ shall live and the Church through him, can never be dissolved by any separation. And this St. Autustine clearly declares in these words: "This is safeguarded in Christ and the Church, which, living with Christ who lives for ever, may never be divorced from Him. The observance of this sacrament is such in the City of God . . . that is, in the Church of Christ, that when for the sake of begetting children, women marry or are taken to wife, it is wrong to leave a wife that is sterile in order to take another by whom children may be had. Anyone doing this is guilty of adultery, just as if he married another, guilty not by the law of the day, according to which when one's partner is put away another may be taken, which the Lord allowed in the law of Moses because of the hardness of the hearts of the people of Israel; but by the law of the Gospel."[36]

Indeed, how many and how important are the benefits   63
which flow from the indissolubility of matrimony cannot escape anyone who gives even a brief consideration either to the good of the married parties and the offspring or to the welfare of human society. First of all, both husband and wife possess a positive guarantee of the endurance of this stability which that generous yielding of their persons and the intimate fellowship of thir hearts by their nature strongly require, since true love never falls away.[37] Besides, a strong bulwark is set up in defence of a loyal chastity against incitements to infidelity, should any be encountered either from within or from without; any anxious fear lest in adversity or old age the other spouse should prove unfaithful is precluded and in its place there reigns a calm sense of security. Moreover, the dignity of both man and wife is maintained and mutual aid is most satisfactorily assured, while through the indissoluble bond, always enduring, the spouses are warned continuously that not for the sake of perishable things nor that they may serve their passions, but that they may procure one for the other high and lasting good have they entered into the nuptial partnership, to be dissolved only by death. In the training and education of children, which must extend over a period

of many years, it plays a great part, since the grave and long enduring burdens of this office are best borne by the united efforts of the parents. Nor do lesser benefits accrue to human society as a whole. For experience has taught that unassailable stability in matrimony is a fruitful source of virtuous life and of habits of integrity. Where this order of things obtains, the happiness and well being of the nation is safely guarded; what the families and individuals are, so also is the State, for a body is determined by its parts. Wherefore, both for the private good of husband, wife and children, as likewise for the public good of human society, they indeed deserve well who strenuously defend the inviolable stability of matrimony.

64   But considering the benefits of the Sacrament, besides the firmness and indissolubility, there are also much higher emoluments as the word "sacrament" itself very aptly indicates; for to Christians this is not a meaningless and empty name. Christ the Lord, by the Institutor and "Perfecter" of the holy sacraments,[38] by raising the matrimony of His faithful to the dignity of a true sacrament of the New Law, made it a sign and source of that peculiar internal grace by which "it perfects natural love, it confirms an indissoluble union, and sanctifies both man and wife."[39]

65   And since the valid matrimonial consent among the faithful was constituted by Christ as a sign of grace, the sacramental nature is so intimately bound up with Christian wedlock that there can be no true marriage between baptized persons "without it being by the very fact a sacrament."[40]

66   By the very fact, therefore, that the faithful with sincere mind give such consent, they open up for themselves a treasure of sacramental grace from which they draw supernatural power for the fulfilling of their rights and duties faithfully, holily, perseveringly even unto death. Hence this sacrament not only increases sanctifying grace, the permanent principle of the supernatural life, in those who, as the expression is, place no obstacle *(obex)* in its way, but also adds particular gifts, dispositions, seeds of grace, by elevating and perfecting the natural powers. By these gifts the parties are assisted not only in understanding, but in knowing intimately, in adhering to firmly, in willing effectively, and in successfully putting

to practice, those things which pertain to the marriage state, its aims and duties, giving them in fine right to the acutal assistance of grace, whensoever they need it for fulfilling the duties of their state.

Nevertheless, since it is a law of divine Providence in the supernatural order that men do not reap the full fruit of the Sacraments which they receive after acquiring the use of reason unless they cooperate with grace, the grace of matrimony will remain for the most part an unused talent hidden in the field unless the parties exercise these supernatural powers and cultivate and develop the seeds of grace they have received. If, however, doing all that lies within their power, they cooperate diligently, they will be able with ease to bear the burdens of their state and to fulfil their duties. By such a sacrament they will be strengthened, sanctified and in a manner consecrated. For, as St. Augustine teaches, just as by Baptism and Holy Orders a man is set aside and assisted either for the duties of Christian life or for the priestly office and is never deprived of their sacramental aid, almost in the same way (although not by a sacramental character), the faithful once joined by marriage ties can never be deprived of the help and the binding force of the sacrament. Indeed, as the Holy Doctor adds, even those who commit adultery carry with them that sacred yoke, although in this case not as a title to the glory of grace but for the ignominy of their guilty action, "as the soul by apostasy, withdrawing as it were from marriage with Christ, even though it may have lost its faith, does not lose the sacrament of Faith which it received at the laver of regeneration."[41]   67

These parties, let it be noted, not fettered but adorned by the golden bond of the sacrament, not hampered but assisted, should strive with all their might to the end that their wedlock, not only through the power and symbolism of the sacrament, but also through their spirit and manner of life, may be and remain always the living image of that most fruitful union of Christ with the Church, which is to be venerated as the sacred token of most perfect love.   68

All of these things, Venerable Brethren, you must consider carefully and ponder over with a lively faith if you   69 would see in their true light the extraordinary benefits on matrimony—offspring, conjugal faith, and the sacrament. No one can fail to admire the divine Wisdom, Holiness and Goodness which, while respecting the dignity and happiness of husband and wife, has provided so bountifully for the conservation and propagation of the human race by a single, chaste and sacred fellowship of nuptial union.

II.

70   When we consider the great excellence of chaste wedlock, Venerable Brethren, it appears all the more regrettable that particularly in our day we should witness this divine institution often scorned and on every side degraded.

71   For now, alas, not secretly nor under cover, but openly, with all sense of shame put aside, now by word again by writtings, by theatrical productions of every kind, by romantic fiction, by amorous and frivolous novels, by cinematographs portraying in vivid scene, in addresses broadcast by radio telephony, in short by all the inventions of modern science, the sanctity of marriage is trampled upon and derided; divorce, adultry, all the basest vices either are extolled or at least are depicted in such colours as to appear to be free of all reproach and infamy. Books are not lacking which dare to pronounce themselves as scientific but which in truth are merely coated with a veneer of science in order that they may the more easily insinuate their ideas. The doctrines defended in these are offered for sale as the productions of modern genius, of that genius namely, which, anxious only for truth, is considered to have *emancipated* itself from all those old-fashioned and immature opinions of the ancients; and to the number of these antiquated opinions they relegate the traditional doctrine of Christian marriage.

72   These thoughts are instilled into men of every class, rich and poor, masters and workers, lettered and unlettered, married and single, the godly and godless, old and young, but for these last, as easiest prey, the worst snares are laid.

73   Not all the sponsors of these new doctrines are carried to the extremes of unbridled lust; there are those who, striving

as it were to ride a middle course, believe nevertheless that something should be conceded in our times as regards certain percepts of the divine and natural law. But these likewise, more or less wittingly, are emissaries of the great enemy who is ever seeking to sow cockle among the wheat.[42] We, therefore, whom the Father has appointed over His field, We who are bound by Our most holy office to take care lest the good seed be choked by the weeds, believe it fitting to apply to Ourselves the most grave words of the Holy Ghost with which the Apostle Paul exhorted his beloved Timothy: "Be thou vigilant . . . Fulfill thy ministry . . . Preach the word, be instant in season, out of season, reprove, entreat, rebuke in all patience and doctrine."[43]

And since, in order that the deceits of the enemy may be **74** avoided, it is necessary first of all that they be laid bare; since much is to be gained by denouncing these fallacies for the sake of the unwary, even though We prefer not to name these iniquities "as becometh saints,"[44] yet for the welfare of souls We cannot remain altogether silent.

To begin at the very source of these evils, their basic prin- **75** ciples lies in this, that matrimony is repeatedly declared to be not instituted by the Author of nature nor raised by Christ the Lord to the dignity of a true sacrament, but invented by man. Some confidently assert that they have found no evidence for the existence of matrimony in nature or in her laws, but regard it merely as the means of producing life and of gratifying in one way or another a vehement impulse; on the other hand, others recognize that certain beginnings or, as it were, seeds of true wedlock are found in the nature of man since, unless men were bound together by some form of permanent tie, the dignity of husband and wife or the natural end of propagating and rearing the offspring would not receive satisfactory provision. At the same time they maintain that in all beyond this germinal idea matrimony, through various concurrent causes, is invented solely by the mind of man, established solely by his will.

How grievously all these err and how shamelessly they **76** leave the ways of honesty is already evident from what we have set forth here regarding the origin and nature of wedlock, its purposes and the good inherent in it. The evil of this teaching is plainly seen from the consequences which its advocates deduce from it, namely, that the laws, institutions and customs by which wedlock is governed, since they take their origin solely from the will of man, are subject entirely to him, hence can and must be founded, changed and abrogated according to human caprice and the shifting circumstances of human affairs; that the generative power which is gounded in nature itself is more sacred and has wider range than matrimony—hence it may be exercised both outside as well as within the confines of wedlock, and though the purpose of matrimony be set aside, as though to suggest that the license of a base fornicating woman should enjoy the same rights as the chaste motherhood of a lawfully wedded wife.

77 Armed with these principles, some men go so far as to concoct new species of unions, suited, as they say, to the present temper of men and the times, which various new forms of matrimony they presume to label "temporary," "experimental," and "companionate." These offer all the indulgence of matrimony and its rights without, however, the indissoluble bond, and without offspring, unless later the parties alter their cohabitation into a matrimony in the full sense of the law.

78 Indeed there are some who desire and insist that these practices be legitimatized by the law or, at least, excused by their general acceptance among the people. They do not seem even to suspect that these proposals partake of nothing of the modern "culture" in which they glory so much, but are simply hateful abominations which beyond all question reduce our truly cultured nations to the barbarous standards of savage peoples.

79 And now, Venerable Brethren, we shall explain in detail the evils opposed to each of the benefits of matrimony. First consideration is due to the offspring, which many have the boldness to call the disagreeable burden of matrimony and which they say is to be carefully avoided by married people not through virtuous continence (which Christian law permits in matrimony when both parties consent) but by frustrating the marriage act. Some justify this criminal abuse on the

ground that they are weary of children and wish to gratify their desires without their consequent burden. Others say that they cannot on the one hand remain continent nor on the other can they have children because of the difficulties whether on the part of the mother or on the part of family circumstances.

But no reason, however grave, may be put forward by which anything intrinsically against nature may become conformable to nature and morally good. Since, therefore, the conjugal act is destined primarily by nature for the begetting of children, those who in exercising it deliberately frustrate its natural power and purpose sin against nature and commit a deed which is shameful and intrinsically vicious. 80

Small wonder, therefore, if Holy Writ bears witness that the Divine Majesty regards with greatest detestation this horrible crime and at times has punished it with death. As St. Augustine notes, "Intercourse even with one's legitimate wife is unlawful and wicked where the conception of the offspring is prevented. Onan, the son of Juda, did this and the Lord killed him for it."[45] 81

Since, therefore, openly departing from the uninterrupted Christian tradition some recently have judged it possible solemnly to declare another doctrine regarding this question, the Catholic Church, to whom God has entrusted the defence of the integrity and purity of morals, standing erect in the midst of the moral ruin which surrounds her, in order that she may preserve the chastity of the nuptial union from being defiled by this foul stain, raises her voice in token of her divine ambassadorship and through Our mouth proclaims anew: any use whatsoever of matrimony exercised in such a way that the act is deliberately frustrated in its natural power to generate life is an offence against the law of God and of nature, and those who indulge in such are branded with the guilt of a grave sin. 82

We admonish, therefore, priests who hear confessions and others who have the care of souls, in virtue of Our supreme authority and in Our solicitude for the salvation of souls, not to allow the faithful entrusted to them to err regarding this most grave law of God; much more, that they keep them- 83 selves immune from such false opinions, in no way conniving in them. If any confessor or pastor of souls, which may God forbid, lead the faithful entrusted to him into these errors or should at least confirm them by approval or by guilty silence, let him be mindful of the fact that he must render a strict account to God, the Supreme Judge, for the betrayal of his sacred trust, and let him take to himself the words of Christ: "They are blind and leaders of the blind: and if the blind lead the blind, both fall into the pit."[46]

84   As regards the evil use of matrimony, to pass over the arguments which are shameful, not infrequently others that are false and exaggerated are put forward. Holy Mother Church very well understands and clearly appreciates all that is said regarding the health of the mother and the danger to her life. And who would not grieve to think of these things? Who is not filled with the greatest admiration when he sees a mother risking her life with heroic fortitude, that she may preserve the life of the offspring which she has conceived? God alone, all bountiful and merciful as He is, can reward her for the fulfilment of the office alloted to her by nature, and will assuredly repay her in a measure full to overflowing.[47]

Holy Church knows well that not infrequently one of the parties is sinned against rather than sinning, when for a grave cause he or she reluctantly allows the perversion of the right order. In such a case, there is no sin, provided that, mindful of the law of charity, he or she does not neglect to seek to dissuade and to deter the partner from sin. Nor are those considered as acting against nature who in the married state use their right in the proper manner although on account of natural reasons either of time or of certain defects, new life cannot be brought forth. For in matrimony as well as in the use of the matrimonial rights there are also secondary ends, such as mutual aid, the cultivating of mutual love, and the quieting of concupiscence which husband and wife are not forbidden to consider so long as they are subordinated to the primary end and so long as the intrinsic nature of the act is preserved.

86   We are deeply touched by the sufferings of those parents who, in extreme want, experience great difficulty in rearing their children.

However, they should take care lest the calamitous state   87
of their external affairs should be the occasion for a much
more calamitous error. No difficulty can arise that justifies
the putting aside of the law of God which forbids all acts
intrinsically evil. There is no possible circumstance in which
husband and wife cannot, strengthened by the grace of God,
fulfil faithfully their duties and preserve in wedlock their
chastity unspotted. This truth of Christian Faith is expressed
by the teaching of the Council of Trent. "Let no one be so
rash as to assert that which the Fathers of the Council have
placed under anathema, namely, that there are precepts of
God impossible for the just to observe. God does not ask the
impossible, but by His commands, instructs you to do what
you are able, to pray for what you are not able that He may
help you."[48]

This same doctrine was again solemnly repeated and con-   88
firmed by the Church in the condemnation of the Jansenist
heresy which dared to utter this blasphemy against the goodness of God: "Some precepts of God are, when one considers
the powers which man possesses, impossible of fulfilment
even to the just who wish to keep the law and strive to do so;
grace is lacking whereby these laws could be fulfilled."[49]

But another very grave crime is to be noted, Venerable   89
Brethren, which regards the taking of the life of the offspring
hidden in the mother's womb. Some wish it to be allowed
and left to the will of the father or the mother; others say it
is unlawful unless there are weighty reasons which they call
by the name of medical, social, or eugenic "indication."
Because this matter falls under the penal laws of the state by
which the destruction of the offspring begotten but unborn is
forbidden, these people demand that the "indication." which
in one form or another they defend, be recognized as such by
the public law and in no way penalized. There are those,
moreover, who ask that the public authorities provide aid for
these death-dealing operations, a thing, which, sad to say,
everyone knows is of very frequent occurrence in some
places.

As to the "medical and therapeutic indication" to which,   90
using their own words, we have made reference, Venerable

Brethren, however much we may pity the mother whose health and even life is gravely imperiled in the performance of the duty allotted to her by nature, nevertheless what could ever be a sufficient reason for excusing in any way the direct murder of the innocent? This is precisely what we are dealing with here. Whether inflicted upon the mother or upon the child, it is against the precept of God and the law of nature: "Thou shalt not kill:"[50] The life of each is equally sacred, and no one has the power, not even the public authority, to destroy it. It is of no use to appeal to the right of taking away life for here it is a question of the innocent, whereas that right has regard only to the guilty; nor is there here question of defense by bloodshed against an unjust aggressor (for who would call an innocent child an unjust aggressor?); again there is no question here of what is called the "law of extreme necessity" which could even extend to the direct killing of the innocent. Upright and skilful doctors strive most praiseworthily to guard and preserve the lives of both mother and child; on the contrary, those show themselves most unworthy of the noble medical profession who encompass the death of one or the other, through a pretence at practicing medicine or through motives of misguided pity.

91   All of which agrees with the stern words of the Bishop of Hippo in denouncing those wicked parents who seek to remain childless, and failing in this, are not ashamed to put their offspring to death: "Sometimes this lustful cruelty or cruel lust goes so far as to seek to procure a baneful sterility, and if this fails the fetus conceived in the womb is in one way or another smothered or evacuated, in the desire to destroy the offspring before it has life, or if it already lives in the womb, to kill it before it is born. If both man and woman are party to such practices they are not spouses at all; and if from the first they have carried on thus they have come together not for honest wedlock, but for impure gratification; if both are not party to these deeds, I make bold to say that either the one makes herself a mistress of the husband, or the other simply the paramour of his wife."[51]

92   What is asserted in favour of the social and eugenic "indication" may and must be accepted, provided lawful and up-

right methods are employed within the proper limits; but to wish to put forward reasons based upon them for the killing of the innocent is unthinkable and contrary to the divine precept promulgated in the words of the Apostle: Evil is not to be done that good may come of it.[52]

Those who hold the reins of government should not forget   **93** that it is the duty of public authority by appropriate laws and sanctions to defend the lives of the innocent, and this all the more so since those whose lives are endangered and assailed cannot defend themselves. Among whom we must mention in the first place infants hidden in the mother's womb. And if the public magistrates not only do not defend them, but by their laws and ordinances betray them to death at the hands of doctors or of others, let them remember that God is the Judge and Avenger of innocent blood which cries from earth to Heaven.[53]

Finally, that pernicious practice must be condemned   **94** which closely touches upon the natural right of man to enter matrimony but affects also in a real way the welfare of the offspring. For there are some who over solicitous for the cause of eugenics, not only give salutary counsel for more certainly procuring the strength and health of the future child—which, indeed, is not contrary to right reason—but put eugenics before aims of a higher order, and by public authority wish to prevent from marrying all those whom, even though naturally fit for marriage, they consider, according to the norms and conjectures of their investigations, would, through hereditary transmission, bring forth defective offspring. And more, they wish to legislate to deprive these of that natural faculty by medical action despite their unwillingness; and this they do not propose as an infliction of grave punishment under the authority of the state for a cime committed, nor to prevent future crimes by guilty persons, but against every right and good they wish the civil authority to arrogate to itself a power over a faculty which it never had and can never legitimately possess.

Those who act in this way are at fault in losing sight of the   **95** fact that the family is more sacred than the State and that men are begotten not for the earth and for time, but for

Heaven and eternity. Although often these individuals are to be dissuaded from entering into matrimony, certainly it is wrong to brand men with the stigma of crime because they contract marriage, on the ground that, despite the fact that they are in every respect capable of matrimony, they will give birth to only defective children, even though they use all care and diligence.

96   Public magistrates have no direct power over the bodies of their subjects; therefore, where no crime has taken place and there is no cause present for grave punishment, they can never directly harm, or tamper with the integrity of the body, either for the reasons of eugenics or for any other reason. St. Thomas teaches this when, inquiring whether human judges for the sake of preventing future evils can inflict punishment, he admits that the power indeed exists as regards certain other forms of evil, but justly and properly denies it as regards the maiming of the body. "No one who is guiltless may be punished by a human tribunal either by flogging to death, or mutilation, or by beating."[5][4]

97   Furthermore, Christian doctrine establishes, and the light of human reason makes it most clear, that private individuals have no other power over the members of their bodies than that which pertains to their natural ends; and they are not free to destroy or mutilate their members, or in any other way render themselves unfit for their natural functions, except when no other provision can be made for the good of the whole body.

98   We may now consider another class of errors concerning conjugal faith. Every sin committed as regards the offspring becomes in some way a sin against conjugal faith, since both these blessings are essentially connected. However, we must mention briefly the sources of error and vice corresponding to those virtues which are demanded by conjugal faith, namely the chaste honour existing between man and wife, the due subjection of wife to husband, and the true love which binds both parties together.

99   It follows therefore that they are destroying mutual fidelity, who think that the ideas and morality of our present time concerning a certain harmful and false friendship with a

third party can be countenanced, and who teach that a greater
freedom of feeling and action in such external relations should
be allowed to man and wife, particularly as many (so they
consider) are possessed of an inborn sexual tendency which
cannot be satisfied within the narrow limits of monogamous
marriage. That rigid attitude which condemns all sensual
affections and actions with a third party they imagine to be
a narrowing of mind and heart, something obsolete, or an
abject form of jealousy, and as a result they look upon whatever penal laws are passed by the State for the preserving of
conjugal faith as void or to be abolished. Such unworthy and
idle opinions are condemned by that noble instinct which is
found in every chaste husband and wife, and even by the
light of the testimony of nature alone,—a testimony that is
sanctioned and confirmed by the command of God: "Thou
shalt not commit adultery,"[55] and the words of Christ:
"Whosoever shall look on a woman to lust after her hath
already committed adultery with her in his heart."[56] The
force of this divine precept can never be weakened by any
merely human custom, bad example or pretext of human
progress, for just as it is the one and the same "Jesus Christ,
yesterday and to-day and the same for ever,"[57] so it is the
one and the same doctrine of Christ that abides and of which
not one jot or tittle shall pass away till all is fulfilled.[58]

The same false teachers who try to dim the lustre of con-   100
jugal faith and purity do not scruple to do away with the
honourable and trusting obedience which the woman owes
to the man. Many of them even go further and assert that
such a subjection of one party to the other is unworthy of
human dignity, that the rights of husband and wife are equal;
wherefore, they boldly proclaim, the emancipation of women
has been or ought to be effected. This emancipation in their
ideas must be threefold, in the ruling of the domestic society,
in the administration of family affairs and in the rearing of
the children. It must be social, economic, physiological:—
physiological, that is to say, the woman is to be freed at her
own good pleasure from the burdensome duties properly
belonging to a wife as companion and mother (We have
already said that this is not an emancipation but a crime);

social, inasmuch as the wife being freed from the cares of children and family, should, to the neglect of these, be able to follow her own bent and devote herself to business and even public affairs; finally economic, whereby the woman even without the knowledge and against the wish of her husband may be at liberty to conduct and administer her own affairs, giving here attention chiefly to these rather than to children, husband and family.

101   This, however, is not the true emancipation of woman, nor that rational exalted liberty which belongs to the noble office of a Christian woman and wife, it is rather the debasing of the womanly character and the dignity of motherhood, and indeed of the whole family, as a result of which the husband suffers the loss of his wife, the children of their mother, and the home and the whole family of an ever watchful guardian. More than this, this false liberty and unnatural equality with the husband is to the detriment of the woman herself, for if the woman descends from her truly regal throne to which she has been raised within the walls of the home by means of the Gospel, she will soon be reduced to the old state of slavery (if not in appearance, certainly in reality) and become as amongst the pagans the mere instrument of man.

102   This equality of rights which is so much exaggerated and distorted, must indeed be recognised in those rights which belong to the dignity of the human soul and which are proper to the marriage contract and inseparably bound up with wedlock. In such things undoubtedly both parties enjoy the same rights and are bound by the same obligations; in other things there must be a certain inequality and due accommodation, which is demanded by the good of the family and the right ordering and unity and stability of home life.

103   As, however, the social and economic conditions of the married woman must in some way be altered on account of the changes in social intercourse, it is part of the office of the public authority to adapt the civil rights of the wife to modern needs and requirements, keeping in view what the natural disposition and temperament of the female sex, good morality, and the welfare of the family demands, and provided always that the essential order of the domestic society remain

intact, founded as it is on something higher than human authority and wisdom, namely on the authority and wisdom of God, and so not changeable by public laws or at the pleasure of private individuals.

These enemies of marriage go further, however, when they substitute for that true and solid love, which is the basis of conjugal happiness, a certain vague compatibility of temperament. This they call sympathy and assert that, since it is the only bond by which husband and wife are linked together, when it ceases the marriage is completely dissolved. What else is this than to build a house upon sand?—a house that in the words of Christ whould forthwith be shaken and collapse, as soon as it was exposed to the waves of adversity "and the winds blew and they beat upon that house. And it fell: and great was the fall thereof."[5 9] on the other hand, the house built upon a rock, that is to say on mutual conjugal chastity and strengthened by a deliberate and constant union of spirit, will not only never fall away but will never be shaken by adversity.

104

We have so far, Venerable Brethren, shown the excellency of the first two blessings of Christian wedlock which the modern subverters of society are attacking. And now considering that the third blessing, which is that of the sacrament, far surpasses the other two, we should not be surprised to find that this, because of its outstanding excellence is much more sharply attacked by the same people. They put forward in the first place that matrimony belongs entirely to the profane and purely civil sphere, that it is not to be committed to the religious society, the Church of Christ, but to civil society alone. They then add that the marriage contract is to be freed from any indissoluble bond, and that separation and divorce are not only to be tolerated but sanctioned by the law; from which it follows finally that, robbed of all its holiness, matrimony should be enumerated amongst the secular and civil institutions. The first point is contained in their contention that the civil act should stand for the marriage contract(civil matrimony, as it is called), while the religious act is to be considered a mere addition, or at most a concession to a too superstitious people. Moreover they want it to be no

105

cause for reproach that marriages be contracted by Catholics with non-Catholic without any reference to religion or recourse to the ecclesiastical authorities. The second point, which is but a consequence of the first is to be found in their excuse for complete divorce and in their praise and encouragement of those civil laws which favour the lossening of the bond itself. As the salient features of the religious character of all marriage and particularly of the sacramental marriage of Christians have been treated at length and supported by weighty arguments in the encyclical letters of Leo XIII, letters which We have frequently recalled to mind and expressly made our own, We refer you to them, repeating here only a few points.

106   Even by the light of reason alone and particularly if the ancient records of history are investigated, if the unwavering popular conscience is interrogated and the manners and institutions of all races examined, it is sufficiently obvious that there is a certain sacredness and religious character attaching even to the purely natural union of man and woman, "not something added by chance but innate, not imposed by men but involved in the nature of things," since it has "God for its author and has been even from the beginning a foreshadowing of the Incarnation of the Word of God."[60] This sacredness of marriage which is intimately connected with religion and all that is holy, arises from the divine origin we have just mentioned, from its purpose which is the begetting and educating of children for God, and the binding of man and wife to God through Christian love and mutual support; and finally it arises from the very nature of wedlock, whose institution is to be sought for in the farseeing Providence of God, whereby it is the means of transmitting life, thus making the parents the ministers, as it were, of the Divine Omnipotence. To this must be added that new element of dignity which comes from the sacrament, by which the Christian marriage is so ennobled and raised to such a level, that it appeared to the Apostle as a great sacrament, honourable in every way.[61]

107   This religious character of marriage, its sublime signification of grace and the union between Christ and the Church, evidently requires that those about to marry should show a

holy reverence towards it, and zealously endeavour to make their marriage approach as nearly as possible to the archetype of Christ and the Church.

They, therefore, who rashly and heedlessly contract mixed   108
marriages, from which the maternal love and providence of the Church dissuades her children for very sound reasons, fail conspicuously in this respect, sometimes with danger to their eternal salvation. This attitude of the Church to mixed marriages appears in many of her documents, all of which are summed up in the Code of Cannon Law: "Everywhere and with the greatest strictness the Church forbids marriages between baptized persons, one of whom is a Catholic and the other a member of a schismatical or heretical sect; and if there is, added to this, the danger of the falling away of the Catholic party and the perversion of the children, such a marriage is forbidden also by the divine law."[62] If the Church occasionally on account of circumstances does not refuse to grant a dispensation from these strict laws (provided that the divine law remains intact and the dangers above mentioned are provided against by suitable safeguards), it is unlikely that the Catholic party will not suffer some detriment from such a marriage.

Whence it comes about not unfrequently, as experience   109
shows, that deplorable defections from religion occur among the offspring, or at least a headlong descent into that religious indifference which is closely allied to impiety. There is this also to be considered that in these mixed marriages it becomes much more difficult to imitate by a lively conformity of spirit the mystery of which We have spoken, namely that close union between Christ and His Church.

Assuredly, also, will there be wanting that close union of   110
spirit which as it is the sign and mark of the Church of Christ, so also should be the sign of Christian wedlock, its glory and adornment. For, where there exists diversity of mind, truth and feeling, the bond of union of mind and heart is wont to be broken, or at least weakened. From this comes the danger lest the love of man and wife grow cold and the peace and happiness of family life, resting as it does on the union of hearts, be destroyed. Many centuries ago indeed, the old

Roman law had proclaimed: "Marriages are the union of male and female, a sharing of life and the communication of divine and human rights."[63] But especially, as We have pointed out, Venerable Brethren, the daily increasing facility of divorce is an obstacle to the restoration of marriage to that state of perfection which the divine Redeemer willed it should possess.

111   The advocates of the neo-paganiam of to-day have learned nothing from the sad state of affairs, but instead, day by day, more and more vehemently, they continue by legislation to attack the indissolubility of the marriage bond, proclaiming that the lawfulness of divorce must be recognised, and that the antiquated laws should give place to a new and more humane legislation. Many and varied are the gounds put forward for divorce, some arising from the wickedness and the guilt of the persons concerned, others arising from the circumstances of the case; the former they describe as subjective, the latter as objective; in a word, whatever might make married life hard or unpleasant. They strive to prove their contentions regarding these grounds for divorce legislation they would bring about, by various arguments. Thus, in the first place, they maintain that it is for the good of either party that the one who is innocent should have the right to separate from the guilty, or that the guilty should be withdrawn from a union which is unpleasing to him and against his will. In the second place, they argue, the good of the child demands this, for either it will be deprived of a proper education or the natural fruits of it, and will too easily be affected by the discords and shortcomings of the parents, and drawn from the path of virtue. And thirdly the common good of society requires that these marriages should be completely dissolved, which are now incapable of producing their natural results, and that legal separations should be allowed when crimes are to be feared as the result of the common habitation and intercurse of the parties. This last, they say must be admitted to avoid the crimes being committed purposely with a view to obtaining the desired sentence of divorce for which the judge can legally loose the marriage bond, as also to prevent people from coming before the courts when it is obvious from the

state of the case that they are lying and perjuring
—all of which brings the court and the lawful authority into
contempt. Hence the civil laws, in their opinion, have to be
reformed to meet these new requirements, to suit the changes
of the times and the changes in men's opinions, civil institutions and customs. Each of these reasons is considered by
them as conclusive, so that all taken together offer a clear
proof of the necessity of granting divorce in certain cases.

Others, taking a step further, simply state that marriage,   112
being a private contract, is, like other private contracts, to be
left to the consent and good pleasure of both parties, and so
can be dissolved for any reason whatsoever.

Opposed to all these reckless opinions, Venerable Brethren,   113
stands the unalterable law of God, fully confirmed by Christ,
a law that can never be deprived of its force by the decrees
men, the ideas of a people or the will of any legislator:
"What God hath joined together, let no man put asunder."[64]
And if any man, acting contrary to this law, shall have put
asunder, his action is null and void, and the consequence remains, as Christ Himself has explicitly confirmed: "Everyone
that putteth away his wife and marrieth another, committeth
adultery: and he that marrieth her that is put away from her
husband committeth adultery."[65] Moreover, these words refer to every kind of marriage, even that which is natural and
legitimate only; for, as has already been observed, that indissolubility by which the loosening of the bond is once and for
all removed from the whim of the parites and from every
secular power, is a property of evvery true marriage.

Let that solemn pronouncement of the Council of Trent   114
be recalled to mind in which, under the stigma of anathema,
it condemned these errors: "If anyone should say that an
account of heresy or the hardships of co-habitation or a
deliberate abuse of one party by the other the marriage tie
may be loosened, let him be anathema;"[66] and again: "If
anyone should say that the Church errs in having taught or
in teaching that, according to the teaching of the Gospel and
the Apostles, the bond of marriage cannot be loosed because
of the sin of adultery of either party; or that neither party,
even though he be innocent, having given no cause for the sin

of adultery, can contract another marriage during the lifetime of the other; and that he commits adultery who marries another after putting away his adulterous wife, and likewise that she commits adultery who puts away her husband and marries another: let him be anathema."[67]

115   If therefore the Church has not erred and does not err in teaching this, and consequently it is certain that the bond of marriage cannot be loosed even on account of the sin of adultery, it is evident that all the other weaker excuses that can be, and are usually brought forward, are of no value whatsoever. And the objections brought against the firmness of the marriage bond are easily answered. For, in certain circumstances, imperfect separation of the parties is allowed, the bond not being severed. This separation, which the Church herself permits, and expressly mentions in her Canon Law in those canons which deal with the separation of the parties as to marital relationship and co-habitation, removes all the alleged inconveniences and dangers.[68] It will be for the sacred law and, to some extent, also the civil law, in so far as civil matters are affected, to lay down the grounds, the conditions, the method and precautions to be taken in a case of this kind in order to safeguard the education of the children and the well-being of the family, and to remove all those evils which threaten the married persons, the children and the State. Now all those arguments that are brought forward to prove the indissolubility of the marriage tie, arguments which have already been touched upon, can equally be applied to excluding not only the necessity of divorce, but even the power to grant it; while for all the advantages that can be put forward for the former, there can be adduced as many disadvantages and evils which are a formidable menace to the whole of human society.

116   To revert again to the expressions of Our predecessor, it is hardly necessary to point out what an amount of good is involved in the absolute indissolubility of wedlock and what a train of evils follows upon divorce. Whenever the marriage bond remains intact, then we find marriages contracted with a sense of safety and security, while, when separations are considered and the dangers of divorce are present, the mar-

riage contract itself becomes insecure, or at least gives ground
for anxiety and surprises. On the one hand we see a wonderful
strengthening of goodwill and cooperation in the daily life of
husband and wife, while, on the other, both of these are miserably weakened by the presence of a facility for divorce. Here
we have at a very opportune moment a source of help by
which both parties are enabled to preserve their purity and
loyalty; there we find harmful inducements to unfaithfulness. On this side we find the birth of children and their
tuition and upbringing effectively promoted, many avenues
of discord closed amongst families and relations, and the
beginnings of rivalry and jealousy easily suppressed; on that,
very great obstacles to the birth and rearing of children and
their education, and many occasions of quarrels, and seeds of
jealousy sown everywhere. Finally, but especially, the dignity
and position of women in civil and domestic society is
reinstated by the former; while by the latter it is shamefully
lowered and the danger is incurred "of their being considered
outcasts, slaves of the lust of men."[6][9]

To conclude with the important words of Leo XIII, since   117
the destruction of family life "and the loss of national wealth
is brought about more by the corruption of morals than by
anything else, it is easily seen that divorce, which is born of
the perverted morals of a people, and leads, as experiment
shows, to vicious habits in public and private life, is particularly opposed to the well-being of the family and of the
State. The serious nature of these evils will be the more
clearly recognised, when we remember that, once divorce has
been allowed, there will be no sufficient means of keeping it
in check within any definite bounds. Great is the force of
example, greater still that of lust; and with such incitements
it cannot but happen that divorce and its consequent setting
loose of the passions should spread daily and attack the souls
of many like a contagious disease or a river bursting its banks
and flooding the land."[7][0]

Thus, as we read in the same letter, "unless things change,   118
the human family and State have every reason to fear lest
they should suffer absolute ruin."[7][1] All this was written
fifty years ago, yet it is confirmed by the daily increasing

corruption of morals and the unheard of degradation of the family in those lands where Communism reigns unchecked.

III.

119   Thus far, Venerable Brethren, We have admired with due reverence what the all wise Creator and Redeemer of the human race has ordained with regard to human marriage; at the same time we have expressed Our grief that such a pious ordinance of the divine Goodness should to-day, and on every side, be frustrated and trampled upon by the passions, errors and vices of men.

120   It is then fitting that, with all fatherly solicitude, We should turn Our mind to seek out suitable remedies whereby those most detestable abuses which We have mentioned, may be removed, and everywhere marriage may again be revealed. To this end, it behooves Us, above all else, to call to mind that firmly established principle, esteemed alike in sound philosophy and sacred theology: namely, that whatever things have deviated from their right order, cannot be brought back to that original state which is in harmony with their nature except by a return to the divine plan which, as the Angelic Doctor teaches,[72] is the exemplar of all right order.

121   Wherefore, Our predecessor of happy memory, Leo XIII, attacked the doctrine of the naturalists in these words: "It is a divinely appointed law that whatsoever things are constituted by God, the Author of nature, these we find the more useful and salutary, the more they remain in their natural state, unimpaired and unchanged; inasmuch as God, the Creator of all things, intimately knows what is suited to the constitution and the preservation of each, and by his will and mind has so ordained all things that each may duly achieve its purpose. But if the boldness and wickedness of men change and disturb this order of things, so providentially disposed, then, indeed, things so wonderfully ordained, will begin to be injurious, or will cease to be beneficial, either because, in the change, they have lost their power to benefit, or because God Himself is thus pleased to draw down chastisement on the pride and presumption of men."[73]

In order, therefore, to restore due order in this matter of marriage, it is necessary that all should bear in mind what is the divine plan and strive to conform to it. 122

Wherefore, since the chief obstacle to this study is the power of unbridled lust, which indeed is the most potent cause of sinning against the sacred laws of matrimony, and since man cannot hold in check his passions, unless he first subject himself to God, this must be his primary endeavour, in accordance with the plan divinely ordained. For it is a sacred ordinance that whoever shall have first subjected himself to God will, by the aid of divine grace, be glad to subject to himself his own passions and concupiscence; while he who is a rebel against God will, to his sorrow, experience within himself the violent rebellion of his worst passions. 123

And how wisely this has been decreed, St. Augustine thus shows: "This indeed is fitting, that the lower be subject to the higher, so that he who would have subject to himself whatever is below him, should himself submit to whatever is above him. Acknowledge order, seek peace. Be thou subject to God, and thy flesh subject to thee. What more fitting! What more fair! Thou are subject to the higher and the lower is subject to thee. Do thou serve Him who made thee, so that that which was made for thee may serve thee. For we do not commend this order, namely, "The flesh to thee and thou to God,' but 'Thou to God, and the flesh to thee.' If, however, thou despisest the subjection of thyself to God, thou shalt never bring about the subjection of the flesh to thyself. If thou dost not obey the Lord, thou shalt be tormented by thy servant."[74] This right ordering on the part of God's wisdom is mentioned by the holy Doctor of the Gentiles, inspired by the Holy Ghost, for in speaking of those ancient philosophers who refused to adore and reverence Him whom they knew to be the Creator of the universe, he says: "Wherefore God gave them up to the desires of their heart, unto uncleanness, to dishonour their own bodies among themselves;" and again: "For this same God delivered them up to shameful affections."[75] And St. James says: "God resisteth the proud and giveth grace to the humble,"[76] without which grace, as the 124 same Doctor of the Gentiles reminds us, man cannot subdue the rebellion of his flesh.[77]

125   Consequently, as the onslaughts of these uncontrolled passions cannot in any way be lessened, unless the spirit first shows a humble compliance of duty and reverence towards its Maker, it is above all and before all needful that those who are joined in the bond of sacred wedlock should be wholly imbued with a profound and genuine sense of duty towards God, which will shape their whole lives, and fill their minds and wills with a very deep reverence for the majesty of God.

126   Quite fittingly, therefore, and quite in accordance with defined norm of Christian sentiment, do those pastors of souls act who, to prevent married people from failing in the observance of God's law, urge them to perform their duty and exercise their religion so that they should give themselves to God, continually ask for His divine assistance, frequent the sacraments, and always nourish and preserve a loyal and thoroughly sincere devotion to God.

127   They are greatly deceived who having underestimated or neglected these means which rise above nature, think that they can induce men by the use and discovery of the natural sciences, such as those of biology, the science of heredity, and the like, to curb their carnal desires. We do not say this in order to belittle those natural means which are not dishonest, for God is the Author of nature as well as of grace, and he has disposed the good things of both orders for the beneficial use of men. The faithful, therefore, can and ought to be assisted also by natural means. But they are mistaken who think that these means are able to establish chastity in the nuptial union, or that they are more effective than supernatural grace.

128   This conformity of wedlock and moral conduct with the divine laws respective of marriage, without which its effective restoration cannot be brought about, supposes, however, that all can discern readily, with real certainty, and without any accompanying error, what those laws are. But everyone can see to how many fallacies an avenue would be opened up and how many errors would become mixed with the truth, if it were left solely to the light of reason of each to find it out,

or if it were to be discovered by the private interpretation of
the truth which is revealed. And if this is applicable to many
other truths of the moral order, we must all the more pay
attention to those things, which appertain to marriage where
the inordinate desire for pleasure can attack frail human
nature and easily deceive it and lead it astray; this is all the
more true of the observance of the divine law, which demands
sometimes hard and repeated sacrifices, for which, as experience points out, a weak man can find so many excuses for
avoiding the fulfilment of the divine law.

On this account, in order that no falsification or corrup-   129
tion of the divine law but a true genuine knowledge of it may
enlighten the minds of men and guide their conduct, it is
necessary that a filial and humble obedience towards the
Church should be combined with devotedness to God and the
desire of submitting to Him. For Christ Himself made the
Church the teacher of truth in those things also which concern the right regulation of moral conduct even though some
knowledge of the same is not beyond human reason. For just
as God, in the case of the natural truths of religion and morals, added revelation to the light of reason so that what is
right and true, "in the present state also of the human race
may be known readily with real certainty without any ad-
mixture of error,"[78] so for the same purpose he has constituted the Church the guardian and the teacher of the whole
of the truth concerning religion and moral conduct; to her
therefore should the faithful show obedience and subject
their minds and hearts so as to be kept unharmed and free
from error and moral corruption, and so that they shall not
deprive themselves of that assistance given by God with such
liberal bounty, they ought to show this due obedience not
only when the Church defines something with solemn judgment, but also, in proper proportion, when by the constitutions and decrees of the Holy See, opinions are prescribed
and condemned as dangerous or distorted.[79]

Wherefore, let the faithful also be on their guard against   130
the overrated independence of private judgment and that
false autonomy of human reason. For it is quite foreign to
everyone bearing the name of a Christian to trust his own

mental powers with such pride as to agree only with those things which he can examine from their inner nature, and to imagine that the Church, sent by God to teach and guide all nations, is not conversant with present affairs and circumstances; or even that they must obey only in those matters which she has decreed by solemn definition as though her other decisions might be presumed to be false or putting forward insufficient motive for truth and honesty. Quite to the contrary, a characteristic of all true followers of Christ, lettered or unlettered, is to suffer themselves to be guided and led in all things that touch upon faith or morals by the Holy Church of God through its Supreme Pastor the Roman Pontiff, who is himself guided by Jesus Christ Our Lord.

131   Consequently, since everything must be referred to the law and mind of God, in order to bring about the universal and permanent restoration of marriage, it is indeed of the utmost importance that the faithful should be well instructed concerning matrimony; both by word of mouth and by the written word, not cursorily but often and fully, by means of plain and weighty arguments, so that these truths will strike the intellect and will be deeply engraved on their hearts. Let them realize and diligently reflect upon the great wisdom, kindness and bounty God has shown towards the human race, not only by institution of marriage, but also, and quite as much, by upholding it with sacred laws; still more, in wonderfully raising it to the dignity of a Sacrament by which such an abundant fountain of graces has been opened to those joined in Christian wedlock, that these may be able to serve the noble purposes of wedlock for their own welfare and for that of their children, of the community and also for that of human relatioship.

132   Certainly, if the latter day subverters of marriage are entirely devoted to misleading the minds of men and corrupting their hearts, to making a mockery of matrimonial purity and extolling the filthiest of vices by means of books and pamphlets and other innumerable methods, much more ought you, Venerable Brethren, whom "the Holy Ghost has placed as bishops, to rule the Church of God, which He hath purchased with His own blood."[80] to give yourselves wholly

to this, that through yourselves and through the priests subject to you, and, moreover, through the laity welded together by Catholic Action, so much desired and recommended by Us, into a power of hierarchical apostolate, you may, by every fitting means, oppose error by truth, vice by the excellent dignity of chastity, the slavery of covetousness by the liberty of the sons of God,[81] that disastrous ease in obtaining divorce by an enduring love in the bond of marriage and by the inviolate pledge of fidelity given even to death.

Thus will it come to pass that the faithful will whole-   **133** heartedly thank God that they are bound together by His command and led by gentle compulsion to fly as far as possible from every kind of idolatry of the flesh and from the base slavery of the passions. They will, in a great measure, turn and be turned away from these abominable opinions which to the dishonour of man's dignity are now spread about in speech and in writing and collected under the title of "perfect marriage" and which indeed would make that perfect marriage nothing better than "depraved marriage," as it has been rightly and truly called.

Such wholesome instruction and religious training in re-   **134** gard to Christian marriage will be quite different from that exaggerated physiological education by means of which, in these times of ours, some reformers of married life make pretence of helping those joined in wedlock, laying much stress on these physiological matters, in which is learned rather the art of sinning a subtle way than the virtue of living chastely.

So, Venerable Brethren, we make entirely Our own the   **135** words which Our predecessor of happy memory, Leo XIII, in his encyclical letter on Christian marriage addressed to the bishops of the whole world: "Take care not to spare your efforts and authority in bringing about that among the people committed to your guidance that doctrine may be preserved whole and unadulterated which Christ the Lord and the apostles, the interpreters of the divine will, have handed down, and which the Catholic Church herself has religiously preserved, and commanded to be observed by the faithful of every age."[82]

136   Even the very best instruction given by the Church, however, will not alone suffice to bring about once more conformity of marriage to the law of God; something more is needed in addition to the education of the mind, namely a steadfast determination of the will, on the part of husband and wife, to observe the sacred laws of God and of nature in regard to marriage. In fine, in spite of what others may wish to assert and spread abroad by word of mouth or in writing, let husband and wife resolve: to stand fast to the commandments of God in all things that matrimony demands; always to render to each other the assitance of mutual love; to preserve the honour of chastity; not to lay profane hands on the stable nature of the bond; to use the rights given them by marriage in a way that will be always Christian and sacred, more especially in the first years of wedlock, so that should there be need of continency afterwards, custom will have made it easier for each to preserve it. In order that they may make this firm resolution, keep it and put it into practice, an oft-repeated consideration of their state of life, and a diligent reflection on the sacrament they have received, will be of great assistance to them. Let them constantly keep in mind, that they have been sanctified and strengthened for the duties and for the dignity of their state by a special sacrament, the efficacious power of which, although it does not impress a character, is undying. To this purpose we may ponder over the words full of real comfort of holy Cardinal Robert Bellarmine, who with other well-known theologians with devout conviction thus expresses himself: "The sacrament of matrimony can be regarded in two ways: first, in the making, and then in its permanent state. For it is a sacrament like to that of the Eucharist, which not only when it is being conferred, but also whilst it remains, is a sacrament; for as long as the married parties are alive, so long is their union a sacrament of Christ and the Church."[83]

137   Yet in order that the grace of this sacrament may produce its full fruit, there is need, as we have already pointed out, of the cooperation of the married parties, which consists in their striving to fulfil their duties to the best of their ability and with unwearied effort. For just as in the natural order men

must apply the powers given them by God with their own toil and diligence that these may exercise their full vigor, failing which, no profit is gained, so also men must diligently and unceasingly use the powers given them by the grace which is laid up in the soul by this sacrament. Let not, then, those who are joined in matrimony neglect the grace of the sacrament which is in them,[84] for, in applying themselves to the careful observance, however laborious, of their duties they will find the power of that grace becoming more effectual as time goes on. And if ever they should feel themselves to be over-burdened by the hardships of their condition of life, let them not lose courage, but rather let them regard in some measure as addressed to them that which St. Paul the Apostle wrote to his beloved disciple Timothy regarding the sacrament of holy Orders when the disciple was dejected through hardship and insults: "I admonish thee that thou stir up the grace which is in thee by the imposition of my hands. For God hath not given us the spirit of fear; but of power, and of love, and of sobriety."[85]

All these things, however, Venerable Brethren, depend in large measure on the due preparation remote and proximate, of the parties for marriage. For it cannot be denied that the basis of a happy wedlock, and the ruin of an unhappy one, is prepared and set in the souls of boys and girls during the period of childhood and adolescence. There is danger that those who before marriage sought in all things what is theirs, who indulged even their impured desires, will be in the married state what they were before, that they will reap that which they have sown;[86] indeed, within the home there will be sadness, lamentation, mutual contempt, strifes, estrangements, weariness of common life, and, worst of all, such parties will find themselves left alone with their own unconquered passions. 138

Let then, those who are about to enter on married life, approach that state well disposed and well prepared, so that they will be able, as far as they can, to help each other in sustaining the vicissitudes of life, and yet more in attending to their eternal salvation and in forming the inner man unto the fulness of the age of Christ.[87] It will also help them, if 139 they behave towards their cherished offspring as God wills: that is, that the father be truly a father, and the mother truly a mother; through their devout love and unwearying care, the home, though it suffer the want and hardship of this valley of tears, may become for the children in its own way a foretaste of that paradise of delight in which the Creator placed the first men of the human race. Thus will they be able to bring up their children as perfect men and perfect Christians; they will instill into them a sound understanding of the Catholic Church, and will give them such a disposition and love for their fatherland as duty and gratitude demand.

140 Consequently, both those who are now thinking of entering upon this sacred married state, as well as those who have the charge of educating Christian youth, should, with due regard to the future, prepare that which is good, obviate that which is bad, and recall those points about which We have already spoken in Our encyclical letter concerning education: "The inclinations of the will, if they are bad, must be repressed from childhood, but such as are good must be fostered, and the mind, particularly of children, should be imbued with doctrines which begin with God, while the heart should be strengthened with the aids of divine grace, in the absence of which, no one can curb evil desires, nor can his discipline and formation be brought to complete perfection by the Church. For Christ has provided her with heavenly doctrines and divine sacraments, that He might make her an effectual teacher of men."[88]

141 To the proximate preparation of a good married life belongs very specially the care in choosing a partner; on that depends a great deal whether the forthcoming marriage will be happy or not, since one may be to the other either a great help in leading a Christian life, or, a great danger and hindrance. And so that they may not deplore for the rest of their lives the sorrows arising from an indiscreet marriage, those about to enter into wedlock should carefully deliberate in choosing the person with whom henceforward they must live continually: they should, in so deliberating, keep before their minds the thought first of God and of the true religion of Christ, then of themselves, of their partner, of the children

to come, as also of human and civil society, for which wedlock is a fountain head. Let them diligently pray for divine
help, so that they make their choice in accordance with Christian prudence, not indeed led by the blind and unrestrained
impulse of lust, nor by any desire of riches or other base influence, but by a true and noble love and by a sincere affection for the future partner; and then let them strive in their
married life for those ends for which the State was constituted by God. Lastly, let them not omit to ask the prudent
advice of their parents with regard to the partner, and let
them regard this advice in no light manner, in order that by
their mature knowledge and experience of human affairs they
may guard against a disastrous choice, and, on the threshold
of matrimony, may receive more abundantly the divine blessing of the fourth commandment: "Honour thy father and
thy mother (which is the first commandment with a promise)
that it may be well with thee and thou mayest be long-lived
upon the earth."[89]

Now since it is no rare thing to find that the perfect ob-   142
servance of God's commands and conjugal integrity encounter
difficulties by reason of the fact that the man and wife are in
straitened circumstances, their necessities must be relieved as
far as possible.

And so, in the first place, every effort must be made to   143
bring about that which Our predecessor Leo XIII, of happy
memory, has already insisted upon, [90] namely, that in the
State such economic and social methods should be adopted
as will enable every head of a family to earn as much as, according to his station in life, is necessary for himself, his wife,
and for the rearing of his children, for "the labourer is worthy
of his hire."[91] To deny this, or to make light of what is
equitable, is a grave injustice and is placed among the greatest
sins by Holy Writ;[92] nor is it lawful to fix such a scanty
wage as will be insufficient for the upkeep of the family in
the circumstances in which it is placed.

Care, however, must be taken that the parties themselves,   144
for a considerable time before entering upon married life,
should strive to dispose of, or at least to diminish, the material obstacles in their way. The manner in which this may be

done effectively and honestly must be pointed out by those who are experienced. Provision must be made also, in the case of those who are not self-supporting, for joint aid by private or public guilds.[93]

145   When these means which We have pointed out do not fulfil the needs, particularly of a larger or poorer family, Christian charity towards our neighbour absolutely demands that those things which are lacking to the needy should be provided; hence it is incumbent on the rich to help the poor, so that, having an abundance of this world's goods, they may not expend them fruitlessly or completely squander them, but employ them for the support and well-being of those who lack the necessities of life. They who give of their substance to Christ in the person of His poor will receive from the Lord a most bountiful reward when He shall come to judge the world, they who act to the contrary will pay the penalty.[94] Not in vain does the Apostle warn us: "He that hath the substance of this world and shall see his brother in need, and shall shut up his bowels from him: how doth the charity of God abide in him?"[95]

146   If, however, for this purpose, private resources do not suffice, it is the duty of the public authority to supply for the insufficient forces of individual effort, particularly in a matter which is of such importance to the common weal, touching as it does the maintenance of the family and married people. If families, particularly those in which there are many children, have not suitable dwellings; if the husband cannot find employment and means of livelihood, if the necessities of life cannot be purchased except at exorbitant prices; if even the mother of the family to the great harm of the home, is compelled to go forth and seek a living by her own labour, if she, too, in the ordinary or even extraordinary labours of childbirth, is deprived of proper food, medicine, and the assistance of a skilled physician, it is patent to all to what an extent married people may lose heart, and how home life and the observance of God's commands are rendered difficult for them, indeed it is obvious how great a peril can arise to the public security and to the welfare and very life of civil society itself when such men are reduced to that condition of des-

peration that, having nothing which they fear to lose, they are emboldened to hope for chance advantage from the upheaval of the state and of established order.

Wherefore, those who have the care of the State and of the public good cannot neglect the needs of married people and their families, without bringing great harm upon the State and on the common welfare. Hence, in making the laws and in disposing of public funds they must do their utmost to relieve the needs of the poor, considering such a task as one of the most important of their administrative duties.   147

We are sorry to note that not infrequently nowadays it happens that through a certain inversion of the true order of things, ready and bountiful assistance is provided for the unmarried mother and her illegitimate offspring (who, of course must be helped in order to avoid a greater evil) which is denied to legitimate mothers or given sparingly or almost grudgingly.   148

But not only in regard to temporal goods, Venerable Brethren, is it the concern of the public authority to make proper provision for matrimony and the family, but also in other things which concern the good of souls. Just laws must be made for the protection of chastity, for reciprocal conjugal aid, and for similar purposes, and these must be faithfully enforced, because, as history testifies, the prosperity of the State and the temporal happiness of its citizens cannot remain safe and sound where the foundation on which they are established, which is the moral order, is weakened and where the very fountainhead from which the State draws its life, namely, wedlock and the family, is obstructed by the vices of its citizens.   149

For the preservation of the moral order neither the laws and sanctions of the temporal power are sufficient, nor is the beauty of virtue and the expounding of its necessity. Religious authority must enter in to enlighten the mind, to direct the will, and to strengthen human frailty by the assistance of divine grace. Such an authority is found nowhere save in the Church instituted by Christ the Lord. Hence We earnestly exhort in the Lord all those who hold the reins of power that they establish and maintain firmly harmony and friendship with this Church of Christ so that through the united activity   150 and energy of both powers the tremendous evils, fruits of those wanton liberties which assail both marriage and the family and are a menace to both Church and State, may be effectively frustrated.

151   Governments can assist the Church greatly in the execution of its important office, if, in laying down their ordinances, they take account of what is prescribed by divine and ecclesiastical law, and if penalties are fixed for offenders. For as it is, there are those who think that whatever is permitted by the laws of the State, or at least is not punished by them, is allowed also in the moral order, and, because they neither fear God nor see any reason to fear the laws of man, they act even against their conscience, thus often bringing ruin upon themselves and their conscience, thus often bringing ruin themselves and upon many others. There will be peril to or lessening of the rights and integrity of the State from its association with the Church. Such suspicion and fear is empty and groundless, as Leo XIII has already so clearly set forth: "It is generally agreed," he says, "that the Founder of the Church, Jesus Christ, wished the spiritual power to be distinct from the civil, and each to be free and unhampered in doing its own work, not forgetting, however, that it is expedient to both, and in the interest of everybody, that there be a harmonious relationship . . . If the civil power combines in a friendly manner with the spiritual power of the Church, it necessarily follows that both parties will greatly benefit. The dignity of the State will be enhanced, and with religion as its guide, there will never be a rule that is not just; while for the Church there will be at hand a safeguard and defence which operate to the public good of the faithful."[96]

152   To bring forward a recent and clear example of what is meant, it has happened quite in consonance with right order and entirely according to the law of Christ, that in the solemn Convention happily entered into between the Holy See and the Kingdom of Italy, also in matrimonial affairs a peaceful settlement and friendly cooperation has been obtained, such as befitted the glorious history of the Italian people and its ancient and sacred traditions. These decrees are to be found in the Lateran Pact: "The Italian State, desirous of

restoring to the institution of matrimony, which is the basis of the family, that dignity conformable to the traditions of its people, assigns as civil effects of the sacrament of matrimony all that is attributed to it in Canon Law."[97] To this fundamental norm are added further clauses in the common pact.

This might well be a striking example to all of how, even   *153* in this our day (in which, sad to say, the absolute separation of the civil power from the Church, and indeed from every religion, is so often taught), the one supreme authority can be united and associated with the other without detriment to the rights and supreme power of either thus protecting Christian parents from pernicious evils and menacing ruin.

All these things which, Venerable Brethren, prompted by   154 Our past solicitude We put before you, We wish according to the norm of Christian prudence to be promulgated widely among all Our beloved children committed to your care as members of the great family of Christ, that all may be thoroughly acquainted with sound teaching concerning marriage, so that they may be ever on their guard against the dangers advocated by the teachers of error, and most of all, that "denying ungodliness and worldly desires, they may live soberly and justly, and godly in this world, looking for the blessed hope and coming of the glory of the great God and Our Saviour Jesus Christ."[98]

May the Father, "of whom all paternity in heaven and   155 earth is named,"[99] Who strengthens the weak and gives courage to the pusillanimous and fainthearted, and Christ Our Lord and Redeemer, "the Institutor and Perfecter of the holy sacraments,"[100] Who desired marriage to be and made it the mystical image of His own ineffable union with the Church, and the Holy Ghost, Love of God, the Light of hearts and the Strength of the mind, grant that all will perceive, will admit with a ready will, and by the grace of God will put into practice, what We by this letter have expounded concerning the holy Sacrament of Matrimony, the wonderful law and will of God respecting it, the errors and impending dangers, and the remedies with which they can be counteracted, so that that fruitfulness dedicated to God will flourish again vigorously in Christian wedlock.

156   We most humbly pour forth Our earnest prayer at the Throne of His Grace, that God, the Author of all graces, the inspirer of all good desires and deeds, [101] may bring this about, and deign to give it bountifully according to the greatness of His liberty and omnipotence, and as a token of the abundant blessing of the same Omnipotent God, We most lovingly grant to you, Venerable Brethren, and to the clergy and people committed to your watchful care, the Apostolic Benediction.

157   Given at Rome, in Saint Peter's, this 31st day of December, of the year 1930, the ninth of Our Pontificate.

The Order of the Purposes of Matrimony
Extract from the Sentence of the
Holy Roman Rota
January 22, 1944

(Exposition of the case.

I. — Discussion of the request for nullity based on the motive of violence and fear.)

II. — *Simulation of Matrimonial consent*

9. — The Law.

Since the asserted simulation of matrimonial consent, in   159
the present case, is strictly connected with the ends of Matrimony, and the Holy Father gloriously reigning, inaugurating
on October 3, 1941, the new juridical year of the Roman
Rota, having spoken in regard to the ends of matrimony,
inviting the Auditors, as it seems, to go deeper into this question and to study it more carefully, it is useful to point out
what follows.

Matrimony has a primary and a secondary end. This is   160
evident from the Constitutions and the numerous Encyclicals
of the Supreme Pontiffs, from the common doctrine of
theologians, canonists and moralists, and from the explicit
words of Canon Law. Canon 1013, #I, says: "The primary
end of Matrimony is the procreation and education of the
children; the secondary end is mutual aid and a remedy for
concupiscence." The word *finis* ("end") in the above-mentioned sources is taken in a technical sense and means a benefit which is meant to be obtained both on the part of nature

and by deliberate intention of the agent. There must also be used in matrimony the well-known distinction between the *finis operis* and the *finis operantis* (which can be one or several). The *finis operis* in matrimony is that benefit which matrimony tends of its very nature to obtain, and which God the Creator gave to the institution of matrimony. If it is true that matrimony "by its very nature is a divine institution" and that "it was governed by laws, confirmed, and elevated by God, the Author Himself of nature, and by the same Restorer of nature, Christ Our Lord," it follows that "the very institution of matrimony, *the ends*, the laws and the benefits also come from God". Beside this the *finis operantis* is that benefit to obtain which the will of the contracting parties tends. It is evident that the *finis operantis* can coincide with the *finis operis*; indeed, Pius XI of happy memory expressly warns the contracting parties "to seek in matrimony those very ends for which it was instituted by God". The Roman Catechism, treating of the causes which direct men to matrimony stresses in the first place one of the *fines operis,* saying: "The prime cause is the society itself between the different sexes, sought by natural instinct and established in the hope of mutual help, so that each one may withstand, more easily with the help of the other, life's hardships and support the weakness of old age". But these two ends do not always coincide. Indeed, it can happen that the *finis operantis* is completely *extra* or *praeter* to the *finis operis*. For example, if the contracting party proposes as the primary end of matrimony the acquirement of riches or the freedom from an evil which would otherwise threaten him. The *finis operantis* can also be contrary to the *finis operis* and this happens every time that a person contracting matrimony has in mind a benefit or an end which is repugnant to one or all of the *fines operis,* namely of matrimony. But now the *fines operis* must be treated separately.

161   10. — Matrimony, considered as a work and institution of nature, is a natural society, one and indivisible, specifically distinct from every other human association. It must have therefore a natural *finis operis*, one and indivisible, specifically proper and distinct from every other end. Now the end, as

the Angelic Doctor testifies, *"est causa formalis, qua plurium unio peragitur atque specificatur talis equalis est."* It follows that when *several fines operis* are assigned to the one and same society, one of these must be *prime* and *principal*, by reason of its formal cause, in which the other ends are contained or to which others are added so that the prime cause can the more easily, surely and fully be achieved. It is necessary therefore that among the ends of matrimony there be determined the order, according to which the other *fines operis* be subordinated to the principal end, which determines the specific nature of matrimony.

11. — A) *The primary end of Matrimony.*   162

The primary and principal, one and indivisible *finis operis*   163
of matrimony which uniquely specifies its nature is the procreation and education of the offspring. This end can be considered a) *active*, b) *passive*, c) *sub utroque respectu.* Considered as *active* it regards the activity of the wedded couples, namely, the wedded couple inasmuch as they procreate and educate the offspring; intended as *passive* it regards the offspring inasmuch as they are procreated and educated; taken *sub utroque resectu* it considers the wedded couple and the offspring together. The secondary ends, then, which are ordained to the primary end, can regard rather one aspect than another—active or passive—but they can also regard in an equal measure both aspects.

12. —a) This *objective ordination* of matrimony to the   164
primary end which is included in its nature, if it is considered in the order of execution, consists in this that the conjugal union (as much *in fieri* as *in facto esse*) contains of its very nature and can supply all that is demanded on the part of human activity and is sufficient to obtain the procreation and the education of the offspring (in a manner suitable to and worthy of human nature). Indeed Christian marriage, of its very nature, comprises the *destination, aptitude* and *sufficiency* to obtain this end, since all those who contract marriage or already married are united and bound by a reciprocal right, exclusive and perpetual, to effecting acts capable of themselves to generate offspring. Therefore, having placed this right in its true light, considering the vehe-

ment urge of the sexual appetite to exercise the generative power, and keeping in mind that it is not lawful to satisfy this appetite outside of marriage, it must necessarily be concluded that the end which is the procreation and the education of the offspring is sufficiently and efficaciously provided for.

165   13. — This natural ordination to the primary end, this aptitude and sufficiency is achieved in *every* valid matrimony (even those of the sterile and of the aged) and is so essential that lacking this no marriage can exist or continue to exist. No marriage can be contracted, no marriage can exist if the basic right over the partner's body relative to the generative acts is not established or does not exist in the wedded couple. If this basic right is wanting or ceases, marriage cannot be contracted, or if it were already contracted, it ceases with the ceasing of this basic right (this happens following a dispensation of a matrimony *ratum et non consummatum*).

166   14. — b) No less so than marriage itself, even the *conjugal act* is subordinated and bound to the primary end, and to such a degree, that the exercise of this act is only permitted if and inasmuch as there is verified and is observed its essential subordination to the primary end of matrimony. This subordination is secured by the fact that husband and wife, when completing the natural conjugal act, can give all that is requested and suffices on the part of human activity for the generation of offspring (the sentence of the Rota, April 25, 1941, before Wynen should be consulted, where there is treated fully this subordination of the conjugal act and of the essentially required elements *in copula* so that this subordination can be said to be of itself apt for the generation of the offspring).

167   15. — This subordination to the primary end which exists through its natural structure in the naturally completed conjugal act, is observed and is verified even in the wedded union of sterile persons and of others who for causes extrinsic to the act cannot generate offspring with the natural use of marriage. The following words of Pius XI of happy memory, taken from the Encyclical *Casti connubii*, refer to such persons: "Nor are husband and wife to be accused of acting against nature if they make use of their right in a proper

and natural manner, even though natural causes (owing to circumstances of time or to certain defects) render it impossible for new life to originate. Both matrimony and the use of the matrimonial right have secondary ends—which husband and wife are quite entitled to have in view, so long as *the intrinsic nature of the act, and therefore its due subordination to its primary end, is safeguarded*).

16. — The Supreme Pontifff gloriously reigning, in his 168 allocution to the Holy Rota, mentioned above, also stresses that the conjugal act is subordinated to the primary end of matrimony; indeed he reproves the manner of those whose writings and judgments either completely separate or isolate beyond due measure the conjugal act from the primary end of matrimony. In the same error fall also those who hold that for the essence of the matrimonial act it is sufficient that such an act be completed in the natural manner in conformity to its external species, even if in its fulfillment it lacks one of the elements which on the part of conjugal activity itself are wholly necessary, and whose absence, if antecedent and incurable, render man incapable of matrimony, according to the constant jurisprudence of the Holy Rota, (cf. the above stated sentence): "for example if the male has not the faculty or the power to emit *true seed*, namely that which is produced in the genital organs, even if it be deprived of spermatozoa. These are the words of Pius XII: "Two extremes. . .are to be avoided: on the one hand, to deny practically or to abase excessively the secondary ends of matrimony and the generative act; on the other, to dissolve and separate beyond measure the conjugal act from the primary end, to which according to all its intrinsic structure it is primarily and principally ordained".

17. — B) *The secondary end of Matrimony*   169
The previously mentioned canon 1013 assigns a double 170 secondary end to matrimony, namely, the *mutuum adiutorium* and the *remedium concupiscentiae*. These ends are *fines operis* and not only *fines operantis*.

18. — a) Only a few things need be said of the other sec- 171 ondary end, the *remedium concupiscentiae* and of its relation to the primary end.

172   It will be easily understood that of its very nature this end
is subordinated to the primary end of generation. Indeed,
concupiscence is remedied *in* matrimony and by *means* of
matrimony with the lawful use of the generative faculty—a
use destined, proportioned and subordinated to the primary
end of matrimony, in the above mentioned manner. Therefore,
even the *sedatio concupiscentiae* as a result of conjugal acts,
is together with these acts subordinated to the primary end
of matrimony.

173   19. — b) The other secondary end is the *mutuum adiutorium*, which includes various services and mutual aids
between the contracting parties, for example, cohabitation,
the same table, the use of material benefits, the acquirement
and the administration of the means of subsistence, the most
personal help in the various conditions of life, in the psychic
and somatic exigencies of life, in the use of the natural
faculties and also in the exercise of the supernatural virtues.

174   20. — Recently, some authors when treating of the ends of
matrimony, explain this *mutuum adiutorium* in a different
manner. They hold that inasmuch as "the personal being" of
the married couple receives a help and a complement, this
evolution and perfection "of the person" of husband and
wife is not secondary but a primary end of matrimony. However, not all of these authors consider the matter in the same
light. These newcomers to matrimonial matters stray from
true and certain doctrine, without being able to apply solid
and proven arguments in favor of their opinions. Putting aside
these teachings of some recent authors, therefore, we must
now examine the order and the interdependence between the
primary and the secondary ends of matrimony, omitting the
remedium concupiscenitae, which we have already treated
briefly above.

175   21. — C) *Relation of the secondary end of matrimony
with the primary end.*

176   Even outside of matrimony there can be a reciprocal help
and common life between two persons of different sex either
in the simple case of brother and sister living together, or
in virtue of an explicit agreement to lend each other reciprocal help and common life, inasmuch as they are called and are

proper to matrimony and its *secondary finis operis* must be
considered according to a special property, which distinguishes them from any other community of life, united to
reciprocal help. They are, then, distinguished *by their internal
relation to the primary end,* which differentiates the conjugal
union from every other human association.

22. — a) This relation between the secondary and the   177
primary end is found first of all in the *origin* of this primary
end in the origin of the corresponding right to mutal aid. It
can be demonstrated thus: The immediate and essential object
of the matrimonial contract is the exclusive and perpetual
right over the body of the partner as regards the acts capable
of generating offspring. As a consequence and natural complement of this right, there follows the right to all that without which the right to generate—and consequently to educate
—the offspring, cannot be satisfied in a manner suitable to
the dignity of human nature. Now it is not possible to satisfy
in the above mentioned manner the right to generate and
educate the offspring if the right to mutual help is not added
to such a principal right, which includes the right to common
life, in other words the right to cohabitation, bed and board,
and help in all the necessities of life. Let it be noted, however,
that it is not a question here of the help lent by fact, but of
the *right* to this mutual *adiutorium,* indeed, as the *principal*
object of the matrimonial contract is not the "offspring",
but the "right" to beget offspring, so the secondary object is
not the *mutuum adiutorium* but the right to it.

23. — From what has been said up to now it follows that   178
the right to life in common and mutual help is a result of the
contracting parties' primary right to beget offspring. It also
follows that a matrimonial contract cannot be concluded,
which aims at mutual help and which prescinds at the same
time from the given and accepted right to the body: such
contract (not conceding any right on the body) cannot be
stipulated between two persons of different sex unless it
be outside of marriage. A matrimonial contract *attempted*
in such a manner would be null and would not establish in
the contracting parties either a principal or a secondary basis
of matrimonial rights. On the contrary, every matrimonial

consent to give and accept the right over the body of its very nature, gives rise to the married couple's right to a life in common and to reciprocal help.

179   24. — However, since this secondary right does not enter into the principal right as its constitutive part, nor is united to it as its prerequisite condition *sine qua non,* a matrimonial contract can be concluded which regards the principal right and explicitly denies the secondary end. In particular, as regards *cohabitation* which is one of the principal benefits united to the secondary end, and of its exclusion in the contract, Wernz-Vidal has to say: "Husband and wife, not being able to satisfy regularly and conveniently the conjugal debt without cohabitation, are, owing to this fundamental right and duty of marital life, also held by an onerous duty not only to observe cohabitation in the same house, but also to participate at the same table and have the same bed, except in cases contemplated by law. This assiduous cohabitation, common bed and board, belongs to the integrity of individual life, not to the essence of conjugal life, and therefore, sometimes, in a particular case, for a reasonable cause, they may be wanting, as in a marriage of conscience, and the obligation of justice to observe these matters admits a certain elasticity". Gasparri on the matter teaches: "The greater number of authors maintain that the condition never to live together is against the substance of matrimony, but if the matrimonial right is truly observed by both parties, we do not think that such a doctrine corresponds to truth, because habitation, bed and board in common do not form part of the substance of matrimony, and indeed, a marriage of conscience is permitted, with such a tacit or expressed condition".

180   25. — These rules are to be taken into account also in the case in which the contracting parties, renouncing the secondary end of cohabitation and the mutal aid connected to it, by common consent agree not to make use of the right given and accepted to the body of the other partner. "Just as it is not contradictory to receive a right already suspended as concerns its use in the very acceptance of the right, as happens when two persons bound by the vow of chastity contract matrimo-

ny, so there is no contradiction in giving by the other party to such an exclusion." The inner reason which renders the matter admissible is this "Husband and wife are not obliged *ad copulam*, unless one or the other party asks for the debt, and one of the parties can renounce to claim this right, obliging himself not to request it; nor are husband and wife obliged to generate offspring positively, but it is sufficient that they do not hinder it positively or kill the offspring." De Smet thus expresses himself: "Nothing prevents on the one hand that reciprocal matrimonial consent, or full mutual power over the other's body be given, and on the other, that the engaged couple agree between themselves and promise by a distinct act *not to use* the right they have, in order to preserve chastity. What is excluded is not the right to use this right, but only its exercise".

While his opinion, according to approved authors, as re-   181
gards the agreement made by the engaged couple is to be held as common teaching, nevertheless, the authors are not of one mind if the pact not to exercise this right is bound to the consent as a *condition sine qua non*. Whatever the outcome of this question, the matrimonial contract cannot in this case be declared null, because the question of law is not certain. But, not withstanding the matters explained above, the following must be added: as in determined circumstances, the firm and definite will not to fulfill can be a sign of defect of will to contract and oblige oneself (this defect must be however demonstrated in another way), likewise the serious and definite will not to concede in any way or at any time the right to common life or mutual help, can be a sign more or less well-founded of the lack of intention in the contractant to concede to the other party the principle right over the body, although from this sign alone there can never arise the moral certainty of the lack of will to contract matrimony and to oblige oneself.

26. — From what has been said the following must be con-   182
cluded. As the *right* to life in common and all mutual help is in its origin intrinsically dependent on the principal *right* to the acts of generation and not vice versa; and as in matrimonial rights there exists a determined order, and a determined

dependence: likewise must it be said of the ends of matrimony—to which these rights are ordered and in view of which
they are conceded by nature—that by reason of their origin
they are arranged in a given order and connected between
themselves. After having determined the principal and
primary end of matrimony, the Author of nature gave matrimony, as an institution of nature, a secondary and complementary end, so that *in* and *by* the same institution
called marriage, there could and must be satisfied that
primary end in a suitable manner.

183   27. — By way of a corollary it may be added that the well
known definition, or more to the fact, description, which
Modestinos gave of Matrimony: "Matrimony is the union of
a man and a woman in a life-long union, the preparation of
divine and human law," groups together the elements, essentially constitutive and naturally consequent, without
clarifying the order and the dependence between them.
Therefore, it is not possible to study the ends of matrimony
from this famous description of matrimony, without proceeding with caution and allowing room for necessary distinctions.
In reality, as it has been noted above, as in the matrimonial
contract "the right to the body" and the "right to aid" are
not coordinated on the one plane but remain between themselves as the principal or super-ordered object and the secondary or subordinated object, so the ends as well, corresponding
to the rights, are not equally principal or coordinate, but one
is principal and the other is secondary and subordinate.

184   28. — b) The order of dependence and subordination
which is described here is not only found in the origin of the
secondary right, which is destined to the attainment of the
secondary end and which assures this attainment but the
same order is pointed out when the marriage is considered *in
facto esse.*

185   Every man, indeed, being of his very nature a "social
being," needs the help of his fellow man. He finds this help
inasmuch as he is a member both of human society in general,
and of a determined civil and domestic society in particular.
In this common help of all men, there must also be considered
the help and complement which one sex (even without any

carnal affection and activity) receives from the nature of the
other sex. Human society is formed of men and women who
exert a reciprocal influence. But this common help cannot
constitute the *finis operis* of matrimony. To constitute this,
it must be further determined by a *specific element,* whence
it appears why "mutual help" was assigned to matrimony by
the Creator as its *finis operis.* This specific element again is
and must be in *relation to the primary end and to the principal right.* Hence husband and wife, by the very nature of matrimony, are bound to the primary end of this institution,
because, by matrimony, they acquired the right and destination to become "authors of a new life," procreating and
educating children, even if in fact this is not verified.

But to satisfy in a due manner this specific destination,   **186**
they need a multiple reciprocal help, and that not only as
regards generative activity properly so-called, but even as
regards the primary end in a complete sense, that, taken both
actively and passively. Indeed, nature desires that those should
become "the authors of a new life" who are burdened by
numerous demands of nature and life, yet adorned with human dignity. Such being the case nature aids this principal
right with various assistances and life in common. This
specific note of mutual matrimonial aid, which emanates
from the innermost structure of matrimony, is also had in
those marriages in which husband and wife do not wish or are
unable to reach effective generation. What the Creator placed
in natura rei, namely in marriage, does not depend on human
will nor is it abolished by an external impediment.

29. — This specific mutual matrimonial aid added to the   **187**
institution itself of matrimony comprises directly only *the
aptitude and the destination* for every necessary help, assured
by means of the transfer of the right properly so-called to
such help, and not the actual assistance in itself. On the other
hand, however, to contract a valid marriage the transfer of
the right to such help is not required: thus it appears clear
that there can be a true marriage, even if husband and wife in
reality do not enjoy this assistance which nature intends to
give to matrimony. It is, moreover, apparent, why the actual
use of mutual aid is not by its nature reserved to the service

of the primary right. Mutual matrimonial aid is given by nature rather as a comfort to the person of husband and wife, inasmuch as they are destined to become, not in any kind of way, but in a suitable and worthy manner, "the authors of a new life," by whom so sustained by due help, the generative activity itself as a result is favored. Indeed, if the persons who generate are placed in a safe position, both themselves and the children, as regards life's difficulties and necessities (which grow further still with the birth of children), then the generative activity is well founded for by that fact. Hence it is clear that every reciprocal help, which emanates from marriage without damage to the primary end, is contained within the limits of the secondary end, and, because of the help and comfort which it gives to the person of husband and wife, it possesses a specific attitude, destination and subordination to the primary end (not withstanding a certain relative independence which, according to what was said, belongs to the secondary end).

188   30. — The matters spoken of up to now of the secondary end of matrimony, considered *in facto esse* can be thus briefly summarized.

189   1⁰ The destination and corresponding right to "mutual aid" derive from the very nature of matrimony and from God's will, and constitute its secondary *finis operis*. Therefore they can never be wanting in a true and perfect domestic society, nor are they ever frustrated as long as there exists the marriage itself with its primary end and its principal right.

190   2⁰ The "mutual assistance," considered as a secondary end of matrimony *in facto esse*, is called a dependent end, subordinate in respect to the primary end, since it was an addition made by the Creator to marriage, in view of the primary end. But it is an adjoined and non-constitutive element *ab extra* only by reason of the *primary end*, but not in respect to marriage *itself*, as it were an *extra-matrimonial end*; it is an "intra-matrimonial" end, although not of the same degree as the primary end.

191   3⁰ The aptitude and the right to *mutuum adiutorium* are not restricted to *generative activity* nor do they regard it in the first place, but rather they regard the *persons who gene-*

ate, inasmuch as these persons, by the marriage contract, are destined to be able to become *authors of a new life*.

4⁰ The secondary end has a certain independence, in that in the person of husband and wife it can be verified and brought to effect in those cases in which either temporarily or perpetually the accomplishment of the primary end is impeded. The reason is that the *mutuum adiutorium* (and equally so the right to it) does not constitute an essential part of the primary right and the primary end. It is rather *extra essentiam* of the primary right and the primary end, though it be something *naturale consequens* of it and properly called matrimonial right.   192

5⁰ Whoever separates the matrimonial *mutuum adiutorium* taken in the widest sense, from its intrinsic subordination to the primary end not only offends objective truth and the intention of the Creator Himself, but necessarily opens the way to disastrous consequences.   193

(Discussion of the fact.)

III. — Discussion of the *inconsummatio* of the marriage.— The Tribunal's conclusions.   194

Address of Pope Pius XII
to the Italian Medical-biological Union of St. Luke
November 12, 1944

Your presence, beloved sons, brings to mind a scene enacted in Paris in December, 1804. In the Grand Hall of the Louvre, where numerous delegations crowded to render homage to the Vicar of Christ and to receive his blessing, five young doctors—among them the celebrated Laënnec —all members of the congregation Auxilium Christianorum founded a few years earlier in that metropolis, were introduced to the Sovereign Pontiff, Pius VII. The Pope could not disguise a reaction of surprise: "Oh!" he said laughingly, "Medicus pius, res miranda!"

196   Into the heavy atmosphere created by a materialist intellectual formation, an Association such as yours—the medical-biological Union of St. Luke,—helps to inject, as it were, a gust of clean, fresh air: above all by placing before men those basic truths of healthy reason and of faith, in which the great questions of medical ethics find their solution, in the second place, by asserting and applying Christian principles in the practical exercise of the medical profession and in the education of young scholars.

197   One of the characters of Rembrandt's famous "Lesson in Anatomy", in striking contrast to his colleagues in their handsome waistcoats, whose main concern seems to be the handing of their portraits down to posterity, attracts the attention of the viewer by the vitality and depth of his expression. With wrapt features, held breath, his eyes probe the

open wound, anxious to read the secrets of those organs, avid to wrest from death the mystery of life. Anatomy, a wonderful science even only in its own field for all that it reveals, has the virtue of introducing the mind to even vaster and nobler spheres. How well the great Morgagni knew and felt this, when he could, during a dissection, drop the scalpel to exclaim: "Ah! if I could only love God as well as I know him!"

While anatomy manifests the power of the Creator in its 198 study of matter, physiology penetrates into the functions and marvels of the organism, biology discovers the laws of life, its conditions, its demands, its generous liberality. Providential arts these: medicine and surgery, which apply all these sciences to the defence of the human body, as fragile as it is perfect, in order to repair its losses, and heal its wounds. What is more, the physician more than others brings to his work his heart no less than his intelligence. He is not dealing with inert matter, however precious. It is a man like himself, a brother, who is suffering at this hands. This patient, furthermore, is not a lone creature, but a human person, with a place and a duty in the family, and a mission, however humble, in society. The Christian doctor, too, will never lose sight of the fact that the sick and injured whom he treats, and who, thanks to his care, will go on living for a certain time, or who despite his efforts die, are on the road to immortality, and their dispositions at the moment of death will determine their eternal beatitude or punishment.

Made up of matter and spirit, an element in the universal 199 order of beings, man is in fact directed in his life here below towards a goal which is beyond time and above nature. Due to this compenetration of matter by spirit in the perfect unity of the human composite, from this man's sharing in the movement of all visible creation, it follows that the doctor will often be sollicited for advice, and decisions, and principles which, though they affect directly the care of the body with its members and organs, will nevertheless concern too the soul and its faculties, and man's supernatural destiny and his role in society.

If the physician does not keep in mind the particular make- 200 up of the human being, man's place and function in the universal order of being, his spiritual and supernatural destiny, then that physician runs the risk of becoming easily entangled in more or less materialist prejudices, and of following the destructive tendencies of utilitarianism, hedonism, and absolute autonomy from the moral law.

201   A captain may be well able to give detailed instructions on the handling of the machinery, or on setting the sails; but if he does not know his goal, and cannot read from his instruments or from the stars shining above him, the position and course of his vessel, where will his mad career not take him?

202   This concept of being and of end opens the way to the loftiest considerations.

203   The complexity of that composite of matter and spirit and of the universal order is such that man cannot tend towards the one and only end of his being and of his personality if not with the harmonious cooperation of his various corporal and spiritual faculties; nor can he take his rightful place in the scheme of things either by cutting himself off from the rest of the world, or by losing himself in it as do the myriad identical molecules in a formless mass. These complexities and this necessary harmony offer certain difficulties, and dictate to the doctor of his duty.

204   In forming man, God regulated each of his functions, assigning them to the various organs. In this way, He distinguished those which are essential to life from those which contribute only to the integrity of the body, however precious be the activity, well-being, and beauty of this last. At the same time, God fixed, prescribed, and limited the use of each organ. He cannot therefore allow man now to arrange his life and the functions of his organs according to his own taste, in a manner contrary to the intrinsic and immanent function assigned them. Man, in truth, is not the owner of his body nor its absolute lord, but only its user. A whole series of principles and norms derives from this fact, governing the use of the body with its members and organs, and the right to dispose of them: principles and norms to which are equally subject the individual concerned and the doctor called in for consultation.

In the case of a conflict of divergent interests, the same   205
rules must govern the solution according to the scale of
values—save always the inviolability of God's commandments.
Hence it will never be permissible to sacrifice eternal interests
for a temporal good, however precious this be. Nor will it be
licit to put this last at the service of common fancies or of the
demands of passion. The doctor often discovers that in such
sometimes tragic conflicts, he is in the position of counsellor,
almost of qualified judge.

The inevitable struggle of conflicting interests raises very   206
delicate problems even when confined within the single human
person, whose unity is so complex. Much more difficult are
the problems raised in society, when it tries to assert its rights
over the body, the corporal integrity, and the very life of
man. To determine in theory the limits is often awkward. In
practice, the doctor no less than the individual directly concerned, may find that he must examine and analyze these
exigencies or presumptions, to measure and estimate their
morality and the binding force of the ethical obligation they
impose.

Here too, reason and faith trace the boundary line between   207
the rights of society and that of the individual. Certainly man
is by nature destined to live in society, but, as is clear from
reason alone, as a general principle society is made for the
man and not man for society. It is not the community but
the Creator Himself Who gives to man dominion over his
body and his life, and to the Creator man must answer for
the use he makes of them. It follows that society cannot
directly deprive man of that right, excepting only if man by a
proportionately grave crime makes himself punishable with
death.

Regarding the body, the life, and the corporal integrity of   208
the individual, the juridical position of society differs essentially from that of the individual himself. Man's power over
his members and organs is a direct—though not unlimited—
power; because these are parts which go to make up his phys-
sical being. Their association in the one being has for goal only
the well-being of the whole physical organism, and hence it is

clear that each of these organs and members can be sacrificed if it puts the whole organism in danger, a danger which cannot in any other way be averted. Quite different is the case with society, which is not a physical being, but a simple community of purpose and action. In virtue of this it can demand of those who make it up and who are called its members, all those services essential for the true common good.

209   Such are the foundations on which must rest every judgment on the moral value of acts and operations concerning the human body, human life, and corporal integrity of the person, which public authority allows or imposes.

210   The truths so far expounded can be known by the light of the reason alone. But there is another fundamental law which appears more to the eyes of the doctor than to others, whose complete meaning and purpose can be revealed and illustrated only the light of revelation: We are thinking of the law of suffering and death.

211   Physical pain has no doubt a natural and salutary function as well: it is a danger signal which gives warning that some hidden sickness has been born and is developing, perhaps secretly; and thus it induces one to seek the remedy. But in the course of his scientific research the doctor inevitably comes upon suffering and death like a locked door to which his mind does not hold the key. In the exercise of his profession, they loom inexorably and mysteriously, a law in the face of which his art often stands helpless and his compassion sterile. He can make his diagnosis according to the principles of the laboratory and clinic, plan the treatment in accordance with all the demands of science. . .but in the depths of his being, as man and scientist, he feels that the explanation of that mystery continues to elude him. He suffers; a cosuming anguish grips him until he asks of faith the answer which though now incomplete—it is complete in the mysterious designs of God and will be revealed as such in eternity—has yet the power of bring him peace of soul.

212   And this is the answer faith gives. God, when He created man, had by a gift of grace made him exempt from that natural law which governs every living material being. God had wished to include man's destiny suffering and death. They

were introduced by sin. But He, the Father of mercy, took them into His own hands, made them pass through the body. the veins, the heart of His beloved Son, God like Himself, become man for the salvation of the world. And thus suffering and death became for every man who accepts Christ, a means of redemption and sanctification. And thus man's pilgrimage here below, continually shadowed by the sign of the cross and the law of suffering and death, develops and purifies the soul, and leads it to happiness without end in eternal life.

To suffer. . .to die. . . .It is truly, to use the bold phrase of the Apostle of the Gentiles, the "folly of God"—a folly which is wiser than all the wisdom of men.[1] In the pale radiance of his weak faith, the poor poet sang: 213

L'homme est un apprenti, la douleur est son maitre,
Et nul ne se connait tant qu'il n'a pas souffert.[2]

In the light of revelation, the holy author of the Imitation of Christ could pen the sublime twelfth chapter of his second book: *De regia via sanctae crucis*, all aglow with the most wonderful understanding of the noblest Christian conception of life.   214

In the face of the insistent problem of pain, what reply can the doctor give? for his own satisfaction first? and to the unhappy person whom sickness has reduced to a blind torpor, and in whom rise a vain sense of rebellion against suffering and death? Only a heart impregnated with a deep and living faith will find the words which carry the sincerity and deep conviction capable of rendering acceptable the words of the divine Master: "It is necessary to suffer and to die, and so enter into glory."[3] The doctor will fight against sickness and death with all the means and methods of his science and art, but not with the desperate resignation of pessimism, nor yet with the "exasperated resolution" which a certain modern philosophy has seen fit to exalt, but with the calm peace of one who sees and knows what suffering and death mean in the salvific designs of the omniscient and infinitely good and merciful Lord.   215

It is therefore clear that the physician, as also all his activity, is constantly in the orbit of the moral order, subject to the authority of its laws. Nothing he ever does or says or   216 counsels can ever be completely outside the field of morality or utterly independent of the basic principles of ethics and religion. For his every word and action he is responsible before God and his own conscience.

217   It is unfortunately true that some reject as an absurdity of the imagination, in theory and in practice, the concept of a "Christian medical science." In their opinion, there cannot be such a thing, just as there cannot be a Christian chemistry or physics, theoretical or applied. The sphere of the experimental sciences, they say, is quite outside the sphere of morality and religion, and hence these sciences neither know nor recognize any laws except those immanent to themselves. What a strange and unjustified restriction of the point of view on the problem! Can they not perceive that the objects of those sciences are not isolated in a vacuum, but are a part of the universe about us? That they have a fixed place and a rung on the scale of values? That they are continually in contact with the objects of other sciences, and that in particular they are subject to the law of intrinsic and transcendent finality which links all things in an ordered whole? We readily admit that in speaking of a Christian attitude in science, it is not so much the science which is being considered, as its representatives and scholars, in which the science lives, grows, and makes itself manifest. Even physics and chemistry, which scientists of conscience apply to the service and prosperity of the individual and of society, can become instead in the hands of wicked men instruments of corruption and of ruin. More than ever in medicine, then, do truth and the demands of the common good oppose any presumed objective or subjective separation of the science from the many bonds and relations which link it to the general order.

218   But your union of Catholic doctors and biologists is not valuable only because the learned discussion it promotes, the scientific contacts it encourages, the faithful adhesion to the teachings of the Church which its members profess, ensure for each of them a wider knowledge and a deeper understanding of the basic truths which limit and govern their field of study and labor. Your union offers another advantage as well: it facilitates in professional practice, the solution of cases

which are particularly difficult, in conformity with the moral law.

But it would be impossible in a brief discourse to list and consider these individual cases. In any case, in Our exhortation given last February to the parish priests and lenten preachers of Rome, We took the opportunity of expounding a series of considerations concerning the Ten Commandments, from which We judge that the Catholic physician too, can draw useful conclusions for the exercise of his profession. **219**

The greatest of all the commandments is the commandment of love: the love of God first of all, and then, as its natural consequence, love of our neighbor. True love, enlightened by reason and faith, does not blind man, but makes him more farseeing. The Catholic physician, in forming his opinions, in undertaking and carrying out the work of care of the sick, will never find a better counsellor than this true love. **220**

"Dilige et quod vis fac;" this succinct axiom of St. Augustine's[4], often quoted out of context, can here be applied in all its rigor. What a reward for the conscientious doctor, when he hears on the day of judgment from the lips of the Lord those words of thanks: "I was sick and you visited Me."[5] Such love is not weak. It will not stand for a careless diagnosis. It will be deaf to the solicitations of passion which would have it as accomplice. It is full of goodness, without envy, without pride, without anger. It takes no pleasure in wrongdoing. It believes, hopes, endures to the last: thus does the Apostolate of the Gentiles describe Christian charity in his remarkable hymn to love.[6] **221**

The fifth commandment-non occides[7]—contains in synthesis the duties concerning life and the integrity of the human body. It is fruitful in lessons not only for the professor in the lecture hall of the university, but also for the medical practitioner. So long as a man commits no crime, his life is intangible, and therefore every action which tends directly towards its destruction is illicit. . .whether this destruction be the goal intended or only a means to an end, whether this life be embrionic, or in full flower, or already approaching its term. Only God is Lord of the life of a man who is not guilty of a crime punishable with death. The physician has no right to **222** dispose either of the life of the child or that of the mother. And no one on earth, no individual, no human authority, can give him the right to its destruction. His office is not to destroy life but to save it. In the course of the last few decades, the Church has found it necessary to proclaim repeatedly and in all clarity these fundamental and immutable principles, in opposition to certain opinions and methods.

223   In the conclusions and decrees of the Magisterium of the Church, the Catholic doctor will find in these matters a reliable guide for his own theoretical judgment, and for his conduct in practice.

224   But there is in the moral order a vast sector which demands that the doctor have particularly clearly in mind the principles which govern his actions: the sector which concerns those mysterious energies which God has placed in the organism of man and woman for the creation of new life. It is a natural power, whose structure and essential activities have been determined by the Creator, as has their specific goal and corresponding obligations they impose. To these man is subject whenever he consciously uses that faculty. The primary goal—to which the secondary ends are essentially subordinate —intended by nature in the use of this faculty is the propagation of life and the upbringing of the offspring. Only matrimony, its essence and properties regulated by God, guarantees both these goals, in accordance with the well-being and dignity of both parents and offspring.

225   This one law it is which enlightens and governs the whole delicate matter. It is to this norm that one must refer the concrete cases, the special difficulties. Only this norm guarantees in this subject, the moral and physical health of the individual and of society.

226   It should not be difficult for the doctor to understand the intrinsic finality deeply rooted in nature. It should not be difficult for him to affirm it, and to apply it in practice in his professional activity. He will often be more readily believed than the theologian, when he declares and warns that whoever transgresses and breaks the laws of natue, will sooner or later have to suffer the tragic consequences in his own person, and in his physical and psychical integrity.

The young man who feels the impulse of his nascent   227
passions has recourse to the physician: the engaged couple
soon to be married, come to him for advice. . .advice which
too often they hope will be in a sense contrary to nature and
right living. Married people come to ask his opinion and
assistance—more than not his connivance—because they say
that there is no solution for the difficulties of life apart from
the voluntary infringement of the duties and obligations
inherent to the married state. Every possible argument—medical, eugenic, social, moral,—will be brought to bear to induce
the physician to give a decision or to lend his aid in favor of
following the instincts of nature, while at the same time
depriving the life-generating force of the possibility of attaining its goal.

How will the doctor be able to stand firm in the face of   228
these assults if he is not clearly conscious and firmly convinced that the Creator Himself, for the good of the human
race, has indissolubly bound up the voluntary use of those
natural energies with their intrinsic purpose. . .a bond which
can never lawfully be loosed or broken?

The eight commandment likewise has its place in the   229
morality of medicine. According to the moral law, no one
may tell a lie. And yet there are cases when a doctor, even
when asked, though he cannot give an answer which is positively untrue, at the same time cannot crudely tell the whole
truth, especially when he knows that the patient has not the
strength to stand such a revelation. But there are other cases
when the doctor has most certainly the duty of speaking out
clearly, a duty before which every other medical or humani-
tarian consideration must give way. It is not lawful to lull the
sick person or his relations into a false sense of security when
there is the risk of compromising the eternal salvation of the
former, or his fulfillment of his duties in justice and charity.
It would be wrong to try to justify or excuse such conduct
under the pretext that the physician alway says what, in his
opinion, will best contribute to the patient's well-being, and
that it is the fault of his hearers if they take his words too
literally.

230   Another of the duties which derive from the eighth commandment is the observance of the professional secret, which must serve and serves the good of the individual and even more of society. In this sector too, there can arise conflicts between the public and private interests, or between different elements and aspects pertaining to the common good. In these conflicts it will be very difficult indeed to measure and weigh justly the pros and cons for speaking out or keeping silent. In such a dilemma, the conscientious doctor seeks his norm in the basic tenets of Christian ethics, which will help him to pick the right course. These norms, in fact, while they clearly affirm the obligation on the physician to preserve the professional secret, above all in the interest of the common good, do not concede to this an absolute value. For that very common good would suffer were the professional secret placed at the service of crime or injustice.

231   We would not like to conclude without saying a word regarding the docor's obligation not only of possessing a sound scientific formation, but also of continuing to develop and integrate his professional knowledge and opinions. This is a moral duty in the strict sense, which binds in conscience before God, because it concerns an activity which has a direct and telling influence on the essential well-being of the individual and the community.

232   For the medical student, this means that during the years of his university formation, he must study seriously to acquire the theoretical knowledge required, and the practical knowledge necessary to apply this in practice.

233   For the university professor, it means that he must teach his students both these things as well as possible, and never give a guarantee of professional capacity unless he is certain— by a conscientious and exhaustive examination—that is merited. To act in any other way would be to commit a grave sin, because it would expose the public and private health to serious danger and incalculable harm.

234   For the medical practitioner there is the obligation of keeping abreast of the developments in medicine, through the reading of scientific works and periodicals, attendance at

congresses and courses, disucssion with colleagues, consultation of the professors of the faculty of medicine. The medical practitioner is obliged in these matters to the extent that his conditions allow it, for the good of the sick and of the community.

It will redound to the great honor of your Union if you   235
demonstrate by facts that its members are not only second to one in the sphere of professional knowledge and capacity, but also that they are among the leaders in the first rank. In this way you will make an effective contribution towards arousing and strengthening faith in the moral principles you profess. As a result, too, of this, the membership of your Association will become a guarantee that whoever sincerely desires of one of you wise counsel, worthy assistance, and conscientious care will not be deluded.

Luke, whom St. Paul called "the beloved physician,"[8]   236
wrote in his Gospel: "And when the sun was going down, all those who had friends afflicted with diseases of any kind brought them to Him: and He laid His hands upon each one of them, and healed them."[9] Although he does not possess such miraculous power, the Catholic doctor, who is really what his profession and his Christianity demand, will find that all human miseries come to him in search of solace, and to beg him to lay his hands upon them. And God will bless his knowledge and art, so that he may heal many, and for those whom he cannot heal obtain at least relief and comfort from their affliction.

(Blessing.)

Address of Pope Pius XII
to Delegates at the Fourth International Congress
of Catholic Doctors
September 29, 1949

Over the centuries, and especially in this our age, medicine has continued to advance. And this progress has been truly complex, for its object includes the most varied branches of speculative and practical science. There has been progress in the study of the body and of the organism, in all the physical, chemical, and natural sciences, in the knowledge of remedies with their properties and their means of utilization; progress, too, in the application of therapeutics, and not only in physiology, but in psychology as well, and in the reciprocal interaction of the physical and moral elements in the person.

238 Careful as he is lest some advantage of such progress escape his attention, the physician is continually on the look-out for all which brings healing, or at least alleviates men's suffering and sickness. As surgeon, he is concerned with rendering less painful those operations which are unavoidable. As gynecologist, his interest is to attenuate the pains of child-birth, without at the same time either compromising health of mother or child, or running the risk of interfering with those sentiments of motherly tenderness which the woman should have for the newly-born.

239 If the elementary spirit of humanity, the natural love of his fellow man, stimulates and guides every conscientious physician in his reasearch, will not a Christian doctor, sustained by divine charity, dedicate himself without considering either

worries or discomfort, for the well-being of those whom he considers—and rightly, as our faith teaches us—his brothers? He will most certainly rejoice from the very depths of his being at the immense progress already made, for the results which his predecessors have attained, for the results continually obtained by his colleagues, bound to those of the past by the continuity of a magnificent tradition. He will be legitimately proud, too, of his own contribution.

Nonetheless, he will never be satisfied. He will always see   240
before him new races to be run, new goals to be reached. And hence he will work passionately. On the one hand, because as a doctor he is wholly dedicated to procuring relief from pain for each and every man, while as a scientist, the discoveries which follow one upon the other give him a taste of the "joy of knowing." On the other hand, as a believer and a Christian, he perceives in the splendors uncovered, in the new horizons which open out before him as far as the eye can see, the greatness and power of the Creator, the inexhaustible goodness of the Father, who, after giving to the organism so many resources for its spontaneous development, defence and healing, in most cases has also provided the remedies for the corporal ills in inert or living matter, in mineral, vegetable and animal nature.

The doctor would not correspond fully to the ideal of his   241
vocation if, in profiting of the most recent developments of science, in the practice of his profession he employed only his intelligence and ability, and did not bring to this practice as well—We would almost say "above all"—his human heart, his delicate, Christian charity. He is dealing in "in anima vili". To be sure, he operates directly on the body, but on the body animated by an immortal, spiritual soul, in such guise that in virtue of the mysterious bond which indissolubly links physical and moral, the physician will not act with efficacy on the body if he does not at the same time act on the soul.

Whether he is dealing with the body or with that unity   242
which is the human composite, the Christian doctor will always have to be on guard against the fascination of science, against the temptation of applying his knowledge and art to purposes other than the care of the patients entrusted to him.

Thank God he will not have to defend himself from another temptation, the criminal temptation of using the gifts of God hidden in the womb of nature, for the service of base interests, unmentionable passions, or inhuman desires. Unfortunately, one need not travel far in order to find concrete examples of such deplorable abuses. The disintegration of the atom, to take an example, and the production of atomic energy is one thing. Another thing again is its destructive use, which eludes all control. One thing is the magnificent progress of modern science in aviation: quite another thing the use of massed squadrons of bombers without any possibility of limiting their action to military or strategic objectives. Above all, one thing is the respectful research which reveals the beauty of God mirrored in His creatures, the power of God in the forces of nature; quite another thing is the deification of nature itself and of material forces, while denying their Author.

243   What does the doctor do who is worthy of his vocation? He takes command of these forces, these natural qualities, to employ them for purposes of healing, to give health and strength, and what is still more worthwhile, to preserve men from sickness and contagion and epidemics. In his hands, the formidable power of radioactivity is hemmed in, and employed to fight those evils which repulse every other cure. The nature of the most deadly posions serves in the preparation of effective remedies. What is more, the most dangerous germs of infection are used in many ways for the preparation of serums to be employed in vaccination.

244   The inviolable laws of natural and Christian morality must be observed everywhere. It is not from emotive considerations nor from a materialist, natural philanthropy that the essential principles of medical ethics derive, but from these laws: the dignity of the human body, the pre-eminence of the soul over the body, the brotherhood of all men, the sovereign dominion of God over life and destiny.

245   On various past occasions, We have touched on a good number of particular points in medical morality.

246   Now there has arisen another pressing problem, which demands, no less urgently than the rest, the light of Catholic

moral doctrine: the problem of artificial insemination. We cannot let this occasion pass without indicating, at least in its broad lines, the moral judgment which governs this matter.

1. When dealing with man, the question of artificial insem-   247
ination cannot be considered either exclusively—nor yet principally—under its biological and medical aspect, leaving aside the moral and juridical point of view.

2. Artificial insemination outside matrimony must be   248
condemned as immoral purely and simply.

In fact the natural law and divine positive law state that   249
the procreation of new life cannot take place except in marriage. Only matrimony safeguards the dignity of the partners —in the present case principally that of the woman—their personal well-being, and guarantees at the same time the well-being of the child and his upbringing.

It follows that there cannot be any difference of opinion   250
among Catholics regarding the condemnation of artificial insemination outside the conjugal union. The child born under these conditions would be by that very fact illegitimate.

3. Artificial insemination in matrimony, but produced by   251
means of the active element of a third person, is equally immoral, and as such is to be condemned without right of appeal.

Only the husband and wife have the reciprocal right on the   252
body of the other for the purpose of generating new life: an exclusive, inalienable, incommunicable right. And that is as it should be, also for the sake of the child. To whoever gives life to the tiny creature, nature imposes, in virtue of that very bond, the duty of protecting and educating the child. But when the child is the fruit of the active element of a third person—even granting the husband's consent—between the legitimate husband and the child there is no such bond of origin, nor the moral and juridicial bond of conjugal procreation.

4. What of the liceity of artifical insemination in matri-   253
mony? For the moment let it suffice to recall these principles of the natural law: the mere fact that the means reaches the goal intended does not justify the use of such a means. Nor does the desire for a child—a completely legitimate desire of

the married people—suffice to prove that recourse to artificial fecundation is legitimate because it would satisfy such a desire.

254   It would be mistaken, too, to consider that the possibility of resorting to this means could render valid a marriage between persons incapable of contracting it because of *impedimentum impotentiae.*

255   Superfluous to add here that the active element can never be licitly procured by acts against nature.

256   Though new methods cannot be excluded a priori simply because they are new, in the case of artificial insemination one should not only keep a very cautious reserve, but must exlude it altogether. This does not necessarily forbid the use of certain artificial means destined simply either to facilitate the natural act, or to enable the natural act, normally carried out, to attain its proper end.

257   Let it not be forgotten that only procreation of a new life according to the will and the plan of the Creator carries with it, to an amazing degree of perfection, the realization of intended aims. It is at the same time in conformity with the corporal and spiritual nature and the dignity of the marriage partners, and with the normal and happy development of the child.

(Blessing.)

Address of Pope Pius XII
to Midwives
October 29, 1951

Beloved daughters, the object of your profession, the secret of its grandeur and its beauty lies in this, that you guard with care the silent, humble cradle wherein Almighty God has infused an immortal soul into the seed provided by the parents, and this you do in order to give your professional assistance to the mother and to prepare a successful birth for the child she carries in her womb.

When you reflect on the wonderful collaboration of the parents, of nature and of God, as a result of which a new human being is born to the image and likeness of the Creator,[1] you cannot help valuing at its proper worth the precious cooperation you contribute to an event of such importance. The heroic mother of the Machabees said to her sons: "I know not how you were formed in my womb; for I neither gave you breath, nor soul, nor life, neither did I frame the limbs of every one of you. But the Creator of the world formed the nativity of man."[2]

Hence whoever approaches this cradle of the formation of life and plays a part there, in one way or another, should know the order the Creator lays down to be followed and the laws that rule this order. For here it is not a question of physical or of biological laws which are automatically obeyed by agents not endowed with reason, or of blind forces, but it is a question of laws, the execution of which are confided to the voluntary and free cooperation of man.

259

260

261   This order, founded by supreme intellect, is directed to the end designed by the Creator. It embraces not only the external acts of man, but also the internal consent of his free will—it covers acts as well as omissions when duty so demands. Nature places at man's disposal the whole chain of the causes which give rise to a new human life; it is man's part to release the living force, and to nature pertains the development of that force, leading to its completion. Once man has fulfilled his part and set in motion the marvellous evolution of life, it is his duty to respect religiously its progress, and the same duty forbids him either to halt the course of nature or to prevent its natural development.

262   Thus the part played by nature and the part played by man are precisely determined. Your professional training and experience enable you to know the part played by nature and by man, together with the rules and laws to which both are subject. Your conscience, enlightened by reason and by faith under the guidance of divine authority, teaches you on the one hand what you may lawfully do, and on the other hand, what you are in duty bound to refrain from doing.

263   In the light of these principles, We now propose to lay before you some considerations on the apostolate to which your profession binds you. Every profession willed by God carries with it a mission—the mission to carry out, within the bounds of the profession itself, the plan and intention of the Creator and to help man to understand the justice and the holiness of the divine scheme and the benefit that will be given to those who carry it out.

264   Your professsional apostolate is carried out first and foremost through your personal influence.

265   Why is your service called for? Because people are convinced that you know your business, because you know what is good for the mother and child, because you are aware of the dangers to which both are exposed and how these same dangers may be avoided and overcome. Your advice and help are expected, limited though they may be and not infallible, but in keeping with the latest developments both in theory and in fact of the profession in which you specialize.

And if all this is expected of you, it is because people have   266
confidence in you, and this confidence is, above all, something
personal. Your character must inspire it. That this confidence
in you be not misplaced is not only your keen desire, but also
something demanded by your office and profession and consequently your bounden duty. Hence you strive to reach the
summit of the knowledge of your craft.

But your professional skill is demanded, too, by the nature   267
of your apostolate. What weight, in point of fact, would your
views on the moral and religious issues connected with your
office carry, if you were seen to be lacking in professional
knowledge? On the other hand, your intervention in the
moral and religious field will be the more effective if, by your
superior technical ability, you command respect. To the
favorable opinion that you will deservedly win for yourselves
there will be added also in the minds of those who seek your
help, the well-founded belief that your Christian convictions,
faithfully put into practice, far from being an obstacle to
your professional worth, will be its support and guarantee. It
will be plain to all that in the exercise of your profession you
are aware of your responsibility before God;

and that it is your faith in God which is the strongest   268
argument encouraging you to give your assistance with greater
devotion in proportion to the gravity of the need. In this
solid religious foundation you find the strength to counter
any unreasonable and immoral claim from whatever quarter,
with a calm, undaunted and unswerving denial.

Esteemed and appreciated as you are for your personal   269
conduct no less than for your knowledge and experience, you
will find the care of mother and child will be readily confided
to you, and, perhaps even without you yourselves realizing it,
you will exercise a profound, often silent, but efficacious
apostolate of a living Christianity. Great, in fact, as may be
the moral authority due to qualities strictly professional,
your personal influence will find its fulfillment chiefly in the
twofold guarantee of genuine human feeling and real Christian living.

The second aspect of your apostolate is your zeal to uphold   270
the value and inviolability of human life.

271   The world today has urgent need of conviction in this regard by the threefold testimony of mind, heart and facts. Your profession offers you the possibility of giving such testimony and even lays upon you the duty of doing so. Sometimes this testimony will take the form of a simple word spoken tactfully at the right moment to the mother or the father; more frequently it will be expressed in your demeanor, and the conscientious way in which you act will have an unobstrusive but effective influence on them both. You, more than anyone else, are in a position to know and appreciate what human life is in itself and to determine its worth in the light of sound reasoning, of your own moral conscience, of civil society, of the Church, and, above all, in the eyes of God. The Lord has made all the other things on earth for man, and man himself, both in his existence and in his essence, has been fashioned for God and not for other creatures, even though, insofar as his behavior is concerned, he has a duty to the community. Now even the unborn child is "man" to the same degree and by the same title as the mother.

272   Furthermore, every human being, even a child in the mother's womb, has a right to life directly from God and not from the parents or from any human society or authority. Hence there is no man, no human authority, no science, no medical, eugenic, social, economic or moral "indication" that can offer or produce a valid juridical title to a direct deliberate disposal of an innocent human life; that is to say, a disposal that aims at its destruction whether as an end or as a means to another end, which is, perhaps, in no way unlawful in itself. Thus for example to save the life of the mother is a very noble end; but the direct killing of the child as a means to that end is not lawful. The direct destruction of the so-called "life without value" whether born or yet to be born, such as was practised very widely a few years ago, cannot in any way be justified. Hence when this practice began, the Church formally declared that it was against the natural law and the divine positive law, and consequently, unlawful to kill even by order of the public authorities, those who were innocent but, on account of some physical or mental defect, rendered useless to the State and a burden upon it.[3] The life

of one who is innocent is untouchable, and any direct attempt or aggression against it is a violation of one of the fundamental laws without which secure human society is impossible. We have no need to teach you in detail the meaning and the gravity in your profession of this fundamental law. But never forget that there rises above every man-made code and above every "indication" the faultless law of God.

The apostolate of your profession demands of you that   273
you pass on to others that knowledge of human life, that regard and respect for it, which your Christian faith nurtures in your hearts. You must, when called upon, be prepared to defend resolutely and to protect, when possible, the helpless and hidden life of the child, following the divine precept "Non occides", Thou shalt not kill.[4] Such defensive action becomes at times most necessary and urgent, but nevertheless, it is not the most noble and important part of your mission. This, in fact, is not purely negative, but is eminently constructive, and it aims at encouraging, edifying and strengthening.   274

Instill into the minds and hearts of the mother and father the esteem and joyous desire of the newborn child so that it is welcomed with love from the moment of its birth. The child, formed in the womb of the mother, is a gift from God,[5] Who confides its care to the parents. With what a delicate and charming touch does Holy Writ describe the children seated at table with their father! They form the reward of the just man, whereas sterility is often the punishment of the sinner. Listen to the divine utterance expressed with the matchless poetry of the psalmist: "Thy wife as a fruitful vine, on the sides of thy house. Thy children as olive plants, round about thy table. Behold thus shall the man be blessed that feareth the Lord!"[6] But of the wicked man it is written: "May his posterity be cut off; in one generation may his name be blotted out."[7]

Hasten to lay the newborn child in the arms of the father   275
as did the Romans of old, but do it for an incomparably higher motive. With the Romans it was a recognition of paternity and of the authority that arises from it; with us, it will be to pay homage to the Creator, to call down God's blessing and to undertake to carry out with devout affection

the office with God has entrusted to him. If Our Lord praises and rewards the faithful servant for having made good use of five talents[8], what praise, what recompense, will He not set aside for the father who has protected and reared for Him the human life which was confided to him; a treasure of greater value than all the gold and silver in the world.

276   Your apostolate, however, is concerned above all with the mother. Without doubt the voice of nature speaks in her and places in her heart the desire, the courage, the love and the will to take care of the child; but in order to overcome the suggestions of faintheartedness from whatever cause, that voice needs to be strengthened and to strike, so to speak a supernatural note. It falls to you by your bearing and manner of acting, rather than by words to make the young mother realize the greatness, the beauty, the nobility of that life which now is awakening, and which is being shaped and quickened in the womb, the life that is born in her, that she carries in her arms and nourishes at her breast. It rests with you to help her to appreciate the greatness of the gift of God's love for her and for her child. The Sacred Scriptures bring to our ears with many examples an echo of the prayers of supplication and, then, of the hymns of grateful joy of many mothers whose prayers at length were heard after having long implored with tears the grace of motherhood.

277   And those sorrows, too, which, after original sin, the mother has to suffer to bring her child into the world, help to bind more tightly the link which unites them. Her love is in proportion to her suffering. This has been expressed with moving and profound simplicity by Him Who has formed the hearts of mothers: "A woman, when she is in labor, hath sorrow because her hour is come; but when she hath brought forth the child, she remembereth no more the anguish, for joy that a man has been born into the world."[9] Besides, the Holy Spirit, by the pen of the Apostle St. Paul, shows once again the grandeur and joy of motherhood: God gives the child to the mother, but in giving it, He makes her cooperate effectively in the unfolding of the flower, the seed of which He had sown in her, and this cooperation becomes the way that leads her to eternal salvation: "Woman will be saved by childbearing."[10]

This perfect agreement between faith and reason gives you   278
a guarantee that you are in the right and that you can pursue
with unconditional security your apostolate of appreciation
and love of the life that is being born. Should you succeed in
exercising this apostolate at the side of the cradle in which
the newly-born utters its first cries, it will not be difficult for
you to achieve what your conscience as midwives, in keeping
with the law of God and of nature, expects you to prescribe
for the good of the mother and the child.

It is not, moreover, necessary for Us to prove to you who   279
have experienced it, how essential nowadays is that apostolate
of appreciation and love for the new life. Unfortunately, cases
are not rare in which even a cautious reference to children
as a "blessing" is enough to provoke a downright denial and
perhaps even derision. Far more frequently, in thought and
in words, the attidude of considering children a heavy "burden" predominates. How opposed is this frame of mind to
the mind of God and to the words of Holy Scripture, and, for
that matter, to sound reason and the sentiment of nature!
Should there be conditions and circumstances in which parents, without violating the law of God, can avoid the "blessing" of children, such cases of force majeure, however, by no
means authorize the perversion of ideas, the disparaging of
values, the belittling of the mother who has had the courage
and the honor to give life.

If what we have said up to now deals with the protection   280
and the care of the natural life, it should hold all the more in
regard to the supernatural life which the newly-born infant
receives with Baptism.

In the present economy there is no other way of com-   281
municating this life to the child who has not yet the use of
reason. But, nevertheless, the state of grace at the moment
of death is absolutely necessary for salvation. Without it, it
is not possible to attain supernatural happiness, the beatific
vision of God. An act of love can suffice for an adult to
obtain sanctifying grace and supply for the absence of Bap-
tims; for the unborn child or for the newly-born, this way is
not open. If, then, we hold that charity towards our neighbor
imposes upon us the obligation of helping him in case of

necessity, this obligation is increased in proportion to the importance of the good to be procured or the evil to be avoided. Again, it is increased when the person in need is unable to help or save himself. It is therefore easy to understand the importance of giving baptism to the infant completely without the use of reason, when it is in serious danger or facing certain danger.

282   Undoubtedly this obligation is binding in the first place on the parents; but in urgent cases, where there is no time to lose, or it is impossible to obtain a priest, yours is the sublime duty of administering Baptism. Do not, then, fail in performing this charitable service and in exercising this active apostolate of your profession. Let the words of Jesus be your comfort and your encouragement: "Blessed are the merciful, for they shall obtain mercy."[11] And what act of mercy is greater or more beautiful than to ensure for the soul of the infant between the threshold of life it has just crossed and that of approaching death, the entrance into a glorious and happy eternity!

283   The third aspect of your apostolate may be described as helping the mother in the prompt and generous fulfillment of her marital duties.

284   Scarcely had Mary Most Holy understood the Angel's message than she replied: "Behold the handmaid of the Lord! Be it done unto me according to thy word."[12] An eager acceptance of the vocation of motherhood! Virginal motherhood incomparably superior to any other; yet a real motherhood in the true and proper meaning of the word.[13] For this reason, when reciting the Angelus and after recalling Mary's acceptance, the faithful finish at once with: "And the Word was made flesh."[14]

285   It is one of the fundamental requirements of the right moral order, that with the use of the conjugal rights, there should correspond a sincere acceptance of the duties of motherhood. On this condition, the woman follows the path traced by the Creator to the end He has appointed for the creature, making her, by the exercise of that function, a sharer in His goodness, His wisdom, and His omnipotence in accordance with the Angel's announcement: "Concipies in

utero et paries"—"Thou shalt conceive in thy womb and shalt bring forth a son."[1][5]

If such then is the biological foundation of your pro-   286
fessional activity, the urgent object of your apostolate will be
to strive to sustain, to reawaken and stimulate the mother's
instinct and the mother's love.

When spouses value and appreciate the honor of producing   287
a new life, and await its coming with a holy impatience, your
part is a very easy one; it will be sufficient to cultivate this
interior sentiment in them; the readiness to welcome and
cherish that growing life follows automatically. Unfortunately,
however, it is not always the case; the child is often not
wanted, worse still, its coming is often dreaded. In such conditions, how can there be a ready response to the call of duty?
Your apostolate in this case must be both powerful and
effective; primarily, in a negative way, by refusing any immoral cooperation; then also in a positive way, by deftly applying
yourselves to the removal of preconceived ideas, various fears
or fainthearted excuses; and as far as possible to remove also
the external obstacles which may cause distress where the acceptance of motherhood is concerned. You may come forward
unhesitatingly where you are asked to advise and help in the
bringing forth of new life, to protect it and set it on its way
towards its full development. But, unfortunately, in how many
cases are you rather called upon to prevent the procreation
and preservation of this life, regardless of the precepts of the
moral order? To accede to such requests would be to abuse
your knowledge and your skill by becoming accomplices in
an immoral act; it would be the perversion of your apostolate.
It demands a calm but unequivocal refusal to countenance
the transgression of God's law or the dictates of your conscience. It follows, therefore, that your profession requires
that you should have a clear knowledge of this divine law, so
that it may be respected and followed without excess or
defect.

Our Predecessor, Pius XI, of happy memory, in his Encyc-   288
lical, "Casti Connubii", December 31, 1930, solemnly proclaimed anew the fundamental law governing the marital act
and conjugal relations; he said that any attempt on the part

of the husband and wife to deprive this act of its inherent force or to impeded the procreation of a new life, either in the performance of the act itself, or in the course of the development of its natural consequences, is immoral, and furthermore, no alleged "indication" or need can convert an intrinsically immoral act into a moral and lawful one.

289   This precept is as valid today as it was yesterday, and it will be the same tomorrow and always, because it does not imply a precept of human law, but it is the expression of a law which is natural and divine.

290   Let these words be your unfailing guide in all cases where your profession and your apostolate demand of you a clear and unequivocal decision.

291   It would be more than a mere want of readiness in the service of life if the attempt made by man were to concern not only an individual act but should affect the entire organism itself, with the intention of depriving it, by means of sterilization, of the faculty of procreating a new life. Here, too, you have a clearly established rule in the Church's teaching which governs your behavior both internally and externally. Direct sterilization—that is, the sterilization which aims, either as a means or as an end in itself, to render child-bearing impossible—is a grave violation of the moral law, and therefore unlawful. Even public authority has no right, whatever "indication" it may use as an excuse, to permit it, and much less to prescribe it or to use it to the detriment of innocent human beings. This principle has already been enunciated in the above-mentioned Encyclical of Pius XI on Marriage. So, therefore, ten years ago, when sterilization came to be more widely used, the Holy See was obliged to make an explicit and solemn declaration that direct sterilization, whether permanent or temporary, of the man or of the woman, is unlawful, and this by virtue of the natural law from which the Church herself, as you well know, has no power to dispense.

292   Do all you can, therefore, in your apostolate, to oppose these perverse tendencies, and refuse your cooperation in them.

The further serious problem presents itself today whether,   293
and how far, the obligation of readiness to fulfill the duty of
motherhood can be reconciled with the ever increasing recourse to the periods of natural sterilty (the so-called agene-
sical periods in the woman), a practice which seems to be the
clear expression of a will opposed to that readiness.

You are rightly expected to be well informed, from the   294
medical point of view, of this well-known theory and of the
progress which can still be foreseen in this matter; and moreover, your advice and help are expected to be based, not on
simple, popular publications, but on scientific facts and the
authoritative judgment of conscientious specialists in medicine and biology. It is your office, and not that of the priest,
to instruct married people by private consultation or through
serious publications on the medical and biological aspect of
the theory, without at the same time allowing yourselves to
be drawn into discussions which are neither right nor becoming.

But in this field, too, your apostolate demands of you as   295
women and as Christians that you know and defend the moral
law to which this theory is subordinated. And here the
Church is competent to speak.

In the first place, there are two hypotheses to be considered.   296
If the application of this theory means nothing more than
that married people use their matrimonial rights even during
the time of natural sterility, there is nothing to be said against
it; by so doing, they do not in any way prevent or prejudice
the consummation of the natural act and its further natural
consequences. It is precisely in this that the application of
the theory We are discussing is essentially distinct from the
abuse of it already mentioned, which consists of a perversion
of the act itself. If, however, a further step is made, that is,
of restricting the marital act exclusively to that particular
period, then the conduct of the married couple must be
examined more attentively.

Here, again, two alternatives must be considered. If, even   297
at the time of the marrige, it was the intention of the man or
the woman to restrict the marital right itself to the periods of

sterility, and not merely the use of that right, in such a way that the other partner would not even have the right to demand the act at any other time, that would imply an essential defect in the matrimonial consent. This would invalidate the marriage itself, because the right deriving from the marriage contract is a permanent right, uninterrupted and not intermittent of each of the partners in respect of the other.

298   If, on the other hand, the limitation of the act to the times of natural sterility refers not to the right itself but only to the use of the right, there is then no question of the validity of the marriage. Nevertheless, the moral lawfulness of such conduct would be affirmed or denied according as to whether or not the intention to keep constantly to these periods is based on sufficient and reliable moral grounds. The sole fact that the couple do not offend against the nature of the act and that they are willing to accept and bring up the child that is born notwithstanding the precautions they have taken, would not of itself alone be a sufficient guarantee of a right intention and of the unquestionable morality of the motives themselves.

299   The reason is that marriage binds to a state of life which, while conferring certain rights, at the same time imposes the accomplishment of a positive work which belongs to the very state of wedlock. This being so, the general principle can now be stated that the fulfillment of a positive duty may be withheld should grave reasons, independent of the good will of those obliged to it, show that such fulfillment is untimely, or make it evident that it cannot equitably be demanded by that which requires the fulfillment—in this case, the human race.

300   The marriage contract which gives the spouses the right to satisfy the inclinations of nature established them in a state of life, the married state. Nature and Creator impose upon the married couple who use that state by carrying out its specific act, the duty of providing for the conservation of the human race. Herein we have the characteristic service which gives their state its peculair value—the good of the offspring. Both the individual and society, the people and the State, and the Church herself, depend for their existence on the order which God has established on fruitful marriage. Hence,

to embrace the married state, to make frequent use of the faculty proper to it and lawful only in that state, while on the other hand, always and deliberately to seek to evade its primary duty without serious reasons, would be to sin against the very meaning of married life.

Serious reasons, often put forward on medical, eugenic, 301 economic and social grounds, can exempt from that obligatory service even for a considerable period of time, even for the entire duration of the marriage. It follows from this that the use of the infertile periods can be lawful from the moral point of view and, in the circumstances which have been mentioned, it is indeed lawful. If, however, in the light of a reasonable and fair judgment, there are no such serious personal reasons, or reasons deriving from external circumstances, then the habitual intention to avoid the fruitfulness of the union, while at the same time continuing fully to satisfy sensual intent, can only arise from a false appreciation of life and from motives that run counter to true standards of moral conduct.

Here you will perhaps urge a point, and say that sometimes, 302 whilst engaged in your profession, you find yourselves face to face with very delicate cases, namely, those in which to run the risk of motherhood cannot be demanded, nay, where motherhood must be absolutely avoided, and where, on the other hand, the use of sterile periods either does not afford a sufficient safeguard, or where, for other reasons, it must be discarded. And so, you ask, how is it still possible to speak of an apostolate in the service of motherhood?

If, in your sure and experienced judgment, the circum- 303 stance definitely demand a "No," that is to say that motherhood is unthinkable, it would be a mistake, a wrong, to prescribe a "Yes." Here it is a question of concrete facts, and therefore a medical, not a theological question, and so it is within your competence. However, in such cases, the married couple do not ask you for a medical answer, an answer which must necessarily be negative, they seek rather your approval of a "technique" of marital relationship that is proof against the risk of motherhood. So, here again, you are called upon to exercise your apostolate, inasmuch as you leave no doubt that, even in extreme cases, every preventive practice and every direct attack on the life and development of the seed is forbidden and banned in conscience, and that there is only one thing to do, and that is, to abstain from any complete use of the natural faculty. In this matter your apostolate demands a clear and certain judgment and a calm firmness.

304   It will be objected, however, that such abstinence is impossible, that heroism such as this is not feasible. At the present time you can hear and read of this objection everywhere, even from those who, because of their duty and authority, should be of quite a different mind. The following argument is brought forward as proof: No one is obliged to do the impossible and no reasonable legislator is presumed to wish by his law to bind persons to do the impossible. But for the married people to abstain for a long time is impossible. Therefore they are not bound to abstain: divine law cannot mean that.

305   In such manner of argument a false conclusion is reached from premises which are only partially true. To be convinced of this, one has simply to reverse the terms of the argument: God does not oblige us to do the impossible. But God obliges married people to abstain if their union cannot be accomplished according to the rules of nature. Therefore, in such cases, abstinence is possible. In confirmation of this argument, we have the doctrine of the Council of Trent which, in the chapter on the necessary and possible observance of the Commandments, referring to a passage in the works of Augustine, teaches: "God does not command what is impossible, but when He commands, He warns you to do what you can and to ask His aid for what is beyond your powers, and He gives His help to make that possible for you.

306   Do not be disturbed when, in the practice of your profession and in your apostolate, you hear this clamor about impossibility. Do not let it cloud your internal judgment, nor affect your exterior conduct. Never lend yourselves to anything whatsoever which is opposed to the law of God and your Christian conscience. To judge men and women of today incapable of continuous heroism is to do them wrong. In these days, for many reasons—perhaps through dire neces-

sity, or even at times under pressure of injustice,—heroism is being practised to a degree and extent that in times past would have been thought impossible. Why then, if circumstances demand it, should this heroism stop at the limits prescribed by passion and the inclinations of nature? It is obvious that he who does not want to master himself, will not be able to do so; and he who thinks he can master himself, relying solely on his own powers and not sincerely and perseveringly seeking divine aid, will be miserably deceived.

Here then, you see how your apostolate can win married   307
people over to a service of motherhood, that is, not one of utter servitude to the promptings of nature, but to the exercise of marital rights and duties, governed by the principles of reason and faith.

Finally there is an aspect of your apostolate that concerns   308
the defence of the right order of values and the dignity of the human person.

"Personal values" and the need to respect them, is a subject   309
that for the past twenty years has kept writers busily employed. In many of their elaborate works, the specifically sexual act, too, has a position allotted to it in the service of the person in the married state. The peculiar and deeper meaning of the exercise of the marital right should consist in this: that the bodily union is the expression and actuation of the personal and affective union.

Articles, pamphlets, books and lectures, dealing in partic-   310
ular even with the "technique of love," have served to spread these ideas and to illustrate them with warnings to the newly-wed as a guide to marriage that will prevent them neglecting, through foolishness, misplaced modesty, or unfounded scrupulosity, what God, Who is Creator also of their natural inclinations, offers to them. If a new life results from this complete reciprocal gift of the husband and wife, it is a consequence that remains outside or, at the most, at the circumference, so to say, of the "personal values"; a consequence that is not excluded, but is not to be considered as a focal point of marital relations.

According to these theories, the dedication of yourselves   311
to the welfare of the life still hidden in the mother's womb,

or to helping the mother to be happily delivered, would be of only minor importance and would take secondary place.

312   Now, if this relative appreciation merely emphasized the value of the persons of the married couple rather than that of the offspring, such a problem could, strictly speaking, be disregarded. But here there is a question of a serious inversion of the order of values and of purposes which the Creator Himself has established. We are face to face with the propagation of a body of ideas and sentiments directly opposed to serene, deep and serious Christian thought. Here again your apostolate must play its part. You may become the confidantes of the mother and wife and be asked questions about the most secret desires and intimate acts of married life. If so, how could you, aware as you are of your mission, make truth and right order prevail in the judgment and relationship of the married couple, unless you yourselves have precise knowledge and a firmness of character necessary to maintain what you know to be true and righteous?

313   The truth is that marriage, as a natural institution, is not ordered by the will of the Creator towards personal perfection of the husband and wife as its primary end, but to the pro-creation and education of a new life. The other ends of marriage, although part of nature's plan, are not of the same importance as the first. Still less are they superior. On the contrary, they are essentially subordinate to it. This principle holds good for all marriages, even if they are unfruitful: just as it can be said that all eyes are intended and constructed to see, even though in abnormal cases, because of particular internal or external conditions, they can never be capable of giving sight.

314   It was precisely for the purpose of putting an end to all uncertainty and wanderings away from the truth, which were threatening to spread mistaken ideas about the order of precedence in the purposes of marriage and the relationship between them, that We ourselves, some years ago (March 10, 1944), drew up a statement placing them in their right order. We called attention to what the very internal structure of their natural disposition discloses, to what is the heritage of Christian tradition, to what the Sovereign Pontiffs have

repeatedly taught, and to what was afterwards definitely stated in the Code of Canon Law.[16] Furthermore, a little while afterwards, to put an end to conflicting opinions, the Holy See, by public Decree, proclaimed that the appeal of certain modern writers who deny that the procreation and education of the child is the primary end of marriage, or teach that the secondary ends are not essentially subordinate to the primary end, but rather are of equal value and are independent of it, cannot be admitted.[17]

Does that mean a denial or a dimishing of what is good and right in the personal values which result from marriage and from the marriage act? Certainly not, because in marriage the Creator has destined human beings, made of flesh and blood and endowed with a mind and a heart, for the procreation of new life, and they are called to be the parents of their progeny as human beings and not irrational animals. It is to this end that God wills the union of married people. Indeed Holy Writ says of God that He created human kind to His image, created them male and female,[18] and willed—as we find repeatedly stated in the Holy Bible—that a man "shall leave father and mother, and shall cleave to his wife, and they shall be two in one flesh."[19]   **315**

All this is therefore true and willed by God, but it must not be disjoined from the primary function of marriage, that is, from the duty to the new life. Not only the exterior common life, but also all the personal wealth, the qualities of mind and spirit, and finally all that there is of the more truly spiritual and profound in married love as such, has been placed by the will of nature and the Creator at the service of the offspring. Of its nature, perfect married life means also the complete self-sacrifice of the parents on behalf of their children, and love of husband and wife in its strength and tenderness is an essential need for the most earnest care of the child and the guarantee that this will be taken.   **316**

To consider unworthily the cohabitation of husband and wife, and the marital act as a simple organic function for the transmission of seed, would be the same as to convert the domestic hearth, which is the family sanctuary, into a mere biological laboratory. For this reason, in Our address of   **317**

September 29, 1949, made to the International Congress of Catholic Doctors, We formally rejected artificial insemination in marriage. The marital act, in its natural setting, is a personal action. It is the simultaneous and direct cooperation of husband and wife which, by the very nature of the agents and the propriety of the act, is the expression of the mutual giving which, in the words of Scripture, results in the union "in one flesh."

318   There is much more than the union of two life-germs, which can be brought about even artifically, that is, without the cooperation of the husband and wife. The marital act, in the order of, and by nature's design, consists of a personal cooperation which the husband and wife exchange as a right when they marry.

319   When, therefore, this interchange of rights is, from the beginning, permanently impossible in its natural form, the object of the marriage contract is essentially vitiated. This is what We have already stated, viz., "Let it not be forgotten: the procreation of a new life according to the will and intention of the Creator alone brings with it, to a most admirable degree of perfection, the realization of the ends and spiritual nature and the dignity of husband and wife, and with the normal and wholesome development of the child."

320   It follows that it is for you to tell the fiancée or the young wife who comes to discuss with you the values of married life, that these personal values in relation to the body, sense or spirit, are really good and true, but that the Creator has put them in the second place in the scale of values, and not in the first.

321   There is a further consideration which can easily be forgotten. All these secondary values, in regard to generation and its processes, are part of the specific duty of husband and wife, namely, to be the parents and educators of the new living being. A high and noble duty! It does not, however, belong to the essence of a complete human being, as though a human being who did not use the generative faculty would suffer some loss of dignity. To renounce the use of that power does not mean any mutilation of personal and spiritual values, especially if a person refrains from the highest motives. Of

such a free renunciation made for the sake of the kingdom of God, the Creator has said: "Non omnes capiunt verbum istud, sed quibus datum est—all men take not this word, but they to whom it is given."[20]

It is therefore a mistake and a departure from the way of moral truth to exalt too highly the generative function even in its right moral setting of married life. This often happens today. Again, it brings the risk of an error of understanding and of misguided affection which hinders and stifles good and noble feelings, especially with young people who have as yet had no experience and unaware of life's snares. After all, what normal person, healthy in mind and body, would want to belong to the number of those lacking character and spirit? 322

Do you however, by your apostolate, wherever you work professionally, enlighten people's minds and instill into them this right order of values, so that men any regulate their judgment and their conduct by it. 323

Our explanation of the apostolic work of your profession would, however, be incomplete were We not able to add a few words more on the defence of human dignity in the use of the generative inclination. 324

The Creator in His goodness and wisdom has willed to make use of the work of the man and the woman to preserve and propagate the human race, by joining them in wedlock. The same Creator has arranged that the husband and wife find pleasure and happiness of mind and body in the performance of that function. Consequently, the husband and wife do no wrong in seeking out and enjoying this pleasure. They are accepting what the Creator intended for them. 325

Still, here too, the husband and wife ought to know how to keep within the bounds of moderation. As in eating and drinking, they ought not to give themselves over completly to the promptings of their senses, so neither ought they to subject themselves unrestrainedly to their sensual appetite. This, therefore, is the rule to be followed: the use of the natural, generative instinct and function is lawful in the married state only, and in the service of the purposes for which marriage exists. It follows from this that, only in the married 326 state and in the observance of these laws, are the desires and enjoyment of that pleasure and satisfaction allowed; because pleasure is subject to the law of action from which it springs, and not vice-versa—action made subject to the law of pleasure. And this law, so reasonable, looks not only to the substance, but to the circumstances of the action; so that, while the substance of the function is still preserved, sin can be committed by the way it is carried out.

327   The transgression of this law is as old as original sin. However, at the present time, there is a danger of losing sight of this fundamental principle. Today, in fact, it is customary in speaking and in writing (even among some Catholics), to uphold the necessity of personal freedom, the peculiar purpose and value of sexual relationship and its use, independently of the purpose of the procreation of offspring. They would like to submit the order established by God to fresh examination and to a new regulation. They would like no other check in the manner of satisfying this instinct than the observance of what is essential to the instinctive act. For the moral obligation to master our passions, they would substitute freedom to make use of the whims and inclinations of nature blindly and without restraint. This must sooner or later result in harm to morality, to conscience, and to human dignity.

328   If the exclusive aim of nature, or at least, its primary aim, had been the mutual giving and possessing of husband and wife in joy and delight; if nature had arranged that act only to make their personal experience happy in the highest possible degree, and not as an incentive in the service of life, then the Creator would have made use of another plan in the formation and constitution of the natural act. Instead, the act is completely subordinate and ordered to the great and unique law, *"generatio et educatio prolis"* (the generating and education of children), that is, to the fulfillment of the primary end of marriage as the origin and source of life.

329   Unfortunately, waves of hedonism never cease to roll over the world. They are thereatening to overwhelm the whole of married life in a rising sea of ideas, desires, and acts, not without grave danger to and serious prejudice of the primary duty of husband and wife.

Too often people are not ashamed of exalting this anti-   330
Christian hedonism as though it were a doctrine, by inculcat-
ing the desire to make the pleasure in the preparation and the
act of conjugal union ever more intense; as if the whole moral
law governing marital relations consisted of the proper fulfillment of this act—as if everything else, no matter how
carried out, finds its justification in the profuse expression of
mutual affection, hallowed by the sacrament of Matrimony
and worthy of praise and reward before God and the conscience of man. All question of man's dignity and of his
dignity as a Christian, both of which are a restraint on sexual
excess, are set aside.

That is false. The seriousness and holiness of the Christian   331
moral law does not permit the unrestrained satisfying of the
sexual instinct, nor such seeking merely for pleasure and
enjoyment. It does not allow rational man to let himself be
so dominated either by the substance or the circumstances
of the act.

Some would like to maintain that happiness in married life   332
is in direct ratio to the mutual enjoyment of marital relations.
This is not so. On the contrary, happiness in married life is in
direct ratio to the respect the husband and wife have for each
other, even in the intimate act of marriage. Not that they
should regard what nature offers them and God has given
them as immoral, and refuse it, but because the respect and
mutual esteem which arise from it, are one of the strongest
elements of a love which is all the more pure because it is the
more tender.

Whilst performing the duties of your profession, do your   333
utmost to repel the attack of this refined hedonism, which is
spiritually an empty thing and therefore unworthy of Christian spouses. Make it clear that nature has undoubtedly given
the instinctive desire for pleasure and sanctioned it in lawful
wedlock, not as an end in itself, but in the service of life.
Banish from your hearts this cult of pleasure, and do your
best to stop the spreading of literature which considers it a
duty to describe the intimacies of married life under the pretext of giving instruction, guidance and reassurance. In general,
common sense, natural instinct, and a short instruction on

the clear and simple maxims of the Christian moral law, will suffice to give peace to husband and wife of tender conscience. If, in certain special circumstances, a fiancée or young married woman has need for further enlightenment on some particular point, it is your duty prudently and tactfully to give them an explanation which is in agreement with the natural law and a healthy Christian conscience.

334   Our teaching has nothing to do with Manichaeism or with Jansenism, as some would like to make out in self-justification. It is simply a defence of the honor of Christian marriage and the personal dignity of husband and wife.

335   To give your services for such a purpose, is a pressing duty of your calling, especially in these days.

336   So We conclude what We had in mind to explain to you.

337   Your profession offers you a vast and varied apostolate, an apostolate not so much of word as of action and guidance; an apostolate that you will be able to exercise usefully only if you are well-informed, in advance, of the object of your mission and of the means to its fulfillment, and, moreover, if you are gifted with a will strong in resolve that is rooted in a deep religious conviction, inspired and enriched by your faith and by Christian charity.

338   Whilst We implore for you the powerful help of divine light and strength, now as a pledge and earnest of a generous bounty of heavenly graces, We bestow on you from Our Heart, Our Apostolic Blessing.

Address of Pope Pius XII
to the Associations of the Large Families
November 26, 1951

In the order of nature, among social institutions there is no other that is dearer to the Church than the family. Christ has elevated Matrimony to the dignity of a Sacrament, which is as it were the root of the family. The family itself has always found, and will always find, in the Church a defender, a support, a protector in all that concerns its inviolable rights, its liberty, the exercise of its high function.

Therefore, We feel a particular happiness, beloved sons and daughters, in giving a welcome in Our home to the national Congress of the "Family Front" and of the large family, and in expressing Our satisfaction for your efforts towards the ends at which you aim, and Our paternal blessing for their successful realization.   **340**

A family movement such as yours, whose aim is to produce   **341** fully in the people the idea of the Christian family, cannot fail, under the impulse of the interior force which animates it and of the necessities of the people itself, in the midst of which it lives and grows, to place itself at the service of that threefold aim which forms the object of your cares: the influence to be exercised on legislation in the vast field which immediately or mediately affects the family, solidarity between families; Christian culture of the family. This third object is the fundamental one, the first two must contribute to second it and promote it.

342   We have often and on the most varied occasions spoke on behalf of the Christian family, and in most cases to come to its help or to call others thereto to save it from the most serious dangers; above all to succor it in the calamity of war. The damage wrought by the First World War was far from being fully repaired, when the second even more terrible conflagration came to increase it to the uttermost. There will be need of time and efforts on the part of men and of an even greater divine help before the deep wounds inflicted on the family by these two wars begin to heal extensively. Another evil, also partly due to devastating wars, but a consequence of over-population and of individual tendencies inexpedient and self-interested, is the housing crisis; all those, legislators, statesmen, members of social welfare, who endeavor to find a remedy accomplish, even if only indirectly, an apostolate of eminent value.

343   The same is true for the struggle against the scourge of unemployment, for the establishment of a sufficient family wage, so that the mother is not obliged, as too often happens, to look for work outside the home, but may devote herself to a greater extent to her husband and children. Work for schools and for religious education is also a precious contribution towards the welfare of the family; as is also the encouraging in it of a healthy naturalness and simplicity of manners, a reinforcement of religious beliefs, a development of an atmosphere of Christian purity, suitable for protecting it from those harmful external influences and from all those morbid excitements that arouse the sordid passions in the minds of adolescents.

344   But there is an even deeper misery, from which the family must be preserved; it is that debasing slavery to which it is reduced by a mentality tending to make it a mere organism at the service of the social community, in order to procreate for such a community a sufficient mass of "human material."

345   Another danger threatens the family, a danger no means recent, but having its roots in the past, which, however, is growing rapidly, and can become disastrous because it attacks the family in its very germ; We mean the extensive revolution in conjugal morals.

In the course of the last few years, We have taken every **346** opportunity to expound one or other of the essential points of that morality, and more recently to indicate it in its entirety, not only by confuting the errors which corrupt it, but also by showing positively its meaning, duty, and importance, its values for the happiness of the married couple, the children and the whole family, for stability and greater social benefit from the domestic hearth even to the State and to the Church herself.

At the center of this doctrine matrimony appeared as an **347** institution at the service of life. In strict relation with this principle, in accordance with the constant teaching of the Church, We expounded a thesis which is one of the essential foundations not only of conjugal morality, but also of social morality in general, that is, that the direct attack on innocent human life, as a means to an end—in the present case to the end of saving another life—is illicit.

Innocent human life, in whatever condition it may be, from **348** the first moment of its existence, is to be preserved from any direct voluntary attack. This is a fundamental right of the human person, of general value in the Christian concept of life; valid both for the still hidden life in the womb and for the new born babe, and opposed to direct abortion as it is to the direct killing of the child, before, during, and after birth. No matter what the distinction between those different moments in the development of the life, already born or still to be born, for profane and ecclesiastical law and for certain civil and penal consequences—according to the moral law, in all these cases it is a matter of a grave and illicit attempt on inviolable human life.

This principle holds good both for the mother as well as **349** the child. Never and in no case has the Church taught that the life of the child must be preferred to that of the mother. It is erroneous to place the question with this alternative: either the life of the child or that of the mother. No; neither the life of the mother nor of the child may be submitted to an act of direct suppression. Both for the one and the other the demand cannot be but this: to use every means to save the life of both the mother and the child.

350   To seek always new ways to assure the life of both is one of the most beautiful and noble aspirations of medicine. If, notwithstanding the progress of science, there still remain, and will remain in future, cases in which the mother's death is certain, when she desires that the life in her womb continue its life's course, and does not desire to destroy it, thus violating God's commandment: do not kill! There remains for man, who to the last moment shall have attempted to help and to save, only to bow down with respect to the laws of nature and to the dispositions of divine Providence.

351   But—it is objected—the life of the mother, especially the mother of a large family, is far superior in value to that of the still unborn child. The application of the theory of the scale of values to the case which here concerns us has already been favorably received in juridical discussions. The reply to this tormenting objection is not difficult. The inviolability of the life of an innocent person does not depend on its greater or lesser value. More than ten years ago, the Church formally condemned the killing of a life deemed "useless"; and those who know the sad antecedents that provoked such a condemnation, those who know how to ponder the disastrous consequences that would follow were the sanctity of an innocent life to be measured according to its value, can easily appreciate the motives which led to such a disposition. On the other hand, who can judge with certainty which of the two lives is in reality the more precious? Who can know what path that child will follow and to what heights of perfection and of work it will reach? Here, two greatnesses are compared, about one of which nothing is known. *(An example.)*

352   It has been Our intention here to use always the expressions *"direct* attempt on the life of the innocent person", *"direct* killing." The reason is that if, for example, the safety of the future mother, independently of her state of pregnancy, might call for an urgent surgical operation, or any other therapeutic application, which would have as an accessory consequence, in no way desired nor intended, but *inevitable,* the death of the foetus, such an act could not be called a *direct* attempt on the innocent life. In these conditions the operation can be lawful, as can other similar medical interventions, provided

that it be a matter of great importance, such as life, and that it is not possible to postpone it till the birth of the child, or to have recourse to any other efficacious remedy.

Therefore, since the primary office of matrimony is to be   353
at the service of life, Our special regard and Our paternal gratitude go to those generous husbands and wives who, for the love of God and trusting in Him, courageously raise a numerous family.

The Church, on the other hand, can understand, with   354
sympathy and comprehension, the real difficulties of matrimonial life in these our days. For this reason, in Our last address on conjugal morality, We affirmed the legitimacy and at the same time the limits—truly very wide—of that controlling of births which, unlike the so-called "birth control," is compatible with God's law. It can be hoped (but in such matters the Church naturally leaves the judgment to medical science) that for such a lawful method a sufficiently certain basis can be found, and recent research seems to confirm this hope.

To overcome the many trials of conjugal life there is above   355
all the most powerful aids of a lively Faith and a frequenting of the Sacraments, whence emerge torrents of strength whose efficacy is hardly clearly known by those who are outside of the Church. We wish to close Our speech by recalling these sublime aids. It may also happen to you, beloved sons and daughters, that, one day or another, you may feel your courage being troubled by the violent storm raging about you, and, even more dangerously, in the midst of your family, by the doctrines which subvert the wholesome and normal concept of Christian marriage. Be trustful! Nature's energies and, above all, those of grace with which God has enriched your souls by the means of the Sacrament of matrimony are like a solid rock, against which the waves of a stormy sea break up powerless. And, if the tragedies of the war and post-war period have inflicted upon matrimony and the family wounds which are still bleeding, nonetheless during those years also, the constant fidelity, the sound perseverance of married couples, and maternal love standing firm in the face of innumerable difficulties, have in many cases truly and splendidly triumphed.

Address of Pope Pius XII
to the XXVI Congress of Urology
October 8, 1953

*(The Holy Father welcomes the members of the Congress.
—The question of the amputation of a healthy organ to
suppress the disease which afflicts another organ.)*

T hree things condition the moral permission of a surgical
operation requiring an anatomical or functional mutilation: firstly, that the preservation or functioning of
a particular organ provokes a serious damage or constitutes a
threat to the complete organism, secondly, that this damage
cannot be avoided, or at least notably diminished, except by
the amputation in question and that its efficacy is well
assured, lastly, that it can be reasonably foreseen that the
negative effect, namely, the mutilation and its consequences,
will be compensated by the positive effect: exclusion of a
damage to the whole organism, mitigation of the pain, etc.

The decisive point is not that the amputated or paralyzed
organ be itself diseased, but that its preservation or functioning directly or indirectly cause a serious threat to the whole
body. It is quite possible that by its healthy functioning a
healthy organ exerts a harmful action on a diseased organ,
capable of aggravating the evil and its repercussion on the
body as a whole. It can also happen that the removal of a
healthy organ and the arrest of its normal function halts the
evil, for example, growth in the case of cancer; or at all events
essentially changes its conditions of existence. If no other

means are available, surgical intervention on the healthy organ is permitted in both these cases.

358   The conclusion at which We have arrived is deduced from the right of disposal which man has received from the Creator as regards his own body, in conformity with the principle of totality, also involved here, by which every particular organ is subordinated to the body as a whole and must be subordinated to it in case of conflict. As a consequence, he who has received the use of the complete organism has the right to sacrifice a particular organ if its preservation or functioning causes a notable damage to the whole, impossible to be avoided in any other way. Since you are sure that, in the case stated, only the removal of the seminal glands permits the disease to be conquered, there is no objection from the moral point of view to this removal.

(At this point, the Holy Father spoke of a special case of surgery, to prevent an erroneous application of the above principle.)

359   We must, however, call your attention to a false application of the principle explained above.

360   It happens often, when gynecological complications call for a surgical operation, or even independently of such an operation, that healthy oviducts are excised or rendered incapable of functioning in order to prevent another pregnancy and the serious dangers which would result therefrom for the health or even the life of the mother, dangers which stem from other diseased organs, such as kidneys, heart, lungs, but which are aggravated in the case of pregnancy. To justify the excision of the oviducts, recourse is had to the principle quoted above, and it is stated that it is morally permissible to operate on healthy organs when the good of the whole requires it.

361   Here, however, recourse is wrongly made to this principle. For in this case the danger which the mother undergoes does not come either directly or indirectly from the presence or the normal functioning or the oviducts, nor from their influence upon the diseased organs, kidneys, lungs, heart. The

danger is verified only if free sexual activity leads to a pregnancy which could threaten these organs already too weak or diseased. The conditions which would justify disposing of a part in favor of the whole in virtue of the principle of totality are lacking. It is not therefore morally permissible to operate on healthy oviducts.

(The second question: the duty of the medical expert in the processes where there is raised the question of nullity of marriage arising from impotence.)

To give an accurate reply to this question, it may be useful   362
first to dispel misunderstandings surrounding the concept of "impotentia" or "potentia generandi." Potentia generandi takes on at times such a wide meaning that it includes all that both partners must possess to procreate new life; the internal or external organs, as well as the aptitude for the functions which correspond to the finality of these organs. The term is also used in a narrower sense and includes then only that which is required on the part of the personal activity of the spouses in order that this activity may really engender life, at least by itself and in a general way. In this sense "potentia generandi" is not the same as "potentia coëundi."

The conditions required for "potentia coëundi" are deter-   363
mined by nature and are deduced from the mechanism of the act. In this the action of the spouses, from a biological point of view, is at the service of the seminal fluid which it transmits and receives. How can we tell whether the "potentia coëundi" really exists and that consequently the act of the spouses is vested with all its essential elements? A practical criterion, although it is not valid without exception in all cases, is the capacity of performing the external act in a normal way. It is true that an element can be lacking without the partners being aware of it. However, this "signum manifestativum" (indication) must suffice in practice in life, for life requires that for an institution as wide as marriage, men should possess in normal cases, a sure and easily recognizable means of ascertaining their aptitude for marriage, this is sufficient because nature is wont to build the human organism in such a way

that the internal reality corresponds to the external form and structure.

364 Further, the "potentia coëundi" includes on the part of the husband the capacity to transmit in a natural way the liquid of the seminal glands, it is not a question of each of the specific and complementary elements which constitute this liquid. The lack of active sperm is not ordinarily a proof that the husband cannot exercise the function of transmission. Thus, azoospermia, oligospermia, asthenospermia, necrospermia have nothing to do by themselves with "impotentia coëundi" because they concern the constitutive elements of the seminal fluid itself, and not the faculty of transmitting it.

365 In all this one must hold that this action of the spouses is and remains at the service of a finality: the bringing forth of new life. It is erroneous to state that medicine and biology have a different concept of "potentia coëundi" than theology and canon law, and that the latter means, by this term, something other than what nature and the Creator have determined. You have but to read the text of canon 1068 on the physical power to see that it is dealing not with positive law, but with natural law.

366 Certainly the good sense of men and the practice of the Church leave no doubt on the fact that personal values are involved in marriage and its consummation; values which surpass by far mere biology and which the spouses often understand much better than the immediately biological ends of nature. But reason and Revelation suggest also and imply that nature introduces this personal and supra-biological element because it calls to marriage not sensitive beings deprived of reason, but men endowed with intelligence, heart and personal dignity, and charges them to procreate and educate new life: because, in marriage, the spouses devote themselves to a permanent task and to a community of life which is indissoluble.

367 Biology and medicine have, today more than ever, the mission of leading contemporary man toward a heightened concept of the biological meaning of the collaboration of the spouses and of the reason why nature authorizes this act only in marriage.

In our day, people heed the physician more readily than   368
they do the priest. But the physician himself must possess a
sure judgment, guided by nature, and enough personal independence to remain faithful to it.

This being said, We can reply to your question: The expert   369
examination required by the ecclesiastical tribunal in cases
"de nullitate ex titulo impotentiae" generally does not consist
in ascertaining the "impotentia generandi," but the "impo-
tenia coëundi," "Impotentia generandi," as opposed to
"impotentia coëundi," is not sufficient, according to ordinary
jurisprudence, to warrant a sentence of nullity. In the very
large majority of the cases, therefore, the microscospic
examination of the sperms could be omitted. It can be shown
in another way, if there is any usefulness to it, that the
seminal tissue still possesses some functional aptitude and,
likewise, that the canals that link these glands with the organs of evacuation are still functioning, are not entirely
deteriorated or definitely obstructed. The examination of the
sperm, by itself alone, can hardly give sufficient security.

Besides, the Holy Office has already decided, on August   370
2, 1929 that "masturbatio directe procurata—ut obtineatur
sperma" is not licit, and this, whatever may be the purpose
of the test.

(Duty of the medical expert.)

SACRA VIRGINITAS
Encyclical Letter of Pope Pius XII
On Holy Virginity
March 25, 1954

Holy virginity and that perfect chastity which is consecrated to the services of God is without doubt among the most precious treasures which the Founder of the Church has left in heritage to the society which He established.

372   2. This assuredly was the reason why the Fathers of the Church confidently asserted that perpetual virginity is a very noble gift which the Christian religion has bestowed on the world. They rightly noted that the pagans of antiquity imposed this way of life on the Vestals only for a certain time;[1] and that, although in the Old Testament virginity is ordered to be kept and preserved, it is only a previous requisite for marriage;[2] and furthermore, as Ambrose writes,[3] "We read that also in the temple of Jerusalem there were virgins. But what does the Apostle say? 'Now all these things happened to them in figure,'[4] that this might be a foreshadowing of what was to come."

373   3. Indeed right from Apostolic times this virtue has been thriving and flourishing in the garden of the Church. When the Acts of the Apostles[5] say that Philip the deacon was the father of four virgins, the word certainly refers to their state of life rather than to their age. And not much later Ignatius of Antioch salutes the virgins,[6] who together with the widows, formed a not insignificant part of the Christian community of Smyrna. In the second century, as St. Justin testifies, "many men and women, sixty and seventy years old, imbued

from childhood with the teaching of Christ, keep their integrity."[7] Gradually the number of men and women who had vowed their chastity to God grew; likewise the importance of the office they fulfilled in the Church increased notably, as We have shown more at length in Our Apostolic Constitution, "Sponsa Christi."[8]

4. Further, the Fathers of the Church, such as Cyprian, Athanasius, Ambrose, John Chrysostom, Jerome, Augustine, and many others, have sung the praises of virginity. And this doctrine of the Fathers, augmented through the course of centuries by the Doctors of the Church and the masters of asceticism, helps greatly either to inspire in the faithful of both sexes the firm resolution of dedicating themselves to God by the practice of perfect chastity and of presevering thus till death, or to strengthen them in the resolution already taken.

374

5. Innumerable is the multitude of those who from the beginning of the Church until our time have offered their chastity to God. Some have preserved their virginity unspoiled, others after the death of their spouse, have consecrated to God their remining years in the unmarried state, and still others, after repenting their sins, have chosen to lead a life of perfect chastity, all of them at one in this common oblation, that is, for love of God to abstain for the rest of their lives from sexual pleasure. May then what the Fathers of the Church preached about the glory and merit of virginity be an invitation, a help, and a source of strength to those who have made the sacrifice to persevere with constancy, and not take back or claim for themselves even the smallest part of the holocaust they have laid on the altar of God.

375

6. And while this perfect chastity is the subject of one of the three vows which constitute the religious state,[9] and is also required by the Latin Church of clerics in major orders[10] and demanded from members of Secular Institutes,[11] it also flourishes among many who are lay people in the full sense: men and women who are not constituted in a public state of perfection and yet by private promise or vow completely abstain from marriage and sexual pleasures, in order to serve

376

their neighbor more freely and to be united with God more easily and more closely.

377   7. To all of these beloved sons and daughters who in any way have consecrated their bodies and souls to God, We address Ourselves, and exhort them earnestly to strengthen their holy resolution and be faithful to it.

378   8. However, since there are some who, straying from the right path in this matter, so exalt marriage as to rank it ahead of virginity and thus depreciate chastity consecrated to God and clerical celibacy, Our apostolic duty demands that We now in a particular manner declare and uphold the Church's teaching on the sublime state of virginity, and so defend Catholic truth against these errors.

379   9. First of all, We think it should be noted that the Church has taken what is capital in her teaching on virginity from the very lips of her Divine Spouse.

380   10. For when the disciples thought that the obligations and burdens of marriage, which their Master's discourse had made clear, seemed extremely heavy, they said to Him: "If the case stands so between man and wife, it is better not to marry at all."[12] Jesus Christ replied that His ideal is not understood by everybody but only by those who have received the gift; for some are hindered from marriage because of some defect of nature, others because of the violence and malice of men, while still others freely abstain of their own will, and this "for the kingdom of heaven." And He concludes with these words, "He that can take it, let him take it."[13]

381   11. By these words the divine Master is speaking not of bodily impediments to marriage, but of a resolution freely made to abstain all one's life from marriage and sexual pleasure. For in likening those who of their own free will have determined to renounce these pleasures to those who by nature or the violence of men are forced to do so, is not the Divine Redeemer teaching us that chastity to be really perfect must be perpetual?

382   12. Here also it must be added, as the Fathers and Doctors of the Church have clearly taught, that virginity is not a Christian virtue unless we embrace it "for kingdom of heav-

en";[14] that is, unless we take up this way of life precisely to be able to devote ourselves more freely to divine things to attain heaven more surely, and with skillful efforts to lead others more readily to the kingdom of heaven.

13.   Those therefore who do not marry because of exaggerated self-interest, or because, as Augustine says,[15] they shun the burdens of marriage, or because like Pharisees they proudly flaunt their physical integrity, an attitude which has been condemned by the Council of Gangra, lest men and women renounce marriage as though it were something despicable instead of because virginity is something beautiful and holy,—none of these can claim for themselves the honor of Christian virginity.[16]

14.   Moreover, the Apostle of the Gentiles, writing under divine inspiration, makes this point: "He that is without a wife, is solicitous for the things that belong to the Lord, how he may please God . . . And the unmarried woman and the virgin thinketh on the things of the Lord, that she may be holy in body and spirit."[17]

15.   This then is the primary purpose, this the central idea of Christian virginity: to aim only at the divine, to turn thereto the whole mind and soul; to want to please God in everything, to think of Him continually, to consecrate body and soul completely to Him.

16.   This is the way the Fathers of the Church have always interpreted the words of Jesus Christ and the teaching of the Apostle of the Gentiles; for from the very earliest days of the Church they have considered virginity a consecration of body and soul offered to God. Thus St. Cyprian demands of virgins that "once they have dedicated themselves to Christ by renouncing the pleasures of the flesh, they have vowed themselves only for their Lord and please only Him."[18] And the Bishop of Hippo, going further, says, "Virginity is not honored because it is bodily integrity, but because it is something dedicated to God . . . Nor do we extol virgins because they are virgins but because they are virgins dedicated to God in loving continence."[19] And the masters of Sacred Theology, St. Thomas Aquinas[20] and St. Bonaventure,[21] supported by the authority of Augustine, teach that virginity does not

383

384

385

386

possess the stability of virtue unless there is a vow to keep it forever intact. And certainly those, who obligate themselves by perpetual vow to keep their virginity, put into practice in the most perfect way possible what Christ said about perpetual abstinence from marriage; nor can it justly be affirmed that the intention of those who wish to leave open a way of escape from this state of life is better and more perfect.

387   17. Moreover the Fathers of the Church considered this obligation of perfect chastity as a kind of spiritual marriage, in which the soul is wedded to Christ; so that some go so far as to compare breaking the vow with adultery.[22] Thus St. Athanasius writes that the Catholic Church has been accustomed to call those who have the virtue of virginity the spouses of Christ.[23] And St. Ambrose, writing succinctly of the consecrated virgin, says, "She is a virgin who is married to God."[24] In fact, as is clear from the writings of this same Doctor of Milan,[25] as early as the fourth century the rite of consecration of a virgin was very like the rite the Church uses in our own day in the marriage blessing.[26]

388   18. For the same reason the Fathers exhort virgins to love their Divine Spouse more ardently then they would love a husband had they married, and always in their thoughts and actions to fulfill His will.[27] Augustine writes to virgins: "Love with all your hearts Him Who is the most beautiful of the sons of men: you are free, your hearts are not fettered by conjugal bonds . . . If then you would owe your husbands great love, how great is the love you owe Him because of Whom you have willed to have no husbands? Let Him Who was fastened to the cross be securely fastened to your hearts."[28] And this in other respects too is in harmony with the sentiments and resolutions which the Church herself requires of virgins on the day they are solemnly consecrated to God by inviting them to recite these words: "The kingdom of this earth and all wordly trappings I have valued as worthless for love of Our Lord Jesus Christ, Whom I have seen, loved, believed, and preferred above all else."[29] It is nothing else but love of Him that sweetly constrains the virgin to consecrate her body and soul entirely to her Divine Redeemer; thus St. Methodius, Bishop of Olympus, places these beauti-

ful words on he lips: "You yourself, O Christ, are my all. For you I keep myself chaste, and holding aloft my shining lamp I run to meet you, my Spouse."[30] Certainly it is the love of Christ that urges a virgin to retire behind convent walls and remain there all her life, in order to contemplate and love the heavenly Spouse more easily and without hindrance; certainly it is the same love that strongly inspires her to spend her life and strength in works of mercy for the sake of her neighbor.

19. As for those men "who were not defiled with women, being virgins,"[31] the Apostle John asserts that, "they follow the Lamb wherever he goes."[32] Let us meditate then on the exhortation Augustine gives to all men of this class: "You follow the Lamb because the body of the Lamb is indeed virginal . . . Rightly do you follow Him in virginity of heart and body wherever He goes. For what does following mean but imitation? Christ has suffered for us, leaving us an example as the Apostle Peter says 'that we should follow in his footsteps.' "[33] Hence all these disciples and spouses in Christ embraced the state of virginity, as St. Bonaventure says, "in order to become like unto Christ the spouse, for that state makes virgins like unto Him."[34] It would hardly satisfy their burning love for Christ to be united with Him by the bonds of affection, but this love had perforce to express itself by the imitation of His virtues, and especially by conformity to His way of life, which was lived completely for the benefit and salvation of the human race. If priests, religious men and women, and others who in any way have vowed themselves to the divine service, cultivate perfect chastity, it is certainly for the reason that their Divine Master remained all His life a virgin. St. Fulgentius exclaims "This is the only-begotten Son of God, the only-begotten son of a virgin also, the only spouse of all holy virgins, the fruit, the glory, the gift of holy virginity, whom holy virginity brought forth physically, to whom holy virginity is wedded spiritually, by whom holy virginity is made fruitful and kept inviolate, by whom she is adorned, to remain ever beautiful, by whom she is crowned, to reign forever glorious."[35]

390   20. And here We think it opportune, Venerable Brothers, to expose more fully and to explain more carefully why the love of Christ moves generous souls to abstain from marriage, and what is the mystical connection between virginity and the perfection of Christian charity. From our Lord's words referred to above, it has already been implied that this complete renunciation of marriage frees men from its grave duties and obligations. Writing by divine inspiration, the Apostle of the Gentiles proposes the reason for this freedom in these words: "And I would have you to be without solicitude . . . But he that is with a wife, is solicitous for the things of the world, how he may please his wife; and he is divided."[36] Here however it must be noted that the Apostle is not reproving men because they are concerned about their wives, nor does he reprehend wives because they seek to please their husbands; rather is he asserting clearly that their hearts are divided between love of God and love of their spouse, and beset by gnawing cares, and so by reason of the duties of their married state they can hardly be free to contemplate the divine. For the duty of the married life to which they are bound clearly demands: "They shall be two in one flesh."[37] For spouses are to be bound to each other by mutual bonds both in joy and in sorrow.[38] It is easy to see, therefore, why persons who desire to consecrate themselves to God's service embrace the state of virginity as a liberation, in order to be more entirely at God's disposition and devote to the good of their neighbor. How, for example, could a missionary such as the wonderful St. Frances Xavier, a father of the poor such as the merciful St. Vincent de Paul, a zealous educator of youth like St. John Bosco, a tireless "mother of emigrants" like St. Frances Xavier Cabrini, have accomplished such gigantic and painful labors, if each had to look after the corporal and spiritual needs of a wife or husband and children.

391   21. There is yet another reason why souls desirous of a total consecration to the service of God and neighbor embrace the state of virginity. It is, as the holy Fathers have abundantly illustrated, the numerous advantages for advancement in spiritual life which derive from a complete renouncement of all sexual pleasure. It is not to be thought that such pleasure,

when it arises from lawful marriage, is reprehensible in itself; on the contrary, the chaste use of marriage is ennobled and sanctified by a special sacrament, as the Fathers themselves have clearly remarked. Nevertheless, it must be equally admitted that as a consequence of the fall of Adam the lower faculties of human nature are no longer obedient to right reason, and may involve man in dishonorable actions. As the Angelic Doctor has it, the use of marriage "keeps the soul from the full abandon to the service of God."[39]

22.   It is that they may acquire this spiritual liberty of body and soul, and they may be freed from temporal cares, that the Latin Church demands of her sacred ministers that they voluntarily oblige themselves to observe perfect chastity.[40] And "if a similar law," as Our predecessor of immortal memory Pius XI declared, "does not bind the ministers of the Oriental Church to the same degree, nevertheless among them too ecclesiastical celibacy occupies a place of honor, and, in certain cases, especially when the higher grades of the hierarchy are in question, it is a necessary and obligatory condition."[41]   **392**

23.   Consider again that sacred ministers do not renounce marriage solely on account of their apostolic ministry, but also by reason of their service at the altar. For, if even the priests of the Old Testament had to abstain from the use of marriage during the period of their service in the Temple, for fear of being declared impure by the Law just as other men,[42] is it not much more fitting that the ministers of Jesus Christ, who offer every day the Eucharistic Sacrifice, possess perfect chastity? St. Peter Damian, exhorting priests to perfect continence, asks: "If Our Redeemer so loved the flower of unimpaired modesty that not only was He born from a virginal womb, but was also cared for by a virgin nurse even when He was still an infant crying in the cradle, by whom, I ask, does He wish His body to be handled now that He reigns, immense, in heaven?"[43]   **393**

24.   It is first and foremost of the foregoing reasons that, according to the teaching of the Church, holy virginity surpasses marriage in excellence. Our Divine Redeemer had already given it to His disciples as a counsel for a more perfect   **394**

life.[44] St. Paul, after having said that the father who gives his daughter in marriage "does well," adds immediately "and he that giveth her not, doth better."[45] Several times in the course of his comparison between marriage and virginity the Apostle reveals his mind, and especially in these words: "for I would that all men were even as myself . . . But I say to the unmarried and to widows: it is good for them if they so continue, even as I."[46] Virginity is preferable to marriage then, as We have said, above all else because it has a higher aim:[47] that is to say, it is a very efficacious means for devoting oneself wholly to the service of God, while the heart of married persons will always remain more or less "divided."[48]

395   25. Turning next to the fruitful effects of virginity, our appreciation of its value will be enhanced; for "by the fruit the tree is known."[49]

396   26. We feel the deepest joy at the thought of the innumerable army of virgins and apostles who, from the first centuries of the Church up to our own day, have given up marriage to devote themselves more easily and fully to the salvation of their neighbor for the love of Christ, and have thus been enabled to undertake and carry through admirable works of religion and charity. We by no means wish to detract from the merits and apostolic fruits of the active members of Catholic Action: by their zealous efforts they can often touch souls that priests and religious cannot gain. Nevertheless, works of charity are for the most part the field of action of consecrated persons. These generous souls are to be found laboring among men of every age and condition, and when they fall, worn out or sick, they bequeath their sacred mission to others who take their place. Hence it often happens that a child, immediately after birth, is placed in the care of consecrated persons, who supply in so far as they can for a mother's love; at the age of reason he is entrusted to educators who see to his Christian instruction together with the development of his mind and the formation of his character; if he is sick, the child or adult will find nurses moved by the love of Christ who will care for him with unwearying devotion; the orphan, the person fallen into material destitution or moral abjection, the prisoner, will not be abandoned. Priests, religious, con-

secrated virgins will see in him a suffering member of Christ's Mystical Body, and recall the words of the Divine Redeemer: "For I was hungry, and you gave me to eat; I was thirsty, and you gave me to drink; I was a stranger, and you took me in, naked, and you covered me; sick, and you visited me; I was in prison, and you came to me . . . Amen I say to you, as long as you did it to one of these my least brethren, you did it to me."[50] Who can ever praise enough the missionaries who toil for the conversion of the pagan multitudes, exiles from their native country, or the nuns who render them indispensable assistance? To each and every one We gladly apply these words of Our Apostolic Exhortation, "Menti Nostare" ". . . by this law of celibacy the priest not only does not abdicate his paternity, but increases it immensely, for he begets not for an earthly and transitory life but for the heavenly and eternal one."[51]

27.   The fruit of virginity is not only in these external works, to which it allows one to devote oneself more easily and fully, but also in the earnest prayer offered for others and the trials willingly and generously endured for their sake, which are other very perfect forms of charity toward one's neighbor. To such also the servants and spouses of Christ, especially those who live within the convent or monastery walls, have consecrated their whole lives.   **397**

28.   Finally, virginity consecrated to Christ is in itself such an evidence of faith in the kingdom of heaven, such a proof of love for our Divine Redeemer, that there is little wonder if it bears abundant fruits of sanctity. Innumerable are the virgins and apostles vowed to perfect chastity who are the honor of the Church by the lofty sanctity of their lives. In truth, virginity gives souls a force of spirit capable of leading them even to martyrdom, if needs be: such is the clear lesson of history which proposes a whole host of virgins to our admiration, from Agnes of Rome to Maria Goretti.   **398**

29.   Virginity fully deserves the name of angelic virtue, which St. Cyprian writing to virgins affirms: "What we are to be, you have already commenced to be. You already possess in this world the glory of the resurrection, you pass through the world without suffering its contagion. In preserving virgin   **399**

chastity, you are the equals of the angels of God."[52] To
souls, restless for a purer life or inflamed with the desire to
possess the kingdom of heaven, virginity offers itself as "a
pearl of great price," for which one "sells all that he has, and
buys it."[53] Married people and even those who are captives
of vice, at the contact of virgin souls, often admire the splendor of their transparent purity, and feel themselves moved to
rise above the pleasures of sense. When St. Thomas states
"that to virginity is awarded the tribute of the highest "beauty."[54] it is because its example is captivating: and, besides,
by their perfect chastity do not all these men and women
give a striking proof that the mastery of the spirit over the
body is the result of a divine assistance and the sign of proven
virtue?

400   30. Worthy of special consideration is the reflection that
the most delicate fruit of virginity consists in this, that virgins make tangible, as it were, the perfect virginity of their
mother, the Church and the sanctity of her intimate union
with Christ. In the ceremony of the consecration of virgins,
the consecrating prelate prays God: "that there may exist
more noble souls who disdain the marriage which consists in
the bodily union of man and woman, but desire the mystery
it enshrines, who reject its practice while loving its mystic
signification."[55]

401   31. The greatest glory of virgins is undoubtedly to be the
living images of the perfect integrity of the union between
the Church and her divine Spouse. For this society founded
by Christ it is a profound joy that virgins should be the marvellous sign of its sanctity and fecundity, as St. Cyprian so
well expresses it: "They are the flower of the Church, the
beauty and ornament of spiritual grace, a subject of joy, a
perfect and unsullied homage of praise and honor, the image
of God corresponding to the sanctity of the Lord, the most
illustrious portion of Christ's flock. In them the glorious
fecundity of our mother, the Church, finds expression and
she rejoices; the more the number of virgins increases, the
greater is this mother's joy."[56]

II

32. This doctrine of the excellence of virginity and of celi-   402
bacy and of their superiority over the married state was, as
We have alread said, revealed by our Divine Redeemer and by
the Apostle of the Gentiles; so too, it was solemnly defined
as a dogma of divine faith by the holy council of Trent,[57]
and explained in the same way by all the holy Fathers and
Doctors of the Church. Finally, We and Our Predecessors
have often expounded it and earnestly advocated it whenever occasion offered. But recent attacks on this traditional
doctrine of the Church, the danger they constitute, and the
harm they do to the souls of the faithful lead Us, in fulfilment
of the duties of Our charge, to take up the matter once again
in this Encyclical Letter, and to reprove these errors which
are so often propounded under a specious appearance of
truth.

33.   First of all, it is against common sense, which the   403
Church always holds in esteem, to consider the sexual instinct as the most important and the deepest of human
tendencies, and to conclude from this that man cannot
restrain it for his whole life without danger to his vital
nervous system, and consequently without injuring the harmony of his personality.

34. As St. Thomas very rightly observes, the deepest natu-   404
ral instinct is the instinct of conservation; the sexual instinct
comes second. In addition, it is for the rational inclination,
which is the distinguishing privilege of our nature, to regulate
these fundamental instincts and by dominating to ennoble
them.[58]

35. It is, alas, true that the sin of Adam has caused a deep   405
disturbance in our corporal faculties and our passions, so that
they wish to gain control of the life of the senses and even of
the spirit, obscuring our reason and weakening our will. But
Christ's grace is given us, especially by the sacraments, to help
us to keep our bodies in subjection and to live by the spirit.[59]
The virtue of chastity does not mean that we are insensible to

the urge of concupiscence, but that we subordinate it to reason and the law of grace, by striving wholeheartedly after what is noblest in human and Christian life.

406   36. In order to acquire this perfect mastery of the spirit over the senses, it is not enough to refrain from acts directly contrary to chastity, but it is necessary also generously to renounce anything that may offend this virtue nearly or remotely; at such a price will the soul be able to reign fully over the body and lead its spiritual life in peace and liberty. Who then does not see, in the light of Catholic principles, that perfect chastity and virginity, far from harming the normal unfolding of man or woman, on the contrary endow them with the highest moral nobility.

407   37. We have recently with sorrow censured the opinion of those who contend that marriage is the only means of assuring the natural development and perfection of the human personality.[60] For there are those who maintain that the grace of the sacrament, conferred ex opere operato, renders the use of marriage so holy as to be a fitter instrument than virginity for uniting souls with God, for marriage is a sacrament, but not virginity. We denounce this doctrine as a dangerous error. Certainly, the sacrament grants the married couple the grace to accomplish holily the duties of their married state, and it strengthens the bonds of mutual affection that unite them; but the purpose of its institution was not to make the employment of marriage the means, most suitable in itself, for uniting the souls of the husband and wife with God by the bonds of charity.[61]

408   38. Or rather does not the Apostle Paul admit that they have the right of abstaining for a time from the use of marriage, so that they may be more free for prayer,[62] precisely because such abstinence gives greater freedom to the soul which wishes to give itself over to spiritual thoughts and prayer to God?

409   39. Finally, it may not be asserted, as some do, that the "mutual help,"[63] which is sought in Christian Marriage, is a more effective aid in striving for personal sanctity than the solitude of the heart, as they term it, of virgins and celibates. For although all those who have embraced a life of perfect chastity have deprived themselves of the expression of human

love permitted in the married state, nonetheless it cannot thereby be affirmed that because of this privation they have diminished and despoiled the human personality. For they receive from the Giver of heavenly gifts something spiritual which far exceeds that "mutual help" which husband and wife confer on each other. They consecrate themselves to Him Who is their source, and Who shares with them His divine life, and thus personality suffers no loss, but gains immensely. For who, more than the virgin, can apply to himself that marvelous phrase of the Apostle Paul: "I live, now not I, but Christ liveth in me."[64]

40. For this reason the Church has most wisely held that the celibacy of her priests must be retained; she knows it is and will be a source of spiritual graces by which they will be evermore closely united with God.   410

41. We feel it opportune, moreover, to touch somewhat briefly here on the error of those who, in order to turn boys and girls away from Seminaries and Religious Institutes, strive to impress upon their minds that the Church today has a greater need of the help and of the profession of Christian virtue on the part of those who, united in marriage, lead a life together with others in the world, than of priests and consecrated virgins, who, because of their vow of chastity, are, as it were, withdrawn from human society. No one can fail to see, Venerable Brothers, how utterly false and harmful is such an opinion.   411

42. Of course, it is not Our intention to deny that Catholic spouses, because of the example of their Christian life, can, wherever they live and whatever be their circumstances, produce rich and salutary fruits as a witness to their virtue. Yet whoever for this reason argues that it is preferable to live in matrimony than to consecrate oneself completely to God, without doubt perverts the right order. Indeed We earnestly wish, Venerable Brothers, that those who have already contracted marriage, or desire to enter this state, be properly taught their serious obligation not only to educate properly and carefully whatever children they have or will have, but also to help others, within their capacity, by the testimony of their faith and the example of their virtue. And yet, as Our   412

duty demands, We cannot but censure all those who strive to turn young people away from the Seminary or Religious Orders and Institutes, and from the taking of sacred vows, persuading them that they can, if joined in marriage, as fathers and mothers of families pursue a greater spiritual good by an open and public profession of their Christian life. Certainly their conduct would be more proper and correct, if, instead of trying to distract from a life of virginity those young men and women, who desire to give themselves to the service of God, too few alas today, they were to exhort with all the zeal at their command the vast numbers of those who live in wedlock to promote apostolic works in the ranks of the laity. On this point, Ambrose fittingly wirtes: "To sow the seeds of perfect purity and to arouse a desire for virginity has always belonged to the function of the priesthood."[65]

413   43. We think it necessary, moreover, to warn that it is altogether false to assert that those who are vowed to perfect chastity are practically outside the community of men. Are not consecrated virgins, who dedicate their lives to the service of the poor and the sick, without making any distinction as to race, social rank, or religion, are not these virgins united intimately with their miseries and sorrows, and affectionately drawn to them, as though they were their mothers? And does not the priest likewise, moved by the example of his Divine Master, perform the function of a good shepherd, who knows his flock and calls them by name?[66] Indeed it is from that perfect chastity which they cultivate that priests and religious men and women find the motive for giving themselves to all, and love all men with the love of Christ. And they too, who live the contemplative live, precisely because they not only offer to God prayer and supplication but immolate themselves for the salvation of others, accomplish much for the good of the Church, indeed, when in circumstances like the present they dedicate themselves to works of charity and of the apostolate, according to the norms which We laid down in the Apostolic Letter "Sponsa Christi,"[67] they are very much to be praised; nor can they be said to be separated from contact with men, since they labor for their spiritual progress in this twofold way.

III

44. From the Church's teaching on the excellence of vir-   414
ginity, let Us now come Venerable Brothers, to some points
which are of practical application.

45. In the first place, it must be clearly stated that because   415
virginity should be esteemed as something more perfect than
marriage, it does not follow that it is necessary for Christian
perfection.

46. Holiness of life can really be attained, even without a   416
chastity that is consecrated to God. Witness to this are the
many holy men and women, who are publicly honored by
the Church, and who were faithful spouses and stood out as
an example of excellent fathers and mothers; indeed it is not
rare to find married people who are very earnest in their
efforts for Christian perfection.

47. It should be pointed out, also, that God does not urge   417
all Christians to virginity, as the Apostle Paul teaches us with
these words: "Now concerning virgins, I have no commandment of the Lord, but I give counsel."[68] We are, therefore,
merely invited by counsel to embrace perfect chastity, as
something which can lead those "to whom it is given"[69] more
safely and successfully to the evangelical perfection they seek,
and to the conquest of the kingdom of heaven. Wherefore it
is "not imposed, but proposed," as St. Ambrose so aptly
observed.[70]

48. Hence, perfect chastity demands, first, a free choice   418
by Christians before they consecrate themselves to God and
then, from God, supernatural help and grace.[71] Our Divine
Redeemer Himself has taught us this in the following words:
"All men take not his word, but they to whom it is given . . .
He that can take it, let him take it."[72] St. Jerome, intently
pondering this sacred phrase of Jesus Christ, exhorts all "that
each one study his own powers, whether he can fulfill the
percepts of virginal modesty. For of itself chastity is charming and attractive to all. But one's forces must be considered,
that he who can may take it. The Lord's word is as it were an

exhortation, stirring on His soldiers to the prize of purity. He that can take it, let him take it: let him who can, fight, conquer and receive his reward."[7][3]

419   49. For virginity is a difficult virtue; that one be able to embrace it there is needed not only a strong and declared determination of completely and perpetually abstaining from those legitimate pleasures derived from marriage; but also a constant vigilance and struggle to contain and dominate rebellious movements of body and soul, a flight from the importuning of this world, a struggle to conquer the wiles of Satan. How true is that saying of Chrysostom: "the root, and the flower, too, of virginity is a crucified life."[7][4] For virginity, according to Ambrose, is as a sacrifical offering, and the virgin "an oblation of modesty, a victim of chastity."[7][5] Indeed, St. Methodius, Bishop of Olympus, compares virgins to martyrs,[7][6] and St. Gregory the Great teaches that perfect chastity substitutes for martyrdom: "Now, though the era of persecution is done, yet our peace has its martyrdom, because though we bend not the neck to the sword, yet with a spiritual weapon we slay fleshly desires in our hearts."[7][7] Hence a chastity dedicated to God demands strong and noble souls, souls ready to do battle and conquer "for the sake of the kingdom of heaven."[7][8]

420   50. Prior, therefore, to entering upon this most difficult path, all who by experience know they are too weak in spirit should humbly heed this wraning of Paul the Apostle: "But if they do not contain themselves, let them marry. For it is better to marry than to be burnt."[7][9] For many, undoubtedly, the burden of perpetual continence is a heavier one than they should be persuaded to shoulder. And so priests, who are under grave obligation of helping by their advice young people who declare they are drawn by some movement of soul to aspire to the priesthood or enter religious life, must urge them to ponder the matter carefully, lest they enter a way which they cannot hope to follow sturdily and happily to its end. They should prudently examine the fitness of candidates, even obtaining, as often as is proper, the opinion of experts; and then, if serious doubt remains, especially if it is based on past experience, they should make use of their authority to

make candidates cease from seeking a state of perfect chastity, nor should these latter ever be admitted to Holy Orders, or to religious profession.

51. And yet, although chastity pledged to God is a difficult virtue, those who after serious consideration generously answer Christ's invitation and do all in their power to attain it, can perfectly and fathfully preserve it. For since they have eagerly embraced the state of virginity or celibacy, they will certainly receive from God that gift of grace, through whose help they will be able to carry out their promise. Wherefore, if there are any "who do not feel they have the gift of chastity even though they have vowed it,"[80] let them not declare they cannot fulfill their obligations in this matter. "For," says the Council of Trent, quoting St. Augustine, " 'God does not command the impossible, but in commanding serves notice that one do what he can, and pray for what he cannot,'[81] and He helps us to accomplish it."[82] This truth, so full of encouragement, We recall to those also whose will has been weakened by upset nerves and whom some doctors, sometimes even Catholic doctors, are too quick to persuade that they should be freed from such an obligation, advancing the specious reason that they cannot preserve their chastity without suffering some harm to their mental balance. How much more useful and opportune it is to help the infirm of this type to strengthen their will, and to advise them that not even to them is chastity impossible, according to the word of the Apostle: "God is faithful, who will not suffer you to be tempted above that which you are able: but will make also with temptation issue, that you may be able to bear it."[83]

52. Here are the helps, commended to us by our Divine Redeemer, by which we may efficaciously protect our virtue: constant vigilance, whereby we diligently do all that we can; moreover, constant prayer to God, asking for what we cannot attain by ourselves, because of our weakness. "Watch and pray, that you enter not into temptation. The spirit indeed is willing, but the flesh is weak."[84] A vigilance which guards every moment of our lives and every type of circumstance is absolutely necessary for us: "For the flesh lusteth against the spirit: and the spirt against the flesh."[85] But if anyone grants

421

422

however little to the enticements of the flesh, he will see himself quickly pulled toward those "works of the flesh" which the Apostle lists,[86] the basest and ugliest vices of man.

423   53.   Hence we must watch particularly over the movements of our passions and of our senses, and so control them by voluntary discipline in our lives and by bodily mortification that we render them obedient to right reason and God's law: "And they that are Christ's have crucified their flesh, with the vices and concupiscences."[87] The Apostle of the Gentiles says this about himself: "But I chastise my body, and bring it into subjection: lest perhaps, when I have preached to others, I myself should become a castaway."[88] All holy men and women have most carefully guarded the movements of their senses and their passions, and at times have very harshly crushed them, in keeping with the teaching of the Divine Master: "But I say to you, that whosoever shall look on a woman to lust after her, hath already committed adultery with her in his heart. And if thy right eye scandalize thee, pluck it out and cast it from thee. For it is expedient for thee that one of thy members should perish, rather than that thy whole body be cast into hell."[89] It is abundantly clear that with this warning Our Saviour demands of us above all that we never consent to any sin, even internally, and that we steadfastly remove far from us anything that can even slightly tarnish the beautiful virtue of purity. In this matter no diligence, no severity can be considered exaggerated. If ill health or other reasons do not allow one heavier corporal austerities, yet they never free one from vigilance and internal self-control.

424   54.   On this point it should be noted, as indeed the Fathers[90] and Doctors[91] of the Church teach, that we can more easily struggle against and repress the wiles of evil and the enticements of the passions if we do not struggle directly against them, but rather flee from them as best we may. For the preserving of chastity, according to the teaching of Jerome, flight is more effective than open warfare: "Therefore I flee, lest I be overcome."[92] Flight must be understood in this sense, that only do we diligently avoid occasions of sin, but especially that in struggles of this kind we lift our minds and hearts to God, intent above all on Him to Whom we have

vowed our virginity. "Look upon the beauty of your "Lover,"[93] St. Augustine tells us.

55. Flight and alert vigilance, by which we carefully avoid   425
the occasions of sin, have always been considered by holy
men and women as the most effective method of combat in
this matter, today however it does not seem that everybody
holds the same opinion. Some indeed claim that all Christians, and the clergy in particular, should not be "separated
from the world" as in the past, but should be "close to the
world"; therefore they should "take the risk" and put their
chastity to the test in order to show whether or not they have
strength to resist; therefore, they say, let young clerics see
everything so that they may accustom themselves to gaze at
everything with equanimity, and thus render themselves
immune to all temptations. For this reason they readily
grant young clerics the liberty to turn their eyes in any direction without the slightest concern for modesty, they may
attend motion pictures, even those forbidden by ecclesiastical
censorship; they may peruse even obscene periodicals; they
may read novels which are listed in the Index of forbidden
books or prohibited by the Natural Law. All this they allow
because today the multitudes are fed by this kind of amuse-
ment and publication and because those who are minded to
help them should understand their way of thinking and
feeling. But it is easily seen that this method of educating and
training the clergy to acquire the sanctity proper to their
calling is wrong and harmful. For "he that loveth danger shall
perish in it";[94] most appropriate in this connection is the
admonition of Augustine: "Do not say that you have a chaste
mind if your eyes are unchaste, because an unchaste eye be-
trayes an unchaste heart."[95]

56. No doubt this pernicious method is based upon serious   426
confusion of thought. Indeed Christ Our Lord asserted of His
Apostles, "I have sent them into the world,"[96] yet previously
He had said of them, "They are not of the world, as I also am
not of the world,"[97] and He prayed to His Heavenly Father
in these words, "I pray not that thou shouldst take them out
of the world, but that thou shouldst keep them from evil."[98]
Motivated by the same principles, and in order to protect

priests from temptations to evil, to which all those are ordinarily subject who are in intimate contact with the world, the Church has promulgated appropriate and wise laws,[99] whose purpose is to safeguard sacerdotal sanctity from the cares and pleasures of the laity.

427   57. All the more reason why the young clergy, because they are to be trained in the spiritual life, in sacerdotal and religious perfection, must be separated from the tumult of the world before entering the lists of combat; for long years they must remain in a Seminary or Scholasticate where they receive a sound and careful education which provides them with a gradual approach to and a prudent knowledge of those problems which our times have brought to the fore, in accordance with the norms which We established in the Apostolic Exhoration "Menti Nostrae."[100] What gardener would expose young plants, choice indeed but weak, to violent storms in order that they might give proof of the strength which they have not yet acquired? Seminarians and scholastics are surely to be considered like young and weak plants who must still be protected and gradually trained to resist and to fight.

428   58. The educators of the young clergy would render a more valuable and useful service, if they would inculcate in youthful minds the precepts of Christian modesty, which is so important for the preservation of perfect chastity and which is truly called the prudence of chastity. For modesty foresees threatening danger, forbids us to expose ourselves to risks, demands the avoidance of those occasions which the imprudent do not shun. It does not like impure or loose talk, it shrinks from the slightest immodesty, it carefully avoids suspect familiarity with persons of the other sex, since it brings the soul to show due reverence to the body, as being a member of Christ[101] and the temple of the Holy Spirit.[102] He who possesses the treasure of Christian modesty abominates every sin of impurity and instantly flees whenever he is tempted by its seductions.

429   59. Modesty will moreover suggest and provide suitable words for parents and educators by which the youthful conscience will be formed in matters of chastity. "Wherefore," as We said in a recent address, "this modesty is not to

be so understood as to be equivalent to a perpetual silence on this subject, nor as allowing no place for sober and cautious discussion about these matters in imparting moral instruction."[103] In modern times however there are some teachers and educators who too frequently think it their duty to initiate innocent boys and girls into the secrets of human generation in such a way as to offend their sense of shame. But in this matter a just temperance and moderation must be used, as Christian modesty demands.

60. This modesty is nourished by the fear of God, that   430
filial fear which is founded on the virtue of profound Christian humility, and which creates in us utter abhorrence for the slightest sin, as Our predecessor, St. Clement I, stated in these words, "He who is chaste in flesh should not be proud, for he whould know that he owes the gift of continence to another."[104] How important Christian humility is for the protection of virginity, no one perhaps has taught more clearly than Augustine. "Because perpetual continence, and virginity above all, is a great good in the saints of God, extreme vigilance must be exercised lest it be corrupted by pride ... The more clearly I see the greatness of this gift, the more truly do I fear lest it be plundered by thieving pride. No one therefore protects virginity, but God Himself Who bestowed it: and "God is charity."[105] The guardian therefore of virginity is charity; the habitat of this guardian is humility."[106]

61. Moreover there is another argument worthy of atten-   431
tive consideration: to preserve chastity unstained neither vigilance nor modesty suffice. Those helps must also be used which entirely surpass the powers of nature, namely prayer to God, the Sacraments of Penance and Holy Eucharist, a fervent devotion to the most holy Mother of God.

62. Never should it be forgotten that perfect chastity is a   432
great gift of God. For this reason Jerome wrote these succinct words, "It is given to those,[107] who have asked for it, who have desired it, who have worked to receive it. For it will be given to everyone who asks, the seeker will find, to the importunate it will be opened."[108] Ambrose adds that the constant fidelity of virgins to their Divine Spouse depends upon prayer.[109] With that fervent piety for which he was noted St.

Alphonsus Liguori taught that there is no help more necessary
and certain for conquering temptations against the beautiful
virtue of chastity than instant recourse to God in prayer.[110]

433   63. To prayer must be added frequent and fervent use of
the Sacrament of Penance which; as a spiritual medicine,
purifies and heals us; likewise it is necessary to receive the
eucharist, which, as Our predecessor of happy memory Leo
XIII asserted, is the best remedy against lust.[111] The more
pure and chaste is a soul, the more it hungers for this bread,
from which it derives strength to resist all temptations to sins
of impurity, and by which it is more intimately united with
the Divine Spouse; "He who eats my flesh and drinks my
blood, abides in me and I in him."[112]

434   64. The eminent way to protect and nourish an unsullied
and perfect chastity, as proven by experience time and again
throughout the course of centuries, is solid and fervent devotion to the Virgin Mother of God. In a certain way all other helps are contained in this devotion, there is no doubt that
whoever is sincerely and earnestly animated by this devotion
is salutarily inspired to constant vigilance, to continual prayer,
to receive the Sacraments of Penance and the Holy Eucharist.
Therefore in a paternal way we exhort all priests, religious
men and women, to entrust themselves to the special protection of the holy Mother of God who is the Virgin of virgins
and the "teacher of virginity," as Ambrose says,[113] and the
most powerful Mother of those in particular who have vowed
and consecrated themselves to the service of God.

435   65. That virginity owes its origin to Mary is the testimony
of Athanasius,[114] and Augustine clearly teaches that "The
dignity of virginity began with the Mother of the Lord."[115]
Pursuing the ideas of Athanasius,[116] Ambrose holds up the
life of the Virgin Mary as the model of virgins. "Imitate her,
my daughters . . .![117] Let Mary's life be for you like the por-
trayal of virginity, for from her, as though from a mirror, is
reflected the beauty of chastity and the ideal of virtue. See
in her the pattern of your life, for in her, as though in a model,
manifest teachings of goodness show what you should correct,
what you should copy and what preserve . . . She is the image
of virginity. For such was Mary that her life alone suffices for

the instruction of all . . .[118] Therefore let holy Mary guide
your way of life."[119] "Her grace was so great that it not only
preserved in her the grace of virginity, but bestowed the grace
of chastity upon those upon whom she gazed."[120] How true
is the saying of Ambrose, "Oh the richness of the virginity of
Mary"![121] Because of this richness it will be very useful for
religious men and women and for priests of our day to contemplate the virginity of Mary, in order that they may more
faithfully and perfectly practice the chastity of their calling.

66. But it is not enough, beloved sons and daughters, to
meditate on the virtues of the Blessed Virgin Mary: with absolute confidence fly to her and obey the counsel of St.
Bernard, "Let us seek grace and seek it through Mary."[122] In
a special way entrust to her during the Marian Year the care
of your spiritual life and perfection, imitating the example of
Jerome who asserted, "My virginity is dedicated in Mary and
to Christ."[123]

67. In the midst of the grave difficulties with which the
Church must contend today, the heart of the Supreme Pastor
is greatly comforted, Venerable Brothers when We see that
virginity, which is flourishing throughout the world, is held
in great honor and repute in the present as it was in past
centuries, even though, as We have said, it is being attacked
by errors which, We trust, will soon be dispelled and pass
away.

68. Nevertheless We do not deny that this Our joy is
overshadowed by a certain sorrow since We learn that in not
a few countries the number of vocations to the priesthood
and to the religious life is constantly decreasing. We have
already given the principal reasons which account for this fact
and there is no reason why We should return to them now.
Rather do We trust that those educators of youth, who have
succumbed to errors in this matter, will repudiate them as
soon as they are detected, and will consequently seriously
resolve both to correct them and to do what they can to
provide every help for the youth entrusted to their care who
feel themselves called by divine grace to aspire to the priesthood or to embrace the religious life, in order that they may
be able to reach so noble a goal. May God grant that new and

436

437

438

larger ranks of priests, religious men and women, equal in number and virtue to the current necessities of the Church, may soon go forth to cultivate the vineyard of the Lord.

439   69.   Moreover, as the obligation of Our Apostolic Office demands, We urge fathers and mothers to willingly offer to the service of God those of their children who are called to it. But if this be a source of trouble, sorrow or regret, let them seriously meditate upon the admonition which Ambrose gave to the mothers of Milan, "The majority of the young women whom I knew wanted to be virgins were forbidden to leave by their mothers . . . If your daughters want to love a man, the laws allow them to choose whom they will. But those who have a right to choose a man, have no right to choose God?"[124]

440   70.   Let parents consider what a great honor it is to see their son elevated to the priesthood, or their daughter consecrate her virginity to her Divine Spouse. In regard to consecrated virgins, the Bishop of Milan writes, "You have heard, parents, that a virgin is a gift of God, the oblation of parents, the priesthood of chastity. The virgin is a mother's victim, by whose daily sacrifice divine anger is appeased."[125]

441   71.   Before We come to the end of this Encyclical Letter, We wish Venerable Brothers, to turn Our mind and heart in a special manner to those men and women, who, vowed to the service of God, are suffering bitter and terrible persecutions in not a few countries. Let them imitate the example of the consecrated virgins of the early Church who with courageous and indomitable hearts suffered martyrdom for the sake of their virginity.[126]

442   72.   May all who have vowed to serve Christ, bravely persevere "even to death."[127] May they realize that their pains, sufferings and prayers are of great value in the sight of God for the restoration of His Kingdom in their countries and in the universal Church; may they be most certain that those "who follow the Lamb wither he goeth,"[128] will sing forever a "new canticle,"[129] which no one else can sing.

443   73.   Our paternal heart is filled with compassion for priests, religious men and women, who are bravely professing their faith even to the extent of martyrdom; and not only for

them, but for all those who in every part of the world are totally dedicated and consecrated to the divine service, We implore God with suppliant prayer to sustain, strengthen and console them. We earnestly invite each and every one of you, Venerable Brothers, and your faithful to pray with Us and to implore for all these souls the consolations, gifts and graces which they need from God.

74. Let the Apostolic Blessing, which with loving heart   444
We impart to you, Venerable Brothers, to all priests and consecrated virgins, to those especially "who suffer persecution for justice's sake"[130] and to all your faithful, be a pledge of heavenly grace and a testimony of Our paternal benevolence.

75. Given at Rome, at St. Peter's, March 25th, Feast of   445
the Annunication of the Blessed Virgin Mary, 1954, in the sixteenth year of Our Pontificate.

Address of Pope Pius XII
to a Group of Catholic Obstetricians and Gynecologists
January 8, 1956

We have received information about a new development in the field of gynecology and We have been asked to pass judgment on it *from the moral and religious point of view*. We are referring to natural and painless childbirth in which, without reliance on artificial means, only the mother's natural forces are used.

447   In Our allocution to the members of the Fourth International Congress of Catholic Doctors, on September 29, 1949 *(Discorsi e Radiomessaggi* vol. XI, p. 221-234), We said that the doctor has the desire at least of mitigating the evils and sufferings that afflict man. We then cited the surgeon, who strives to avoid, as much as possible, causing pain in the operations he must perform. We cited, too, the gynecologist who tries to lessen the sufferings connected with birth, without endangering mother or child and without doing harm to the ties of motherly affection which—we are told—are ordinarily formed at that moment. This last remark was a reference to a procedure then in use in the maternity hospital of a large modern city: in order to save the mother from suffering, she was plunged into a deep hypnosis. But it was noted that this procedure resulted in an emotional indifference toward the child, although some believe that this fact can be explained otherwise.

448   In the light of this experience, care was subsequently taken to wake the mother for a few moments at several intervals

during labor. In this way it was possible to avoid the feared effect. Somewhat the same observation could be made during a prolonged narcosis.

The new method of which We wish to speak at present   449
does not entail this danger. It leaves the mother at childbirth fully conscious from beginning to end and with full use of her psychic forces (intellect, will, emotions); it suppresses, or, according to others, it diminishes, the pain alone.

What attitude is to be taken toward it from the moral and   450
religious point of view?

First of all, painless childbirth considered as an actual fact   451
is in clear contrast with general human experience today as well as with that of the past and of earliest times.

The most recent research indicates that some mothers give   452
birth without feeling any pain though no analgesic or anaesthetic has been used. It also shows that the degree of intensity of the suffering is less among primitive peoples than among the civilized. If there is a moderate degree of pain for many mothers, for most there is a high degree and, not seldom, the pain is unbearable. These are the current observations.

The same must be said of past ages, in so far as historical   453
sources permit us to verify the fact. The pains of women in labor were proverbial; they were referred to in order to express the most violent and agonizing suffering, and literature, both profane and religious, furnishes proof of this fact. This manner of speaking is, in fact, customary even in the biblical texts of the Old and the New Testament, especially in the writings of one of the prophets. We shall cite a few examples. Isaias compares his people to a woman who in childbirth is in pain and cries out (cf. Is. 26, 17); Jeremias, as he views the approaching judgment of God, says: "I hear cries like those of a woman in labor, cries of anguish, like those of a woman who gives birth for the first time" (Jer. 4, 31). The evening before His death, our Lord compares the situation of His Apostles to that of a mother awaiting the moment of childbirth: "A woman about to give birth has sorrow, because her hour has come. But when she has brought forth the child, she no longers remembers the anguish for her joy that a man is born into the world" (John 16, 21).

454 All this allows us to affirm, as a fact accepted among men of the past and of the present, that a mother gives birth in pain. This is what the new method opposes.

455 Two general considerations, presented by its supporters, offer guidance and orientation to the one who wishes to outline its principal features: the first concerns the difference between the painless activity and the painful activity of the organs and members; the second concerns the origin of the pain and its connection with organic function.

456 The functions of the organism, so they say, are not accompanied by any painful sensations when they are normal and are carried out in the proper manner. Such painful sensations denote the presence of some complication, otherwise nature would contradict herself, for she associates pain with such a process in order to provoke a defense reaction and a protection against what would be harmful to her. Normal childbirth is a natural function and should consequently take place without pain. Whence, then, does the pain come?

457 The answer is given that the sensation of pain is set in motion and regulated by the cerebral cortex, where stimuli and signals are received from the whole organism. The central organ reacts to these stimuli in very different ways; some of these reactions (reflexes) have by nature a precise character and are associated by nature with determined processes (absolute reflexes); others, on the contrary, have neither their character nor their connections fixed by nature but are determined by other factors (conditioned reflexes).

458 Sensations of pain are among the reflexes (absolute or conditioned) which arise from the cerebral cortex. Experience has proved that it is possible, by means of arbitrarily established associations, to provoke sensations of pain, even when the stimulus which arouses them is, by itself, totally incapable of doing so.

459 In human relations, these conditioned reflexes have as their agent a most efficacious one and one most frequently used, language, the spoken or written word, or, if you will, the opinion which prevails in a given milieu and which everyone shares and expresses in language.

Thus the origin of the sharply painful sensations felt in   460
childbirth is understandable. These sensations are considered
by certain authors to be due to contrary conditioned reflexes
set in motion by false ideological and emotional reflexes.

The disciples of the Russion Pavlov (physiologists, psychol-   461
ogists, gynecologists), profiting by their master's research into
conditioned reflexes, presents the question substantially as
follows:

Childbirth has not always been painful, but it has become   462
so in the course of time because of "conditioned reflexes."
These may have originated in a first painful childbirth; perhaps heredity also plays a part but there we would be dealing
only with secondary factors. The principal cause of these reflexes is language and the opinion of the group manifested by
language. Childbirth, so the talk goes, is "the mother's difficult hour," it is a torture imposed by nature which hands the
defenseless mother over to unbearable sufferings. This association of ideas created by the people in the environment
provokes fear of childbirth and fear of the terrible pains
which accompany it. Thus, when the muscular contractions
of the uterus are felt at the beginning of labor, a defense
reaction against pain sets in. This pain provokes a muscular
cramp which in turn causes an increase in suffering. The pains
therefore are real but they result from a falsely interpreted
cause. In childbirth there are indeed normal contractions of
the uterus and accompanying organic sensations but these
sensations are not interpreted by the central nervous system
for what they really are, namely, simple natural functions;
because of conditioned reflexes, and particularly because of
extreme "fear," they are diverted into the domain of painful
sensations. Such would be the genesis of the pains of childbirth.

Thus we seek what the purpose and task of painless obstet-   463
rics will be. By applying the scientific knowledge that has
been acquired, this method must first dissociate the already
existing associations between the normal sensations of the
contractions of the uterus and the pain reactions of the
cerebral cortex. In this way negative conditioned reflexes are

suppressed. At the same time, new, positive reflexes must be created which will replace the negative reflexes.

464   As for the practical application, it consists in first giving the mothers (long before the time of childbirth) intensive instruction, adapted to their intellectual capacities, concerning the natural processes which take place in them during pregnancy and particularly at the time of delivery. These natural processes they already recognized to a certain extent but often without clearly perceiving their interconnection. There were many things, too, that remained enveloped in mysterious obscurity and were even susceptible of false interpretations. The characteristic conditioned reflexes also acquired a considerable influencing force and kept nurturing anxiety and fear. All these negative elements would be eliminated by the aforesaid instruction.

465   At the same time a repeated appeal is made to the mother's will and emotions in order to preclude the feelings of fear which are, and which have been proved to her to be, unfounded. One must also dispel from the mother's mind any impression of pain, which perhaps might tend to manifest itself but which, in any case, is unjustified, being based only on a false interpretation, as she has been taught, of the natural organic sensations of the contracting uterus. Mothers are especially induced to realize the natural nobility and dignity of what they accomplish at the time of delivery. They are also given detailed technical explanations on what they must do to insure a successful delivery. They are instructed, for example, in exactly how to exert their muscles and how to breathe properly. This instruction consists especially in practical exercises so that the technique may be familiar to them at the moment of delivery. The object therefore is to guide the mothers and to bring them to a state of mind in which they will not go through childbirth in a purely passive way, as an inevitable process, but will adopt an active attitude toward it, bringing to bear on it the influence of their intellect, will, and emotions so as to bring the confinement to term in the manner intended by nature and in cooperation with nature.

466   Throughout the duration of labor, the mother is not left to herself. She profits by the assistance and the constant

supervision of a personnel trained according to the new techniques, who remind her of what she has learned and point out at the proper time what she should do or avoid or modify. They also immediately right her mistakes, as occasion arises, and help her to correct the anomalies which may present themselves.

Such is, in essence, the theory and practice of painless   467 childbirth according to the Russian researchists. For his part, the Englishman, Grantly Dick Read, has perfected a theory and technique which are analogous in a certain number of points. In his philosophical and metaphysical postulates, however, he differs substantially, for he does not rely, as the Russians do, on a materialistic concept.

Regarding the extension and success of the new method   468 (called psycho-prophylactic method), the claim is made that, in Russia and in China, it has already been used in hundreds of thousands of cases. It has also been implanted in various countries of the West; some municipal maternity hospitals are said to have reserved special sections for it. Maternity hospitals organized exclusively according to these principles would still seem to be few in the West: France, among others, has one (communist) in Paris; also in France two Catholic institutions, at Jollieu and Cambrai, have completely adopted this method among their services, without sacrificing what has previously proved successful.

As for its success, it is alleged to be very imporant: 85% to   469 90% of the births taking place in this manner are said to have been really painless.

After having thus given an outline of this method, We pass   470 on to its evaluation. In documentation which has been made available to us there is found this characteristic note: "For the personnel, the primary indispensable requirement is unreserved faith in the method." Can an absolute faith of this kind be required on the basis of the scientific results attained?

The method unquestionably contains elements that must   471 be considered as scientifically established; there are other elements that have only a high probability, and still others which remain as yet (at least for the present) problematical. It is scientifically established that, in a general sense, conditioned reflexes do exist; that fixed ideas or emotional states can be associated with certain events and that this can also hold true for sensations of pain. But at the present time it is not evident to all that it has been proved (or at least that it can be proved from the above) that the pains of delivery are due exclusively to this cause. Serious judges of the matter also harbor reservations regarding the axiom which is stated as *quasi a priori*: "All normal physiological acts, and therefore normal childbirth likewise, ought to take place without pain; otherwise, nature would contradict herself." They do not admit that this axiom can be applied universally and without exception, or that nature would contradict herself if she made childbirth an intensely painful act. In fact, they say, it would be perfectly understandable, physiologically and psychologically, for nature, in her solicitude for the mother who gives birth and for the infant who is born, to impress upon the mother, in an inescapable way, a consciousness of the importance of this act and to try to compel her to take the measures required in her own interest and in that of the child.

472   Let us leave the scientific verification of these two axioms, which some claim to be certain and others hold to be debatable, to the competent specialists. But, in order to discern the true from the false, we must keep to the decisive objective criterion: "The scientific character and value of a discovery should be evaluated exclusively according to its agreement with objective reality." It is important here not to neglect the distinction between "truth" and "affirmation" ("interpretation," "subsumption," "systematization") of the truth. If nature rendered childbirth painless in factual reality, if it became painful subsequently because of conditioned reflexes, if it can become painless again, if all this is not merely asserted, interpreted, or systematically constructed, but demonstrated as real, it follows that the scientific results are true. If it is not possible, or at least not yet possible to obtain complete certitude in this matter, one should abstain from any absolute affirmation and consider the conclusions arrived at as scientific "hypotheses."

But, refraining for the moment from forming a definitive   473
judgment on the degree of scientific certitude of the psycho-
prophylactic method, We pass on to examine it from the
moral point of view.

Is this method morally irreproachable? The answer, which   474
must take into consideration the object, end, and motive of
the method, is briefly: "In itself it contains nothing that can
be critized from the moral point of view."

The instruction given in regard to nature's travail in child-   475
birth, the correction of the false interpretation of organic
sensations and the invitation to correct them; the influence
exercised to avoid groundless anxiety and fear; the assistance
afforded to help the mother collaborate opportunely with
nature and remain calm and under self-control; an increased
consciousness of the nobility of motherhood in general, and
particularly of the moment when the mother brings forth the
child, all these are positive values in which there is nothing to
criticize; they are benefits for the mother in labor and they
are completely in conformity with the will of the Creator.
Viewed and understood in this way, the method is a natural
form of self-training which protects the mother from superficiality and levity. It is a positive influence for the development of her personality so that, at the very important moment of childbirth, she may manifest the firmness and solidity
of her character.

Under still other aspects, the method can lead to positive   476
moral achievements. If pain and fear are successfully eliminated from childbirth, that very fact lessens any inducement
to commit immoral acts in the use of marriage rights.

As for the motives and purpose of the aids afforded the   477
mother in childbirth, the material action, as such, does not
imply any moral justification, either positive or negative; that
is the concern of the one who renders his aid. It can and
should be done from motives and for a purpose which are
irreproachable, such as the interest presented by a purely
scientific fact; the natural and noble sentiment which creates
esteem and love for the human person in her mother and
which wants to do her good and help her, a deeply religious

and Christian attitude which is inspired by the ideals of a living Christianity. But it can happen that the help may be given for a purpose or from motives which are immoral. In this case, it is the personal action of the one who furnishes aid which is to be judged wrong; the immoral motive does not change the assistance, which is good, into something evil, at least so far as its objective structure is concerned. Conversely, an assistance which is good in itself cannot justify an evil motive or prove the evil motive to be good.

478   There remains to be said a word of theological and religious evaluation, in so far as there is a distinction between this and the moral value in the strict sense. The new method is often presented in the context of a materialistic philosophy and culture and in opposition to Holy Scripture and Christianity.

479   The ideology of a researchist and of a scholar is not in itself a proof of the truth and value of what he has discovered and expounded. The theorem of Pythagoras or (to remain in the realm of medicine) the observations of Hippocrates which have been recognized as exact, the discoveries of Pasteur, or Mendel's laws of heredity, do not owe the truth of their content to the moral and religious ideas of their authors. They are not "pagan" because Pythagoras and Hippocrates were pagan nor are they Christian because Pasteur and Mendel were Christians. These scientific achievements are true for the reason and to the extent that they correspond with reality.

480   Even a materialistic research scholar can make a real and valid scientific discovery, but this contribution does not in any way constitute an argument in favor of his materialistic ideas.

481   The same reasoning holds good for the culture to which a scholar belongs. His discoveries are not true or false according as he has descended from this or that culture from which he has received inspiration and which has left its mark deeply impressed upon him.

482   The laws, the theory, and the technique of natural painless childbirth are undoubtedly valid, but they have been elaborated by scholars who, for the most part, profess a materialistic culture. This ideology and culture are not true because the scientific results cited above are true. It is still much less

accurate to say that the scientific results are true and are demonstrated as such because their authors and the cultures from which they derive have a materialistic orientation. The criteria of truth lie elsewhere.

The convinced Christian finds nothing in his philosophical   483
ideas and his culture which prevents him from occupying himself seriously, in theory and practice, with the psychoprophylactic method. He knows, as a general rule, that reality and truth are not identical with their interpretation, subsumption, or systematization, and that consequently, he can at the same time accept the one entirely and reject the other altogether.

A criticism of the new method from the theological point   484
of view must in particular take into account Holy Scripture, for materialistic propaganda claims to find a glaring contradiction between the truth of science and that of Scripture. In Genesis (Gen. 3, 16) we read: *"In dolore paries filios"* ("In pain shall you bring forth children"). In order to understand this saying correctly, it is necessary to consider the condemnation declared by God in the whole of its context. In inflicting this punishment on our first parents and their descendants, God did not wish to forbid and did not forbid men to seek after and make use of all the riches of creation; to make progress step by step in culture, to make life in this world more bearable and more beautiful, to lighten the burden of fatigue, pain, sickness, and death, in a word, to subdue the earth (Gen. 1, 28).

Similarly, in punishing Eve, God did not wish to forbid   485
and did not forbid mothers to make use of means which render childbirth easier and less painful. One must not look for loopholes in the words of Scripture, these words remain true in the sense intended and expressed by the Creator, namely, motherhood will give the mother much to endure. In what precise manner did God conceive this chastisement and how will He carry it out? Scripture does not say. Some claim that originally childbirth was entirely painless and became painful only at a later date (perhaps because of an erroneous interpretation of the judgment of God) as a result of autosuggestion and heterosuggestion, arbitrary associations of ideas,

conditioned reflexes, and because of the faulty behavior of mothers in labor. To date, however, these assertions on the whole have not been proved. On the other hand, it may be true that incorrect behavior, psychic or physical, on the part of women in labor is capable of increasing considerably the difficulties of delivery and has in reality increased them.

486   Science and technique can, therefore, use the conclusions of experimental psychology, of physiology, and of gynecology (as in the psycho-prophylactic method) in order to eliminate the sources of error and painful conditioned reflexes, and to render childbirth as painless as possible. Scripture does not forbid it.

487   By way of conclusion, let Us add some remarks on Christian obstetrics.

488   Christian charity has always taken an interest in mothers at the time of their confinement. It has tried and still tries today to render them efficacious assistance, psychic and physical, in accordance with the state of advancement of science and technique. This can be applied at the present time to the new findings of the psycho-prophylactic method, in the measure in which they meet the approval of serious scholars. Christian obstetrics can here incorporate into its principles and its methods all that is correct and justified.

489   However, it must not be content with this for persons who are capable of receiving more, nor must it abandon anything of the religious values which has been turning to profit up to the present. In Our allocution to the Congress of the Italian Association of Catholic Midwives on October 29, 1951 *(Discorsi e Radiomessaggi* vol. XIII, p. 333-353), We spoke in detail of the apostolate which Catholic midwives are capable of exercising and which they are called upon to practice in their profession. Among other things We mentioned the personal apostolate, namely, that which they exercise by means of their knowledge and their art and by the solidity of their Christian faith (1.c. p. 334ff). They also exercise the apostolate of motherhood by endeavoring to remind mothers of its dignity, its seriousness, and its nobility. What We have said today can be applied here, since they assist the mother in the hour of her delivery. The Christian mother draws from

her faith and from her life of grace the light and strength to put full confidence in God, to realize that she is under the protection of Providence, and likewise to accept willingly what God asks her to endure. It would therefore be a pity if Christian obstetrics limited itself to rendering her an assistance of a purely natural order, that is, psycho-prophylactic services.

Two points deserve to be emphasized here: Christianity   490
does not interpret sufferings and the cross in a merely negative fashion. If the new technique spares the mother the sufferings of childbirth or lessens them, she can accept it without any scruple of conscience, though she is not obliged to do so. In the event of only partial success or of failure, she knows that the suffering can be a source of good, if it is borne with God and in obedience to His will. The life and sufferings of our Lord, the pains which so many great men have borne and even sought and through which they have matured and risen to the heights of Christian heroism, the everyday examples We see of resignation to the cross: all these reveal the significance of suffering and of the patient acceptance of pain in the present economy of salvation, during the time of this earthly life.

A second remark: Christian thought and life, and therefore   491
Christian obstetrics, do not attribute an absolute value to the progress of science and the perfection of technique. That attitude, on the contrary, is regarded as natural by materialistic thought and by the concept of life which materialism inspires. For them it serves as a religion or as a substitute for religion. Although the Christian applauds new scientific discoveries and makes use of them, he rejects every materialistic apotheosis of science and culture. He knows that science and culture occupy a place on the scale of objective values but that, while they are not the lowest, neither are they the highest. Even with regard to them, he repeats today as ever and always: "Seek first the kingdom of God and His justice" (Matt. 6, 33). The highest, the ultimate value of man is found, not in his science and his technical capabilities, but in the love of God and devotion to His service. For these reasons, when faced with the scientific discovery of painless child-

birth, the Christian is careful not to admire it unreservedly and not to use it with exaggerated haste. He judges it in a positive and reflective manner, in the light of sane natural reason and in the more vivid light of faith and love which emanate from God and the cross of Christ.

Address of Pope Pius XII
to the Second World Congress on Fertility and Sterility
May 19, 1956

You, gentlemen, have expressed the desire to come and present your respects to Us on the occasion of the Second World Congress on Fertility and Sterility, which you are now holding in Naples. We eagerly respond to your wish and We express the very special pleasure We experience in receiving an imposing group of scientists and practitioners from so many different countries. You lend yourselves to the study of a subject which is difficult and delicate, because it concerns one of the principal functions of the human body and because the results of your labors can have consequences that are weighty significance in the lives of many men and in the evolution of society.

Involuntary conjugal sterility, for which you propose to find a remedy, creates an obstacle to the attainment of the principal end of marriage. It likewise develops in the couple a profound uneasiness, often concealed by an instinctive modesty but filled with danger for the stability of the marriage itself. That is why, in view of the inability of modern medicine to treat successfully many cases of this kind, you formed in 1951 this "International Association of Fertility." 493

The first Congress, held in New York in 1953, proposed in its Order of the Day three principal resolutions: to aid by every possible means the study of fertility and research into its problems; to promote and spread this speciality among doctors so that a sufficient number of them might be able to 494 lend efficacious help to sterile couples; and to stress the necessity of establishing clinics, services, and fertility centers in hospitals, under the direction of competent personnel.

495   This present Congress, like its predecessor, manifests the desire to develop to the maximum the knowledge which we have, to disseminate that knowledge among doctors in all parts of the world, and likewise to bring about a coordination of efforts on certain points which will terminate in more significant results.

496   You will hear a remarkable number of reports and communications, which examine the endocrine and metabolic factors of fertility and sterility, their professional and toxic factors, the new methods of diagnosis and treatment of sterility in man and woman, the diagnosis of ovulation and spermatogenesis and the treatment of their disorders, and surgical intervention in sterility.

497   A series of memoranda will also consider the experimental researches conducted on this subject and the problems relative to one of the principal functions of man. This collection of studies brilliantly illustrates the interest which this Congress arouses and the manner in which eminent specialists, on all sides, have wished to make their contribution to the common effort.

498   It is not Our province to pass judgment on the strictly technical aspects of your work. We wish rather to consider briefly certain moral implications of the questions, which you approach from the scientific point of view.

499   Your previous Congress, in its last resolution, pointed out that involuntary conjugal sterility raises an economic and social problem of great importance, that it contributes to the lowering of the fertility index of populations and that it can thereby influence the life and destiny of peoples. Sometimes one does not get beyond this relatively obvious and easily grasped point. It will then be said that the birth rate must be increased to ensure a nation's vitality and its development in all its domains. It is true that an increased birth rate is a manifestation of the creative energies of a people or of a family, it illustrates the courage men show in the face of life with its risks and its difficulties, and it emphasizes man's

constructive and progressive will. With reason do we say that the physical impossibility of exercising paternity and maternity easily becomes a source of discouragement and introversion. Life, which ardently longs to continue and to reproduce itself, is thrown back on itself, so to speak, and many hearths, alas, succumb to this trial.

It is with pleasure that We should like to mention here one consideration which you yourselves have placed in relief. If your zeal in pursuing research into matrimonial sterility and the means of overcoming it presents a scientific aspect worthy of attention, it is abundantly true that it also involves lofty spiritual and ethical values which must be taken into account. This We have indicated above. It is a profoundly human trait for the married couple to see and find in their child the true and complete expression of their reciprocal love and of their mutual giving of self. It is not difficult to understand why the unsatisfied desire for paternity or maternity is deeply felt as a sad and painful sacrifice by parents who are animated by sound and noble sentiments. Moreover, involuntary sterility in a marriage can become a serious danger to the union and even to the stability of the family. `500`

But, in reality, this social aspect serves but to conceal a more intimate and more serious fact. Marriage, in effect, unites two persons in a common destiny, in their progress toward the realization of an ideal which implies, not complete earthly happiness, but the attainment of spiritual values of a transcendent order which Christian revelation in particular proposes in all their grandeur. This ideal the married couple pursue together by dedicating themselves to the attainment of the primary end of marriage, the generation and education of children. `501`

Several times already We have believed it necessary to recall how the individual aims of the married couple, their life in common, and their personal perfection could be considered only a subordinate to the goal which surpasses them, that is, paternity and maternity. "Not only the common task of eternal life," We said in an allocution addressed to midwives on October 29, 1951, "but also every form of personal progress, even intellectual and spiritual progress, to the extent `502` that there is greater depth and spirituality in conjugal love as such, has been put by the will of nature and the Creator at the service of posterity." (*Discorsi e Radiomessaggi*, vol. xiii, pag. 348-349). Such is the constant teaching of the Church. It has rejected every concept of marriage which would threaten to throw it back on itself and to make of it an egotistic quest for emotional and physical satisfaction in the interest of the spouses alone.

503 But the Church has likewise rejected the opposite attitude which would pretend to separate, in generation, the biological activity in the personal relation of the married couple. The child is the fruit of the conjugal union when that union finds full expression by bringing into play the organic functions, the associated sensible emotions, and the spiritual and disinterested love which animates the union. It is in the unity of this human act that we should consider the biological conditions of generation. Never is it permitted to separate these various aspects to the positive exclusion either of the procreative intention or of the conjugal relationship. The relationship which unites the father and the mother to their child finds its root in the organic fact and still more in the deliberate conduct of the spouses who give themselves to each other and whose will to give themselves blossoms forth and finds its true attainment in the being which they bring into the world.

504 Furthermore, only this consecration of self, begun in generosity and brought to realization in hardship, by the conscious acceptance of the responsibilities which it involves, can guarantee that the task of educating the children will be pursued with all the care and courage and patience which it demands. It can therefore be affirmed that human fecundity, beyond the physical factors, takes on essential moral aspects which must necessarily be considered, even when the subject is treated from the medical point of view.

505 It is quite evident that, when the scholar and the physician approach a problem in their specialized field, they have the right to concentrate their attention on its strictly scientific elements and to solve the problem on the basis of these data alone. But when one is confronted with practical applications

to man, it is impossible not to take into account the repercussions which the proposed methods will have on the person and his destiny. The importance of a human act consists precisely in going beyond the moment itself at which the act is posited to consider the entire orientation of a life, and to bring it into relation with the absolute. This is already true of everyday activity; how much more is it true of an act which involves, with the reciprocal love of the spouses, their future and that of their posterity.

We also believe that it is of capital importance for you, 506 gentlemen, not to neglect this perspective when you consider the methods of artificial fecundation. The means by which one tends toward the production of a new life take on an essential human significance inseparable from the desired end and susceptible of causing grave harm to this very end if these means are not conformable to reality and to the laws inscribed in the nature of beings.

We have been asked to give some directives on this point 507 also. On the subject of the experiments in artificial human fecundation *"in vitro,"* let it suffice for Us to observe that they must be rejected as immoral and absolutely illicit. With regard to the various moral problems which are posed by artificial fecundation, in the ordinary meaning of the expression, or "artificial insemination," We have already expressed Our thought in a discourse addressed to physicians on September 29, 1949 (*Discorsi e Radiomessaggi*, vol. xi, pp. 221 ff.). For the details We refer you to what We said then and We confine Ourself here to repeating the concluding judgment given there: "With regard to artificial fecundation, not only is there reason to be extremely reserved, but it must be absolutely rejected. In speaking thus, one is not necessarily forbidding the use of certain artificial means destined solely to facilitate the natural act or to achieve the attainment of the natural act normally performed." but since artificial fecundation is being more and more widely used, and in order to correct some erroneous opinions which are being spread concerning what We have taught, We have the following to add:

Artifical fecundation exceeds the limits of the right which 508 spouses have acquired by the matrimonial contract, namely that of fully exercising their natural sexual capacity in the natural accomplishment of the marital act. The contract in question does not confer on them a right to artificial fecundation, for such a right is not in any way expressed in the right to the natural conjugal act and cannot be deduced from it. Still less can one derive it from the right to the "child," the primary "end" of marriage. The matrimonial contract does not give this right, because it has for its object not the "child," but the "natural acts" which are capable of engendering a new life and are destined to this end. It must likewise be said that artificial fecundation violates the natural law and is contrary to justice and morality. . . . [1]

509   If fecundity responds to certain demands of the organism and satisfies powerful instincts, it involves immediately, as We have said, psychological and moral elements. The task of education surpasses, by its significance and its consequences, that of generation. The communication of soul with soul which operates between parents and children, with all the seriousness, the delicacy, and self-forgetfulness which it demands, very soon obliges parents to go beyond the state of emotional possession to think of the personal destiny of those who are confided to them. Most often the children, when they reach adult age, leave their family and go far away to respond to the necessities of life or to answer the call to a higher vocation. The thought of this normal separation, painful as it may be for the parents, should help them to rise to a nobler appreciation of their mission and to a purer vision of the significance of their efforts. Under penalty of at least partial loss, the family is called upon to become an integral part of society, to enlarge the circle of its affections and its interests, and to orient its members toward wider horizons, in order that they may think not only of themselves but also of works of social service.

510   The Catholic Church finally, the depository of divine purposes, teaches the superior fecundity of lives entirely consecrated to God and to neighbor. Here the comple renunciation of family life permits a totally disinterested spiritual activity which proceeds, not from any fear of life or its entanglements but from the perception of the true destinies

of man, created in the image of God and seeking a universal love which no carnal attachment succeeds in limiting. Such is the most sublime and most enviable fecundity that man can wish for, a fecundity which transcends the biological realm to enter straightway into that of the spirit.

We did not wish to conclude this allocution, gentlemen, without opening up these perspectives. To some they may appear rather far removed from the objectives which now occupy you. But that is not at all true. They alone, in fact, make it possible for you to give your work the place which belongs to it and to appreciate the value of it. What you wish is not only to increase the number of men but to raise the moral level of mankind together with its beneficent forces and its will to grow physically and spiritually. You wish to bring a new fervor to the affection of so many couples who are saddened by an empty hearth. Far from hindering their full development, it is your ambition to put at their service all your knowledge so that there may be awakened in them all those admirable resources which God has hidden in the hearts of fathers and mothers to help them mount up, themselves and their whole family, to Him. 511

We dare to hope that, imbued with such a responsibility, you will pursue with growing ardor your scientific labor and the practical results at which you are aiming. Invoking on you, on your families and on all those who are dear to you the most abundant divine favors, We wholeheartedly bestow on you Our Apostolic Benediction. 512

Address of Pope Pius XII
to a Pilgrimage Sponsored by the
Federation of Italian Women
October 14, 1956

Beloved daughters of the Italian Federation of Women! You have asked that We speak a word to your meeting at the dear Shrine of Loreto, a place full of meaning, one that sets the hearts of the faithful aglow with memories of the adorable mystery of the Incarnation that took place in the womb of her whom the Archangel hailed as "full of grace" and "blessed among women." *(Luke* 1, 28).

514 We are happy to grant your request. And We are grateful to you for the fervent prayers which you have promised to offer up to the Mother of God for Us, as well as for the fresh opportunity you give Us to set out on a spiritual pilgrimage and to make Our poor voice heard in a place which echoes with the footsteps and the words of Our holy Predecessors and of many saints, who were all deeply devoted to Mary.

515 How We would like to see all the women of Italy and of the world crowd around the throne of the Virgin with your spirit and ardor, so that her lofty example might teach them the secret of all greatness and the best way to carry out in their own lives the plans of God, which correspond to the deepest and purest aspirations of their hearts! The constant tradition of the Church in proposing Mary to Christian women as the sublime model of a Virgin and a Mother shows the high esteem that Christianity nourishes for womanhood and the immense trust which the Church herself rests in woman's

power for good and her mission on behalf of the family and
of society.

The dedicated legions of Italian women who meet and
work together in your Federation are well aware of this,
among other reasons because We Ourselves have taken special
care, whenever it was necessary, to reawaken an awareness of
the great dignity of woman, this was particularly true during
those critical moments in the life of the nation, when a tur-
bulent period of decline, due principally to the after effects
of war, had shaken the confidence of many people. "Be the
rebuilders of the home, the family, society" was what We
urged in the troubled October of 1945, in a talk in which We
spoke at length of the duties of women in social and political
life.[1]

516

Now, eleven years later, it is a great consolation to Us to
realize that the Italian Women's Federation (which was then
no more than a promising seed that had been planted), along
with the Women of Catholic Action, who were also present
on that occasion, took Our words to heart, and made that
exhortation of Ours the rule and basis for all their activity.
The influence of this activity is something that is now felt
throughout the Peninsula, and it finds expression in many
activities of mutual aid and social service.

517

Will your old ardor grow weak now that a somewhat more
peaceful light has begun to shine over your country? Is there
no longer any need to extend, reinforce, and perfect the
work you have undertaken in the hope of reawakening in
your sisters an awareness of their dignity and of their lofty
mission?

518

Have false theories, frivolous customs, and bad company
stopped trying to undermine womankind and to beat down
what God has lifted up, to demolish what the Church is trying
to build, to separate all those whom you are struggling might-
ily to unite? Sad to say, they have not.

519

Woman, the crown of creation, and in a certain sense its
masterpiece, woman, that gentle creature, to whose delicate
hands God seems to have entrusted the future of the world to
such a great extent, insofar as she is man's helper; woman,
the expression of all that is best, kindest, most lovable here

520

below, still finds that, despite the deceptive appearances of being placed on a pedestal, she is often the object of a lack of respect, and sometimes of a subtle but positive contempt on the part of a world with tendencies toward paganism.

521   So it really is necessary for you to carry on your noble work and make your organization just what you like to call it—a "movement," a "school," a "force," in a word, a dynamic center of thought and action, which is determined to assert and defend the real value of woman, by establishing her rights as well as her duties.

522   In the first place, your Federation is supposed to be a *"movement"* in the modern sense of the term, that is, an activity aimed at attracting as many women as possible to an ideal, by stirring their consciences out of their lethargy, giving due consideration to their problems, and helping them to achieve any special aims they may have.

523   At the basis of every movement, you have to have an idea which is truly fruitful and truly binds it together; you must have an ideal, the longing for which serves as the heart of the movement by transmitting a vital, irresistible force to all the members. The only possible basic idea for your movement is the one that urged you on to found your Federation in the first place, the one We pointed out at that time: "the preservation and growth of that dignity which womankind has received from God." *(ibid,* p. 227) The dignity of woman!

524   People are always talking about this dignity, but they do not always display a true and adequate understanding of it, one that will prevent false conclusions, unjustified complaints, and the occasional vindictive claims which are made without any real basis.

525   Even now, you can still find some people who tend to play down or even completely ignore the Church's meritorious role in restoring womankind to its original dignity. They never tire of claiming that the Church is actually bitterly opposed to the so-called "emancipation of woman from a feudal regime." They use false or fragmentary evidence and give a superficial interpretation of customs and laws which were inspired by necessary proprieties of the day; and they do this in an attempt to associate the Church with something that it has

firmly opposed from its very beginning—that unjust status of personal inferiority to which paganism often condemned women.

Do I have to recall the famous sentence of St. Paul which is reflected in the internal nature and external attitude of all Christian civilization? "(There is) neither Jew nor Greek; there is neither slave nor freeman; there is neither male nor female. For you are all one in Christ Jesus." *(Gal. 3, 28)*. This does not mean that Christian law does away with the limitations or proper subjection which arise from the demands of nature, of human and Christian propriety, or from the needs of life together, which cannot last long without some authority, even in its smallest unit, the family.   526

Then there are those who, although they know nothing of the Church's doctrine as to the basis for woman's dignity, make unjustifiable comparisons between this doctrine of the Church and certain erroneous theories which supposedly offer a "broader basis." This succeeds in stirring up suspicion even in the minds of women of good will toward women's associations which are promoted or encouraged by the Church.   527

Need We repeat what the real foundation for the dignity of woman is? It is precisely the same as the basis of the dignity of man: both are children of God, redeemed by Christ, with the same supernatural destiny. How can anyone speak of woman as having an incomplete personality, or speak of a minimization of her value, or of a supposed moral inferiority, and still claim to derive all that from Catholic doctrine?   528

There is another basis for dignity that is identical for both the sexes: divine Providence has given both man and woman a common destiny here on earth, the destiny toward which all human history is moving, and which is indicated in the command which the Creator gave to our first parents together: "Increase and multiply, and fill the earth and subdue it, and rule over it . . ."(*Gen.* I, 28).   529

Because of this temporal goal, there is no field of human activity which must remain closed to woman; her horizons reach out to the regions of politics, labor, the arts, sports; but always in subordination to the primary functions which   530

have been fixed by nature itself. The Creator with His wonderful ways of bringing harmony out of variety has established
a common destiny for all mankind, but He has also given the
two sexes different and complementary functions, like two
roads leading to the same destination.

531   That is why men and women have a different physical and
psychological structure: different attitudes, characteristics,
and inclinations, which are balanced off by the wonderful
law of compensation, and which fit together to lend a marvelous harmony to the work of each. So we have an absolute
equality in personal and fundamental values, but different
functions which are complementary and superbly equivalent,
and from them arise the various rights and duties of the one
and the other.

532   There can be no doubt that the primary function and the
sublime mission of woman is motherhood, and, in accordance
with the lofty goal which the Creator Himself has set in the
order He has chosen, this dominates the life of woman intensively and extensively. Her very physical structure, her spiritual qualities, the richness of her sentiments, combine to
make woman a mother, to such an extent that motherhood
represents the ordinary way for woman to reach her true
perfection (even in the moral order) and, at the same time, to
achieve her double destiny—that on earth and that in heaven.
Motherhood is not the ultimate foundation of woman's
dignity but it does give her such splendor and so great a role
in the working out of human destiny that this by itself is
enough to make every man on the face of the earth, great or
small as he may be, bow with reverence and love in the
presence of his own mother.

533   On other occasions, We have explained that the perfection
of woman, who is naturally ordained to physical motherhood,
can also be achieved in other ways, through many different
kinds of good works, and especially through the voluntary
acceptance of a higher calling, whose dignity is to be measured
by the divine summits of virginity, charity, and the Christian
apostolate.

534   The radiant truth which shines forth in this series of considerations is that woman, both as a person and as a mother,

derives all of her dignity from God and His wise dispositions. As a result, natural law makes it an inalienable and inviolable dignity which women are obliged to preserve, protect, and increase.

Let this be the basic idea that you spread, and the funda-   535
mental ideal that you set for your sisters; this ideal ought to inspire your Federation, for it is the best criterion for a just estimate of your rights and duties. When you approach society and its institutions in search of your own proper place in your own specific field of activity, along with the rights and privileges to which you may justly lay claim, make your Christian dignity the ultimate basis for those claims. Other points remain secondary, and a proper consideration of them must be based on the principles We have just explained. (We are thinking especially of the so-called "equality of the sexes," which has been the cause of so much spiritual discontent and consequent bitterness for women who do not have a clear view of their own special value.)

Your Federation ought to be a *"school"* as well, or rather   536
an institution which not only promotes the study of problems affecting women, but, above all, enlightens and guides them in the fulfillment of their duties.

You are certainly right in thinking that a school of this   537
kind will be extremely useful to all those who have been prevented by circumstances from learning the right road to follow, to others who are edging along it timidly and fearfully because of a feeling of being alone, and to the many who may find that they have lost their way because of errors which are being spread in frank or subtle form in books, newspapers, and films, and at public meetings. But what should you teach in this school?

Your teaching should aim, first of all, at interior formation   538
of each individual in accordance with her own state in life, and then at putting her on the road toward external, social action. It should always be in agreement with the doctrine and counsel of the Church. This does not mean that you have to mistrust all discoveries and teachings of modern education on matters affecting you or that you must, as a matter of principle, reject attitudes which are now generally accepted.

539   At the same time, there is only one way to be really sure of possessing truth and a sound moral outlook and to be certain of success, and that is to see to it that you do not accept teachings which contradict the doctrine and practice of the Church. The priceless treasury of Catholic training with its long tradition and outstanding teachers has attached a well-deserved importance to problems affecting women. And, look where you may, it would be hard to find anywhere else an ideal of womankind as lofty and perfect as that which Christianity has frequently brought to full realization in long lines of young girls, wives, mothers, and widows, who are the boast and the true hope of our people.

540   If the teaching of your Federation becomes a part of this solid tradition, it will lay special stress on persuasion and example as means of imparting lessons in how to live. You are certainly in a better position than anyone else to know just how much many of your sisters need this. You can see the causes and the remedies for that kind of weariness which is characteristic of the married life of the woman of today, and you are best able to decide how to inspire them with courage and perseverance in their daily struggles, and how to give them the strength they need to remain calm in the face of the many radical changes which take place at different periods of a woman's life.

541   After this fundamental instruction on "how to live" in the most Christian sense of the word, it would be well to add other courses of what we might term a technical nature—for example, the proper care of the house, the education of children, the choice of suitable employment, provision for the future, and woman's role in our present society. A woman is well-instructed, firm in her convictions, at peace with herself, and sure of the support and cooperation of a large group of women just like herself, has good reason to expect that she can make a real contribution toward the improvement of society.

542   Last of all, you are going to work to bring women fully into the life of the nation as a beneficial *"force"* for the welfare of all.

Although this linking of the notions of woman and of strength seems to be characteristic of modern times, it is well to remember that Christian tradition always preserved that description of the energetic, virtuous woman which we find in the sacred book of Proverbs. The sacred writer answers the question: "Who shall find a valiant woman?" (*Prov.* 31, 10), by tracing out a living model, one which has often been recalled through the course of the centuries.

543

In what will this force, which you hope to achieve through the harmonious cooperation of the women of the self-same nation, consist? What is its purpose? What is the secret of making it grow and become more effective? For the women who take an active part in your movement, this force will consist principally in the attractive influence of your example; without this, neither your programs nor your schools will stir up any confidence in the ideal you proclaim, or any enthusiasm for it.

544

As for its growth and effectivenes, the force of this Federation of women can best be displayed by definite planned action in every field, even those of politics and law, with the specific aim of making institutions, laws, and customs pay some attention and respect to the special needs of women.

545

It is quite true that modern states have taken long steps toward meeting the basic aims of women. But what we might call their psychological and emotional demands are still treated somewhat carelessly, as if they did not deserve any serious consideration.

546

These demands are indefinable and almost intangible from a statistical point of view, but they are still real values, which We cannot affort to neglect, for they have their roots in nature, and they are intended to play a part in human society by restraining extreme tendencies in important decisions and by establishing a fairer distribution of burdens and benefits among all citizens.

547

A woman's sensibilities play a great part in the life of a family, and often actually determine its course, and these same sensibilities should play their part in the life of the nation and of mankind as a whole. There is no good reason why

548

men alone whould feel at home in questions that concern the whole human family, even those affecting its psychological life.

549   Specifically, if more attention were paid to the anxieties of feminine sentiment, the work of consolidating the peace would move ahead more rapidly, those nations which are well-supplied with the goods of this world would be more hospitable and more generous toward those who are in want, those in charge of public property would often be more cautious in their business dealings, and the organizations set up to take care of community needs in the fields of housing, education, hospitals, and employment would get more done and be more foresighted. For failures in each of these matters often bring in their wake an indescribable suffering to mothers and wives, who see their dear ones languishing in misery if forced separation or an untimely death has not already robbed them of their affection.

550   With reference to work, the physical and moral make-up of woman calls for prudent discrimination as to its quantity and its quality. The idea of using women in construction work, in the mines, and for various types of heavy labor—which is praised and practiced in certain countries which claim to be progressive—is not a modern achievement at all; instead it is more like a sad return toward an age that Christian civilization laid to rest long ago.

551   It is true that woman is a force to be reckoned with in the economy of a nation, but only on the condition that she continue to carry out the lofty functions which are rightfully hers. She is certainly not an industrial force (to use the common terminology) such as man is, for a greater expenditure of physical energy can be expected of the latter. That genteel respect which every man of refined upbringing shows women whenever he meets them ought to be put into practice by the civil laws and institutions of the nation as well.

552   We have pointed out a few definite aims toward which you can direct the constructive force of your movement, to the immediate advantage of your own group and, indirectly, to the benefit of the country as a whole. Safeguard this beneficial power and make it grow. Its real strength does not lie in

agitation in the streets and squares, but in persuasion and in the trust which you will be able to inspire and which you are already stirring up in the midst of your own people, who are endowed by nature with a spirit that is open to justice, goodness, tenderness of feeling and family values.

Beloved daughters listening to Our words on the green   553
stones of the Shrine of Loreto, and all of you who are in the equally sacred intimacy of your own homes, We could not say good-bye to you without coming back to the spiritual presence of her who is Blessed amongst women, Mary, in the hope of drawing inspiration and a promise of efficacious assistance from her maternal Heart, as a final seal on this exhortation of Ours.

When the Archangel Gabriel told the humble Handmaid of   554
the Lord of the loft mission that God had marked out for her, her profound humility could not see anything in herself proportionate to the grandeur of the destiny announced to her. With the voice of a Handmaid who is ready and willing to serve but ignorant of how to do so, She answered, *"Quomodo fiet istud"*—"How shall this happen." (*Luke* 1, 34) The Archangel reassured her, reminding her of the power of the Most High and that nothing is impossible to God. (Cfr. *ibid.*, 35 and 37).

The program just traced out may seem too much for your   555
powers, beloved daughters, or it may look like one that will not be welcomed by present-day society, or that will meet sharp opposition. We say to you again: Almighty God has deigned to inspire your minds with high ideals and your hearts with generous impulses, and you have begged for His help through the intercession of His Most Holy Mother; depend upon Him to give you the courage and perseverance to carry out your aims fully. Begin without delay by working on yourselves and on your families, and then your action will begin to extend profoundly, but without being noticed, into ever wider circles. Have confidence in your own work, for We are depending heavily on you, and so are society and the nation.

We invoke the blessings of God and of His blessed Mother   556
on all of you members of the Italian Women's Federation and on all the women of Italy, in particular those who are

most beset by misfortune, in the hope that through you the world may come to know better days, and with all Our heart We impart to you Our paternal Apostolic Blessing.

Address of Pope Pius XII
to the World Union of Family Organizations
September 16, 1957

We are pleased to welcome the participants in the "International Family Days," organized by the World Union of Family Organizations. During the past years you have studied many of the economic, social and educational problems which are related to family life. We congratulate you for the results you have achieved and the improvements you have succeeded in obtaining in a field so dear to Our heart.

The subject you are dealing with this year certainly de-   558
serves the greatest attention and the active sympathy of all: families deprived of a father. Until lately this subject has not been given sufficient attention, partly because of the helplessness of these families in the sphere of social action. It is, therefore, the duty of organizations such as yours to undertake a systematic examination of the conditions of life, always difficult and sometimes even crushing, which burden widows and orphans.

In a preliminary inquiry you collected statistical infor-   559
mation on the number and status of these families. You then sought to clarify their legal position. On the basis of these data, you then dealt with related economic, professional, psychological, and educational problems.

We hope that the results of this research and these discus-   560
sions will soon be published, and that they will constitute, for all who are striving to improve the conditions of these severly

tried families, a starting point for serious and prolonged action aimed at remedying, in the greatest measure possible, so much actual suffering.

561   Without dealing specifically with the questions you are studying, We intend to say a few words here on the spiritual and religious problems of widowhood, and to emphasize the interior attitudes and dispositions that befit a Christian widow and should direct her life. We think especially, with paternal concern, of those who are still young and have a family to raise, and who are therefore the most heavily stricken by the loss of their husbands.

562   It is noticeable that the very word "widow" produces in those who hear it a sadness and even a sort of aversion, and so some widows refuse to bear this name and do everything possible to make people forget their condition. They give the excuse that widowhood is a humiliation, gives rise to pity, and places them in a position of inferiority which they wish to escape and even forget. Many regard this as a normal reaction but—let Us speak plainly—it is hardly a Christian reaction. Doubtless it reveals a more or less instinctive apprehension in the face of suffering, but it also betrays ignorance on profound realities.

563   When death strikes down the head of a family in his prime and takes him away from his home, it plants a very heavy cross and an indelible pain in the heart of his wife—the pain of one who has lost the better part of herself, the loved one who was the center of her affection, the ideal of her life, the quiet and gentle strength on which she leaned with such trust, the comforter who could understand and soften all her sorrows. Suddenly the woman finds herself alone, abandoned, bending under the burden of her sorrow and the responsibilities she must face. How can she provide sustenance for herself and her children? How can she solve the cruel dilemma: whether to devote her time to her children, or to leave home to earn her daily bread? How can she preserve her independence despite necessary appeals for help to close relatives or other families? We need only call to mind these questions in order to understand the degree of the widow's dejection and why she rebels under the immense bitterness which heaps

itself upon her and before the anguish which surrounds her like an unscalable wall.

As a result, some widows abandon themselves to a kind of passive resignation. They lose interest in life and refuse to come out of their sufferings. Others, on the contrary, try to forget, they create excuses for themselves which dispense them from facing their real responsibilities in a loyal and courageous manner.   564

During the early centuries of the Church's existence, the Christian communities assigned a specific role to widows. In His mortal life, Christ showed them particular kindness and the Apostles after Him recommended them to the affection of Christians and gave them rules of life and perfection. St. Paul described the widow as "she who. . . has set her hope on God and continues in supplications and prayers night and day" (1 *Tim*. 5, 5).   565

Although the Church does not condemn remarriage, she shows her predilection for souls who wish to remain faithful to their spouse and to the perfect symbolism of the sacrament of marriage. She rejoices when she sees the spiritual riches being cultivated which are proper to this state. The first of these, it seems to Us, is a strong conviction that, far from destroying the bonds of human and supernatural love which are contracted in marriage, death can perfect them and strengthen them.   566

It is true that legally, and on the plane of perceptible realities, the matrimonial institution does not exist any more, but that which constituted its soul, gave it strength and beauty—conjugal love with all its splendor and its eternal vows— lives on just as the spiritual and free beings live on who have pledged themselves to each other.   567

When one of the spouses, loosed from his mortal bonds, enters into the divine intimacy, God frees him from every weakness and all the dregs of selfishness. He also invites the one who is left on earth to enter into a more pure and spiritual state of mind. Since one of the spouses has consummated his sacrifice, should not the other be willing to detach herself more from the world, and to renounce the intense but fleeting joys of sensible and carnal affection which bound the husband   568 to the home and monopolized her heart and energies? By accepting the cross of separation, and by renouncing the presence of her dear one, another presence is gained which is more intimate, more profound, and stronger. It is a purifying presence also, for he who sees God face to face will not tolerate in those whom he loved most while on earth retirement into themselves, discouragement, or attachments which are without sound foundation.

569   The sacrament of marriage, symbol of Christ's redeeming love for the Church, applies to the husband and wife the reality of this love. It transfigures them; it renders the husband similar to Christ who delivers Himself to save mankind, and the wife similar to the redeemed Church which accepts its part in the sacrifice of Christ. Widowhood thus becomes, in some manner, the natural outcome of this mutual consecration. It represents the present life of the Church Militant, deprived of the vision of its heavenly spouse, but still unfailingly untied with Him, walking with Him in faith and hope, living on that love which sustains it in all its trials, and eagerly awaiting the final fulfillment of the promises that were made in the beginning.

570   Such is the greatness of widowhood, when it is lived as a prolongation of the graces of matrimony and as a preparation for the flowering in the light of God. What human consolation could ever equal this marvelous prospect? But one must also be worthy of penetrating their meaning and import, and ask for that understanding through humble and attentive prayer and the corageous acceptance of the Lord's will.

571   It is relatively easy for a woman who lives her Christianity intensely and whose marriage has never known any grave crisis, to elevate herself to this plane. But some, during their married life, have undergone times of distress because of the lack of understanding or the misconduct of their husbands. Others have heroically borne their sufferings so as not to desert a home which only brought them disappointments, humiliations, and physical and moral exhaustion. In such cases the death of the husband can appear to be a providential liberation from a yoke that had become too heavy.

Yet, when faced with the mystery of death and the divine 572
judgment, remembering the promises of mercy and resurrection in Christian revelation, the unhappy and guiltless wife
may not harbor feelings any different than those of Christ
Himself for sinful men: feelings of willing forgiveness and of
generous intercession.

Past wounds and saddening memories then become an 573
effective means of redemption. Offered to God for the soul
of the deceased who died in Christ's love, they expiate his
sins and hasten for him the advent of the beatific vision.
Is not such an attitude, inspired by a deep appreciation of the
conjugal union and its redemptive value, the only true Christian solution? Is it not capable of healing still bleeding wounds,
of erasing bitterness and vain regrets, and of restoring that
which seemed irremediably lost?

How wrong it would be, on the other hand, to take advan- 574
tage of widowhood to free oneself from the reserve and prudence proper to single women, and to abandon oneself to the
vanities of an easy and superficial life. This would be to
ignore the weakness of the human heart, which is too eager
to fill an unpleasant solitude, and to gloss over the dangers
of apparently harmless companionships, too often followed
by unfortunate falls.

We strongly hope, then, that the efforts expended to spread 575
an appreciation for the greatness of Christian widowhood will
be pursued with perseverance. We know that a great number of
widows, thanks to the direction of competent spiritual guides
and the help of their associations, have opened their hearts to
the sublime teachings of the faith.

She whose companion has been called back to God should 576
realize the urgent necessity of cultivating her spiritual life if
she wishes to preserve her interior peace and face all her tasks
unflinchingly. She should not let a single day go by without
devoting some time to meditation, a few privileged moments
when she will feel closer to the Lord and to the husband who
continues to watch over her and her home. May she also set
aside every year a few days dedicated more exclusively to
reflection and prayer, far from the noise and oppression of

her daily cares. She will thus find an indescribable security that will enlighten all her decisions and will allow her to firmly assume her responsibilities as the head of the family. This prayer will be accompanied, naturally, by reception of the sacraments, participation in the liturgy, and the use of other means of sanctification which will help her defend herself against insidious temptations, particularly those of the heart and of the senses.

577   In her home the widow will continue to give of herself, as she promised on her wedding day. Her children expect everything from her since she is also taking the father's place. The widow, for her part, directs to her children the love she bore her husband, she becomes tenderly attached to them and yet, in this also, she must remain faithful to her mission.

578   She must suppress the insistent appeals of a heart which has become very sensitive, to insure for her children a virile and strong upbringing, open to society, and to leave them that freedom to which they have a right, especially in the choice of a state in life.

579   It would be fatal if she were to pine away in vain regrets, or take her pleasure in fading memories, or, at the other extreme, allow herself to be terrified by the somber prospects of the future. The widow will undoubtedly consecrate herself to her duty as educator with all the delicacy and tactfulness of a mother, but will remain united in spirit to her husband, who will suggest to her in God the attitudes she must take, and will give her authority and discernment.

580   The memory of the deceased one, instead of preventing or hindering her generous impulses and her application to the work at hand, should inspire courage to accomplish them fully.

581   In her social relations the widow cannot renounce the place that belongs to her. Undoubtedly she will appear outwardly to have an air of more pronounced reserve, for she participates more strongly in the mystery of the cross; the seriousness of her bearing betrays God's imprint on her life.

582   But for this very reason she has a message for those about her. She lives more on faith, who through her sorrow has won access to a more serene and supernatural world; she does not

seek support from an abundance of temporal goods, but from her confidence in God; to those who are too self-enclosed or withdrawn into themselves and have not yet discovered the full meaning of conjugal love, she will teach purification, necessary detachment, and the unwavering fidelity that love requires.

In regard to other widows in particular, she will feel herself bound in a special way to help them fulfill their sacrifice and understand its significance by raising themselves above a merely human perspective in order to see that sacrifice's eternal prolongation.   583

For all, she will be the one whose silent and tactful charity hastens to render service with a word or a gesture wherever a more pressing need or a greater sorrow shows itself. In her family or professional relations, or with her friends, she will introduce the distinctive note that characterizes her apostolate: the testimony of her faithfulness to a beloved memory, and of her having found in this faithfulness and the renunciation it involves a more profound, more stable, more luminous happiness than that which she had to renounce.   584

In the more austere moments and in temptations to discouragement she will recall the chaste heoine Judith, who did not hesitate to run the greatest risks to save her people from ruin and who placed all her trust in God. She will think especially of the Virgin Mary, also a widow, who after her Son's departure remained behind with the primitive Church and whose prayer, interior life, and hidden dedication constantly drew heaven's blessings on the community.   585

When the widow feels even more her declining physical strength, her poverty, her inability to work or to take part in the activities of charity or of the apostolate, she should remember Christ's words when He saw the rich men place their offerings in the treasury, and after them a poor widow who put two little coins in it: "Truly I say to you, this poor widow has put in more than all" (*Luke* 21, 2-3). What the Lord said about this modest offering also applies to the smallest services a widow can render if they spring from a heart belonging to God. For a heart that has grown through trial is closer to those it loves and is capable of spreading   586 around it the purest reflections of the love which possesses it.

587   As a token of the divine favors which We call upon you, your families, and all those who are dear to you, as well as upon all those who throughout the whole world are discovering in widowhood a road leading toward the full discovery of divine love, We heartily grant you Our Apostolic Benediction.

Address of Pope Pius XII
to the 14th Congress of the World Union of
Catholic Women's Organizations
September 29, 1957

You are gathered around Us today, beloved daughters of the World Union of Catholic Women's Organizations, out of a desire to offer to the common Father, as a token of respect and affectionate devotion, the fruit of five years of apostolic work and generous devotion in the service of the Church. We are deeply touched by this proof of your filial devotion. In expressing our joy and satisfaction to you, We congratulate, through you, the thirty-six million Catholic women who are registered members of the national organizations which form your Union and which you represent here.

We are pleased, first of all, to stress the importance of your 589
association and the great influence it exercises, since you now enjoy an advisory status in the Economic and Social Councils of the United Nations, in UNESCO, in FAO, in ILO, in UNICEF, on the Council of Europe, and in the Organization of American States. You are, therefore, in a position to make known to the most varied sectors of public opinion the ideas of the Church on the development of the personality of the woman and on her mission in the modern world.

This problem, commonly referred to by the phrase "*Pro-* 590
motion de la femme," is a basic preoccupation of many international women's associations—representing attitudes as diverse as those of Protestant, Marxist, and non-sectarian groups—as well as of official international organizations.

591   Present-day society is undergoing a vast upheaval, particularly in recently constituted nations. Many new problems are arising which you wish to approach with a maximum of confidence in a spirit of complete adherence to Christian doctrine. You want to be certain that your actions interpret the wish of the Church, which puts her trust in you and expects of your efforts the Christian renewal of a civilization contaminated by laicism and Marxism, and bewildered by erring religious movements.

592   This is why you have asked Us to give you directives which will guide you in your conduct and offer incentive in your work. You can and must adopt, without reservation, the program of advancing womanhood—a program which offers such great hope to the vast numbers of your sisters who are still subjected to degrading customs, who are still the victims of misery, illiterate environments, or of a total lack of the means of culture and education. But you want to see an elevation of woman that is conceived on Christian principles, in the light of the faith, in the perspective of the Redemption and your supernatural vocation.

593   Your investigations, carried out in various countries of Latin America, Asia, and Africa, have revealed to you all too clearly an urgent need in those areas which calls for a truly understanding and satisfactory answer, valid for every aspect of individual and social life, and which, above all, can meet real spiritual needs.

594   To help you in this difficult task, We will speak to you of the mission and apostolate of Catholic women under its three aspects: the apostolate of truth; the apostolate of love; the apostolate of action.

595   To bring a gravely bewildered civilization back to the right road, the erroneous principles and ideas which determine, in practice, the adoption of its attitudes must first of all be corrected. In addition, any properly conceived apostolate should start by taking into consideration basic intellectual truths on which all subsequent action will be based.

596   We will limit Ourselves here to three basic points which should form your personal convictions and guide your apos-

tolic activity: woman's relation to God; her relationship with Christ; her dependency upon the Church.

The truth most ignored by men of today, at least in their current attitudes, and yet most fundamental for you, is the relation of woman to God.   597

Woman comes from God: it is to God that she owes her existence, her personal characteristics, her earthly task, and the eternal destiny which will crown the loyal fulfillment of her mission. This truth, which reason discloses, acquires its full meaning and absolute certainty in the light of faith. This should be of considerable help to you when you find yourselves at the mercy of the ebb and flow of ideas which novels, movies, and the theater circulate among the masses and which give a thoroughly distorted picture of womanhood.   598

You are sufficiently aware of the teachings of the Catholic Faith on the origin of man and woman to need no detailed instruction on that subject. God created them both in His image, that is to say, as intelligent and free beings, capable of knowing Him, of loving Him, capable also of perpetuating their kind, of dominating cration, and of using it to their own advantage and in His service.   599

This divine origin of the human being is not simply an event which took place millennia ago; it is a present fact, a constant reality, because it is God who constantly is giving life to each human being, who makes him aware of His presence, who places in his heart an invincible attraction toward the good, toward the absolute, toward perfect beatitude.   600

The meaning of human life can be summed up in a phrase, "the search for God," the search for Him who constantly calls His creaturs to Him so that He can increasingly heap upon them the benefits of the fullness of His life and love.   601

What attitude does the present-day world adopt toward this fundamental truth of the divine origin of man and woman? You know what it is from the direct experience you have in your own environs and by the studies carried out by woman's organizations in different parts of the world on the condition of womanhood.   602

The idea of God seems to be superfluous in a world which has fallen victim to the work of man's hands, to the power   603 of science and technical progress, a world from which cumbersome beliefs and superstitions have been eliminated. This atmosphere of atheism, whether militant or latent, is a greater threat to woman than it is to man, both in her personal life and in her social role, because—and We will return to this point later—by reason of her innate inclinations and the functions to which she is called by nature, woman is more in harmony with spiritual realities.

604 She perceives spiritual realities more easily, is more conscious of them, interprets them and makes them felt by others, particularly by those entrusted to her care in her capacity as mother and wife. Her personal dignity and the respect due to her are based primarily on the necessity of safeguarding that spiritual mission, and therefore, in the last analysis, on her proximity to God. The respect for woman and recognition of the true part she plays are closely bound to the religious concepts of the social group to which she belongs.

605 You can see, then, what the primary objective of your apostolate in the service of truth will be: to restore in its integrity faith in God, because God is the source of your being and the ultimate end that you pursue, and because the first step toward improvement of woman's position must be to strengthen the very principles which are the basis of this position.

606 Not only did God give life to woman, but her personality, in its physical and psychological structure, also corresponds to the Creator's intent. Both man and woman are images of God; in their own way they are equal in dignity and have the same rights.

607 It cannot be claimed that woman is inferior. She is called upon to cooperate with man in the propagation and development of the human race, and in this task she assumes the difficult and sublime role of maternity. This entails joy and sorrow to an uncommon degree, because it involves the immense responsibility of bringing a child into the world, protecting and feeding it, caring for its growth and early education, following it with solicitude during the difficult years of adolescence, and preparing it for adult responsibilities.

God endowed woman with precious gifts which enable her   608
to transmit not only physical life but also those inner dispositions of soul and those qualities of the spiritual and moral
order which determine human character.

Modern studies of psychology testify to the complexity   609
and uniqueness of woman's nature so fully that We need not
dwell on the subject. These qualities are of value in all fields
of social and cultural life; in these fields they even constitute
an essential contribution, and civilizations which ignore them
or thrust their influence aside cannot help but undergo more
or less serious deformations which retard their development
and condemn them sooner or later to sterility and decline.

Though woman normally expresses the gift of herself by   610
marriage and motherhood, she can also fulfill the divine
intentions in a more direct manner and make her spiritual
riches bear fruit by a consecrated virginity, which, far from
being a withdrawal into herself, or an escape from the burdens of existence, fulfills her desire to make a more total,
pure, and generous gift.

In Christian and missionary countries, the woman who re-   611
nounces marriage and devotes herself freely to the care of the
sick and unfortunate, to the education of children, and to
improving the condition of families, thus brings to less enlightened minds the presence and action of God. In this field
she acquits herself of her vocation with the highest fidelity
and maximum effectiveness.

You can easily realize, dear daughters, the consequences   612
for your apostolate of the principles and facts We have called
to your attention. Since you propose to expend all your
efforts in raising the status of woman and in developing her
influence in the social field, you should undertake to develop
these gifts with a Christian perspective, which is the only one
capable of giving them their true and full value.

What marvelous progress there would be throughout the   613
world and what a radical improvement there would be in the
social and cultural status of nations if all women were conscious of God's dominion over them and devoted their
influence to making this dominion known and loved!

614   The second truth We wish to stress as a basis of the Catholic woman's apostolate is her relationship to Christ. This fact is clearly expressed in several places in the Holy Scriptures; it is confirmed by the very nature of the work of the Redemption. How can you save others if you do not bring Christ to them? And how can you bring others to Christ if you do not possess Him yourselves? "All are yours," said the Apostle of the Gentiles, "and you are Christ's" (I *Cor.* 3, 22-23).

615   This is the deep conviction which pervades every Christian soul, governs its life, guides its apostolate. You transmit to others the truth and the grace of Christ. The Gospel, the sacraments, the liturgy, the promises of resurrection and eternal life apply to you in all their fullness, and though it may not seem necessary to prove this truth in Christian countries, it must be made to shine forth in Asia and Africa, wherever pagan cults still keep alive concepts of womanhood which belittle her or relegate her to an inferior position.

616   It is enough to read the Gospel and the history of the Church to realize immediately that woman is capable of every form of heroism and saintliness, and that in the work of the apostolate she has held in the past, and still holds, many indispensable assignments.

617   The realationship of woman to Christ is given special emphasis in marriage, and is stressed by St. Paul in his letter to the Ephesians. He writes: "Husbands, love your wives, just as Christ also loved the Church, and delivered himself up for her" (*Eph.* 5, 25). "Let wives be subject to their husbands as to the Lord. . . .Just as the Church is subject to Christ, so also let wives be to their husbands in all things" (*Ibid.* 5, 22-24).

618   By raising marriage of the baptized to the dignity of a sacrament, Christ conferred incomparable dignity upon the husband and the wife and assigned to their union a redeeming function.

619   When St. Paul affirms that women must be subject to their husbands as the Church is subject to Christ, he makes very clear the difference between husband and wife, but in so doing he illustrates the force which links them and maintains the indissolubility of the bond uniting them.

Modern states and those young nations which have obtained   620
independence since the last war or still aspire to it, show an
increasing tendency to introduce into their customs and
legislation a concept of equality between man and woman in
the family and on the social, political, and professional
levels. This development has legitimate aspects and others
which are less legitimate, particularly when they are inspired
by materialistic principles. We do not wish to treat such a
vast question here, but We simply remind you that your
apostolate must firmly maintain the Christian concept of the
wife and the part which woman must play in family life. Only
this concept among all the others inspires mutual esteem,
unqualified devotion, complete fidelity, and, above all, a love
that is ready to sacrifice and forgive.

The union between Christ and the woman has its greatest   621
charm and most perfect fulfillment in the person of the Virgin
Mary. "And the Word was made flesh and dwelt among us"
(*John* 1, 14). It was through the Virgin Mary that God assumed human nature and joined the race of the sons of Adam.
Her dignity as Mother of God brought singular graces and
extraordinary privileges upon Mary: preservation from original sin and all personal fault, the splendor of the virtues and
the gifts of the Holy Spirit, an intimate participation in all
the mysteries of the life of Christ, in His sufferings, in His
death and resurrection, in the continuation of His work within
the Church, and in His Sovereignty over all creatures. She was
given all this because she was the Mother of God, and because
as such she was called upon to play a unique role in the redemption of the world.

What are the consequences of all this for you and your   622
apostolate? First, you should derive from it a great pride in
your sex. It was a woman whom the power of the Most High
covered with His shadow, it was a woman from whom the
second person of the Trinity took flesh and blood, without
the cooperation of man. Though life shows the depths of vice
and degradation to which women may sometimes sink, Mary
shows the heights to which women can rise, in Christ and
through Christ, attaining a position far above all other creatures.

623   What civilization or religion has ever urged women to attain such heights and such perfection? Modern humanism, laicism, Marxist propaganda, the most developed and widespread non-Christian cults offer nothing comparable to this vision, so glorious and so humble, so transcendent and yet so easily accessible!

624   We wanted to outline for you the ideal of womanhood as faith presents it; you find it in Mary and it can be explained by the intimacy of the bonds which united her to Christ. In the conduct of your personal life and in the exercise of your apostolate, never lose sight of her example. Let it inspire your words, your attitudes, and your efforts in your work of empashizing the dignity of woman and the nobility of her mission.

625   However, it is not enough simply to know Mary and her greatness. One must also draw closer to her and live in the light of her presence. It would be almost a contradiction if a Catholic woman working in the apostolate did not foster fervent devotion for the Mother of God. Devotion to Mary will make possible in you a better understanding of Christ and a more intense union with His mysteries. You will receive Christ from the arms of His Mother and she will permit you to love and imitate Him. Pray to her that she might give you the strength to follow Him to the end with faith and ardent love! Pray to her that she might help you to lead today's women along the road that leads to Him!

626   As soon as she enters into apostolic work, the Catholic woman immediately finds herself faced with a swarm of ideas, opinions, trends, and systems which call for her attention on all sides. It is important, then, that she have facility in orienting herself according to the circumstances she encounters. For this she must have firm standards by which to map out a course of action, as well as the necessary moral strength to remain faithful to it and to discover and correct errors which may occur. Where can she find these established standards of thought and action except in the heart of the Christian community, in the Catholic Church?

627   The Church is, by the will of its divine Creator, the depository, custodian, and only authoritative interpreter of super-

natural revelation. The teaching authority which it exercises with regard to this sacred trust entails the right to adjudge all truth, since the eternal destiny of man is single and nothing in his life escapes this finality. Cultural, political, social, and moral realities influence the whole orientation of man's conduct. The Church, entrusted with the mission of leading man to God, and possessing the infallible means of discerning good from evil, is capable of assessing the true value of intellectual and moral principles and that conduct which corresponds to the requirements of truth in concrete circumstances of individual and social life.

Hence, both in her personal conduct and in the exercise of her apostolate, the Catholic woman must take care to remain in close contact with the source of life and light which the Lord has placed in His Church. As long as woman remains under the Church's direction, accepts its teachings and observes its directives, she will enjoy a most precious security which will give to all her undertakings an authority and stability similar to that of the Church itself.   628

Some have wished to limit the jurisdiction of the ecclesiastical magisterium to the field of principles, and to exclude it from the domain of facts, of concrete life. They claim that the latter is the responsibility of the layman, that there the layman is on his own ground and brings to bear a competence which is lacking to ecclesiastical authority.   629

We will simply repeat that this position cannot be sustained. Where there is a question not merely of ascertaining the existence of a material fact, but of evaluating the religious and moral implications which the fact entails, the supernatural destiny of man is at stake, and, therefore, the responsibility of the Church is most certainly involved. The Church can and must, by virtue of its divine mission, define the extent of truth and error involved in a given line of conduct or a particular manner of acting.   630

Though the Church refuses to allow the extent of its activity to be unduly limited, it does not thereby suppress or diminish the freedom and initiative of its children. The ecclesiastical hierarchy is not the whole Church, and it does not exercise its power from without as does civil authority,   631 for example, which deals with its subjects only on a legal basis.

632   You are members of the Mystical Body of Christ, joined to it as a member to a body animated by one Spirit, living one and the same life. The union of the members with the head does not imply that they abdicate their autonomy or renounce the exercise of their functions. On the contrary, it is from the head that they receive the constant impulse which enables them to act with strength and precision, in perfect coordination with the other members, to the benefit of the whole body.

633   May Catholic women rejoice to belong with their whole being to the Body of the Church, as free and responsible people, certain, on their part, of the tasks which are reserved to them, and which contribute to the Church's growth and expansion!

634   The apostolate of truth, for which We have outlined a few directives, would remain ineffective to a great extent were it not extended into the apostolates of love and action. These two apostolates, in fact, constitute two aspects of one and the same reality, because true love desires to express itself in deeds, whereas what seem to be the most heroic acts are valueless if they are not also messengers of sincere love.

635   However, since woman is by nature called upon to manifest the presence and the role of affection, We must give this very special attention and define the place it holds in the apostolic activities of your associations.

636   Let us first of all recall what the Catholic apostolate is and what are its means of action.

637   You know that it is not simply the transmission of doctrine, of a broad outline of dogmas and rules of conduct. However necessary such teachings may be, they constitute but the foundation stone: the essential thing is the practice of these truths in living charity which inspires good works and is absolutely required for the plenitude of faith. The person who exercises the apostolate must obviously be filled with this charity; he passes it on as he teaches the Gospel, or even before this. It is charity which he will see come to life and bloom in the hearts of his proteges, like a flower grown

from the seed he has planted. The first token of success in your apostolate will be your possession in abundance of this treasure of the love of God which penetrates human love, develops it, sanctifies it, and renders it capable, through the most humble signs, of reaching those regions of the soul where the free and responsible person renounces his pride, selfishness, and disordered attachments in order to surrender to the divine love which envelops him and leads him forward according to its own designs.

If your charity is to attain this result, it will probably set   638
out on roads which are long and strewn with obstacles, for do not expect to make the gifts of God accepted and understood by sinning men, blinded by their passions, unless you have carefully prepared them for it.

The economy of the Redemption disposes human beings   639
to receive and bear the divine; it accepts them as they are, in their misery and weakness, and undertakes to renew, purify, and perfect them, just as a mother accepts the child God has given her, loves it and devotes her time and strength to it, that one day it may become a man ready to face life. The grandeur and heroism of love are normally measured by its faithfulness in providing all the necessities of life, with great delicacy and to the smallest detail, for those in one's care.

You have learned in your investigations that your help is   640
needed on behalf of the world's needy peoples in three fields: spiritual, cultural, and material. Only a program carried out simultaneously in these three fields can effectively prevent the progress of materialism, communism, and pagan sects.

The work of evangelization would be betrayed if it were   641
limited to a simple proclamation of the Christian message and neglected its practical implications, particularly those which the social doctrine of the Church has made evident. True charity requires that you love men as Christ loves them—He who could not send His listeners home before they had something to eat, lest they faint on the way (*Mark* 8, 3).

But people must realize without question that your atten-   642
tions are inspired by love of God, and not simply by natural pity or sympathy. It matters little whether or not you awaken in your neighbor a feeling corresponding to your efforts. You

do not work to win gratitude or approval. Let your disinterestedness be a sign of your purity of intention, as St. Paul suggests in his well-known hymn to charity: "Charity is patient, is kind, charity does not envy, is not pretentious, is not puffed up, is not ambitious, is not self-seeking, is not provoked; thinks no evil, does not rejoice over wickedness, but rejoices with the truth, bears with all things, believes all things, hopes all things, endures all things" (I *Corinthians* 13, 4-7).

643   Charity will also help you to sense instinctively the needs of your neighbor. It will make you aware of the call of the Kingdom of God and will indicate to you those critical areas in which your intervention is most needed. It will permit you to overcome your apprehensions and to conquer that indolence which relies on others to do the most tiring work or to show the greatest initiative. It will suggest to you the means best suited for attaining your goal.

644   The most sincere dedication must not give way, without discernment, to impulsive action; it must accept regulation and clearly defined limitations. One sometimes meets very generous souls who are incapable of moderating their impulses, of accepting the counsel of discretion and prudence, of leaving necessary freedom of actions to others, or accepting the restrictions that must come with any kind of cooperation. It is not always easy to renounce a particular good which gives a personal attraction and satisfaction, and submit to the austere demands of the common good. In brief, let your charity be judicious and well ordered.

645   Here you perceive the importance of what We said previously concerning submission to the Church and her directives; this submission is all the more necessary since woman's nature makes her more amenable to the influence of emotional factors.

646   One of the normal consequences of the apostolate of charity will be its growth and purification within you. Among the conclusions to the first study of Latin America that was undertaken by the World Union of Catholic Women's Organizations, you noted the fact that Latin America's spiritual, familial, and social heritage embodies a deep rooted basic

religious sentiment, a strong spirit of sacrifice in the woman, an obvious generosity, and a great desire for development.

We are certain that similar observations could be made of many other regions. Generally, the women you deal with already posses undeniable spiritual resources which have often remained hidden and undeveloped because of their condition of life. Do not approach them with a feeling of superiority, as if you had everything to give them and nothing to receive. 647

True charity, on the contrary, effaces itself in the presence of the person it approaches. It seeks to be receptive to the greatest degree, to enhance and cultivate what another has to give. It is thus open to self-improvement even when in contact with the poorest and most needy people. 648

For this is the profound law of love, that it wishes the happiness of the beloved and his betterment. Its principle of growth urges detachment from self: instead of believing that it alone can fully satisfy its neighbor, it realizes its lack of power and relies more and more on the activity of Him who alone possesses all hearts, God. 649

When it reaches its full growth, divine charity will easily preserve the unity and harmony of those duties and affections which occupy your heart. Without neglecting any of your duties to your family and your social environment, you will still find abundant time and opportunity to devote yourselves to the apostolic activities which the service of the Church calls for. 650

We thus reach the third part of this address: the apostolate of action. Enlightened by the truths of faith, and motivated by an ardent and burning love of God which is ready for any sacrifice, you will communicate supernatural gifts to those around you, through your advice, example, and actions you will become for others a guiding light, a sustaining and encouraging force. 651

Here again, Catholic doctrine and the centuries-old experience of the Church provide you with valuable norms which will orientate your apostolate and give it increased effectiveness. We will, therefore, first consider some of the general 652 characteristics of your action, and then We will give you some specific directives.

653   We believe that the first point to be remembered is the need for action, action clearly conceived and strongly desired. You must reject every attitude of passive acceptance or indifference, every form of apathetic quietism.

654   You cannot in any way expose yourselves to the reproaches of the Master who takes His servant to task because he has buried his talent in the earth instead of making it bear profit (cf. *Matt.* 25, 24-27). Imitate rather the Good Samaritan of the parable (cf. *Luke* 10, 30-37) who understood his duties to his neighbor and whom the Lord set as an example to His questioner, saying: "Go and do likewise."

655   But it is not your intention to give help only when the immediate need arises. You aim at active initiative and spontaneous devotion; you follow in the footsteps of the Lord, who was not compelled to come to earth and, in doing so, merely obeyed the tendencies of His merciful kindness. May all your actions constantly correspond to the impulse of generosity inspired by a love which is thoroughly unselfish!

656   Furthermore, Christ, before ascending into Heaven, entrusted to His Apostles and through them to His whole Church, the task of preaching the Gospel to the world in His name. Every Christian must therefore realize that part of this responsibility rests on his shoulders and that no one can assume it in his stead!

657   A third characteristic of your action will be its universality. It is your duty to assist others as opportunties and needs arise. This universality is expressed partially the work which each of you do, but it is obviously expressed more in your Union considered as a whole.

658   When thirty-six million Catholic women throughout the world work for the fulfillment of a common program based on the demands of faith and Christian living, their association must necessarily bear the mark of that catholicity which is at the base of its very origin. Why call an international congress, exchange the ideas and experiences of different countries for the past five years, unless precisely to affirm the universality of your action?

Let us point out a typical characteristic which differentiates   659
your Union from other international women's groups. Ultimately it is God Himself who enhances all your undertakings
and makes them effective and successful. His Providence,
with its unforeseeable ways, is always surrounded by a halo
of mystery. If, on occasions, results do not correspond to
your expectations, if insurmountable obstacles stop your
advance in some direction, if your purest intentions are
misinterpreted, you still have no reason to give way to discouragement.

You may rest assured that none of your efforts are lost,   660
because God sees them and takes them into account. He also
has His plans; He sees the entirety of His work and disposes
of its various elements as He deems fit. Leave the final decisions to Him, then, without slackening your step or failing
in any way in what He expects of you. Thus you will also
more easily avoid the bitterness and envy that might disturb
the cordiality and harmony of your relations with others who
share the same field of apostolate.

Regarding the field of your apostolate itself and the work   661
it involves, We have noticed that for a few decades it has been
spreading continuously in almost all directions.

This has been and continues to be due to the most diverse   662
of causes—industrialization, social upheavals, increases in the
standards of living and culture, and the creation of new
branches in technical fields. At present women are to be found
in almost all the professions, in cultural, social, and political
organizations and in international organizations. Like others,
the Catholic woman also plays her part in these movements;
she cannot and must not evade it. On the contrary, she must
assume her responsibilities in all these fields of action and
face the requirements of an effective apostolate.

In all those areas where the Catholic woman works—in the   663
family, as wife and mother; in the schools, as teacher; in
legislative, administrative, and legal bodies, in international
relations—she must follow the specific religious and moral
principles which the Church, and particularly the Popes, have
usefully and clearly defined. When circumstances were not

sufficiently clear, they have usually indicated the limits which should not be overstepped.

664   The Apostolic See does not simply tolerate your action; it enjoins you to exercise the apostolate, to devote your efforts to fulfilling the Christian's great missionary duty, that all the lost sheep may be assembled in one fold and under one shepherd (cf. *John* 10, 16).

665   Individual initiative has its place along with action that is organized and applied through various associations. This initiative of the lay apostolate is perfectly justified even without a prior explicit "mission" from the hierarchy. The mother of a family who devotes herself to the religious formation of her children, the woman who devotes herself to charitable works, the one who shows courageous fidelity in guarding her dignity or the moral climate of her environment, all practice a real apostolate.

666   Personal initiative plays a great part in protecting the faith and Catholic life, especially in countries where contacts with the hierarchy are difficult or practically impossible. In such circumstances, the Christians upon whom this task falls must, with God's grace, assume all their responsibilities. It is clear, however, that—even so—nothing can be undertaken against the explicit and implicit will of the Church or contrary in any way to the rules of faith or morals, or to ecclesiastical discipline.

667   We are happy to see members of the young associations of Africa and Asia among you. These associations are now faced with considerable and arduous tasks, for the fulfillment of which they need the help of their more experienced sisters. We do not doubt that this Congress will strengthen bonds of solidarity and give them the assurance of effective help within the framework of your Union.

668   Insofar as Latin America is concerned, it would seem that prompt action is needed in two directions. The first is that of safeguarding against the spread of doctrines propagated by non-Catholic sects, a faith which has often become superficial and lacks sufficient priests to sustain it. You propose, therefore, to develop personal religious convictions and take care of the development of a Christian way of life.

In the second place, you propose widespread social action   669
to improve the seriously inadequate position of a great part
of the rural population and important areas of the urban
population. It is an urgent matter to stimulate the leading
classes to an awareness of the demands of social justice and
the necessity for personal dedication in the tasks of charitable
assistance. But above all, the formation of a popular elite in
rural and urban classes should be undertaken without delay,
in order that they might work from within like yeast mixed
with dough. Such an elite would play a valuable role in improving the religious and social standards of abandoned
people.

At the beginning of this discourse We emphasized the fact   670
that the World Union of Catholic Women's Organizations has
an advisory status in several international organizations. It
can therefore, in neutral circles, voice Catholic opinion on
the development of woman's personality and her mission in
the modern world. We hope that you will be able to draw
profit from these relations and increase your sphere of influence.

This undoubtedly is an indirect form of apostolate, but it   671
is of the greatest importance. Even if all the positive results
one hopes to reach cannot be attained, it is often possible to
prevent the formation of deviations or of dangerous trends.

As We conclude this discussion, We thank the Lord for all   672
that He has already done for your associations, and look
confidently to the future. True, serious threats still hang over
a humanity which is divided into hostile blocs and grapples
with the advancing menace of a ruthless materialism which,
in the form of selfish enjoyment of earthly goods, or the
more repulsive form of collective oppression of whole peoples and nations, pretends to give man back to man by
separating him completely from God.

You, on the other hand, want to bring the message of   673
Redemption on both temporal and spiritual planes to individuals, families, and societies by the united action of all
Catholic women who, thanks to your Union, are becoming
more conscious of their common mission, of their vocation—

as living members of one Church—to make the reign of Christ penetrate everywhere.

674   To you the final triumph of the Christian faith may still seem far away, but you are aware that the stones for the Holy City, where one day all the children of the Father will be gathered together in joy and love, must be gathered one by one. The building is rising slowly but surely. Far from allowing yourselves to be swayed by doubt or pessimism, remember that the Lord has promised His constant help and His glorious coming. "In the world you will have affliction. But take courage, I have overcome the world" (*John* 16, 33).

675   As a token of divine protection and of Our fatherly affection, We grant you, for yourselves and for all the members of your Union and their loved ones, Our Apostolic Benediction.

Address of Pope Pius XII
to the Directors of the Association
for Large Families of Rome and Italy
January 20, 1958

Beloved sons and daughters, Officers and Representatives of the Associations for Large Families of Rome and of Italy, this visit of yours has to be listed among those that bring deepest pleasure to Our heart.

You are well aware of the lively interest We have in family life, of how We never miss an opportunity to point out its many-sided dignity, to re-assert its rights and defend them, to inculcate the duties it involves—in a word, We make it a key-point of Our pastoral teaching. 677

It is this same anxious interest in families that makes Us agree so readily to spend at least a few moments with family groups that come to Our home (whenever the duties of Our office do not make this impossible), and this is why, on occasion, We consent to be photographed in the midst of them, so as to leave some kind of lasting record of Our joy and theirs. 678

The Pope in the midst of a family! Isn't that right where he belongs? Isn't he (in the loftiest spiritual sense of the word) the *Father* of the whole human family that has been reborn in Christ and in the Church? Is it not through him, the Vicar of Christ on earth, that the wonderful plan of creative Wisdom is put into effect—a plan that has conferred on all human fatherhood the destiny of preparing a chosen family for heaven, where the love of the One and Triune God will 679 enfold them in a single eternal embrace and give them Himself as the inheritance that will make them perfectly happy?

680   But you do not represent just any families at all; you are and represent large families, those most blessed by God and specially loved and prized by the Church as its most precious treasures. For these families offer particularly clear testimony to three things that serve to assure the world of the truth of the Church's doctrine and the soundness of its practice, and that redound, through good example, to the great benefit of all other families and of civil society itself.

681   Wherever you find large families in great numbers, they point to: the physical and moral health of a Christian people; a living faith in God and trust in His Providence; the fruitful and joyful holiness of Catholic marriage.

682   We would like to say a few words about each of these points.

683   Surely, one of the most harmful aberrations that has appeared in modern society with its pagan tendencies is the opinion of those who are eager to classify fruitfulness in marriage as a "social malady," and who maintain that any nation that finds itself thus afflicted must exert every effort and use every means to cure the disease. This is the basis for the propaganda that goes under the name of "planned parenthood"; at times it is promoted by persons and organizations who command respect because of their positions in other fields, but who, unfortunately, have taken a stand in this matter which must be condemned.

684   Sad as it is to realize how widespread doctrines and practices of this kind have become, even among the traditionally healthy classes, it is comforting to see indications and proofs of a healthy reaction in your country, both in the legal and in the medical fields. As you know, article 31 of the current Constitution of the Italian Republic, to cite just one source, pays "special attention to large families," and the prevailing teaching among Italian doctors is along a line of opposition ever more strongly against birth-control practices.

685   This does not mean that the danger has passed and that we have destroyed the prejudices which tend to make marriage and its wise norms submit to the aims of reprehensible pride

and selfishness on the part of society or of individuals. We particularly deplore that section of the press that every so often takes up the question once again with the obvious intention of confusing good people and drawing them into error with misleading evidence, questionable polls, and even falsified statements from some cleric or other.

On the part of Catholics, We must urge the wide dissem-   686
ination of the principle, firmly founded on truth, that the only way to protect the physical and moral health of the family and of society is through whole-hearted obedience to the laws of nature, or rather of the Creator, and most of all by fostering a sacred, heart-felt respect for them.

In this matter, everything depends on the intention. You   687
can multiply laws and make the penalties heavier; you can give irrefutable proofs of the stupidity of birth-control theories and of the harm that comes from putting them into practice; but as long as there is no sincere determination to let the Creator carry on His work as He chooses, then human selfishness will always find new sophistries and excuses to still the voice of conscience (to the extent it can), and to carry on abuses.

Now the value of the testimony offered by the parents of   688
large families lies not only in their unequivocal and forceful rejection of any deliberate compromise between the law of God and human selfishness, but also in their readiness to accept joyfully and gratefully these priceless gifts of God—their children—in whatever number it may please Him to send them.

This kind of attitude frees married couples from oppressive   689
anxieties and remorse, and, in the opinion of outstanding doctors, creates the ideal psychological conditions for the healthy development of children born of the marriage. For, right at the beginning of these new lives, it eliminates all those worries and disturbances that can so easily leave physical or psychological scars on the mother or child.

Apart from exceptional cases—and We have had occasion   690
to speak of these before—nature's law is basically one of harmony, and it leads to discord and contradictions only in cases where its normal operation is upset by particular cir-

cumstances which are for the most part abnormal, or by deliberate opposition from a human will. There is no eugenics that can improve upon nature: it is good as a science only so long as it aims at gaining a profound knowledge of nature's laws and respects these laws—although in some cases it may be wise to dissuade people who suffer from serious defects from getting married (cfr. Enc. *Casti connubii*, Dec. 31, 1930: A.A.S. 22 (1930) p. 565).

691   Again, good common sense has always and everywhere looked upon large families as a sign, a proof, and a source of physical health, and history makes no mistake when it points to violation and abuse of the laws governing marriage and procreation as the primary cause of the decay of peoples.

692   Far from being a "social malady," large families are a guarantee of the moral and physical health of a people. Virtues flourish spontaneously in homes where a baby's cries always echo from the crib, and vice is put to flight, as if it has been chased away by the childhood that is renewed there like the fresh and invigorating breath of spring.

693   So let the weak and selfish take their example from you; let the nation continue to be loving and grateful toward you for all the sacrifices you have taken upon yourselves to raise and educate its citizens; just as the Church is pleased with you for enabling her to offer, along with you, ever healthier and larger groups of souls to the sanctifying activity of the divine Spirit.

694   In the modern civil world a large family is usually, with good reason, looked upon as evidence of the fact that the Christian faith is being lived up to, for the selfishness that We just pointed out as the principal obstacle to an increase in the size of a family group cannot be successfully overcome without recourse to ethical and religious principles.

695   In recent times we have seen how so-called "demographic politics" have failed to achieve any noteworthy results; it is easy to see why, for the individual interest will almost always win out over the collective pride and selfishness which this idea so often expresses, and the aims and methods of this policy debase the dignity of the family and the person by placing them on the same level as lower species.

Only the divine and eternal light of Christianity gives full   696
life and meaning to the family and this is so true that right
from the beginning and through the whole course of its history, large families have often been considered as synonymous
with Christian families.

Respect for divine laws has made them abound with life;   697
faith in God gives parents the strength and vigor they need to
face the sacrifice and self-denial demanded for the raising of
their children, Christian principles guide them and help them
in the hard work of education; the Christian spirit of love
watches over their peace and good order, and seems to draw
forth from nature and bestow the deepest family joys that
belongs to parents, to children, to brothers and sisters.

Even externally, a large, well-ordered family is a kind of   698
visible shrine: the sacrament of Baptism is not an exceptional
event for them but something constantly renewing the joy
and grace of the Lord. The series of happy pilgrimages to the
Baptismal font is not yet finished when a new one to Confirmation and first Communion begins, aglow with the same
innocence. The youngest of the children will scarcely have
put away his little white suit among the dearest memories of
life, when the first wedding veil appears to bring parents,
children, and new relatives together at the foot of the altar.
More marriages, more Baptisms, more first Communions
follow each other like ever-new springtimes that, in a sense,
make the visits of God and of His grace to the home un-
ending.

But God also visits large families with His Providence, and   699
parents, especially those who are poor, give clear testimony
to this by resting all their trust in Him when human efforts
are not enough. A trust that has a solid foundation and is
not in vain! Providence—to put it in human words and ideas—
is not a sum total of exceptional acts of divine pity; it is the
ordinary result of harmonious activity on the part of the
infinite wisdom, goodness and omnipotence of the Creator.
God will never refuse a means of living to those He calls into
being.

The Divine Master has explicitly taught that "life is worth   700
more than food, and the body more than clothing" (cfr. *Matt*

6, 25). If single incidents, whether small or great, seem to contradict this, it is a sign that man has placed some obstacle in the way of divine order, or else, in exceptional cases, that God has higher plans for good; but Providence is something real, something necessary since God is the Creator.

701   The so-called problem of over-population of the earth is partly real and partly unreasonably feared as an imminent castrophe for modern society, but undoubtedly the rise of this problem and the continued failure to arrive at a solution of it is not due to some mixup or inertia on the part of divine Providence, but rather to disorder on man's part—especially to his selfishness and avarice.

702   With the progress that has been made in technology, with the ease of transportation, and with the new sources of energy that are just beginning to be tapped, the earth can promise prosperity to all those who will dwell on it for a long time to come.

703   As for the future, who can foresee what new and unsuspected resources may be found on our planet, and what surprises may be uncovered outside of it by the wonderful scientific achievements that have just barely begun? And who can be sure that the natural rhythm of procreation will be the same in the future as it is now? Is it not possible that some law that will moderate the rhythm of expansion from within may come into play? Providence has reserved the future destiny of the world to itself.

704   It is strange to find that the fears of some individuals are able to change well-founded hopes for prosperity into catastrophic spectres at the very moment when science is changing what used to be considered the dreams of wild imaginations into useful realities.

705   So overpopulation is not a valid reason for spreading illicit birth control practices. It is simply a pretext used by those who would justify avarice and selfishness—by those nations, for instance, who fear that the expansion of others will pose a danger to their own political position and cause a lowering of the general standard of living, or by individuals, especially those who are better off, who prefer the greatest possible enjoyment of earthly goods to the praise and merit of bringing

new lives into existence. The final result is that they break the fixed and certain laws of the Creator under the pretext of correcting supposed errors on the part of His Providence.

It would be more reasonable and useful if modern society   706
would make a more determined, universal effort to correct its own conduct, by removing the causes of hunger in the overpopulated or "depressed areas," through a more active use of modern discoveries for peaceful aims, a more open political policy of collaboration and exchange, a more far-seeing and less nationalistic economy; above all, by reacting to all suggestions of selfishness with charity, to those of avarice with a more concrete application of justice.

God is not going to ask men for an accounting of the   707
general destiny of mankind, that is His business; but He will demand an accounting of the single acts that they have deliberately performed in accordance with or against the dictates of conscience.

As for you, parents and children of large families, keep on   708
giving a serene and firm testimony of your trust in divine Providence, and be assured that He will not fail to repay you with the testimony of His daily help and, whenever necessary, with those extraordinary helps that many of you have been happy to experience already.

And now a few words on your third testimony—words that   709
may give new strength to those who are fearful and bring you a little comfort.

Large families are the most splendid flower-beds in the   710
garden of the Church; happiness flowers in them and sanctity ripens in favorable soil. Every family group, even the smallest, was meant by God to be an oasis of spiritual peace. But there is a tremendous difference: where the number of children is not much more than one, that serence intimacy that gives value to life has a touch of melancholy or of pallor about it; it does not last as long, it may be more uncertain, it is often clouded by secret fears and remorse.

It is very different from the serenity of spirit to be found   711
in parents who are surrounded by a rich abundance of young lives. The joy that comes from the plentiful blessings of God breaks out in a thousand different ways and there is no fear

that it will end. The brows of these fathers and mothers may be burdened with cares, but there is never a trace of that inner shadow that betrays anxiety of conscience or fear of an irreparable return to loneliness. Their youth never seems to fade away, as long as the sweet fragrance of a crib remains in the home, as long as the walls of the house echo to the silvery voices of children and grandchildren.

712   Their heavy labors multiplied many times over, their redoubled sacrifices and their renunciation of costly amusements are generously rewarded even here below by the inexhaustible treasury of affection and tender hopes that dwell in their hearts without ever tiring them or bothering them.

713   And the hopes soon become a reality when the eldest daughter begins to help her mother to take care of the baby and on the day the oldest son comes home with his face beaming with the first salary he has earned himself. That day will be a particularly happy one for parents, for it will make the spectre of an old age spent in misery disappear, and they will feel assured of a reward for their sacrifices.

714   When there are many children, the youngsters are spared the boredom of loneliness and the discomfort of having to live in the midst of adults all the time. It is true that they may sometimes become so lively as to get on your nerves, and their disagreements may seem like small riots; but even their arguments play an effective role in the formation of character, as long as they are brief and superficial. Children in large families learn almost automatically to be careful of what they do and to assume responsibility for it, to have a respect for each other and help each other, to be openhearted and generous. For them, the family is a little proving-ground, before they move into the world outside, which will be harder on them and more demanding.

715   All of these precious benefits will be more solid and permanent, more intense and more fruitful if the large family takes the supernatural spirit of the Gospel, which spiritualizes everything and makes it eternal, as its own particular guiding rule and basis. Experience shows that in these cases, God often goes beyond the ordinary gifts of Providence, such as

joy and peace, to bestow on it a special call—a vocation to the priesthood, to the religious life, to the highest sanctity.

With good reason, it has often been pointed out that large families have been in the forefront as the cradles of saints. We might cite, among others, the family of St. Louis, the King of France, made up of ten children, that of St. Catherine of Siena who came from a family of twenty-five, St. Robert Bellarmine from a family of twelve, and St. Pius X from a family of ten.   716

Every vocation is a secret of Providence; but these cases prove that a large number of children does not prevent parents from giving them an outstanding and perfect upbringing; and they show that the number does not work out to the disadvantage of their quality, with regard to either physical or spiritual values.   717

One last word to you, Directors and Representatives of the Associations for Large Families of Rome and of Italy.   718

Be careful to imprint the seal of an ever more vigilant and fruitful dynamism on the action that you intend to carry out in behalf of the dignity of large families and for their economic protection.   719

With regard to the first of these aims, keep in line with the directives of the Church, with regard to the second, you have to shake out of its lethargy that part of society that is not yet aware of its social responsibilities. Providence is a divine truth and reality, but it chooses to make use of human cooperators. Ordinarily it moves into action and comes to our aid when it has been summoned and practically led by the hand by man; it loves to lie hidden behind human activity. While it is only right to acknowledge that Italian legislation can legitimately boast of being most advanced in this area of affording protection to families and especially to large families, We should not close our eyes to the fact that there are still a considerable number of them who are tossed back and forth between discomfort and real privation, through no fault of their own. Your action must aim at bringing these people the protection of the laws, and in more urgent cases the help of charity. Every positive achievement in this field is like a solid stone   720 set into the structure of the nation and of the Church; it is the very best thing you can do as Catholics and as citizens.

721   Calling down the divine protection upon your families and those of all Italy, placing them once again under the heavenly protection of the Holy Family of Jesus, Mary and Joseph, We impart to yo with all Our heart Our paternal Apostolic Blessing.

Address of Pope Pius XII
to Members of the Young Women's Section
of Italian Catholic Action
July 13, 1958

About four months ago, beloved daughters, a throng of joyful youth crowded this St. Peter's Square, and We were encouraged to confide to them Our hope that a better future was in the making for the Church and, through the Church, for the entire world.

This was not the result of that sudden enthusiasm which   723
might easily have come in the presence of such a superb spectacle. Nor did it rise from a desire to stir the young to action and to a peaceful struggle for the advent of Christ's Kingdom.

Rather, We were moved by a need to express Our con-   724
victions to that immense crowd of young folk, evoking the picture of a spring that comes after a cruel winter and forebodes a fertile summer laden with fruit.

This expectation of Ours is strengthened today as We   725
observe the happiness of your faces, think of the perfume of your souls, and contemplate the divine life that is in you, radiating from your whole being.

You, my beloved daughters, are certainly in the flower of   726
your youth, in the flower of life. You are therefore the flower of the Church, the flower of humanity, the flower of the world. You are flowers that are always marvelous in their nearly countless variety.

There is a great variety among flowers as a result of the   727
places where they grow, the seasons of blooming, the culti-

vation they require, the differences of color and perfume, and the variety of uses to which they are put.

728   The first gift of spring is the primrose, little stars filled with perfumed nectar, often level with the grass or bent over by their own weight on a delicate stem.

729   There are flowers that bloom alone at the end of a stem or that join in groups of varied forms or compactness.

730   There are flowers that bloom from the bottom to the top of but a single stem, and others that bloom at the end of their stems in various length and on many branches, giving the impression of one large flower.

731   There are mountain flowers, exposed to the rigors of cold, to showers of torrential waters, to the powerful lash of the winds.

732   There are field flowers that bud and grow almost without order or particular care. Some of these are gathered and others are left to fade or be trodden under foot.

733   There are garden flowers which lie waiting during the last days of winter and then suddenly, almost unexpectedly, burst into a multi-colored carpet.

734   There are flowers of specially chosen types for which the earth is cultivated and special plant food obtained.

735   And there are hothouse flowers, grown in that adjunct to the garden which is designed for the cultivation of plants that would not bloom in the open air or would come to flower slowly: flowers from an area where everything is conditioned —light, heat, humidity—where they blossom and grow and multiply with hardly any contact with the outside atmosphere, but at the same time must have air, when the temperature permits it, so that they will not rot or grow in a weakened condition.

736   We were speaking of flowers, my beloved daughters, and Our thoughts turned constantly to you.

737   May it not be, perhaps, that some of you are like the mountain flowers, exposed to the assaults of the winds and the buffets of the tempest? What then must be the mockery that you sometimes bear, and the insinuations by which some try to lessen the splendor of your spiritual charm?

What are the acts of contempt by which men seek to dis-   738
courage you, and the invitation to evil which would attempt
to entwine your souls and even bind them in the shackles of
guilt?

Others are like the field flowers, because in their case there   739
is no one to attend to them properly—little wild flowers that
the Young Women's Association of Italian Catholic Action
has not discovered and gathered together—like so many of
you who would have been deprived of help and would not
have developed, or would have seen their stems bent and
their petals scattered, but who now embellish and adorn the
world in which they live.

However, it can be said that the greater part of you were   740
born and grew up in well cultivated gardens. The association
was able to take you in its arms when you were still very
small: it supported you when you were babies; it guided you,
holding you by the hand when you were children; and it was
with you when, as teenagers, you took your first steps along
the road of the spiritual life and of apostolic action, with fear
and trembling.

Today, as young women, it comforts you, illuminates you   741
and instructs you in the first encounter with life, in the first
conflicts of your sometimes tormented youth. Those of you
who live as if in greenhouses—we refer to the students who
live in religious institutions—certainly find in the Association
of Catholic Action, as in other similar organizations that the
Church blesses and recommends, a suitable means to profit
more and more from the particularly intense care that is
given you.

While We were speaking of the varied assortment of flow-   742
ers, We hinted at the different uses for which they are destined.

Here We should like to pause for a moment and meditate   743
on two types of flowers that in one way or another should
include all of you.

There are flowers that remain as such always and are   744
destined to be plucked without ever germinating new life.
There are other flowers that beautify the plant and, when
their petals have fallen, give way to fruit.

745 Some of you—not all and not the majority—will be called by God to a life of consecrated virginity. We would be doing an injustice to your generosity and to your constant enthusiasm if We feared to speak frankly to you, as a father should who confides his anxieties to his daughters and knows that they are all ready, anxious and unconditionally dedicated to Christ and the Church.

746 Look at the world, my beloved daughters. It seems to be indifferent to spiritual values, often even hostile to things that remind it of God, His demands and desires. At the same time it invokes the presence of Christian virgins whenever there is weakness that needs support, wherever there is comfort to be given or there are tears to be dried.

747 Orphans need a mother; the sick require disinterested and loving help; the aged beg for filial support; parents and guardians ask for schools and institutes directed by Religious; missions cry out for legions of women consecrated to God.

748 The Pope knows the numerous requests that come in every day, that, although so many young folk in different walks of life are idle and complain sadly *"nemo nos conduxit"* (*Matt.* 20, 7), "no man has hired us," it should be a case of repeating almost in anguish, *"messis quidem multa"* (*Matt.* 9, 37), "the harvest indeed is great, but the laborers are few."

749 Therefore, should it be that the Lord really calls you, answer generously with a "Yes," renouncing father and mother, a human spouse and children. If the Lord really calls you, you must give them all up and must even sacrifice yourselves.

750 But have no fear. This sacrifice offers an indescribably profound joy on this earth and a special crown of glory in heaven because you will be among those who "follow the Lamb wherever He goes" (*Apocalypse* 14, 4).

751 There are others among you—and they are the large majority—whom God has called, or soon will call, to be flowers who will not remain as they are, because one day they will have to bear fruit, if God so wills, in a holy family.

752 On various occasions We have had to correct the error of those who maintain that the Christian virgin is a mutilated and incomplete thing, something that does not fulfill the perfection of its own being. On the contrary, virginity is like

an angelic way of life and by its excellence is a state superior to that of matrimony (cf. Encyclical *"Sacra Virginitas,"* March 25, 1954, A.A.S., 46 (1954), pp. 151-191). But on the other hand, this superiority does not in any way decrease the beauty and grandeur of married life.

Therefore, my beloved daughters, be conscious (from this moment on) of the greatness of the Christian wife and the Christian mother. If your awareness of this fact is clear and timely, you will be induced to omit nothing that will help to prepare you adequately for the sublime mission that awaits you.   753

One day—We wish it for you paternally—you will kneel at the foot of the altar and beside you will be a young man who is resolved to spend his life with you. That day you will be bound by a tie which has God as its author, the substance of which is most noble and the consent to which is sacred.   754

Marriage is a contract which Jesus deigned to elevate to the dignity of a Sacrament, including it thus among the things that seem to be, and are, the meaningful and salutary effects of the Incarnation.   755

Being truly God made man, human nature became the true instrument of life for the Divine Word, the Second person of the Blessed Trinity. Thus the human works of Christ were the works of God, and consequently have a divine value. Since the Incarnation is the mystery by which a human body and soul, together with the Divine nature of the Word from one single person, so it was that the Apostle John could write, 'The Word was made flesh" (*John* 1, 14).   756

The effect of grace, which is conferred "according to the measure of Christ's bestowal" (*Eph.* 4, 7), is that men with their soul, intelligence, will, and action, and also with their body, are made really participants in the divine nature and become children of God. In this way also Christian marriage acquires a special dignity, and by virtue of the Sacrament of Matrimony a human institution—the family community—is transformed into an instrument of divine action. Therefore it is directly sanctified and your conjugal union itself receives a very particular imprint of God.   757

758 But if your state one day will be so great, if one day you will be called to be the cooperator of God in the transmission of life, it is necessary that there be born in you, and always grow stronger, the determined will to be holy, and to be so as brides in your conjugal union itself and in the very exercise of your love.

759 Side by side with the pure ranks of the virgins, which We hope will grow larger with each passing day, there will also be in this manner multitudes of holy spouses.

760 These will not be satisfied with asking God for the simple blessing of their love and their union, but they will beg Him to plant a mystic seed in their souls, made almost as one with their husbands—a seed that will flower and bear fruit in the sanctification of themselves and of their offspring.

761 Beloved youth of Catholic Action, in this springtime of the Church, you must flourish: *"florete flores."* All attempts to make you wither and rob you of the perfume that is your charm must find you indomitable and prepared for any trial.

762 Blossom, beloved daughters, and multiply. Multiply as the flowers multiply: those that are jealously guarded in greenhouses; those cultivated in gardens; those scattered in the fields, and those that wave on the crest of the mountains.

763 Blossom and multiply, but try to acquire more and more every day the consciousness that there are other flowers and other flowerbeds in the magnificent garden of the Church. Beloved daughters, look upon all the flowers and all the flowerbeds with great affection and with an unshakeable spirit of cooperation. The very blossoming of your souls will be subject to the blossoming of charity among you.

764 There is a Woman, as you know, upon whom God willed to rest His gaze with infinite tenderness, having destined her to be His Mother.

765 His omnipotent love kept her crown of virginity intact and at the same time gave her the honor of bride and the dignity of motherhood. Look to her as your unsurpassed and unsurpassable model.

766 Look to Mary, lily of the valley, who nevertheless bore fruit by the Holy Spirit and gave Jesus to the world.

If you look to her, if you imitate her, your freshness will   767
remain intact, your perfume will remain unaltered and your
charm unchanged.

Address of Pope Pius XII
to the Seventh International Hematological Congress
in Rome
September 12, 1958

The Seventh International Congress on Hematology, which has gathered together in Rome more than a thousand specialists from different countries, is the occastion, gentlemen, of this visit. We are very pleased, and cordially welcome you. Your congress was preceded by the International Congress on Blood Tranfusion, which We have also had the pleasure of addressing.

769   A quick glance at the subjects listed in your program suffices to show the many different problems faced by hematology today. Among the subjects treated in the general sessions, We note the questions concerning immuno-hematology, hemorrhagic illnesses, leukemia, the spleen and the recticular endothelial system, anemia, and the use of radioactive isotopes in hematology. There were also symposia at which papers were read and discussed. You have thus had an opportunity to increase your scientific knowledge and to apply it better in everyday life to the individuals and families for whom this acquisition of knowledge is eventually destined.

770   It can be said that problems of blood, inherited from past generations, and of which men are very conscious today—with astonishment and at times even fear—have a universal character that amply justifies your efforts and emphasizes, among other things, the broadly international character of your congress.

A book We mentioned in Our earlier address on the subject   771
of genetic consultation (Sheldon Reed, *Counseling in Medical
Genetics*) points out the various solutions which are currently
envisaged for problems of defective heredity.

It is there reported that, since the discovery of the tech-   772
nique of artificial insemination, "semi-adoption" has been
used on a large scale for having children when the husband is
sterile or when the couple has discovered that he is the
carrier of a dangerous recessive gene. Where the adoptive
father has doubts regarding the legitimacy of the child which
his wife has borne by this method, there is a simple remedy:
legal adoption. A scientific report published in 1954 emphasizes that couples who suspect one another of sterility
tend to want to determine which one of them is at fault by
turning to voluntary adultery. To prevent tragic experiments
of this sort, a clinic on problems of fertility can be of great
help.

Another typical case occurs when a woman turns to genetic   773
consultation because she knows she is the carrier of a hereditary sickness, and, since she cannot consent to techniques
for preventing conception, intends to submit to sterilization.

The first case mentioned above envisages, as a solution to   774
the husband's sterility, artificial insemination, which evidently
presumes a donor, unknown to the couple. We have already
had an opportunity to take a stand against this practice in
the address delivered to the Fourth International Congress
of Catholic Doctors on September 29, 1949. We absolutely
condemned insemination between people who are not married
to one another, and even between spouses.[1]

We returned to this question on May 19, 1956, in Our   775
address to the World Congress on Fertility and Sterility;
We condemned once again all types of artificial insemination,
on the ground that this practice is not included among the
rights of married couples and because it is contrary to the
natural law and Catholic morals. As for artificial insemination
between unmarried persons, We declared in 1949 that this
practice violates the principle of the natural law that new life
may be procreated only in a valid marriage.

776   Solution by voluntary adultery is patently immoral, regardless of any biological, eugenic, or legal ground on which its justification is attempted.

777   A married person cannot assign his conjugal rights to a third person, and any attempt to renounce these rights is invalid and can draw no support from the juridical axiom *"volenti non fit iniuria."*

778   Sterilization, either of the person or of the act alone, has also been advanced as a solution. On biological and eugenic grounds these two methods now have many proponents; they are growing in favor because of new drugs which are more effective and convenient to use.

779   The reaction of some groups of theologians to this state of things is symptomatic and quite alarming. It reveals a deviation of moral judgment, along with an exaggerated haste to revise commonly accepted positions in favor of new techniques. This attitude comes from a praiseworthy intention, which in order to help those in difficulty, refuses to exclude too quickly new possibilities of solution. But this effort at adaption is applied here in an unfortunate way because certain principles either are misunderstood or are given a meaning or implication which they cannot have. The Holy See then finds itself in a situation similar to that of Blessed Innocent XI who was more than once obliged to condemn theses on morality advanced by theologians animated by imprudent zeal and short-sighted temerity.[2]

780   Several times already We have taken a position on the subject of sterilization. We have stated, in substance, that direct sterilization is not authorized by man's right to dispose of his own body and cannot be considered a valid way to prevent transmission of an hereditary disease.

781   "Direct sterilization," We said on October 29, 1951, "that is to say, sterilization which aims, as a means or as an end, at rendering procreation impossible, is a grave violation of the moral law and is therefore illicit. Nor has public authority the right to permit it on any pretext, much less to prescribe it or to have it carried out on innocent persons. This principle has already been announced in *Casti connubii,* Pius XI's Encyclical on marriage.

When, about ten years ago, sterilization began to be more   782
widely applied, it became necessary for the Holy See to declare expressly and publicly that direct sterilization, permanent or temporary, of a man or a woman, is illict by virtue
of the natural law from which the Church herself, as you
know, has no power to dispense."[3]

By direct sterilization We mean an act whose aim to make   783
procreation impossible whether this is intended as a means
or an end; but We do not apply the term to every act which,
in fact, renders procreation impossible. Man does not always
intend to produce the consequences of his acts, even though
he has foreseen them. Thus, for example, the removal of diseased ovaries entails as a necessary consequence the impossibility may not be intended either as an end or as a means.

In Our discourse of October 8, 1953, to a congress of   784
urologists, We explained these matters in detail. The same
principles apply to the present case and prohibit one from
regarding as licit the removal of glands or of sexual organs for
the purpose of impeding the transmission of defective hereditary characteristics.

It also answers the question that is often discussed today   785
among doctors and moralists: Is it licit to impede ovulation
by pills used to remedy undue reaction of the uterus and the
organism, when this medicine, while impeding ovulation, also
renders fecundation impossible? Is its use permitted to married
women, who in spite of this temporary sterility, desire to
have relations with their husbands?

The answer depends on the intention of the person. If a   786
woman takes such medicine, not to prevent conception, but
only on the advice of a doctor as a necessary remedy because
of the condition of the uterus or the organism, she produces
indirect sterilization, which is permitted according to the
general principles governing acts with a double effect. But a
direct and, therefore, illicit sterilization results when ovulation
is stopped to protect the uterus and the organism from the
consequences of a pregnancy which it is not able to sustain.
Some moralists contend that it is permissible to take medi-
cines with this latter intention, but they are in error.

787   It is likewise necessary to reject the view of a number of doctors and moralists who permit these practices when medical indications make conception undesirable, or in other similar cases, which cannot be discussed here. In these cases the use of medication has as its end the prevention of conception by preventing ovulation. They are instances, therefore, of direct sterilization.

788   In an attempt to justify such sterilization, a principle of morality, correct in itself but badly interpreted, is often cited: *"licet corrigere defectus naturae."* And since in practice it suffices, for the application of this principle, to have a reasonable probability, it is maintained that there is a question in the present case of correcting a natural defect.

789   If this principle had an absolute value, eugenics could, without hesitation, use drugs to stop the transmission of a hereditary defect. But it is still necessary to examine the means by which natural defects are corrected and to avoid the violation of other principles of morality.

790   It is also suggested that contraceptives and the Ogino-Knaus method be used to prevent the transmission of hereditary defects.

791   Some experts in eugenics who condemn their use absolutely when there is simply a question of giving rein to passion, approve of both these systems when there are serious hygienic indications. They consider them a less serious evil than the procreation of tainted children. Even if some approve of this position, Christianity has followed and continues to follow a different tradition.

792   Our Predecessor, Pius XI, explained the Christian position in a solemn way in his Encyclical *Casti connubii* of December 31, 1930. He characterizes the use of contraceptives as a violation of natural law, an act to which nature has given a capacity of a human will: *"quemlibet matrimonii usum,"* he wrote, *"in quo exercendo, actus, de industrium hominum, naturali sua vitae procreandae vi destituatur, Dei et naturae legem infringere, et eos qui tale quid commiserint gravis noxae labe commaculari."*[5]

793   On the other hand, to take advantage of natural temporary sterility, as in the Ogino-Knaus method, does not violate the

natural order as does the practice described above, since the conjugal relations comply with the will of the Creator. When this method is used for proportionately serious motives (and the indications of eugenics can have a serious character), it is morally justified.

We have spoken on this subject in Our address of October 29, 1951, not to expound on the biological or medical point of view, but to allay the qualms or conscience of many Christians who used this method in their conjugal life. Moreover, in his Encyclical of December 31, 1930, Pius XI had already formulated the position of principle: *"Neque contra naturae ordinem agere ii dicendi sunt coniuges, qui iure suo recte et naturali ratione utuntur, etsi ob naturales sive temporis sive quorundam defectuum causas nova inde vita oriri non possit."*[6]

794

We stated in the discourse delivered in 1951 that married couples who make use of their conjugal rights have a positive obligation, in virtue of the natural law governing their state, not to exclude procreation. The Creator, in effect, wished human beings to propagate themselves precisely by the natural exercise of the sexual function. But to this positive law We applied the principle which holds for all the others: that these positive laws are not obligatory to the extent that their fulfillment involves great disadvantages which are neither inseparable from the law itself nor inherent in its accomplishment, but which come from another source and which the law-maker did not intend to impose on men when he promulgated the law.

795

The last method mentioned above and on which We wish to express Our opinion is that of adoption.

796

When parents who wish to have a child must be advised against natural procreation because of hereditary defects, one may suggest that they adopt a child. It has been proved that this advice generally produces happy results and gives happiness, peace, and serenity to the parents.

797

From a religious and moral point of view, adoption raises no objections. It is an institution recognized in almost all civilized states. Although certain laws contain morally unacceptable demands, this does not affect the institution itself.

798

From the religious point of view, it is necessary that the children of Catholics be adopted by Catholics, for in practice, parents generally will impose their own religion on adopted children.

799   After having discussed the solutions that are currently proposed to problems raised by hereditary defects, We have still to answer the questions you have asked Us.

800   These questions are all inspired by a desire to clarify the moral obligations arising from those findings of eugenic studies which can be regarded as certain.

801   There is question, in the various cases under discussion, of a general obligation to avoid all more or less serious danger or damage to the interested party, his spouse and his descendants. This obligation is proportionate to the seriousness of the possible damage, to its greater or less probability, to the intensity and proximity of the harmful influence exercised, to the seriousness of the reasons that one has for performing the dangerous acts and for permitting their pernicious consequences.

802   These questions are for the most part questions of fact to which only the interested party, the doctor, and the specialists they consult can give an answer. From the moral point of view it can be said in general that a person has no right to disregard real risks of which one is aware.

803   According to this basic principle, one can reply affirmatively to the first question which you ask: *Should one advise, in general, a prenuptial examination and, in particular, a blood test with respect to Italy and the Mediterranean Basin?*

804   This examination is advisable and, if the danger is really serious, may even be made obligatory in certain regions or localities. In Italy, in the entire Mediterranean Basin, and in countries which receive groups of emigrants from these countries, special attention must be given to the "Mediterranean hematological sickness."

805   The moralist will avoid a categorical yes or no in individual cases. Only a study of all the facts of a given case will permit one to decide whether he is faced with a serious obligation.

806   You also asked *whether it is permitted to advise against the marriage of a couple where the blood test reveals the*

When a subject is the carrier of the Mediterranean hemato- 807
logical illness, one may advise him against marriage but one
cannot forbid it. Marriage is one of the fundamental human
rights, the use of which may not be prevented.

If it is difficult at times to understand the general point of 808
view of the Church, this is because the underlying concept
which Pius XI expounded in the Encyclical on marriage,
Casti connubii, has been lost sight of; Man is created, first
and foremost, not for this world or for his life in time, but
for heaven and eternity. This basic principle seems foreign
to the concerns of eugenics. Still, it is applicable; it is, indeed,
the only completely valid one.

Pius XI also stated, in the same encyclical, that, even if a 809
couple is, in spite of everything, incapable of having healthy
children, no one has the right to prevent them from marrying
or from implementing their legitimately contracted marriage.

In practice, it will often be difficult to make the two points 810
of view—that of eugenics and that of morality—concide. But
to guarantee objectivity in the discussion, each must know
the point of view of the other and be familiar with his reasons.[7]

The same principles give an answer to the third question: 811
*If, after marriage, one discovers the hematological Mediterra-
nean sickness in the couple, is it permissible to advise them
against having children?*

You may advise a couple not to have children but you can- 812
not forbid it. On the other hand, it remains to be seen what
method the adviser (whether he is a doctor, a hematologist,
or a moralist) will suggest to them. Specialized works on the
subject provide no answer, leaving the responsibility of deciding to the couples. But the Church cannot be satisfied with
this negative attitude. She must take a position.

As We have explained, there is no objection to complete 813
continence, to the Ogino-Knaus method, or to the adoption
of children.

The following question concerns the validity of the mar- 814
riage contract between couples who are carriers of the
hematological Mediterranean illness: *If the spouses are unaware of their condition at the time of their marriage, can*

this be reason for the nullity of the marriage? Aside from cases in which a party has laid down as a condition (*Canon* 1092) the absence of all hereditary disease, neither simple ignorance, nor fraudulent hiding of an hereditary defect, nor even positive error which would have halted the marriage if it had been known, is sufficient to render a marriage invalid.

815   The object of the marriage contract is too simple and too clear for one to claim ignorance. The ties contracted with another person must be presumed voluntary because of the sanctity of marriage, the dignity of the spouses, and the security of the children; the contrary must be proved with clarity and certainty. A grave error inherent in the contract (*Canon* 1084) may be undeniable, but this does not prove the absence of a real intention to contract marriage with a determined person. What is decisive in the contract is not what one would have done if one had known a certain circumstance, but what one in reality desired and did because he actually did not know this circumstance.

816   In your seventh question, you ask *if one can consider the "Rh situation" as a reason for the nullity of marriage when it has caused the death of children from the first pregnancy?*

817   You assume the couple did not intend to contract to have children who would be the victims of an early death because of an hereditary trait. But the simple fact that hereditary defects lead to the death of children does not prove the absence of a wish to consummate a marriage. This situation is obviously tragic, but such reasoning depends on a consideration that does not apply.

818   The object of the matrimonial contract is not the child, but the performance of the natural matrimonial act, or—more precisely—the right to perform the matrimonial act. But this right is completely independent of the hereditary traits of the begotten child and of its capacity to live.

819   In the case of a couple in the "Rh situation," you have also asked, *is it always permitted to advise against procreation or is it necessary to wait for a first incident?*

820   Specialists in genetics and eugenics are more competent than We are in this area. It is a question of fact which depends on numerous factors of which you are competent judges.

From the point of view of morals, it suffices to apply the principles which We have explained above, with certain neccessary distinctions.

Finally, you ask *if it is permissible to publish technical* 821 *data showing the inherent dangers of marriage between kinsfolk.* Without any doubt, it is useful to inform the public of the serious risks which marriage of this kind entails. One must also take into account the gravity of the danger in order to judge the moral obligation.

With wisdom and perseverance you are attempting to ex- 822 plore all possible solutions to the many difficult situations. You ceaselessly try to prevent and cure human suffering and misery. Even if there is need for greater accuracy and some modification at certain points, this does not detract from the incontestable merit of your work.

We are pleased to encourage this work. We deeply appre- 823 ciate the active and serious cooperation which allows various opinions to be expressed freely but is not stopped by negative criticism. That is the only open road to real progress, not only for the acquisition of new theoretical knowledge but also for clinical application.

May you continue your work with courage and with a 824 constant desire to safeguard the high spiritual values which alone can worthily crown your efforts.

In token of divine favor and Our goodwill, We accord to 825 you to your dear ones Our Apostolic Blessing.

Explosion or Backfire?
The 1959 Statement on Birth Control
by the National Conference of Catholic Bishops
November 19, 1959

For the past several years a campaign of propaganda has been gaining momentum to influence international, national, and personal opinion in favor of birth prevention programs. The vehicle for this propaganda is the recently coined terror technique phrase, "population explosion." The phrase, indeed, alerts all to the attention that must be given to population pressures, but it also provides a smoke screen behind which a moral evil may be foisted on the public and for obscuring the many factors that must be considered in this vital question.

827   More alarming is the present attempt of some representatives of Christian bodies who endeavor to elaborate the plan into a theological doctrine which envisages artifical birth prevention within the married states as the "will of God." Strangely too, simply because of these efforts and with callous disregard of the thinking of hundreds of millions of Christians and others who reject the position, some international and national figures have made the statement that artificial birth prevention within the married state is gradually becoming acceptable even in the Catholic Church. This is simply not true.

828   The perennial teaching of the Catholic Church has distinguish artificial birth prevention, which is a frustration of the marital act, from other forms of control of birth which are morally permissible. Method alone, however, is not the only

question involved. Equally important is the sincere and objective examination of the motives and intentions of the
couples involved, in view of the nature of the marriage contract itself. As long as due recognition is not given to these
fundamental questions, there can be no genuine understanding
of the problem.

At the present time, too, there is abundant evidence of a   829
systematic, concerted effort to convince United States' public
opinion, legislators and policy makers that United States national agencies, as well as international bodies, should provide
with public funds and support, assistance in promoting artificial birth prevention for economically under-developed countries. The alleged purpose, as already remarked, is to prevent
a hypothetical "population explosion." Experts, however,
have not yet reached agreement on the exact meaning of this
phrase. It is still a hypothesis that must stand the test of
science. Yet, pessimistic population predictors seizing on the
popular acceptance of the phrase, take little account of
economic, social and cultural factors and changes. Moreover,
it would seem that if the predictors of population explosion
wish to avail themselves of the right to foretell *population
increases*, they must concede the right to predict *production
increases* of food as well as of employment and educational
opportunities.

The position of United States Catholics to the growing   830
and needy population of the world is a realistic one which is
grounded in the natural law (which, it should be made clear,
is not the law of the jungle, as sometimes erroneously supposed) and in respect for the human person, his origin, freedom, responsibility and destiny. They believe that the goods
of the earth were created by God for the use of all men and
that men should not be arbitrarily tailored to fit a niggling
and static image of what they are entitled to, as conceived by
those who are more fortunate, greedy or lazy. The thus far
hidden reservoirs of science and of the earth unquestionably
will be uncovered in this era of marvels and offered to
humanity by dedicated persons with faith in mankind, and
not by those seeking short cuts to comfort at the expense
of the heritage of their own or other peoples.

831   United States Catholics believe that the promotion of artificial birth prevention is a morally, humanly, psychologically and politically disastrous approach to the population problem. Not only is such an approach ineffective in its own aims, but it spurns the basis of the real solution, sustained effort in a sense of human solidarity. Catholics are prepared to dedicate themselves to this effort, already so promisingly initiated in national and international circles. They will not, however, support any public assistance, either at home or abroad, to promote artificial birth prevention, abortion or sterilization whether through direct aid or by means of international organizations.

832   The fundamental reason for this position is the well considered objection to promoting a moral evil—an objection not founded solely on any typically or exclusively Catholic doctrine, but on the natural law and on basic ethical considerations. However, quite apart from the moral issue, there are other cogent reasons why Catholics would not wish to see any official support or even favor given such specious methods of "assistance."

833   Man himself is the most valuable productive agent. Therefore, economic development and progress are best promoted by *creating conditions* favorable to his *highest development*. Such progress implies discipline, self-control and the disposition to postpone present satisfactions for future gains. The widespread use of contraceptives would hinder rather than promote the acquisition of these qualities needed for the social and economic changes in underdeveloped countries.

834   Immigration and emigration—even within the same country—have their role to play in solving the population problem. It has been said that migration to other countries is no ultimate solution because of difficulties of absorbing populations into other economies. But it is a matter of record that migration has helped as a solution. Sixty million people migrated successfully from Europe to the Americas in the last 150 years. When the nomadic Indians roamed the uncultivated plains of North America before the coming of these immigrants, the entire country with its estimated Indian population of only 500,000 and its shortage of food, would have been

regarded as "over-populated" according to the norms of the exponents of Planned Parenthood. Yet, the same plains today are being retired into a "land bank" because they are over-productive in a land of 175 millions. It is, therefore, apparent that to speak of a population explosion in the United States in these circumstances is the sheerest kind of nonsense.

The Soviets in their wooing of economically underdeveloped countries do not press artificial birth prevention propaganda on them as a rememdy for their ills. Rather they allure them in to the communist orbit by offering education, loans, technical assistance and trade, and they boast that their economic system is able to use human beings in constructive work and to meet all their needs. The Russian delegate to the relatively recent meeting of the United Nations Economic Commission on Asia and the Far East proclaimed, "The key to progress does not lie in a limitation of population through artificial reduction of the birth rate, but in the speedy defeat of the economic backwardness of these countries." The communist record of contempt for the value of human life gives the lie to this hypocritical propaganda, but to peoples aspiring to economic development and political status, the deceit is not immediately evident. Confronted on the one hand by the prospect of achieving their goals without sacrificing natural fertility and on the other by the insistance that reducing natural fertility is essential to the achievement of such goals, how could these peoples be reasonably expected to reject communism? Yet, the prophets of "population explosion" in alleging that contraception will thwart communism naively emphasize its specious attractiveness in these areas.

United States Catholics do not wish to ignore or minimize the problem of population pressure, but they do deplore the studious omission of adequate reference to the role of modern agriculture in food production. The "population explosion" alarmists do not place in proper focus the idea of increasing the acreage or the acreage yield to meet the food demands of an increasing population. By hysterical terrorism and bland misrepresentation of data they dismiss these ideas as requiring too much time for the development of extensive education and new distribution methods and for the elimination of

835

836

apathy, greed and superstition. Such arguments merely beg the question, for the implementation of their own program demands the fulfillment of the same conditions. It seems never to dawn on them that in a chronic condition where we have more people than food, the logical answer would be, not to decrease the number of people but to increase the food supply which is almost unlimited in potential.

837   We make these observations to direct attention to the very real problem of population pressures. Such remarks are not intended to exhaust this complex subject, nor to discourage demographers, economists, agricultural experts and political scientists in their endeavors to solve the problem. Rather our intention is to reaffirm the position of the Catholic Church that the only true solutions are those that are morally acceptable under the natural law of God. Never should we allow the unilateral "guesstimates" of special pleaders to stampede or terrorize the United States into a national or international policy inimical to human dignity. For, the adoption of the morally objectionable means advocated to forestall the so-called "population explosion" may backfire on the human race.[1]

838   *Signed by members of the Administrative Board, National Catholic Welfare Conference, in the name of the Bishops of the United States*:

FRANCIS CARDINAL SPELLMAN, Archbishop of New York

JAMES FRANCIS CARDINAL McINTYRE, Archbishop of Los Angeles

JOHN CARDINAL O'HARA, C.S.C., Archbishop of Boston

RICHARD CARDINAL CUSHING, Archbishop of Boston

ALOIS MUENCH, CARDINAL-DESIGNATE, Bishop of Fargo, North Dakota

ALBERT MEYER, CARDINAL-DESIGNATE, Archbishop of Chicago

KARL J. ALTER, Archbishop of Cincinnati

WILLIAM O. BRADY, Archbishop of St. Paul

PATRICK A. O'BOYLE, Archbishop of Washington

LEO BINZ, Archbishop of Dubuque

EMMET M. WALSH, Bishop of Youngstown

JOSEPH M. GILMORE, Bishop of Helena
ALBERT R. ZUROWESTE, Bishop of Belleville
JOSEPH T. McGUCKEN, Bishop of Sacramento
ALLEN J. BABCOCK, Bishop of Grand Rapids
LAWRENCE J. SHEHAN, Bishop of Bridgeport

Address of Pope John XXIII
to the Sacred Roman Rota
October 25, 1960

I t brings Us the deepest consolation to extend a welcome for the second time to those who make up the Sacred Roman Rota: the corps of judges, the officials of the Tribunal and the advocates who work there.

840   Beloved sons, once again, as the judicial year opens, you have all joined together in a prayer that gives you strength as it begs the consoling spirit to pour down His priceless gifts of wisdom, counsel, and fortitude, and the help of the divine light into your minds that have to be constantly engaged in the exercise of prudence and sound judgment.

841   Beloved sons! You, my dear Dean, have directed Our attention to the great amount of work accomplished during the year just past.

842   We are very happy to tell you how much real satisfaction We feel at this new proof of the learning and devotion of all those who make up the Tribunal, and We would like to use it as a point of departure for some more general considerations that automatically come to mind when We think of the cases which you are handling; considerations and warnings that reflect the Church's interests and cares, and that We hope will be welcomed by everyone in the world who shares your heartfelt interest in protecting and strengthening the sacredness of the marriage bond and family life.

843   The report that you have presented to Us makes it most obvious that marriage cases are, for all practical purposes,

the main item in the work of the Sacred Rota. And it is easy to imagine that there may be times when, aside from the juridical procedure involved—and this in itself requires of you a great deal of study and of careful ministry—the parties concerned not only may present arguments for or against the existence of the bond, but also, more or less knowingly, may call into question the most sacred aspects of Christian life.

There cannot be any doubt that there is something in our times almost imperceptibly serving to spread far and wide the dangers that threaten the whole concept of the family, and serving to lend greater force to the pitfalls that weaken it. This is happening in a more insistent, a more beguiling, a more deceptive way than in the past.   **844**

The Church has never failed to raise its voice in a cry of alarm when dangerous concessions have been made by the consciences of individuals and of society as a whole in this area that is so delicate and pregnant with consequences for the life of society: encyclicals, documents, the talks of Our predecessors are there to bear witness to the watchful, maternal care of the Church. Even today, she does not fall short in carrying out the commandment she has received from Christ Himself. Above and beyond all else, she continues, better and more effectively, to promulgate her teachings, which are always appropriate, however severe they may be.   **845**

This is why, beloved sons, We would like to draw the attention of all men—jurists, sociologists, educators, and the entire faithful—to the very serious question of the holiness of marriage, so that the dangers We have just mentioned may be driven off ever more effectively. Here are just a few brief ideas that We humbly offer to all for their thoughtful consideration. They touch on three points of pastoral practice and of authentic apostolate; the duty of instruction for all; strength and solidity of doctrine in those who are to educate, counsel, judge; the constant recalling of the fatherhood of God.   **846**

First of all the duty of instruction on the dignity and obligations of married life.   **847**

On April 22, 1942, Pius XII, speaking to a group of newly-weds, reminded them that "marriage is not just a natural   **848** contract; for Christian souls it is a great sacrament, a great sign of grace and of something sacred—namely, Christ's espousal with His Church, which He won and made His own with His own blood in order to bring forth the sons of men who believe in His name to a new life of the spirit . . . The seal and the light of the sacrament which, We might say, change the very nature of the natural contract, give marriage a nobility and a sublime goodness that takes in and unites within itself not only indissolubility, but also all that has to do with the meaning of the sacrament."[1]

849   Now the radiant beauty of this Christian teaching on the essence of matrimony calls first of all for a continuous and persuasive instruction of the faithful, that will reach all levels of society. It is particularly necessary and even urgent for this instruction to reach the young people who are approaching matrimony, and for it to make an impression on them and make them conscious of the very serious duty of religious instruction in this very delicate matter.

850   We of course know that on all sides there are various endeavors under way that have been using the means made available by the press and by modern techniques to make this important work of instruction more effective and more attractive: scientific publications, counsellors, courses of study, special sermons. We want to express Our deep pleasure at these efforts; gradually developed, carefully planned and duly approved by higher ecclesiastical authority, they enkindle wonderful hope for an ever more consoling harvest of good fruit.

851   We must move ahead in this direction with vigor and with sincerety: the conditions of the time demand that we do so without delay. Sometimes the time of youth—and the period of engagements in particular—can smother the brightness and clarity of ideals in the fog of a feeling and expression of love that is mistaken or not sufficiently controlled. These words do not exaggerate the facts; the proof is in the suggestions of the press, the radio, the movies, expressed in terms devoid of any moral foundation. Besides, just look at the whole crowd of affairs and celebrations that create an artifical environment, and make themselves felt in a thousand seductive

—that go against conscience—that change traditional customs for the worse and have the bad training of youngsters as their first and most ruinous effect.

When We consider the seriousness of the danger, which comes not so much from specific individual cases (upon which you can put your finger) as from a general relaxation of sound moral standards on a wide scale, We find an invitation rising to Our lips automatically and We repeat it ardently in *visceribus Jesu Christi*.   852

First of all We ask the pastors of souls to use every means in instructions and in catechisms, through the spoken word and through writings that will spread far and wide, to make their duty clear to the consciences of parents and of youngsters.   853

And We extend this invitation to all who have the means and the inclination to influence public opinion. We ask them to see to it that their influence always serves to clarify rather than confuse, and to promote strong character and respect for the greatest and most precious good in the life of society: the integrity of marriage.   854

This duty calls for a particular *strength and solidity of doctrine* in all those whose specific profession or vocation obliges them often to take an interest in these problems.   855

And this is especially true of you jurists: a strength nourished at the fonts of natural and positive law, that will not give in to any wiles or weakness and that is, at the same time, accompanied by a perfectly balanced judgment that comes from a full awareness of the conditions of the times in which we live.   856

Strength in educators and doctors, too. We can never sufficiently deplore the harm done in this area by a concept of life that is first of all naturalistic and then materialistic, especially with regard to marriage and the family. The steady efforts to snatch this sphere and the defense of it away from the maternal vigilance of the Church and to reduce both (marriage and the family) to the level of merely human institutions has gradually succeeded in weakening their structure and stability more and more.   857

858   And, on the other hand, We can never sufficiently stress the fact that unsullied moral principles, sound training of the emotions, and esteem for human values viewed in their harmony with the supernatural, all avoid or check at the very beginning situations which, if left to the courts, will always leave internal wounds that will never heal. Here again, you have to keep in mind what the actual state of things is as a result of original sin, and that this state necessarily demands that we have recourse to grace, it is the only thing that can restore the equilibrium that man has lost through being wounded, and if it is withdrawn from and deliberately ignored, married life is deprived of its most effective support.

859   Now this is also the duty of educators and of doctors who want to look at their profession not just from one point of view but in the light of the whole, real situation of the man to be healed; for the natural and the supernatural work together in fruitful harmony to cure him.

860   The levity with which people often approach the problem of marriage and the worrisome undermining of moral ramparts are caused not only by a lack of sufficient religious instruction—as We have pointed out—but also by a want of clear and precise ideas on this subject among those whose profession puts them in the position of serving as lights and guides for the younger generation. Fluctuation in their own convictions, superficiality and even error in their philosophical and religious training and—it hurts Us to say it—sometimes a malicious desire to attack the Church's efforts, are the source of the first blow that strikes at the firmness of many consciences; for many, encounters with antichristian teachers and doctors have been the occasion and cause of sad surrenders of principle.

861   Hence strength and solidity of conviction, of doctrine, of resolution, along with constant study, and a humble and sincere attitude of soul that knows that true and profound learning never does go and never can go against the dictates of Revelation and the teaching of the Church.

862   There is a third means that seems to Us to be quite timely for firmly establishing the security of the family, and it fits in perfectly with all that We have said up to now. And that is

the constant recalling of the fatherhood of God *"ex quo omnis paternitas in caelis et in terris nominatur."*[2]

The profound, eternal fruitfulness that is in the bosom of God is, in a certain sense, reflected in an active and generous form in the sons of men who are elevated to the lofty dignity and duty of procreators.   863

In the family we have the closest and most wonderful cooperation of man with God: two human persons created to the image and likeness of God are called not just to the great work of carrying on and prolonging the work of creation through giving physical life to new beings, in whom the life-giving Spirit will infuse the powerful principle of immortal life, but also to the nobler role that completes and perfects the former—that of providing for the human and Christian education of their offspring.   864

A firm conviction of this kind, based on so lofty a truth, is enough to assure stability to every matrimonial bond and to make parents aware of the responsibilities they take on before God and before men.   865

Teachers and pastors of souls know from experience how effective are thoughts of this kind in stirring up holy enthusiasm in young people who are getting ready for marriage, and in stirring up an impressive seriousness that takes the form of accepting advice and making resolutions with all their generosity of spirit.   866

So let every means at your disposal be used to spread a joyous awareness of this majestic nobility of man, of the father and mother of a family, who are primary collaborators with God in carrying on His work in the world, in giving new members to the Mystical Body of Christ, in peopling Heaven with the elect who will sing the glory of the Lord forever.   867

Beloved sons, at Our first meeting with the Sacred Roman Rota on October 19th of last year, We took time to consider the animating spirit of this Tribunal and the tasks entrusted to it by the Supreme Pontiffs beginning with John XXII, down to St. Pius X who, in 1908, reorganized its valuable and praiseworthy activity. You have been most kind and courteous and have shown an appreciation of the reasons lying behind Our words today. As a matter of fact, sometimes the   868 causes that are submitted to the Rota cause Our priestly heart, like your own, to beat with sadness and anxiety over something that is under attack, that needs protection, and that demands courage in investigation and in making a decision, as well as firmness in ideals and in apostolic activity.

869   This is why We wanted to confide some thoughts of a pastoral nature to you, for We felt sure that they would meet with full agreement on your part and that they are already a motivating force in your daily labor. We like to think that Our words will find an echo in the form of serious reflection among an ever wider circle of the faithful who are open and sensitive to the words of their Father.

870   At the conclusion of the present audience, We call upon the Lord to offer you special help toward a perfect fulfillment of the serious responsibilities and tasks committed to you; and We invite you to pray to Him ardently using the profound words of Scripture that apply so well to your activity: *"Da mihi sedium tuarum assistri cem sapientiam. . .Mitte illam de caelis sanctis tuis et a sede magnitudinis tuae, ut mecum sit et mecum laboret, ut sciam quid acceptum sit apud te; . . . deduct me in operibus meis sobrie, et custodiet me in sua potentia."*[3]

871   With such light as an aid, your work will continue to be of great usefulness to the Church and to reflect great credit on each of you. To confirm this most cordial wish, We are happy to offer you proof of how pleased We are in the form of a special, propitiatory Apostolic Blessing, which we bestow upon all of you present here, your families and all of those dear to you.

Address of Pope John XXIII
to the Italian Center for Women
December 7, 1960

It brings Us great pleasure and joy to meet you once again, beloved daughters from the Italian Center for Women, as you celebrate your tenth national congress. The joy and enthusiasm of the souls gathered around the Pope here today take on new beauty from the reflection of a double light, which emits a spirit of candor and gentleness: the Immaculate Virgin, who attracts our hearts with the brillance of her person, which is "full of grace," and her blessed Son, Christ Jesus, to whom peoples turn with fervent longing during this time of Advent. *"Egredietur virga de radice Jesse, et flos de radice ejus ascendet."*[1] The morning star that announces the day of the Incarnation has come into view; the most pure stem has sprouted, from which the most beautiful flower of creation—Jesus, Son of God, Son of Mary—will blossom forth. Today's meeting has been enkindled by this light, and acquires sweetness and grace from it.

The joy that this heart-to-heart talk with you brings Us is born from a vision of the good that the Italian Center for Women has carried forward from its very beginning and is still accomplishing now, as it carries on its lofty mission; above all we take joy from the knowledge that your Center has remained faithful to the supernatural principles that inspire its work of welfare, education, and charity.

873

We are not going to go into a list of the good accomplished and the results achieved, even though we have received an

874

extensive report on them. Beloved daughters! The Pope is well-satisfied with all you have done to stir up the good efforts of women by calling on them to take their place in every sector of family, civic, and social life. The Pope is with you, supporting you, and he joins you in encouraging all those throughout the world who are promoting and helping women's movements, and drawing their inspiration for the same ideals of unity, apostolic zeal, and most ardent generosity that inspire you.

875   The theme of your congress has to do with woman in the family and at work. The topic you have chosen is one of great interest and importance and it offers Us the opportunity of entrusting a few thoughts to you as a reminder of your days in Rome.

876   Family and work: two centers of attraction, two basic structures upon which the life of woman rests. They well deserve a word of attention and of thoughtful consideration.

877   First of all, *woman in the family.*

878   In a talk to you last year, on the 1st of March, We had the opportunity of touching upon some aspects of the family, "taken as the natural environment for the development of human personality, and as a providential refuge, where the storms of life become calm and gentle."[2]

879   We are more than happy to come back to this subject, but Our tone is somewhat sadder, as We repeat the warning that burst from Our lips at that time: "This sanctuary—We say it with sorrow in Our heart—is threatened by so many snares. A propaganda that at times goes beyond all control makes use of the powerful means of the press, shows, and entertainment to spread the wicked seeds of corruption, especially among young people. It is necessary for the family to defend itself, for women to take their places in this work with courage and with a keen sense of responsibility and to be tireless in keeping on the watch, in correcting, in teaching others to distinguish good from evil, taking advantage, where necessary, of the protection provided by civil law."[3]

880   We wanted to repeat this invitation, for the dangerous situations that We complained of then unfortunately have not been eliminated, and in addition there are more and more

new attacks being launched on the sanctity of the family. Those who have responsibility and a proper outlook as Christians and as human beings should neglect no means or effort that will help us to succeed in getting back to conditions that are healthier for the development and defense of the family.

The family is a gift of God: it involves a vocation that ·881 comes from on high and that does not admit of any ready substitute. It is the basis for good, true education, the family is everything, or almost everything for a human being. For example: for the infant who comes into contact with life in his first unforgettable experiences within it, for the adolescent and the young man, to whom it offers a model for emulation as well as a bulwark against the wicked spirit of evil; for the married couple themselves, whom it defends from the crises and loss of direction that sometimes face them, finally, for old people, who can enjoy in it the hard-earned fruits of long fidelity and constancy.

In this picture of the family, there is an irreplaceable role 882 that belongs to woman. There is a voice in the home that everyone will listen to, if it knows how to make itself heard, if it has always made itself respected: it is the watchful and prudent voice of the woman, wife and mother. She can claim the testament of the dying Moses as her own and say to her children, and through them to future generations: "I call heaven and earth to witness this day that I have set before you life and death . . . choose therefore life, that both thou and thy seed may live; and that thou mayest love the Lord thy God, and obey his voice, and adhere to him."[4]

When the voice of the mother encourages, invites, entreats, 883 it remains engraved deep in the heart of her own, and is never again forgotten. Oh, only God knows how much good is stirred up by this voice and what benefits it brings to the Church and to human society!

Beloved daughters, make women aware of their great 884 mission, keep on working in breadth and depth to elicit from the ardent and generous ranks of Chrisitan women a drive toward a lasting renewal of public and private morals and toward an effective strengthening of family and civil life in the light of the teachings of the Gospel.

885   Besides its extensive program dealing with woman in the family, your congress is also taking up the position of woman *at work* as part of its theme.

886   In this regard, we are facing new situations, involving a vast expansion of things to be done and of responsibilities to be met, some of which were not even dreamed of before.

887   This problem touches everyone to some small extent, and it particularly affects parents around the time their daughters reach the full flower of girlhood and the problems of eking out a living and meeting urgent family needs start them thinking about sources of employment and income, or about preparing them in school for the various professions and occupations of tomorrow.

888   There has been and still is some discussion over how wise it is, from certain points of view, to employ women in certain specified types of labor and certain professions. But we have to face facts as they are and they make it clear that there is an ever greater flow of women toward sources of employment, of labor, and an ever more widespread desire on their part for some kind of activity that can make them economically independent and free from want.

889   But even if the economic independence of women brings certain advantages, it also results in many, many problems with regard to their fundamental mission of forming new creatures! Hence we have new situations that are serious and urgent, and that call for preparation and for a spirit of adaptability and of self-sacrifice. These arise in the area of family life: in the care and education of youngsters; in homes that are left without the presence of someone that they need so much; in the loss or disturbance of rest resulting from the assumption of new responsibilities; and, above all, in keeping feast days holy and, in general, in fulfilling those religious duties which are the only thing that can make the mother's work of training her children really fruitful.

890   Everyone knows that outside work, as you might naturally expect, makes a person tired and may even dull the personal-

ity, sometimes it is humiliating and mortifying besides. When a man comes back to his home after being away for long hours and sometimes after having completely spent his energies, is he going to find in it a refuge and a source for restoring his energies and the reward that will make up for the dry, mechanical nature of the things that have surrounded him?

Here again, there is a great task waiting for women: let them promise themselves that they will not let their contacts with the harsh realities of outside work dry up the richness of their inner life, the resources of their sensitivity, of their open and delicate spirit; that they will not forget those spiritual values that are the only defense of their nobility, last of all, that they will not fail to go to the fonts of prayer and sacramental life for the strength to maintain themselves on a level with their matchless mission.   891

They are called to an effort perhaps greater than that of men, if you take into consideration women's natural frailty in certain respects and the fact that more is being asked of them. At all times and in all circumstances, they are the ones who have to be wise enough to find the resources to face their duties as wives and mothers calmly and with their eyes wide open, to make their homes warm and peaceful after the tiring labors of daily work, and not to shrink from the responsibilities involved in raising children.   892

So the work that awaits you is a great and noble one, beloved daughters, if by your presence you are really going to enlighten, sustain, direct. Do not let the many difficulties involved in this task frighten you, have confidence in the generosity and willingness of Christian women, in the healthy spiritual resources of this marvelous legion of beautiful souls, who are nourished with faith and with love and are satisfied to give themselves in sacrifice for their families, without asking for anything in return, without complaining if no reward is forthcoming.   893

But especially trust in God, who is close to you and "of his good pleasure works in you both the will and the performance."[5] He strengthens you and inspires you and He will make your work ever more fruitful.   894

895   Our Immaculate Heavenly Mother is always keeping an eager watch with her love and her grace over these thoughts of our minds and these concerns so dear to our hearts.

896   With the assurance of this motherly protection, We are very pleased to pour forth the full strength and comfort of Our Apostolic Blessing on each of you here present, and to extend it, first of all to your chaplains and then to all those who are working with you for the spread of the Kingdom of God and the safeguarding of the dignity of womanhood.

897   May We be permitted a word of fatherly, joyful congratulations to the members of the Girls Branch of Catholic Action who were winners in the National Christian Doctrine Contest.

898   You have heard Our remarks and you understand what We are so concerned about, good daughters. If We had given you a talk all to yourselves, We could not have offered you any different instructions or pointed out any different road.

899   From this moment forward, you must find the ideal for your role in the picture of the woman who, in a sense, presides over the spiritual running of her home, just as she is described in a passage in the Bible that is so familiar to Our mind: *"Os suum aperuit sapientiae, et lex clementiae in lingua ejus."*[6]

900   Applying yourselves to the study of catechism is the first condition and the basis for the life you will lead tomorrow in the environment of the home and for the relationships you may eventually have in outside labor.

901   So presevere in your search for truth and its beauties; do honor both to really genuine beauty and to truth; experience in yourselves the warmth and sweetness as well as the strength of the doctrine you are studying.

902   The angels of the Lord will go before you, and your youth will offer the beautiful and persuasive testimony of a life that is upright, noble, Christian.

903   Your apostolate will be convincing because of the power of your example, which will make you apostles of those eternal truths that give light to the intellect and warmth to the heart.

And so We bless each of you and your aims and all of the   904
dear ones who are the object of your love or your anxious
care, with the fatherly wish that your presence, which today
is a foretaste of Spring, may tomorrow become the delight
and consolation of Holy Church and of your families.

Address of Pope John XXIII
to Several Italian Women's Associations
September 6, 1961

Beloved sons and daughters. Having gathered in Rome for a course of studies sponsored by the Catholic University of the Sacred Heart on the theme "Woman and the Professions," you desired to have a meeting with the Father.

906   We receive this filial homage with great joy, well aware of its significance and thoughtfulness. It is all the more agreeable to Us inasmuch as it affords Us the very fatherly satisfaction of seeing both the worthy organizers of the course and a large representation from the excellent Catholic Women's Movements, namely, the Women's Association of Catholic Action and the Italian Women's Center. We are, therefore, happy to take this opportunity to address to you a few words of exhortation, and to convey to you the interest and the confidence which We fell in your activity.

907   First of all, We congratulate you on the spirit of fraternal harmony in which, during these days, you are examining a problem of such great import and timeliness. By pooling the fruits of your experience and of surveys conducted in various areas, you are in a better position to coordinate your individual initiatives on a national level, and thus to achieve successful results.

908   We said that you have undertaken to discuss a topic of great import and timeliness. Indeed, one result of the dynamic rhythm of technological and social progress in the last fifty

years has been to take women outside the four walls of their homes and to place them in direct contact with public life. We thus see women working in factories, offices, and businesses, and entering almost all the professions, a field of life and action once reserved almost exclusively to men.

We do not wish to discuss whether this situation corresponds to woman's true ideal—even less do We wish to indulge in regrets and recriminations. On the contrary, Catholics are duty-bound to face this fact, and, in the light of Christian teaching, to ascertain what measures can be taken to mitigate the difficulties of modern woman's situation and to ward off the dangers which such a state of affairs undoubtedly involves.   909

Without going into the details of this far-reaching and complex problem, We shall confine Ourselves to stressing a few points of fundamental importance for the proper orientation of your work.   910

In the first place, any consideration of a woman's occupation cannot disregard the unmistakable characteristics with which God has marked her nature. It is true that living conditions tend to bring about almost complete equality of the sexes. Nevertheless, while their justly-proclaimed equality of rights must extend to all the claims of personal and human dignity, it does not in any way imply equality of functions. The Creator endowed woman with natural attributes, tendencies, and instincts, which are strictly hers, or which she possesses to a different degree from man; this means that woman was also assigned specific tasks.   911

To overlook this difference in the respective functions of men and women or the fact that they necessarily complement each other, would be tantamount to opposing nature: the result would be to debase woman and to remove the true foundations of her dignity.   912

We should also like to remind you that the end for which the Creator fashioned woman's whole being is motherhood. This vocation to motherhood is so proper to her and so much a part of her nature that it is operative even when actual generation of offspring does not occur. Therefore, if women are to be assisted in their choice of an occupation, and in prepar-   913 ing and perfecting their qualifications, it is necessary that, in the practice of their profession, there be some means for continuously developing a maternal spirit.

914   What a contribution to society it would be if she were given the opportunity to use these precious energies of hers to better advantage, especially in the fields of education, social work, and religious and apostolic activity, thereby transforming her occupations into various forms of spiritual motherhood! Today's world has need of maternal sensibilities to dispel the atmosphere of violence and grossness in which men are often struggling.

915   Finally, one must always keep in the foreground the very special claims of the family, which is the most important center of woman's activity and the place where her presence is indispensable. Unfortunately, economic necessity often forces women to work outside their homes. No one will fail to realize how such dissipation of effort and prolonged absence from home place woman in the position of being unable to fulfill her duties as wife and mother. This causes a loosening of family ties, home ceases to be the pleasant, warm, and restful haven where everyone straightens out his life in the warmth of family love. It was precisely to bring wives and mothers back to their proper functions in the home that We, in Our encyclical *Mater et Magistra,* just as Our predecessors did in memorable documents, expressed Our concern that salaries be big enough to support workers and their families.

916   Beloved sons and daughters, modern social structures are still far from allowing woman, in the exercise of her professions, to achieve the fulfillment of her personality, and they do not allow her to make the contribution which the Church and society expect from her. Hence the urgency of finding new solutions, if we are to achieve an order and a balance more commensurate with woman's human and Christian dignity.

917   Hence, too, the need for the forces of Catholic women to be come aware of their obligations. Such obligations do not end, as they did once upon a time, within the confines of the family circle. Woman's gradual ascent to all the responsi-

bilities of a shared life requires her active intervention on the social and political plane. Woman is as necessary as man to the progress of society, especially in all those fields which require tact, delicacy, and maternal intuition.

Beloved sons and daughters, you must diligently carry out these lofty ideals by your words, your example, your actions. You must tirelessly continue to enlighten consciences in a spirit of truth, justice and love.   918

In order that these wishes of Ours may be fulfilled, and a new flame of zeal may be enkindled among the members of your associations, We entreat upon each one of you a profusion of Divine favors, by the pledge of the fatherly Apostolic Blessing, which We impart to you with all Our heart, as We turn prayerful, trusting eyes toward the greatest woman in God's creation, the holy and most sweet Mother of Jesus and our Mother.   919

Address of Pope Paul VI
to the Special Papal Commission
Examining the Problems of Population Growth,
Family Planning, and Birth Regulation
March 27, 1965

Dear Sons, We are happy to see you gathered together around Us on the occasion of the plenary session of your Commission. We know very well just how delicate is the mission and how heavy the responsibility that We have entrusted to you. You are dealing with a problem that impassions world opinion, that preoccupies married couples and their pastors—with good reason.

921   Along with Our pleasure at getting to know each of you goes Our gratitude for your promptness in responding to Our invitation and agreeing to take part in these labors. Your high competence in moral theology, in pastoral theology, in medicine, in economics, in psychology, in demography, in sociology, keeps you from minimizing the exigencies of this work.

922   The list of documents prepared for this fourth session of the Commission is itself an eloquent testimony to the seriousness with which you have undertaken these labors, and We like to look upon this as in itself a pledge of the success that will eventually crown them.

923   We would like to add to this expression of Our gratitude some words of paternal encouragement to carry on your labor with perseverance. It is possible that your keen awareness of the need to allow certain problems to ripen may impose some reasonable delays upon you. But We ask you insistently not to lose sight of the urgency of a situation that calls for unam-

bigous directions from the Church and from her Supreme Authority. The consciences of individuals cannot be left exposed to the uncertainties that nowadays too often keep married life from opening out and developing according to the plan of the Lord. In addition, over and above the pressing problems of married couples, there are also certain economic and social problems being posed—problems, as We said in Our allocution last June 23rd, that the Church will take care not to neglect.

These are, dear Sons, the levels on which your researches are situated: on the one hand, a better knowledge of physiological laws, psychological and medical data, population shifts and social upheavals, on the other hand, and above all, the level of the higher light cast upon these facts by the data of Faith and the traditional teaching of the Church. Like an attentive mother, the Church has at all times had an interest and concern about supplying an answer that is adapted to the great problems posed by men. In keeping with the counsel of the Lord, and with this aim in mind, she welcomes *nova et vetera,*[1] in order to provide the divine leaven of the Gospel with all its richness and to obtain for men an abundance of the supernatural life.   924

In the present case, the problem posed can be summed up like this: in what form and according to what norms ought married couples, in exercising their love for each other, to fulfill this life-giving function to which their vocation calls them? The Christian answer will always be inspired by an awareness of the duties of the married state, of its dignity— the love of the Christian spouses being ennobled by the grace of the sacrament—and of the grandeur of the gift bestowed upon the child who is called to life.   925

The Church, as the guardian of God's natural and positive law, will not allow anyone to underestimate the value of life, nor the sublime originality of a love that is capable of going beyond itself in the spouses' gift of themselves to each other, and then in the gift that is more unselfish still, of each of them to a new being.   926

Our times have become more sharply aware of all these elements than possibly any time in the past. If very diffi-   927 cult problems have arisen—the very ones that We are asking you to examine calmly and with full liberty of mind—then doesn't the thorough-going study to which We have just alluded serve as a harbinger of solutions to some problems that at the present day seem so difficult to solve? We like to think so and to hope so.

928   We wanted to have the basis for your researches enlarged, to have the various currents of theological thought better represented there, to make it possible for the countries that face serious difficulties on the sociological plane to have their voices heard among you, and to have lay people, and married couples in particular, have qualified representatives in such a serious undertaking.

929   Now you are engaged in a new and decisive stage of your labors. We are confident that you will be able to carry them through to the end courageously. We told you just a while ago: the question is too important, the uncertainties of some people too painful, for you not to feel urged on by the demands of charity toward all those to whom We owe an answer. Your labors will, We hope, furnish Us with the elements of that answer.

930   And so apply yourselves wholeheartedly to your task, let whatever has to ripen, ripen, but listen to the anguished cry of many souls and work diligently, without any concern for criticism or difficulties. You are in the service of the Church and of the Vicar of Jesus Christ, who calls down enlightenment from on high upon your Commission and paternally blesses you, your families, and your labors.

GAUDIUM ET SPES
Excerpt from the Pastoral Constitution
on the Church in the Modern World
December 7, 1965

Chapter I

The Dignity of the Human Person

Man as Made in God's Image

According to the almost unanimous opinion of believers and unbelievers alike, all things on earth should be related to man as their center and crown.

But what is man? About himself he has expressed, and 932 continues to express, many divergent and even contradictory opinions. In these he often exalts himself as the absolute measure of all things or debases himself to the point of despair. The result is doubt and anxiety.

The Church understands these problems. Endowed with 933 light from God, she can offer solutions to them so that man's true situation can be portrayed and his defects explained, while at the same time his dignity and destiny are just acknowledged.

For sacred Scripture teaches that man was created "to the 934 image of God," is capable of knowing and loving his Creator, and was appointed by Him as master of all earthly creatures that he might subdue them and use them to God's glory. "What is man that thou art mindful of him or the son of man that thou visitest him? Thou hast made him a little less than the angels, thou hast crowned him with glory and honor: thou hast set him over the works of thy hands, thou hast subjected all things under his feet" (Ps. 8:5-6).

935   But God did not create man as a solitary. For from the beginning "male and female he created them" (Gen. 1:27). Their companionship produces the primary form of interpersonal communion. For by his innermost nature man is a social being, and unless he relates himself to others he can neither live nor develop his potential.

936   Therefore, as we read elsewhere in holy Scripture, God saw "all the things that he had made, and they were very good" (Gen. 1:31).

Sin

937   13. Although he was made by God in a state of holiness, from the very dawn of history man abused his liberty, at the urging of personified Evil. Man set himself against God and sought to find fulfillment apart from God. Although he knew God, he did not glorify Him as God, but his senseless mind was darkened and he served the creature rather than the Creator.

938   What divine revelation makes known to us agrees with experience. Examining his heart, man finds that he has inclinations toward evil too, and is engulfed by manifold ills which cannot come from his good Creator. Often refusing to acknowledge God as his beginning, man has disrupted also his proper relationship to his own ultimate goal. At the same time he became out of harmony with himself, with others, and with all created things.

939   Therefore man is split within himself. As a result, all of human life, whether individual or collective, shows itself to be a dramatic struggle between good and evil, between light and darkness. Indeed, man finds that by himself he is incapable of battling the assults of evil successfully, so that everyone feels as though he is bound by chains.

940   But the Lord Himself came to free and strengthen man, renewing him inwardly and casting out that prince of this world (c. Jn. 12:31) who held him in bondage of sin. For sin has diminished man, blocking his path to fulfillment.

941   The call to grandeur and the depths of misery are both a part of human experience. They find their ultimate and simultaneous explanation in the light of God's revelation.

The Make-Up of Man

14. Though made of body and soul, man is one. Through 942
his bodily composition he gathers to himself the elements of
the material world. Thus they reach their crown through him,
and through him raise their voice in free praise of the Creator.

For this reason man is not allowd to despise his bodily life. 943
Rather, he is obliged to regard his body as good and honorable
since God has created it and will raise it up on the last day.
Nevertheless, wounded by sin, man experiences rebellious
stirrings in his body. But the very dignity of man postulates
that man glorify God in his body and forbid it to serve the
evil inclinations of his heart.

Now, man is not wrong when he regards himself as superior 944
to bodily concerns, and as more than a speck of nature or a
nameless constituent of the city of man. For by his interior
qualities he outstrips the whole sum of mere things. He
attains to these inward depths whenever he enters into his
own heart. God, who probes the heart, awaits him there.
There he discerns his proper destiny beneath the eyes of God.
Thus, when man recognizes in himself a spiritual and immortal soul, he is not being mocked by a deceptive fantasy spring-
ing from mere physical or social influences. On the contrary
he is getting to the depths of the very truth of the manner.

The Dignity of the Mind; Truth; Wisdom

15. Man judges rightly that by his intellect he surpasses the 945
material universe, for he shares in the light of the divine mind.
By relentlessly employing his talents through the ages, he has
indeed made progress in the practical sciences, teachnology,
and the liberal arts. In our times he has won superlative victo-
ries, especially in his probing of the material world and in
subjecting it to himself.

Still he has always searched for more penetrating truths, 946
and finds them. For his intelligence is not confined to ob-
servable data alone. It can with genuine certitude attain to

reality itself as knowable, though in consequence of sin that certitude is partly obscured and weakened.

947   The intellectual nature of the human person is perfected by wisdom and needs to be. For wisdom gently attracts the mind of man to a quest and a love for what is true and good. Steeped in wisdom, man passes through visible realities to those which are unseen.

948   Our era needs such wisdom more than bygone ages if the discoveries made by man are to be further humanized. For the future of the world stands in peril unless wiser men are forthcoming. It should also be pointed out that many nations, poorer in economic goods, are quite rich in wisdom and can offer noteworthy advantages to others.

949   It is, finally, through the gift of the Holy Spirit that man comes by faith to the contemplation and appreciation of the divine plan.

The Dignity of the Moral Conscience

950   16. In the depths of his conscience, man detects a law which he does not impose upon himself, but which holds him to obedience. Always summoning him to love good and avoid evil, the voice of conscience can when necessary speak to his heart more specifically: do this, shun that. For man has in his heart a law written by God. To obey it is the very dignity of man, according to it he will be judged.

951   Conscience is the most secret core and sanctuary of a man. There he is alone with God, whose voice echoes in his depths. In a wonderful manner conscience reveals that law which is fulfilled by love of God and neighbor. In fidelity to conscience, Christians are joined with the rest of men in the search for truth, and for the genuine solution to the numerous problems which arise in the life of individuals and from social relationships. Hence the more that a correct conscience holds sway, the more persons and groups turn aside from blind choice and strive to be guided by objective norms of morality.

952   Conscience frequently errs from invisible ignorance without losing its dignity. The same cannot be said of man who cares but little for truth and goodness, or of a conscience

which by degrees grows practically sightless as a result of habitual sin.

The Excellence of Liberty

17. Only in freedom can man direct himself toward goodness. Our contemporaries make much of this freedom and pursue it eagerly, and rightly so, to be sure. Often, however, they foster it perversely as a license for doing whatever pleases them, even if it is evil.

953

For its part, authentic freedom is an exceptional sign of the divine image within man. For God has willed that man be left "in the hand of his own counsel" so that he can seek his Creator spontaneously, and come freely to utter and blissful perfection through loyalty to Him. Hence man's dignity demands that he act according to a knowing and free choice. Such a choice is personally motivated and prompted from within. It does not result from blind internal impulse nor from mere external pressure.

954

Man achieves such dignity when, emancipating himself from all captivity to passion, he pursues his goal in spontaneous choice of what is good, and procures for himself, through effective and skillful action, apt means to that end. Since man's freedom has been damaged by sin, only by the help of God's grace can he bring such a relationship with God into full flower. Before the judgment seat of God each man must render an account of his own life, whether he had done good or evil.

955

The Mystery of Death

18. It is in the face of death that the riddle of human existence becomes most acute. Not only is man tormented by pain and by the advancing deterioration of his body, but even more so by a dread of perpetual extinction. He rightly follows the intuition of his heart when he abhors and repudiates the absolute ruin and total disappearance of his own person.

956

Man rebels against death because he bears in himself an eternal seed which cannot be reduced to sheer matter. All the

957

endeavors of technology, though useful in the extreme, cannot calm his anxiety. For a prolongation of biological life is unable to satisfy that desire for a higher life which is inescapably lodged in his breast.

958   Although the mystery of death utterly beggars the imagination, the Church has been taught by divine revelation, and herself firmly teaches, that man has been created by God for a blissful purpose beyond the reach of earthly misery. In addition, that bodily death from which man would have been immune had he not sinned will be vanquished, according to the Christian faith, when man who was ruined by his own doing is restored to wholeness by an almighty and merciful Savior.

959   For God has called man and still calls him so that with his entire being he might be joined to Him in an endless sharing of a divine life beyond all corruption. Christ won this victory when He rose to life, since by His death He freed man from death. Hence to every thoughtful man a solidly established faith provides the answer to his anxiety about what the future holds for him. At the same time faith gives him the power to be united in Christ with his loved ones who have already been snatched away by death. Faith arouses the hope that they have found true life with God.

Part II

Some Problems of Special Urgency

Preface

960   46. This council has set forth the dignity of the human person and the work which men have been destined to undertake throughout the world both as individuals and as members of society. There are a number of particularly urgent needs characterizing the present age, needs which go to the roots of the human race. To a consideration of these in the light of the gospel and of human experience, the Council would now direct the attention of all.

961   Of the many subjects arousing universal concern today, it may be helpful to concentrate on these: marriage and the family, human culture, life in its economic, social, and po-

litical dimensions, the bonds between the family of nations, and peace. On each of these may there shine the radiant ideals proclaimed by Christ. By these ideals may Christians be led, and all mankind enlightened, as they search for answers to questions of such complexity.

Chapter I

Fostering the Nobility of Marriage and the Family

Marriage and Family in the Modern World

47. The well-being of the individual person and of human and Christian society is intimately linked with the healthy condition of that community produced by marriage and family. Hence Christians and all men who hold this community in high esteem sincerely rejoice in the various ways by which men today find help in fostering this community of love and perfecting its life, and by which spouses and parents are assisted in their lofty calling. Those who rejoice in such aids look for additional benefits from them and labor to bring them about.   962

Yet the excellence of this institution is not everywhere reflected with equal brilliance. For polygamy, the plague of divorce, so-called free love, and other disfigurements have an obscuring effect. In addition, married love is too often profaned by excessive self-love, the worship of pleasure, and illicit practices against human generation. Moreover, serious disturbances are caused in families by modern economic conditions, by influences at once social and psychological, and by the demands of civil society. Finally, in certain parts of the world problems resulting from population growth are generating concern.   963

All these situations have produced anxious consciences. Yet, the power and strength of the institution of marriage and family can also be seen in the fact that time and again, despite the difficulties produced, the profound changes in modern society reveal the true character of this institution in one way or another.   964

Therefore, by presenting certain key points of Church doctrine in a clearer light, this council wishes to offer guidance   965 and support to those Christians and other men who are trying to keep sacred and to foster the natural dignity of the married state and its superlative value.

The Sanctity of Marriage and the Family

966   48. The intimate partnership of married life and love has been established by the Creator and qualified by His laws. It is rooted in the conjugal covenant of irrevocable personal consent. Hence, by that human act whereby spouses mutually bestow and accept each other, a relationship arises which by divine will and in the eyes of society too is a lasting one. For the good of the spouses and their offspring as well as of society, the existence of this sacred bond no longer depends on human decisions alone.

967   For God Himself is the author of matrimony, endowed as it is with various benefits and purposes. All of these have a very decisive bearing on the continuation of the human race, on the personal development and eternal destiny of the individual members of a family, and on the dignity, stability, peace, and prosperity of the family itself and of human society as a whole. By their very nature, the institution of matrimony itself and conjugal love are ordained for the procreation and education of children, and find in them their ultimate crown.

968   Thus a man and a woman, who by the marriage covenant of conjugal love "are no longer two, but one flesh" (Mt. 19:6), render mutual help and service to each other through an intimate union of their persons and of their actions. Through this union they experience the meaning of their oneness and attain to it with growing perfection day by day. As a mutual gift of two persons, this intimate union, as well as the good of the children, imposes total fidelity on the spouses and argues for an unbreakable oneness between them.

969   Christ the Lord abundantly blessed this many-faceted love, welling up as it does from the fountain of divine love and structured as it is on the model of His union with the Church. For as God of old made Himself present to His people through a covenant of love and fidelity, so now the Savior of men and the Spouse of the Church comes into the lives of married Christians through the sacrament of matrimony. He abides

with them thereafter so that, just as He loved the Church and handed Himself over on her behalf, the spouses may love each other with perpetual fidelity through mutual self-bestowal.

Authentic married love is caught up into divine love and is governed and enriched by Christ's redeeming power and the saving activity of the Church. Thus this love can lead the spouses to God with powerful effect and can aid and strengthen them in the sublime office of being a father or a mother.   970

For this reason, Christian spouses have a special sacrament by which they are fortified and receive a kind of consecration in the duties and dignity of their state. By virtue of this sacrament, as spouses fulfill their conjugal and family obligations, they are penetrated with the spirit of Christ. This spirit suffuses their whole lives with faith, hope and charity. Thus they increasingly advance their own perfection, as well as their mutual sanctification, and hence contribute jointly to the glory of God.   971

As a result, with their parents leading the way by example and family prayer, children and indeed everyone gathered around the family hearth will find a readier path to human maturity, salvation, and holiness. Graced with the dignity and office of fatherhood and motherhood, parents will energetically acquit themselves of a duty which devolves primarily on them, namely education, and especially religious education.   972

As living members of the family, children contribute in their own way to making their parents holy. For they will respond to the kindness of their parents with sentiments of gratitude, with love and trust. They will stand by them as children should when hardships overtake their parents and old age brings its loneliness. Widowhood, accepted bravely as a continuation of the marriage vocation, will be esteemed by all. Families will share their spiritual riches generously with other families too. Thus the Christian family, which springs from marriage as a reflection of the loving covenant uniting Christ with the Church, as a participation in that covenant, will manifest to all men the Savior's living presence in the world, and the genuine nature of the Church. This the family will do by the mutual love of the spouses, by their generous   973 fruitfulness, their solidarity and faithfulness, and by the loving way in which all members of the family work together.

Conjugal Love

974   49. The biblical Word of God several times urges the betrothal and the married to nourish and develop their wedlock by pure conjugal love and undivided affection. Many men of our own age also highly regard true love between husband and wife as it manifests itself in a variety of ways depending on the worthy customs of various peoples and times.

975   This love is an eminently human one since it is directed from one person to another through an affection of the will. It involves the good of the whole person. Therefore it can enrich the expressions of body and mind with a unique dignity, ennobling these expressions as special ingredients and signs of the friendship distinctive of marriage. This love the Lord has judged worthy of special gifts, healing, perfecting, and exalting gifts of grace and of charity.

976   Such love, merging the human with the divine, leads the spouses to a free and mutual gift of themselves, a gift proving itself by gentle affection and by deed. Such love pervades the whole of their lives. Indeed, by its generous activity it grows better and grows greater. Therefore it far excels mere erotic inclination, which, selfishly pursued, soon enough fades wretchedly away.

977   This love is uniquely expressed and perfected through the marital act. The actions within marriage by which the couple are united intimately and chastely are noble and worthy ones. Expressed in a manner which is truly human, these actions signify and promote that mutual self-giving by which spouses enrich each other with a joyful and a thankful will.

978   Sealed by mutual faithfulness and hallowed above all by Christ's sacrament, this love remains steadfastly true in body and in mind, in bright days or dark. It will never be profaned by adultery or divorce. Firmly established by the Lord, the unity of marriage will radiate from the equal personal dignity of wife and husband, a dignity acknowledged by mutual and total love.

The steady fulfillment of the duties of this Christian voca-   979
tion demands notable virtue. For this reason, strengthened by
grace for holiness of life, the couple will painstakingly cultivate and pray for constancy of love, largeheartedness, and the
spirit of sacrifice.

Authentic conjugal love will be more highly prized, and   980
wholesome public opinion created regarding it, if Christian
couples give outstanding witness to faithfulness and harmony
in that same love, and to their concern for educating their
children, also, if they do their part in bringing about the
needed cultural, psychological, and social renewal on behalf
of marriage and the family.

Especially in the heart of their own families, young people   981
should be aptly and seasonably instructed about the dignity,
duty, and expression of married love. Trained thus in the
cultivation of chastity, they will be able at a suitable age to
enter a marriage of their own after an honorable courtship.

The Fruitfulness of Marriage

50. Marriage and conjugal love are by their nature ordained   982
toward the begetting and educating of children. Children are
really the supreme gift of marriage and contribute very substantially to the welfare of their parents. The God Himself
who said, "It is not good for man to be alone" (Gen. 2:18)
and "who made man from the beginning male and female"
(Mt. 19:4), wished to share with man a certain special participation in His own creative work. Thus He blessed male
and female, saying: "Increase and multiply" (Gen. 1:28).

Hence, while not making the other purposes of matrimony   983
of less account, the true practice of conjugal love, and the
whole meaning of the family life which results from it, have
this aim: that the couple be ready with stout hearts to
cooperate with the love of the Creator and the Savior, who
through them will enlarge and enrich His own family day by
day.

Parents should regard as their proper mission the task of   984
transmitting human life and educating those to whom it has
been transmitted. They should realize that they are thereby
cooperators with the love of God the Creator, and are, so to

speak, the interpreters of that love. Thus they will fulfill their task with human and Christian responsibility. With docile reverence toward God, they will come to the right decision by common counsel and effort.

985   They will thoughtfully take into account both their own welfare and that of their children, those already born and those which may be foreseen. For this accounting they will reckon with both the material and the spiritual conditions of the times as well as of their state in life. Finally, they will consult the interests of the family group, of temporal society, and of the Church herself.

986   The parents themselves should ultimately make this judgment, in the sight of God. But in their manner of acting, spouses should be aware that they cannot proceed arbitrarily. They must always be governed according to a conscience dutifully conformed to the divine law itself, and should be submissive toward the Church's teaching office, which authentically interprets the law in the light of the gospel. That divine law reveals and protects the integral meaning of conjugal love, and impels it toward a truly human fulfillment.

987   Thus trusting in divine Providence and refining the spirit of sacrifice, married Christians glorify the Creator and strive toward fulfillment in Christ when, with a generous human and Christian sense of responsibility, they acquit themselves of the duty to procreate. Among the couples who fulfill their God-given task in this way, those merit special mention who with wise and common deliberation, and with a gallant heart, undertake to bring up suitably even a relatively large family.

988   Marriage to be sure is not instituted solely for procreation. Rather, its very nature as an unbreakable compact between persons, and the welfare of the children, both demand that the mutual love of the spouses, too, be embodied in a rightly ordered manner, that it grow and ripen. Therefore, marriage persists as a whole manner and communion of life, and maintains its value and indissolubility, even when offspring are lacking—despite, rather often, the very intense desire of the couple.

Harmonizing Conjugal Love with Respect for Human Life

51. This Council realizes that certain modern conditions   989
often keep couples from arranging their married lives harmoniously, and that they find themselves in circumstances where
at least temporarily the size of their family should not be
increased. As a result, the faithful exercise of love and the full
intimacy of married life is broken off, it is not safe for its
faithfulness to be imperiled and its quality of fruitfulness
ruined. For then the upbringing of the children and courage
to accept new ones are both endangered.

To these problems there are those who presume to offer   990
dishonorable solutions. Indeed, they do not recoil from the
taking of life. But the Church issues the reminder that a true
contradiction cannot exist between the divine laws pertaining
to the transmission of life and those pertaining to the fostering
of authentic conjugal love.

For God, the Lord of life, has conferred on men the sur-   991
passing ministry of safeguarding life—a ministry which must
be fulfilled in a manner which is worthy of man. Therefore
from the moment of its conception life must be guarded with
the greatest care, while abortion and infanticide are unspeakable crimes. The sexual characteristics of man and the human
faculty of reproduction wonderfully exceed the dispositions
of lower forms of life. Hence the acts themselves which are
proper to conjugal love and which are exercised in accord
with genuine human dignity must be honored with great
reverence.

Therefore when there is question of harmonizing conjugal   992
love with the responsible transmission of life, the moral aspect
of any procedure does not depend solely on sincere intentions
or on an evaluation of motives. It must be determined by
objective standards. These, based on the nature of the human
person and his acts, preserve the full sense of mutual self-
giving and human procreation in the context of true love.
Such a goal cannot be achieved unless the virtue of conjugal
chastity is sincerely practiced. Relying on these principles,
sons of the Church may not undertake methods of regulating
procreation which are found blameworthy by the teaching
authority of the Church in its unfolding of the divine law.

993   Everyone should be persuaded that human life and the task
of transmitting it are not realities bound up with this world
alone. Hence they cannot be measured or perceived only in
terms of it, but always have a bearing on the eternal destiny
of men.

All Must Promote the Good Estate of Marriage and the Family

994   52. The family is a kind of school of deeper humanity. But
if it is to achieve the full flowering of its life and mission, it
needs the kindly communion of minds and the joint deliberation of spouses, as well as the painstaking cooperation of
parents in the education of their children. The active presence of the father is highly beneficial to their formation. The
children, especially the younger among them, need the care of
their mother at home. This domestic role of hers must be
safely preserved, though the legitimate social progress of
women should not be underrated on that account.

995   Children should be so educated that as adults they can,
with a mature sense of responsibility, follow their vocation,
including a religious one, and choose their state of life. If
they marry, they can thereby establish their family in favorable moral, social, and economic conditions. Parents or guardians should by prudent advice provide guidance to their young
with respect to founding a family, and the young ought to
listen gladly. At the same time no pressure, direct or indirect,
should be put on the young to make them enter marriage or
choose a specific partner.

996   Thus the family is the foundation of society. In it the various generations come together and help one another to grow
wiser and to harmonize personal rights with the other requirements of social life. All those, therefore, who exercise influence over communities and social groups should work ef-
ficiently for the welfare of marriage and the family.

997   Public authority should regard it as a sacred duty to recognize, protect, and promote their authentic nature, to shield
public morality, and to favor the prosperity of domestic life.
The right of parents to beget and educate their children in
the bosom of the family must be safeguarded. Children, too,
who unhappily lack the blessing of a family should be pro-

tected by prudent legislation and various undertakings, and provided with the help they need.

Redeeming the present time, and distinguishing eternal realities from their hanging expressions, Christians should actively promote the values of marriage and the family, both by the example of their own lives and by cooperation with other men of good will. Thus when difficulties arise, Christians will provide, on behalf of family life, those necessities and helps which are suitably modern. To this end, the Christian instincts of the faithful, the upright moral consciences of men, and the wisdom and experience of persons versed in the sacred sciences will have much to contribute.   998

Those, too, who are skilled in other sciences, notably the medical, biological, social, and psychological, can considerably advance the welfare of marriage and the family, along with peace of conscience, if by pooling their efforts they labor to explain more thoroughly the various conditions favoring a proper regulation of births.   999

It devolves on priests duly trained about family matters to nurture the vocation of spouses by a variety of pastoral means, by preaching God's Word, by liturgical worship, and by other spiritual aids to conjugal and family life; to sustain them sympathetically and patiently in difficulties, and to make them courageous through love. Thus families which are truly noble will be formed.   1000

Various organizations, especially family associations, should try by their programs of instruction and action to strengthen young people and spouses themselves, particularly those recently wed, and to train them for family, social, and apostolic life.   1001

Finally, let the spouses themselves, made to the image of the living God and enjoying the authentic dignity of persons, be joined to one another in equal affection, harmony of mind, and the work of mutual sanctification. Thus they will follow Christ who is the principle of life. Thus, too, by the joys and sacrifices of their vocation and through their faithful love, married people will become witnesses of the mystery of that love which the Lord revealed to the world by His dying and His rising up to life again.   1002

Second Vatican Council
Message to Women
December 8, 1965

(Read by Leon Cardinal Duval of Algiers, assisted by Julius Cardinal Doepfner of Munich and Raul Cardinal Silva of Santiago [Chile].)

And now it is to you that we address ourselves, women of all states—girls, wives, mothers, and widows, to you also, consecrated virgins and women living alone—you constitute half of the immense human family. As you know, the Church is proud to have glorified and liberated woman, and in the course of the centuries, in diversity of characters, to have brought into relief her basic equality with man. But the hour is coming, in fact has come, when the vocation of woman is being achieved in its fullness, the hour in which woman acquires in the world an influence, an effect, and a power never hitherto achieved. That is why, at this moment when the human race is undergoing so deep a transformation, women impregnated with the spirit of the gospel can do much to aid mankind in not falling.

1004   You women have always had as your lot the protection of the home, the love of beginnings, and an understanding of cradles. You are present in the mystery of a life beginning. You offer consolation in the departure of death. Our technology runs the risk of becoming inhuman. Reconcile men with life and above all, we beseech you, watch carefully over the future of our race. Hold back the hand of man who, in a moment of folly, might attempt to destroy human civilization.

Wives, mothers of families, the first educators of the human race in the intimacy of the family circle, pass on to your sons and your daughters the traditions of your fathers at the same time that you prepare them for an unsearchable future. Always remember that by her children a mother belongs to that future which perhaps she will not see.   1005

And you, women living alone, realize what you can accomplish through your dedicated vocation. Society is appealing to you on all sides. Not even families can live without the help of those who have no families. Especially you, consecrated virgins, in a world where egosim and the search for pleasure would become law, be the guardians of purity, unselfishness, and piety. Jesus, who has given to conjugal love all its plentitudes, has also exalted the renouncement of human love when this is for the sake of divine love and for the service of all.   1006

Lastly, women in trial, who stand upright at the foot of the cross like Mary, you who so often in history have given to men the strength to battle unto the very end and to give witness to the point of martyrdom, aid them now still once more to retain courage in their great undertakings, while at the same time maintaining patience and an esteem for humble beginnings.   1007

Women, you who know how to make truth sweet, tender, and accessible, make it your task to bring the spirit of this Council into institutions, schools, homes, and daily life. Women of the entire universe, whether Christian or non-believeing, you to whom life is entrusted at this grave moment in history, it is for you to save the peace of the world.   1008

Address of Pope Paul VI
to Participants in the 13th National Congress
of the Italian Women's Center
February 12, 1966

It gives us great satisfaction and pleasure to extend Our greetings to the 13th National Congress of the Italian Women's Center, and We are glad to have an opportunity to offer some words of encouragement and praise to the fine people who are taking part in it. From the very beginning We have been acquainted with the aims and purposes, the activities, and the achievements of the federated movement. Its lofty and genuinely Christian inspiration and the breadth and openness of its organizational framework have won it the well-deserved confidence of large numbers of Italian women. We also know of the practical and intelligent work it is carrying on both in the field of training women for a knowledgeable participation in public life and in the field of welfare.

1010   Therefore We feel an obligation to express Our gratitude to all the men and women who have contributed to this work with their support, advice, activity, and especially their persevering and loyal dedication (and We are thinking of your wonderful officers in particular). We want once again to express a hope that the program represented and promoted by the Italian Women's Center will be frankly adopted by all Italian women, for it is up to them to reassert the validity of Christianity's moral and spiritual values and of our people's civilized tradition in modern life, as well as to make woman's influence in society intelligent, positive and strong in nature.

We have been encouraged to formulate these evaluations 1011
and wishes by the program of your Congress. We wish it the
heartiest success, feeling sure that the sponsors and the
speakers who have been so carefully chosen for their competence will make everyone taking part in it aware of its seriousness, spirituality, and practicality.

Because of this confidence, We won't comment on your 1012
work. Instead, We will pause over one point on your program,
the question of the family, and take the liberty of dwelling
on this subject for a few moments, recalling what the Ecumenical Council has laid down in the form of a synthesis on
this subject. An exhaustive treatment of the matter was not
possible within the Council itself, especially as far as the serious and complicated problem of the principles dealing with
birth are concerned. It still isn't possible to do away with the
reservation that We expressed in Our talk in June, 1964.
But in the meantime, with the expectation of being able to
offer more detailed teachings later on, We feel it would be a
good idea for Us to speak a few words of pastoral encouragement in this regard.

Our thoughts turn now in a special way to the Christian 1013
spouses and parents who have for the first time in the history
of the Church been admitted to active participation in an
ecumenical council, as spokesmen and representatives of all
the spouses and parents in the Church, indeed of all the families in the world.

Your presence at the Council, beloved children, means 1014
that today's Church is directing a special gaze filled with love
and concern toward families and their problems. It has always
followed the example of its divine Founder in blessing the
family and human love, but nowadays it is more aware than
ever that mankind's physical and moral life and even the real
spread of the kingdom of God depend on the family's health
and its full sharing in the spiritual life.

The Church is also acquainted with the dangers that threat- 1015
en the family's solidity and moral health, and with the difficulties that are trying to undermine them. For this reason
the Council Fathers devoted special attention to that chapter
of the Pastoral Constitution on the Church in the Modern

World which deals with marriage and the family and with their problems.

1016   As We were saying, not all the problems that Christian married people want answered and are waiting to hear about could be treated. Some of them, because of their complexity and delicacy, couldn't very well be discussed in such a large assembly. Others called for and still call for more profound study. For this purpose, as you know, a special papal commission has been set up with the task of going into these problems more deeply from all points of view—scientific, historical, sociological and doctrinal—while making abundant use of the advice of bishops and experts.

1017   We invite you to await the results of these studies and to accompany them with your prayers. The magisterium of the Church cannot propose moral norms unless it is sure that it is interpreting God's will. In reaching this certitude, the Church is not excused from carrying out research nor from examining all the many questions proposed for its consideration from every corner of the world. Sometimes these operations take a long time and are anything but easy.

1018   Meanwhile, the Council has approved a text on this subject and We, in full agreement with the Council Fathers, have promulgated it. We are speaking of the first chapter of the second part of the pastoral Constitution on the Church in the Modern World, which is devoted specifically to a consideration of the great dignity that the Church attributes to marriage and the family. We would like to draw out of it some basic principles of Church doctrine which can throw some light on the course that has to be followed for the good of the family and of all its members. These can be considered the Council's message to the married couples and families of the world and to Christian married people in particular. We will give you the mission of making everyone acquainted with them and of being their first loyal spokesmen through your words and the example you give by your life.

1019   Marriage and the family are not the work of man alone, not some kind of human construction produced by historical and environmental conditions and governed by them in its innermost being, and as changeable as they are. Mar-

riage and the family come from God. They are the work
of God and they correspond to an essential plan that He Himself has traced out and that rises above the changing circumstances of the times, remaining unchanged throughout all
of them. It is God who wants to use marriage and the family
to make men sharers in His most lofty prerogatives: His
love for men and His power to bring life into being. Hence
marriage and the family have a transcendent relationship to
God, they come from Him and they are ordained to Him.
Families are founded on earth and live on earth, but they are
destined to get together once again in heaven.

Any doctrine or concept that does not pay sufficient at-   1020
tention to this essential relationship of marriage and the family to their divine origin and to a destiny which transcends
human experience, would not be grasping the most profound
truth about them and would not be able to find the correct
way to solve their problems.

God has made use of marriage and the family to wisely   1021
unite two of the greatest elements in human existence: the
mission of transmitting life and the legitimate mutual love of
man and woman, by which they are called to complete each
other in a reciprocal giving of themselves that is not just
physical but above all spiritual. Or to put it better, God
wanted to make married people share in His love—the personal love that He has for each of them, by means of which
He calls them to help each other and to give themselves to
each other to achieve the fullness of their personal lives,
and the love that He bears toward mankind and all His sons,
by means of which He wants the sons of men to multiply
so that they may share in His life and in His eternal happiness.

Marriage is born of God's paternal, creative love and it   1022
finds the basic norm for its moral value in a human love corresponding to God's plan and His will: in the mutual love
of the partners, by which each one pledges himself wholly
to helping the other be what God wants him to be, in the desire they share to faithfully express the love of God, Creator
and Father, by generating new lives. "In carrying out the
office of transmitting life and of raising those to whom it has
been transmitted—and this should be regarded as their own

special mission—married couples ought to realize that they are cooperating with the love of God and serving, in a sense, as His spokesmen."[1]

1023   If they look at things in this light, married couples will regard the laws of unity, indissolubility and mutual fidelity (which, when love is missing, can seem to be just a burden) as normal and necessary. They will discover unsuspected wellsprings of generosity, wisdom, and strength enabling them to give life to others.

1024   This God-given mission of serving as spokesmen for His creative and paternal love demands of married couples today an increased awareness of their natural and Christian responsibility in transmitting life.

1025   Present-day living conditions, which are different in many ways from those of times past and vary from one country to another, certainly do not justify pride, selfishness, or a timid lack of trust in God in the fulfillment of this primary mission assigned to married couples. They call rather for a mature decision that takes into account all aspects of seeking the greater good, especially the responsibilities in raising children.

1026   Here again we have a problem that God willed to have regulated by laws that would come from Him—the author of marriage and the family—and be inscribed in the very nature and the manifold purpose of these divine institutions. Hence Christian spouses will find in the duty of charity the light to solve their personal problems in this regard. In the observance of the divine law, God has entrusted the task and the joy of transmitting life to their responsible decision and no one else can take their place or force their wills. But they too must look to a charity that is truly full and universal—charity, first of all, toward God, whose glory and the spread of whose kingdom they must desire, secondly, charity toward their children, putting into action the principle that "charity. . . does not seek its own interest"[2]; and mutual charity, by means of which each seeks the good of the other and tries to anticipate the other's good desires rather than impose his own will. This attitude of charity, enlightened by the law of God, will make it easier to find the way to truth, which means to a correct solution of their problem: the one corresponding to God's will for them, the one they will not regret at the end of their lives, and the one whose fruits they will enjoy for all eternity.

May the Second Vatican Council that has just ended radiate this spirit of generosity among Christian married couples so as to expand the new people of God. May it also stir up in them a desire to have children to offer to God in the priesthood and the religious life, for the salvation and the service of their brethren and for His greater glory. May they always remember that the spread of God's kingdom and the Church's capability of penetrating mankind to bring about its eternal and terrestrial salvation are entrusted to their generosity too.   1027

The law of charity toward God, towards one's spouse and toward one's children, along with the responsibilities that follow upon it, gives a clear indication that Christian marriage and family life call for a moral commitment. This is not an easy road of Christian life, even though the most common, the one most of the children of God are called upon to travel. Instead it is a long journey toward sanctification, which is nourished on the joys and sacrifices of every day, of a life that is clearly more normal when it is guided by God's law and bathed in love.   1028

But Christian married couples know too that they are never alone. The Council reminds them: "In the sacrament of Matrimony, the Saviour of men and Spouse of the Church comes to married people. He stays with them so that just as He has loved the Church and has given Himself for her, so too the spouses may love each other with perpetual fidelity. Legitimate married love is taken up into divine love. It is governed and enriched by Christ's redemptive power and by the salvific work of the Church, so that the spouses may be effectively led toward God and may be helped and strengthened in their sublime mission of being fathers and mothers."[3]   1029

We entrust to you, Christian married people and parents, and to the many undertakings in the Church that are today promoting the spirituality of married life, the task of studying every more deeply the riches of the sacrament of matrimony and its repercussions on the life of married couples, families and society. We entrust to you the task of helping all Christian couples to become aware of the gift they have received.   1030

1031   Within the framework of this compelling moral commitment and of the grandeur of the sacramental gift of matrimony, the Council reminds married Christians of another virtue they ought to cultivate. It is the virtue of conjugal chastity, which was traced out in sharp lines by His Holiness Pius XI and recalled by Pius XII.

1032   This isn't a new or inhuman law. It is the doctrine of rectitude and wisdom that the Church has always taught under God's enlightenment, and that indissolubly binds legitimate expressions of married love to the service of God in the mission of transmitting life derived from Him. It is the doctrine that has ennobled and sanctified Christian married love, purifying it from the selfishness of the flesh and the pride of the spirit, from a superficial pursuit of the ephemeral things of this world in preference to giving oneself to something eternal. It is the doctrine and the virtue that has, in the course of the centuries, redeemed womankind from the slavery of a duty undergone by force and with humiliation; and it has refined the spouses' sense of mutual respect and mutual esteem.

1033   May married couples grasp what moral strength is stirred up and what spiritual wealth fed by the virtue of purity in married life when it is faithfully observed in accordance with God's laws. Serenity, peace, greatness of soul, an unsullied spirit! May they grasp in particular the inestimable value it possesses to prepare them for their task as educators! It is just as true today as it was in the past and will always be, that children's most profound training in loyalty to God is found in the lives of their parents; while parents find in obedience to God an assurance of the grace they need to carry out their task of raising children as Christians, which is so difficult today.

1034   Let them not be discouraged by the difficulties they may encounter, nor abandon their loyalty to the Church because of this. Rather, confidently trusting in the strength of the divine grace which they will constantly ask for in their prayers, let them raise themselves up to the loftiness of the divine ideal instead of reducing the divine law to the measure of their own wills. And let them renew their good resolutions each day and serenely begin their own journey once again—a jour-

that has as its goal eternal life with God and as its reward here on earth a more profound love that brings with it greater happiness. "Blessed are the pure of heart for they shall see God."[4]

The whole People of God has prayed insistently these past few years for a new Pentecost of the Church, which we hope God in His mercy will be bound to give to His Church. The new Pentecost cannot possibly be a time of greater moral ease, but instead one of greater commitment for everyone, Christian married people included. "Enter through the narrow gate. . .the gate is narrow and the road is strait that leads to life."[5]   1035

These words of Ours are intended first of all for Christian couples, but We would like to extend them to all married people. We hope that all the sons of the Church will listen to the voice of their Mother. And We hope that, with their generosity, they will win for the people of God and for all men the light needed for a full understanding of God's laws governing matrimony, and that they will obtain for the Church the light it needs to solve, in keeping with God's will, the difficulties and problems still under study.   1036

With this in mind We ask Christian couples to have the spirit of faith, the trust in God and love for Him, for each other and for their children, that will make them a "sign" in the world of the holiness of the Church, faithful and glorious spouse of Christ the Lord "without stain and without defect. . . , but holy and spotless."[6]   1037

We utter these words before this fine gathering of the Italian Women's Center, which lists among its activities and achievements that of honoring, aiding, instructing and defending the family and particularly the woman of the family. A woman finds in her family not just a greater share of cares and concerns but also her most natural and loving mission, her best recognized dignity, her surest guarantee of salvation and of reward. "Her salvation," says St. Paul, "will be in motherhood, provided that she remains modest and holy in faith and charity."[7]   1038

It is up to you, beloved daughters of the Italian Women's Center, and to your fine chaplains and teachers to accept these words and to spread them with Our Apostolic Blessing.   1039

The Theological Report of the Papal Commission on Birth Control
June 26, 1966

Introduction

The Pastoral Constitution on the Church in the Modern World (*Gaudium et Spes*) has not answered all aspects of the question of responsible parenthood. To those problems as yet unresolved, a response is to be given in what follows. This response, however, can only be understood if it is grasped in an integrated way within the universal concept of salvation history.

1041   In creating the world God gave man the power and the duty to form the world in spirit and freedom and, through his creative capacity, to actuate his own personal nature. In his Word, God himself, as the first efficient cause of the whole evolution of the world and of man, is present and active in history. The story of God and of man, therefore, should be seen as one of shared work. And it should be seen that man's tremendous progress in the control of matter by technical means, and the universal and total "intercommunication" that has been achieved, correspond perfectly to the divine decrees.[1]

1042   In the fullness of time the Word of the eternal Father entered into history and took his place within it, so that by his work humanity and the world might become sharers in salvation. After his ascension to the Father, the Lord continues to accomplish his work through the Chruch. As God became man, so his Church is really incarnate in the world. But because the world, to which the Church ought to represent the mystery of Christ, is in a continual process of change, the Church is itself necessarily and continually in pilgrimage. Its essence and fundamental structures remain always unchangeable; and yet no one can say of the Church that at any time it is sufficiently understood or bounded by definition.[2]

The Church was constituted in the course of time by Christ, its principle of origin is the Word of creation and salvation. For this reason the Church not only draws understanding of its own mystery from the past, but standing in the present time and looking to the future, assumes within itself the whole progress of the human race. The Church is constantly being made more sure of this. What John XXIII wished to express by the word *"aggiornamento,"* Paul VI took up, using the phrase "dialogue with the world," and in his encyclical *Ecclesiam Suam* says the following: "The world cannot be saved from the outside. As the Word of God became man, so must a man to a certain degree identify with the forms of life of those to whom he wishes to bring the message of Christ. Without invoking privileges which would but widen the separation, without employing unintelligible terminology, he must share the common way of life—provided that it is human and honourable—especially of the most humble, if he wishes to be listened to and understood."[3]

1043

In response to the many problems posed by the changes occurring today in almost every field, the Church in the Second Vatican Council has entered into the way of dialogue. "The Church guards the heritage of God's Word and draws from it religious and moral principles, without always having at hand the solution to particular problems. She desires thereby to add that the light of revealed truth to mankind's store of experience, so that the path which humanity has taken in recent times will not be a dark one."[4]

1044

In fulfilment of its mission the Church must propose obligatory norms of human and Christian life from the deposit of faith in an open dialogue with the world. But since moral obligations can never be detailed in their concrete particularities, the personal responsibility of each individual must always be called into play. This is even clearer today because

1045

of the complexity of modern life: the detailing of concrete moral norms to be followed must not be pushed to extremes.

1046   In the present study, dealing with problems relating to responsible parenthood, the Holy Father through his ready willingness to enter into dialogue has given this dialogue an importance unprecedented in history. After several years of study, a Commission of experts called together by him, made up for the most part of laymen from various fields of competency, has prepared material for him, which was lastly examined by a special group of bishops.

1. Fundamental Principles

I. The Fundamental Values of Marriage

1047   "The well-being of the individual person and of human and Christian society is intimately linked with the healthy condition of that community produced by marriage and the family. Hence Christians and all men who hold this community in high esteem sincerely rejoice in the various ways by which men today find help in fostering this community of love and perfecting its life, and by which spouses and parents are assisted in their lofty calling. Those who rejoice in such aid look for additional benefits from them and labour to bring them about."[5]

1048   Over the course of centuries the Church, with the authority conferred on it by Christ our Lord, has constantly protected the dignity and essential values of this institution whose author is God himself, who has made man to his image and raised him to share in his love. It has always taught this to its faithful and to all men. In our day it again intends to offer those numerous families who are seeking a right way guidance as to how, in the conditions of our times, they will be able to live and develop fully the higher gifts of this community.

1049   A couple (*unio conjugum*) ought to be considered above all as a community of persons which has in itself the beginning of new human life. Therefore those things that strengthen and make more profound the union of persons within this community must never be separated from the procreative finality which makes the conjugal community specifically what it is. Pius XI, in *Casti Connubii*, far back as 1930, referring to the tradition expressed in the Roman Catechism, said: "This mutual inward moulding of a husband and wife, this determined effort to perfect each other, can in a very real sense be said to be the chief reason and purpose of matrimony, provided matrimony be looked at not in the restricted sense as instituted for the proper conception and education of the child, but more widely as the blending of life as a whole and the mutual interchange and sharing thereof."[6]

But conjugal love, without which marriage would not be a true union of persons, is not exhausted in the simple mutual giving in which one party seeks only the other. Married people know well that they are only able to perfect each other and establish a true community if their love does not end in a merely egotistic union but according to the condition of each is made truly fruitful in the creation of new life. Nor on the other hand can the procreation and education of a child be considered a truly human fruitfulness unless it is the result of a love existing in a family community. Conjugal love and fecundity are in no way opposed, but complement one another in such a way that they constitute an almost indivisible unity.   1050

Unfolding the natural and divine law, the Church urges all men to be true dispensers of the divine gifts, to act in conformity with their own personal nature and to shape their married life according to the dictates of the natural and divine law. God created man male and female so that, joined together in the bonds of love, they might perfect one another through a mutual, corporal and spiritual giving and that they might carefully prepare their children, the fruit of this love, for a truly human life. Let them regard one another always as persons and not as mere objects. Therefore eveything should be done in marriage so that the benefits conferred on this institution can be attained as perfectly as possible and so that fidelity and moral rightness can be served.   1051

II. Responsible Parenthood and the Regulation of Conception

1052   To cultivate and realize all the essential values of marriage, married people should become ever more deeply aware of the profundity of their vocation and the breadth of their responsibilities. In this spirit and with this awareness let married people seek how they might better be "co-operators with the love of God the Creator and (be), so to speak, the interpreters of that love" for the task of procreation and education.[7]

1. Responsible Parenthood

1053   Responsible parenthood (that is, generous and prudent parenthood) is a fundamental requirement of a married couple's true mission. Enlightened by faith, the spouses understand the scope of their whole task; helped by divine grace, they try to fulfil it as a true service, carried out in the name of God and Christ, orientated to the temporal and eternal good of men. To save, protect and promote the good of the offspring, and thus of the family community and of human society, the married partners will take care to consider all values and seek to realize them harmoniously in the best way they can, with proper reverence towards each other as persons and according to the concrete circumstances of their life. They will make a judgment in conscience before God about the number of children to have and educate according to the objective criteria indicated by Vatican Council II.[8]

1054   This responsible, generous and prudent parenthood always carries with it new demands. In today's situation both because of new difficulties and because of new possibilities for the education of children, couples are hardly able to meet such demands except with generosity and sincere deliberation.

1055   With a view to the education of children let couples more and more build the community of their whole life on a true and magnanimous love, under the guidance of the spirit of Christ.[9] For this stable community between man and woman, shaped by conjugal love, is the true foundation of human fruitfulness. This community between married people through which an individual finds himself by opening himself to another provides the best framework for the fully integrated education of children. Through developing their communion and intimacy in all its aspects, married partners are able to provide that environment of love, mutual understanding and humble acceptance which is the necessary condition of authentic human education and maturation.

Responsible parenthood—through which married persons   1056
intend to observe and cultivate the essential values of matrimony with a view to the good of persons (the good of the children to be educated, of the couples themselves and of the while of human society)—is one of the conditions and expression of a true conjugal chastity. For genuine love, rooted in faith, hope and charity, ought to inform the whole life and every action of a couple. By the strength of this chastity the partners bring about the existence of that true love precisely inasmuch as it is conjugal and fruitful. They accept their task generously and prudently, with all its values, combining them in the best way possible according to the particular circumstances of their life and in spite of difficulties.

Married people know well that very often a time of absti-   1057
nence will be required of them, and sometimes not just for a brief period, because of the habitual conditions of their life, for example, the good of one of the spouses (physical or psychic well-being), or because of what are called professional necessities. A chaste couple know and accept this abstinence as a condition of progress into a deeper mutual love, fully conscious that the grace of Christ will sustain and strengthen them for it.

Seeing their vocation in all its depth and breadth and ac-   1058
cepting it, the couple follow Christ and try to imitate him in a true evangelical spirit.[10] Comforted by the spirit of Christ in the inner man and rooted and grounded in love,[11] they try to build up a total life community, "with all lowliness and meekness, with patience, forebearing one another in love."[12] They will have the peace of Christ in their hearts and give thanks to God the Father as his holy and elected sons.

The partners are then able to ask and expect that they will   1059
be helped by all in such a way that they are progressively able

to approach increasingly responsible parenthood. They need the help of all in order that they can fulfill their responsibilities with full liberty and in the most favourable material, psychological, cultural and spiritual conditions. By the development of the family, then, the whole society is built up with regard to the good of all men in the whole world.[13]

2. Regulation of Conception

1060   The regulation of conception appears necessary for many couples who wish to achieve a responsible, open and reasonable parenthood in the circumstances of today. If they are to observe and cultivate all the essential values of marriage, married people need decent and human means for the regulation of conception. They should be able to expect the collaboration of all, especially of men of learning and science, so that they can have at their disposal means agreeable and worthy of man in the fulfilling of his responsible parenthood.

1061   It is proper to man, created in the image of God, to use what is given in physical nature in such a way that he may develop it to its full significance with a view to the good of the whole person. This is the cultural commission that the Creator has entrusted to men, whom he has made his co-operators. According to the requirements of human nature and with the progress of the sciences, men should discover means more and more apt and adequate so that married people will be able to fulfil their "ministry which must be fulfilled in a manner which is worthy of man."[14]

1062   This intervention of man in physiological processes, an intervention ordained to the essential values of marriage and first of all to the good of children, is to be judged according to the fundamental principles and objective criteria of morality which are considered below, in section four of this Chapter.

1063   "Marriage and conjugal love are by their nature ordained toward the begetting and educating of children."[15] A right ordering toward the good of the child within the conjugal and familial community pertains to the essence of human sexuality. Therefore the morality of sexual acts between married people takes its meaning first of all and specifically from the ordering of their responsible, generous and prudent parenthood. It does not then depend upon the direct fecundity of each and every particular act. Moreover the morality of every marital act depends upon the requirements of mutual love in all its aspects. In a word, the morality of sexual actions is thus to be judged by the true requirements of the nature of human sexuality, whose meaning is maintained and promoted especially by conjugal chastity, as we have said above.

More and more clearly, for a conscience correctly formed, a willingness to raise a family with full acceptance of the various human and Christian responsibilities is altogether distinguished from a mentality and way of married life which in its totality is egoistically and irrationally opposed to fruitfulness. This truly "contraceptive" mentality and practice has been condemned by the traditional doctrine of the Church and will always be condemned as gravely sinful. 1064

III. The Continuity of Doctrine and Its Deeper Understanding

The tradition of the Church which is concerned with the morality of conjugal relations goes back to the beginning of the Church. It should be observed, however, that the tradition developed in argument and conflict with heretics such as the Gnostics, the Manichaeans and later the Cathars, all of whom condemned procreation or the transmission of life as something evil, and nonetheless indulged in moral vices. Consequently this tradition has always, although in differing terms, sought to protect two fundamental values: the good of procreation and the rightness of marital intercourse. Moreover the Church has always taught another truth equally fundamental, although hidden in mystery, namely original sin. This had wounded man in his various faculties, including sexuality. Man could only be healed of this wound by the grace of a Saviour. This is one of the reasons why Christ took marriage and raised it to a sacrament of the New Law. 1065

It is not surprising that in the course of centuries this tradition has always been interpreted in expressions and formulas proper to the times, or that the words in which it was expressed 1066 and the reasons on which it was based have been changed by knowledge which is now obsolete. Nor was a correct balance between all the elements always maintained. Some authors even used expressions which depreciated the matrimonial state. But what is of real importance is that the same values were reaffirmed again and again. Consequently an egoistical, hedonistic and contraceptive approach, which arbitrarily turns the practice of married life away from its ordination to a human, generous and prudent fecundity is always against the nature of man and can never be justified.

1067   The large amount of knowledge and facts which throw light on the world of today suggest that it is not to contradict the genuine sense of this tradition and the purpose of the previous doctrinal condemnations if we advocate the regulation of conception by using human and decent means, ordered to favouring fecundity in the totality of married life and toward the realization of the authentic values of a fruitful matrimonial community.

1068   The reasons supporting this affirmation are of several kinds: social changes in matrimony and the family, especially in the role of the woman; lowering of the infant mortality rate; new bodies of knowledge in biology, psychology, sexuality and demography; a changed estimation of the value and meaning of human sexuality and of conjugal relations; most of all, a better grasp of the duty of man to humanize and to bring to greater perfection for the life of man what is given in nature. Then the *sensus fidelium*, sense of the faithful must be considered: according to it, condemnation of a couple to a long and often heroic abstinence as the means to regulate conception, cannot be founded on the truth.

1069   A further step in the doctrinal evolution, which it seems now should be developed, is founded less on these facts than on a better, deeper and more correct understanding of conjugal life and of the conjugal act when these other changes occur. The doctrine on marriage and its essential values remains the same and whole, but it is now applied differently out of a deeper understanding.

1070   This maturation has been prepared and has already begun. The magisterium itself is in evolution. Leo XIII spoke less

explicitly in his encyclical *Arcanum* than did Pius XI in his
wonderful doctrinal synthesis of *Casti Connubii* which gave a
fresh start to so many beginnings in a living conjugal spirituality. He proclaimed, using the very words of the Roman
Catechism, the importance, in a true sense the primary importance, of true conjugal love for the community of matrimony.
The notion of responsible parenthood which is implied in the
notion of a prudent and generous regulation of conception,
advanced in Vatican Council II, had already been prepared by
Pius XII. The acceptance of a lawful application of the calcu-
lated infertile periods of the woman—that the application is
legitimate presupposes right motives—makes a separation
between the sexual act which is explicitly intended and its
reproductive effect which is intentionally excluded.

The tradition has always rejected seeking this separation   1071
with a contraceptive intention for motives spoiled by egoism
and hedonism, and such seeking can never be admitted. The
true opposition is not sought between some material conformity to the physiological processes of nature and some
artifical intervention. For it is natural to man to exercise human control over what is given by physical nature. The opposition is really to be sought between one way of acting which
is contraceptive and opposed to a prudent and generous fruitfulness and another way which is in an ordered relationship
to responsible fruitfulness and which has a concern for education and all the essential, human and Christian values.

In such a conception the substance of tradition stands in   1072
continuity and is respected. The new elements which today
are discerned in tradition under the influence of new knowledge and facts were found in it before; they were undifferen-
tiated but not denied; so that the problem in today's terms is
new and has not been proposed before in this way. These
elements are being explained and made more precise in the
light of the new data. The moral obligation of following
fundamental norms and fostering all the essential values in a
balanced fashion is strengthened, not weakened. The virtue
of chastity by which a couple positively regulates the practice
of sexual relations is all the more demanded. Human and
Christian criteria or morality therefore demand and at the

same time foster in married life, a spirituality which is more profound, with faith, hope and chairty informed according to the spirit of the Gospel.

IV. The Objective Criteria of Morality

1073   We must now tackle the problem, which many men rightly think to be of great importance, at least practically: what are the objective criteria by which to choose a method of reconciling the needs of marital life with a right ordering of this life to fruitfulness in the procreation and education of offspring?

1074   It is obvious that the method is not to be left to purely arbitrary decision.

1075   1. In resolving the similar problem of responsible parenthood and the appropriate determination of the size of the family. Vatican Council II has shown the way. The objective criteria are the various values and needs duly and harmoniously evaluated. These objective criteria are to be applied by the couples, acting from a rightly formed conscience and according to their concrete situation. In the words of the Council: "Thus they will fulfil their task with human and Christian responsibility. With docile reverence toward God, they will come to the right decision by common counsel and effort. They will thoughtfully take into account both their own welfare and that of their children, those already born and those which may be foreseen. For this accounting they will reckon with both the material and the spiritual conditions of the times as well as of their state in life. Finally they will consult the interests of the family group, of temporal society, and of the Church herself . . . But in their manner of acting, spouses should be aware that they cannot proceed arbitrarily. They must always be governed according to a conscience dutifully conformed to the divine law itself, and should be submissive toward the Church's teaching office, which authentically interprets that law in the light of the Gospel."[16]

1076   In other questions relating to conjugal life, one should proceed in the same way. There are various objective criteria which are concretely applied by couples themselves acting with a rightly formed conscience. All for example, know that objective criteria prohibit that the intimate acts of conjugal life, even if carried out in a way which could be called "natural," be practised if there is a loss of physical or psychic health or if there is neglect of the personal dignity of the spouses or if they are carried out in an egoistic or hedonistic way. These objective criteria are formed by each couple, and are to be applied by them to their concrete situation, avoiding pure arbitrariness in forming their judgment. It is impossible to determine exhaustively by a general judgment and in advance of each individual case what these objective criteria will demand in the concrete situation of a particular couple.

2. Likewise, there are objective criteria as to the means to   1077
be chosen for responsibly determining the size of the family: if they are rightly applied, the couples themselves will find and determine the way of proceeding.

In grave language, Vatican Council II has reaffirmed that   1078
abortion is altogether to be excluded from the means of responsibly preventing birth. Indeed, abortion is not a method of preventing conception but of eliminating offspring already conceived. The affirmation about acts which do not spare an offspring already conceived is to be repeated in regard to those interventions which give serious grounds for suspecting that they are abortive.

Sterilization, since it is a drastic and irreversible intervention   1079
in a matter of great importance, is generally to be excluded as a means of responsibly avoiding conception.

Moreover, the natural law and reason illuminated by Chris-   1080
tian faith dictate that a couple proceed in choosing means not arbitrarily but according to objective criteria. These objective criteria for the right choice of methods are the conditions for keeping and fostering the essential values of marriage as a community of fruitful love. If these criteria are observed, then a right ordering of the human act according to its object, end and circumstances is maintained.

Among these criteria, this must be put *first*: the action   1081
must correspond to the nature of the person and of his acts so that the whole meaning of the mutual giving and of human procreation is kept in a context of true love.[17]

1082   *Secondly*, the means which are chosen should have an effectiveness proportionate to the degree of right or necessity of averting a new conception temporarily or premanently.

1083   *Thirdly*, every method of preventing conception—not excluding either periodic or absolute abstinence—carries with it some negative element of physical evil of which the couple will be aware to a greater or lesser extent. This negative element or physical evil can arise under different aspects: account must be taken of the biological, hygienic and psychological aspects, of the personal dignity of the spouses, and of the possibility of expressing sufficiently and aptly the interpersonal relation or conjugal love. The means to be chosen, where several are possible, is the one that carries with it the smallest possible negative element, according to the concrete situation of the couple.

1084   *Fourthly*, then, in choosing concretely among means, much depends on what means may be available in a certain region or at a certain time or for a certain couple; and this may depend on the economic situation.

1085   Therefore not arbitrarily, but as the law of nature and of God commands, let couples form an objectively founded judgment taking all the criteria into consideration. This they may do without major difficulty, and with peace of mind, if they take common and prudent counsel before God. They should, however, as far as possible, be instructed about these criteria by competent persons and be educated as to the right application of the criteria. Well instructed, and prudently educated as Christians, they will prudently and serenely decide what is truly for the good of the couple and of the children, and does not neglect their own personal Christian perfection, and is, therefore, what God, revealing himself through the natural law and Christian revelation, sets before them to do.

2. Pastoral Necessities

I. The Task and Fundamental Conditions of Educational Renewal

When sometimes a new aspect of human life comes to oc- 1086
cupy a special place in the area of man's responsibility, a task
of educational renewal is imposed in a seriously binding way.

For married people to take up the duty of responsible par- 1087
enthood, they must, more than in the past, grasp the meaning
of fruitfulness and experience a desire for it. To give married
life its unitive value, and do so in service of its procreative
function, they must develop an increasingly purer respect for
their mutual needs, the sense of community and the acceptance of their common Christian vocation.

It will not be a surprise that this conviction of a greater 1088
responsibility will come about as the effect and crown of a
gradual development of the meaning of marriage and conjugal
spirituality. For several generations, in ever increasing numbers, couples have sought to live their proper married vocation
in a more profound and more conscientious way. The teaching
of the magisterium and the encyclical *Casti Connubii* in
particular have notably contributed to and strengthened this
formation of conscience by giving it its full meaning.

The more urgent the appeal is made to observe mutual love 1089
and charity in every expression of married life, the more
urgent is the necessity of forming consciences. Of educating
spouses to a sense of responsibility and of awakening a right
sense of values. This new step in the development of conjugal
life cannot bear all its fruits, unless it is accompanied by an
immense educational activity. No one will regret that these
new demands stirred by the Holy Spirit call the entire human
race to this profound moral maturity.

Couples who might think they find in the doctrine as it has 1090
just been proposed an open door to laxism or easy solutions
make a grave mistake, of which they will be the first victims.
The conscientious decision to be made by married couples
about the number of children they should have is not a matter of minor importance. On the contrary it imposes a more
conscientious fulfilling of their vocation to fruitfulness in the
consideration of the whole complex of values that is involved
here. The same is true of the responsibility of the married
couple for the development of their common life in such a
way that it will be a source of continual progress and perfection.

1091   The God who created man male and female, in order that they might be two in one flesh, in order that they might bring the world under their control, in order that they might increase and multiply,[18] is the God who has elevated their union to the dignity of a sacrament and so disposed that in this world it is a special sign of his own love for his people. He himself will gird the spouses with his strength, his light, his love and his joy in the strength of the spirit of Christ. Who then would doubt that couples, all couples, will be able to respond to the demands of their vocation?

II. Further Consideration: Application of the Doctrine of Matrimony to Different Parts of the World

1092   1. It seems very necessary to establish some pontifical institute or secretariat for the study of the sciences connected with married life. In this commission there could be continual collaboration in open dialogue among experts competent in various areas. The aim of this institute (or secretariat) would, among other duties, be to carry further the research and reflection begun by the commission. The various studies which the commission has already produced could be made public. A special task for this institute would be to study how the doctrine of matrimony should be applied to different parts of the world and to contribute to the formation of priests and married couples dedicated to the family apostolate by sending experts to them.[19]

1093   2. Universal principles and the essential values of matrimony and married life became actual in ways that differ to a certain degree according to different cultures and different mentalities. Consequently there is a special need for episcopal conferences to institute their own organizations for investigation and dialogue between families, between representatives of the different sciences and pastors of souls. They would also have the task of judging which would be in practice the most suitable pastoral means in each region to promote the healthy formation of consciences and education to a sense of responsibility.

Episcopal conferences should make it their particular con-   **1094**
cern that priests and married lay persons be adequately formed
in a more spiritual and moral understanding of Christian
matrimony. Thus they will be prepared to extend pastoral
action to the renewal of families in the spirit of "aggiornamento" initiated by the Constitution on the Church in the
Modern World.

Under their guidance there should also in each religion be   **1095**
action to start the genuine fostering of all families in a context of social evolution which should be truly human. The
fostering of the role of women is of special importance here.

There are many reforms and initiatives needed to open the   **1096**
way to decent and joyful living for all families. Together with
all men of goodwill, Christians must undertake this great
work of human development, without which the betterment
of families can never take effect. Christianity does not teach
some ideal for a small number of elect, but the vocation of
all to the essential values of human life. It cannot be that
anyone would wish to better his own family without at the
same time actively dedicating himself to opening a way for
similiar betterment for all families in all parts of the world.

III. Demographic Fact and Policy

The increase of inhabitants cannot in any way be said to   **1097**
be something evil or calamitous for the human race. As children are "the most excellent gift of matrimony"[20] and
the object of the loving care of the parents, which demands
from them many sacrifices, so the great number of men pertaining to a certain nation and constituting the whole human
race spread over the globe is the foundation of all social sharing and cultural progress. Thus there should be afforded to it
all those things which according to social justice are due to
men as persons.

The Church is not ignorant of the immense difficulties and   **1098**
profound transformations which have arisen from the conditions of contemporary life throughout the world and especially in certain regions where there has been a rapid rise in
population. That is why it again and again raises its voice to

urge various nations and the whole human family to help one another in truly human progress, united in true solidarity and excluding every intention of domination. Then they might avoid all those things both in the political and in the social order which restrict or dissipate in an egotistical way the full utilization of the goods of the earth which are destined for all men.

1099   The Church by its doctrine and by its supernatural aids intends to help all families so that they may find the right way in undertaking their generous and prudent responsibility. Governments, which have the care of the common good, should look with great concern on sub-human conditions of families and "beware of solutions contradicting the moral law, solutions which have been promoted publicly or privately, and sometimes actually imposed."²¹ These solutions have contradicted the moral law in particular by propagating abortion or sterilization. Political demography can be called human only if the rights of parents with regard to the pro-creation and education of children are respected and conditions of life are fostered with all vigour so that parents are enabled to exercise their responsibilities before God and society.

IV. The Inauguration and Further Development of Means for Education of Couples and Youth

1100   1. Couples are burdened by multiple responsibilities throughout the whole of life; they seek light and aid. With the favour of God means of helping married people in their task of building families and continual development that have already been initiated in some regions, often by the married couples themselves, will be established in many more.

1101   Maximum help is to be given to parents in their educational task. They strongly desire to provide the best for their children. The more parents are conscious of their office of fruitfulness, which is extended over the whole time in which the education of their children is accomplished, so much the more do they seek a way of acquiring better preparation to carry out this responsibility. Moreover, in exercising this educational office, parents mature more deeply in it themselves, create a unity, become rich in love, and apply themselves with the lofty aim of giving themselves with united energies to the high task of giving life and education.

2. The building up of the conjugal and family community   1102
does not happen without thought. Therefore it is fitting everywhere to set up and work out many better means of remote and immediate preparation of youth for marriage. This requires the collaboration of everyone. Married people who are already well educated will have a great and indispensable part to play in this work. In these tasks of providing help to those already married and to the young who are preparing to build and develop a conjugal and family community, priests and religious will co-operate closely with the families. Without this co-operation, in which each one has his own indispensable part, there will never be apt methods of education to those responsibilities of the vocation that place the sacrament in clear light so that its full and profound meaning shines forth.

The Church, which holds the deposit of the Gospel, has to   1103
bring this noble message to all men in the entire world. This announcing of the Gospel, grounded in love, illumines every aspect of married and family life. Every aspect, every task and responsibility of the conjugal and family community shines with a clear light, in love towards one's neighbour—a love which is rich with human values and is formed by the divine interpersonal love of Father, Son and Holy Spirit. May the spirit of Christ's love more and more penetrate families everywhere so that together with John, the beloved disciple of Jesus, married couples, parents and children may always understand more deeply the wonderful relation between love of God and love of one another.[22]

Papal Commission on Birth Control
Pastoral Approaches
June 26, 1966

Today, as throughout the course of her history, the Church wishes to remain the institution divinely established to lead men to their salvation in Jesus Christ, through the different states of life to which they have been called. Of these, marriage is the one to which the greater part of mankind is destined, and in which it lives. It is the Church's task to defend and promote the holiness of this state in fidelity to the principles of the Gospels.

1105   No one can be ignorant of the guidance she has lavished on all, emphasizing the greatness of the institution of marriage which is, on earth, a sign of that other fruitful union sealed on the Cross between Christ and the Church (cf. *Eph.* 5. 25-32). No one can fail to be aware of her efforts to make this doctrine inform her way of life, efforts which give rise to institutions appropriate to the needs of the times, so as to help humanity towards the evangelical ideal of the Christian family.

1106   Without going back beyond more recent times, we can recall that Leo XIII, anxious to demonstrate the Christian teaching to the modern world in a positive way, published his encyclical on Marriage, *Arcanum*. A few decades later, faced with a world in which the stability and unity of the family were being threatened by various forms of legislation, in which formerly prosperous nations seemed to be losing their grip and sliding towards death, Pius XI forcefully recalled the great benefits of marriage understood in a Christian way: children, conjugal fidelity, the holiness of the sacrament.

Pius XII not only upheld the whole of this teaching, particularly during the war years which caused such suffering to families, frequently endangering their very existence, but in certain documents he showed the deepening of the doctrine that had come about in the meantime and clarified the various ends of the marriage union. 1107

All this teaching, it must be stressed with joy, has, in many countries, produced lay and Christian family movements which have contributed very powerfully to a deeper understanding of marriage and the demands of the marriage union. It has also stimulated pastors and laymen, theologians, doctors and psychologists to undertake a more rigorous investigation of the conditions and difficulties involved in a more exact and generous observance of the laws that must govern the family, and of the meaning and value of human sexuality. At the same time the conscience of married couples has been faced with a different situation: no longer the threat of nations slowly disappearing through a lack of generosity towards life, but the difficulties provided both by the accelerated pace of human development and by other important social factors, such as people's increased mobility in search of work to support themselves, the massive concentration of populations in towns where the living space vital to families is more strictly limited, or, finally, the social advancement of women. 1108

It was this development of reflection and of experience of family life lived most generously by an ever increasing number of Christian couples, and also livelier appreciation of the dignity of the human person, of the sense of his free and personal responsibility for carrying out God's plan for humanity, that led the Fathers of the Council to reaffirm strongly the stability and holiness of the family institution, based on the God-willed love of two people for each other, two people who have decided to become one flesh for the sake of the life-work ordained for them and entrusted to them by the Creator—the exercise of a joint responsible and generous parenthood. 1109

1110   Through all these teachings and all this rich experience of the faithful, the Church remains faithfully attached to the divine imperatives of the unity, stability and fecundity of marriage: "Be faithful, multiply and fill the earth" (*Gen.* 1. 28; 9. 1); "they shall be two in one flesh" (*Matt.* 19. 6). She remains attached, also, to other related commandments: the solemn task of bringing up children (cf. *Eph.* 6. 4; I *Tim.* 2. 15) and man's urge to dominate creation according to God's plan (cf. *Gen.* 2. 24).

1111   So faithful believers, nourished by the Holy Spirit (cf. *Lumen Gentium* § 12), have been led to find all the riches of the Church's teaching, and all its implications, in the experience of their married life. They have come to realize that human acts are charged with multiple responsibilities; the Magisterium listens to the expression of these, clarifies it, controls it and authenticates it, so that it can bear it in mind when pronouncing on the morality of these acts. Today's needs invite us to give particular emphasis to this aspect. Today, thanks to the progress made in reflection on the subject, and without in any way detracting from the importance of procreation, which, allied to true love, is one of the ends of marriage, we have a clearer view of the multiple responsibilities of married couples: towards each other, first, so that they can live a love that leads them to unity; towards their children, whose development and education—more and more demanding—they must assure; then towards the institution of marriage, whose stability (cf. I *Cor.* 7. 10-11) and unity they are to maintain through the quality of their love and respect for each other's dignity (cf. I *Pet.* 3. 1-7); and finally towards society, since the family is its basic unit.

1112   All this creates a complex of obligations which, far from eliminating duties, invites one to take account of them so that they can all be undertaken together as far as is humanly possible, with due respect for their hierarchy and relative importance. So the Church, particularly through the teaching of Pius XII, has come to realize more fully that marriage has another meaning and another end besides that of procreation alone, even though it remains wholly and definitely ordered to procreation, though not always immediately.

What has been condemned in the past and remains so today   1113
is the unjustified refusal of life, arbitrary human intervention
for the sake of moments of egoistic pleasure; in short, the
rejection of procreation as a specific task of marriage. In the
past, the Church could not speak other than she did, because
the problem of birth control did not confront human consciousness in the same way. Today, having clearly recognized
the legitimacy and even the duty of regulating births, she
recognizes too that human intervention in the process of the
marriage act for reasons drawn from the finality of marriage
itself should not always be excluded, provided that the criteria
of morality are always safeguarded.

If an arbitrarily contraceptive mentality is to be condemned,   1114
as has always been the Church's view, an intervention to
regulate conception in a spirit of true, reasonable and generous charity (cf. *Matt.* 7. 12; *John* 13. 34-5; 15. 12-17; *Rom.*
13. 8-10) does not deserve to be, because if it were, other
goods of marriage might be endangered. So what is always to
be condemned is not the regulation of conception, but an
egoistic married life, refusing a creative opening-out of the
family circle, and so refusing a truly human—and therefore
truly Christian—married love. This is the anti-conception that
is against the Christian ideal of marriage.

As for the means that husband and wife can legitimately   1115
employ, it is their task to decide these together, without drift-
ing into arbitrary decisions, but always taking account of the
objective criteria of morality. These criteria are in the first
place those that relate to the totality of married life and
sexuality.

Sexuality in marriage must be a unifying force. Husband   1116
and wife have to solder their community more and more
strongly together, as this engages them as complete people.

This community is entirely creative; furthermore, it is in   1117
the tasks they undertake together, and particularly in bringing
children into the world and educating them, that husband
and wife together come to effect that deep exchange and
communion of love that belong to the state of marriage.

The act of love, like all expressions of intimacy between   1118
them, needs to be humanized, progressively refined. The phys-

ical expressions of love will enrich their love for each other, but it will grow through abstention too, when this better fits the wishes or needs of one or the other.

1119   Continence is one of the indispensable forms of married love. If it is freely accepted, it will help to prevent intimate life together from becoming stale, and help to protect its quality and meaning. There is an ascesis in this, whose rule, at once supple and very demanding, will be the human quality and growth of their love.

1120   So the means chosen should be suitable for exercising a healthy and responsible parenthood, in the light of certain guiding principles: besides being effective, they should have regard for the health of the parents and their eventual offspring; they should not violate respect for the personal dignity of either husband or wife, who must never be treated as objects—this applies to women, who are still kept in a state unworthy of them in many countries, as much as to men; they should pay attention to any possible psychic consequences they might entail, depending on the person and circumstances; and finally they should not hinder the power of expression of an increasingly close union between two persons.

1121   None of this in any way implies that it can be legitimate for anyone to attack already existing human life, even in the first moments of its existense. The Church has always condemned abortion as a particularly vile form of murder in that it destroys a helpless and innocent human being.

1122   This renewed formulation of conjugal morality might lead some people to believe that they have been wrong to act as they did in the past, since the rules to which they submitted faithfully have now had to evolve. This immediate reaction, however understandable, would not be correct since the views we hold now are not a turning-back on traditional values, but a deepening of them. And this new stage is only possible today thanks to the sacrifices and faithfulness of those who have gone before us. If the Church seems to them to have taken a long time to express what she thinks now, to act on this deepening of values and on the factors that our age has produced for her to reflect on, they should recognize that because of the importance of the subject in question, the Church owed it to her children not to make a pronouncement except with extreme and wise caution. And let not legitimate modifications be taken as casting doubt on the meaning and value of different attitudes on the past. It will always remain true that for Christians procreation confers the dignity of co-operating with God the creator, and that children will always be a great good and joyful responsibility: husbands and wives will only be convinced that they should deprive themselves of them with the greatest sorrow.

The whole of this developed doctrine can only appear to those who reflect on it as an enrichment, in full continuity with the deep, but more rigorous, moral orientations of the past. Its proclamation in a renewed formulation is not giving way in any sense to laxity. It is not an invitation to the faithful to let themselves go on a quest for exclusively selfish pleasure; on the contrary, it is an invitation calling married couples to a truer, more complete love, in which each should be able to forget himself, or herself, to go out to meet the other, so that together they find a joint will to responsible and generous parenthood. The Church is calling them to a deeper understanding of their love, to a more conscious self-mastery in the service of the life ministry that God has entrusted to them. **1123**

The Church knows from experience how difficult it is for human beings, wounded as they are by sin, to love truly. She knows that selfishness watches from deep inside them, spying on the impulse to love which God, who is Love (I *John* 4. 8-16), has placed in mankind, created in his image. But she also knows that Christ is present in the People of God through his Spirit, particularly in the sacraments which the Church dispenses. **1124**

She also knows that any just point of view, like any indisputable right, can lead to abuses on the part of those who start from bad intentions. This is why she is convinced that only an enlightened and thorough process of education can instill the Christian ideal of the family into men's minds. So she invites all her children to promote an immense effort to form men's minds and hearts, so as to allow everyone to discipline the God-given force of sexuality so that it will serve in **1125** the accomplishment of his life's work. Those intending to marry should also receive a clearer, more delicate and more generous preparation for their family vocation; and, finally, those already married should be helped to overcome their difficulties, to live in a harmony of love, service to each other and to the children they have called into life. Obviously, looking back to those Christian families who have already contributed so much to a better understanding of the family, the Church must make a special appeal to them still to intensify this educational effort.

1126   Priests and married couples are called to a close collaboration in this education in responsibility and all the values of marriage. Through this collaboration, in a climate of respect for the specific tasks and gifts of each, mutual knowledge and respect will grow.

1127   The Church also knows that frequently the generous will of parents comes up against difficulties of a physical, psychological or material nature. So she must invite all those who work in professions devoted to the improvement of physical or mental health to participate in this work of helping young people and married couples. And she must also renew her insistent and repeated appeals for more generous mutual aid and more equitable social and economic justice, not only among members of the same nation, but also between nations, to make excessive differences in living conditions disappear as soon as possible, so that all families can develop, not of course in wealth, but in the relative well-being that virtue requires.

1128   So, in response to the questioning of her children, and beyond them, of the whole world, this is the beautiful but demanding teaching worthy of a humanity redeemed by the blood of Christ, all of whose members are called on to form the family of God, that the Church proposes to the people of today. Through this teaching, today as in the past, the Church, protected from error in proclaiming the values whose essence has been confided to her through the word of her well-beloved Head, wishes to promote the Christian advancement of the family.

SACERDOTALIS CAELIBATUS
Encyclical Letter of Pope Paul VI
on Priestly Celibacy (Excerpt)
June 24, 1967

Priestly celibacy has been guarded by the Church for centuries as a brilliant jewel, and retains its value undiminished even in our time when mentality and structures have undergone such profound change.

Amid the modern stirrings of opinion, a tendency has also been manifested, and even a desire expressed, to ask the Church to re-examine this characteristic institution of hers. It is said that in the world of our time its observance has come to be of doubtful value and almost impossible.

2. This state of affairs is troubling consciences, perplexing some priests and young aspirants to the priesthood; it is a cause for alarm in many of the faithful and constrains us to fulfill the promise we made to the Council Fathers. We told them that it was our intention to give new luster and strength to priestly celibacy in the world of today.[1] Since saying this we have over a considerable period of time earnestly implored the enlightenment and assistance of the Holy Spirit and have examined before God opinions and petitions which have come to us from all over the world, notably from some pastors of God's Church.

3. The great question concerning the sacred celibacy of the clergy in the Church has long been before our mind in its deep seriousness: must that grave, ennobling obligation remain today for those who have the intention of receiving major orders? Is it possible or appropriate nowadays to observe

1130

1131

1132

such an obligation? Has the time not come to break the bond linking celibacy with the priesthood in the Church? Could the difficult observance of it not be made optional? Would this not be a way to help the priestly ministry and facilitate ecumenical approaches? And if the golden law of sacred celibacy is to remain, what reasons are there to show that it is holy and fitting? What means are to be taken to observe it, and how can it be changed from a burden to a help for the priestly life?

1133   4. Our attention has rested particularly on the objections which have been and are still made in various forms against the retention of sacred celibacy. In virtue of our apostolic office we are obliged by the importance and indeed complexity, of the subject to give faithful consideration to the facts and the problems they involve, at the same time bringing to them as it is our duty and our mission to do, the light of truth which is Christ. Our intention is to do in all things the will of Him who has called us to this office and to show what we are in the Church, the servant of God's servants.

1134   5. It may be said that today ecclesiastical celibacy has been examined more penetratingly than ever before and in all its aspects. It has been examined from the doctrinal, historical, sociological, psychological and pastoral point of view. The intentions prompting this examination have frequently been basically correct although reports may sometimes have distorted them.

1135   Let us look openly at the principal objections against the law that links ecclesiastical celibacy with the priesthood.

1136   The first seems to come from the most authoritative source, the New Testament which preserves the teaching of Christ and the Apostles. It does not demand celibacy of sacred ministers but proposes it rather as a free act of obedience to a special vocation or to a special spiritual gift (cf. Matt. 19:11-12). Jesus Himself did not make it a prerequisite in His choice of the Twelve, nor did the Apostles for those who presided over the first Christian communities (cf. 1 Tim. 3:2-5; Tit. 1:5-6).

1137   6. The close relationship that the Fathers of the Church and ecclesiastical writers made over the centuries between the ministering priesthood and celibacy has its origin in a mentality and historical situations far different from ours. In patristic texts more frequently we find exhortations to the clergy to abstain from marital relations rather than those which recommend that they observe celibacy, and the reasons justifying the perfect chastity of the Church's ministers seem often to be based on an over-pessimistic view of man's earthly condition or on a certain notion of the purity necessary for contact with sacred things. In addition, it is said that the old arguments no longer are in harmony with the different social and cultural milieus in which the Church today, through her priests, is called upon to work.

7. Many see a difficulty in the fact that in the present discipline concerning celibacy the gift of a vocation to the priesthood is identified with that of perfect chastity as a state of life for God's ministers. And so people ask whether it be right to exclude from the priesthood those who, it is claimed, have been called to the ministry without having been called to lead a celibate life.　　1138

8. It is asserted, moreover, that the maintaining of priestly celibacy in the Church does great harm in those regions where the shortage of the clergy—a fact recognized with sadness and deplored by the same Council[2]—gives rise to critical situations; that it prevents the full realization of the divine plan of salvation and at times jeopardizes the very possibility of the initial proclamation of the Gospel. Thus the disquieting decline in the ranks of the clergy is attributed by some to the heavy burden of the obligation of celibacy.　　1139

9. Then there are those who are convinced that a married priesthood would remove the occasions for infidelity, waywardness and distressing defections which hurt and sadden the whole Church. These also maintain that a married priesthood would enable Christ's ministers to witness more fully to Christian living, by including the witness of married life, from which they are excluded by their state of life.　　1140

10. There are also some who strongly maintains that priests by reason of their celibacy find themselves in a situation that is physically and psychologically detrimental to the development of a mature and well-balanced human personality. And　　1141

so it happens, they say, that priests often become hard and lacking in human warmth; that, excluded from sharing fully the life and destiny of the rest of their brothers, they are obliged to live a life of solitude which leads to bitterness and discouragement.

1142   Is all this perhaps indicative of unwarranted violence to nature and an unjustified disparagement of human values which have their source in the divine work of creation and have been made whole through the work of the redemption accomplished by Christ?

1143   11. Again, in view of the way in which a candidate for the priesthood comes to accept an obligation as momentous as this, the objection is raised that in practice this acceptance results, not from an authentically personal decision, but rather from an attitude of passivity, the fruit of a formation that is neither adequate nor one that make sufficient allowance for human liberty. For the degree of knowledge and power of decision of a young person and his psychological and physical maturity fall far below—or at any rate are disproportionate to—the seriousness of the obligation he is assuming, its real difficulties and its permanence.

1144   12. We well realize that there are other objections that can be made against priestly celibacy. It is a very complex question and one which touches intimately on the ordinary view of life, to which it brings the shining light of divine revelation. A never-ending series of difficulties will present themselves to those who "cannot receive this precept" (Matt. 19:11), and who do not know or who forget the "gift of God" (cf. John 4:10), and who are unaware of the higher logic of that new concept of life, its wonderful efficacy and abundant riches.

1145   13. The sum of these objections would appear to drown out the solemn and age-old voice of the pastors of the Church and of the masters of the spiritual life and to nullify the living testimony of the countless ranks of saints and faithful ministers of God, for whom celibacy has been the object of the total and generous gift of themselves to the mystery of Christ, as well as its outward sign. But no, this voice, still strong and untroubled, is the voice not just of the past but of the present too. Ever intent on seeing things as they are, we cannot close our eyes to this magnificent, wonderful reality: that there are still today in God's holy Church, in every part of the world where she exercises her beneficent influence, great numbers of her ministers—subdeacons, deacons, priests and bishops—who are living their life of voluntary and consecrated celibacy in the most exemplary way. Nor can we overlook the immense ranks of religious men and women at their side, of laity and of young people too, united in the faithful observance of perfect chastity. They live in chastity, not out of disdain for the gift of life, but because of a greater love for that new life which springs from the paschal mystery. They live this life of courageous self-denial and spiritual joyfulness with exemplary fidelity and also with relative facility. This magnificent phenomenon bears testimony to an exceptional facet of the Kingdom of God living in the midst of modern society, to which it renders humble and beneficial service as the "light of the world" and the "salt of the earth" (cf. Matt. 5:13-14). We cannot withhold the expression of our admiration, the spirit of Christ is certainly breathing here.

14. Hence we consider that the present law of celibacy should today continue to be firmly linked to the ecclesiastical ministry. This law should support the minister in his exclusive, definitive and total choice of the unique and supreme love of Christ; it should uphold him in the entire dedication of himself to the public worship of God and to the service of the Church; it should characterize his state of life both among the faithful and in the world at large.   **1146**

15. The gift of the priestly vocation dedicated to the divine worship and to the religious and pastoral service of the People of God, is undoubtedly distinct from that which leads a person to choose celibacy as a state of consecrated life (cf. #5:7). But the priestly vocation, although inspired by God, does not become definitive or operative without having been tested and accepted by those in the Church who hold power and bear responsibility for the ministry serving the ecclesial community. It is therefore the task of those who hold authority in the Church to determine in accordance with the varying conditions of time and place, who in actual practice are to be considered suitable candidates for the religious   **1147**

and pastoral service of the Church, and what should be required of them.

1148   16. In a spirit of faith, therefore, we look on this occasion afforded us by Divine Providence as a favorable opportunity for setting forth anew and in a way more suited to the men of our time, the fundamental reasons for sacred celibacy. If difficulties against faith "can stimulate the mind to a more accurate and penetrating grasp" of it,[3] the same is true of the ecclesiastical discipline which guides and directs the life of the faithful.

1149   We are deeply moved by the joy this occasion gives us of contemplating this aspect of the divine riches and beauty of the Church of Christ. Her beauty may not always be immediately apparent to the human eye, because it is the fruit of the love of the divine Head of the Church and because it reveals itself in that perfection of holiness (cf. Eph. 5:25-27) which moves the human spirit to admiration, since it finds the resources of the human creature inadequate to account for it.

1150   17. Virginity undoubtedly, as the Second Vatican Council declared, "is not, indeed, demanded by the very nature of the priesthood, as is evident from the practice of the primitive Church and from the tradition of the Eastern Churches."[4] But at the same time the Council did not hesitate to confirm solemnly the ancient, sacred and providential present law of priestly celibacy. In addition, it set forth the motives which justify this law for those who, in a spirit of faith and with generous fervor, know how to appreciate the gifts of God.

1151   18. Consideration of the "manifold suitability" *(loc. cit.)* of celibacy for God's ministers is not something recent. Even if the explicit reasons have differed with different mentalities and different situations, they were always inspired by specifically Christian considerations; and from these considerations we can get an intuition of the more fundamental motives underlying them. These can be brought into greater evidence only under the influence of the Holy Spirit, promised by Christ to His followers for the knowledge of things to come (cf. John 16:13) and to enable the People of God to increase in the understanding of the mystery of Christ and of the

Church. In this process the experience gained through the ages from a deeper penetration of spiritual things also has its part.[5]

19. The Christian priesthood, being of a new order, can be understood only in the light of the newness of Christ, the Supreme Pontiff and eternal Priest, who instituted the priesthood of the ministry as a real participation in His own unique priesthood.[6] The minister of Christ and dispenser of the mysteries of God (1 Cor. 4:1), therefore, looks up to Him directly as his model and supreme ideal (cf. 1 Cor. 11:1). The Lord Jesus, the only Son of God, was sent by the Father into the world and He became man, in order that humanity which was subject to sin and death might be reborn, and through this new birth (John 3:5; Tit. 3:5) might enter the kingdom of heaven. Being entirely consecrated to the will of the Father (John 4:34; 17:4), Jesus brought forth this new creation by means of His paschal mystery (2 Cor. 5:17; Gal. 6:15), thus, He introduced into time and into the world a new form of life which is sublime and divine and which transforms the very earthly condition of human nature (cf. Gal. 3:28).   **1152**

20. Matrimony according to the will of God continues the work of the first creation (Gen. 2:18); and considered within the total plan of salvation, it even acquires a new meaning and a new value. Jesus, in fact, has restored its original dignity (Matt. 19:3-8), has honored it (John 2:1-11) and has raised it to the dignity of a sacrament and of a mysterious symbol of His own union with the Church (Eph. 5:32). Thus, Christian couples walk together toward their heavenly fatherland in the exercise of mutual love, in the fulfillment of their particular obligations, and in striving for the sanctity proper to them. But Christ, Mediator of a more excellent Testament (Heb. 8:6), has also opened a new way, in which the human creature adheres wholly and directly to the Lord, and is concerned only with Him and with His affairs (1 Cor. 7:33-35), thus, he manifests in a clearer and more complete way the profoundly transforming reality of the New Testament.   **1153**

21. Christ, the only Son of the Father, by the power of the Incarnation itself was made Mediator between heaven and earth, between the Father and the human race. Wholly in   **1154**

accord with this mission, Christ remained throughout His whole life in the state of celibacy, which signified His total dedication to the service of God and men. This deep connection between celibacy and the priesthood of Christ is reflected in those whose fortune it is to share in the dignity and in the mission of the Mediator and eternal Priest; this sharing will be more perfect the freer the sacred minister is from the bonds of flesh and blood.[7]

1155   22.   Jesus, who selected the first ministers of salvation, wished them to be introduced to the understanding of the mysteries of the kingdom of heaven (Matt. 13:11; Mark 4:11; Luke 8:10), to be co-workers with God under a very special title, and His ambassadors (2 Cor. 5:20). He called them friends and brethren (John 15:15, 20:17), for whom He consecrated Himself so that they might be consecrated in truth (John 17:19), He promised a more than abundant recompense to anyone who should leave home, family, wife and children for the sake of the kingdom of God (Luke 18:29-30). More than this, in words filled with mystery and hope, He also commended[8] an even more perfect consecration to the kingdom of heaven by means of celibacy, as a special gift (Matt. 19:11-12). The motive of this answer to the divine call is the kingdom of heaven (*ibid.* v. 12); similarly, the ideas—of this kingdom (Luke 18:30), of the Gospel (Mark 10:29), and of the name of Christ (Matt. 19:29), are what motivate those invited by Jesus to the difficult renunciations of the apostolate, by a very intimate participation in His lot (cf. Mark *loc. cit.*).

1156   23.   This, then, is the mystery of the newness of Christ, of all that He is and stands for; it is the sum of the highest ideals of the Gospel and of the kingdom; it is a particular manifestation of grace, which springs from the paschal mystery of the Saviour and renders the choice of celibacy desirable and worthwhile on the part of those called by Our Lord Jesus. Thus, they intend not only to participate in Christ's priestly office, but also to share with Him His very condition of living.

1157   24.   The response to the divine call is an answer of love which Christ has shown us so sublimely (John 15:13; 3:16).

This response is included in the mystery of that special love
for those souls, who have accepted His most urgent appeals
(cf. Mark 10:21). Grace with a divine force increases the
longings of love. And love, when it is genuine, is total, exclusive, stable and lasting, an irresistible spur to all forms of
heroism. And so, the free choice of sacred celibacy has always
been considered by the Church "as something that signifies
and stimulates charity":[9] it signifies a love without reservations, it stimulates to a charity which is open to all. Who can
see in such a life so completely dedicated and motivated as
shown above, the sign of a spiritual poverty, of self-seeking,
and not rather see that celibacy is and ought to be a rare and
very meaningful example of a life whose motivation is love,
by which man expresses his own unique greatness? Who can
doubt the moral and spiritual richness of such a consecrated
life, consecrated not to any human ideal no matter how
noble, but to Christ and to His work to bring about a new
form of humanity in all places and for all generations?

25. This biblical and theological vision associates our min-   1158
isterial priesthood with the priesthood of Christ; it is modeled
on the total and exclusive dedication of Christ to His mission
of salvation, and makes it the cause of our assimilation to the
form of charity and sacrifice proper to Christ our Saviour.
This vision seems to us so profound and rich in truth, both
speculative and practical, that we invite you, Venerable Brothers, and we invite you, eager students of Christian doctrine
and masters of the spiritual life, and all priests who have
gained a supernatural insight into your vocation—to persevere
in the study of this vision, and to go deeply into the inner
recesses and wealth of its reality. In this way, the bond between the priesthood and celibacy will be seen in an ever
improving union, owing to its clear logic and to the heroism
of a unique and limitless love for Christ the Lord and for His
Church.

26. "Made captive by Christ Jesus" (Phil. 3:12) unto the   1159
complete abandonment of one's entire self to Him, the priest
takes on the likeness of Christ most perfectly, even in the
love with which the eternal Priest has loved the Church His
Body and offered Himself entirely for her sake, in order to

make her a glorious, holy and immaculate Spouse (cf. Eph. 25-27).

1160   The consecrated celibacy of the sacred ministers actually manifests the virginal love of Christ for the Church, and the virginal and supernatural fecundity of this marriage, by which the children of God are born but not of flesh and blood (John 1:13).[10]

HUMANAE VITAE
Encyclical Letter of Pope Paul VI
on the Regulation of Birth
July 25, 1968

The most serious duty of transmitting human life, for which married persons are the free and responsible collaborators of God the Creator, has always been a source of great joys to them, even if sometimes accompanied by not a few difficulties and by distress.

At all times the fulfillment of this duty has posed grave   1162
problems to the conscience of married persons, but, with the recent evolution of society, changes have taken place that give rise to new questions which the Church could not ignore, having to do with a matter which so closely touches upon the life and happiness of men.

2. The changes which have taken place are in fact note-   1163
worthy and of varied kinds. In the first place, there is the rapid demographic development. Fear is shown by many that world population is growing more rapidly than the available resources, with growing distress to many families and developing countries, so that the temptation for authorities to counter this danger with radical measures is great. Moreover, working and lodging conditions, as well as increased exigencies both in the economic field and in that of education, often make the proper education of a larger number of children difficult today. A change is also seen both in the manner of considering the person of woman and her place in society, and in the value to be attributed to conjugal love in marriage, and also in the

appreciation to be made of the meaning of conjugal acts in relation to that love.[1]

1164   Finally and above all, man has made stupendous progress in the domination and rational organization of the forces of nature, such that he tends to extend this domination to his own total being: to the body, to psychical life, to social life and even to the laws which regulate the transmission of life.

1165   3. This new state of things gives rise to new questions. Granted the conditions of life today, and granted the meaning which conjugal relations have with respect to the harmony between husband and wife and to their mutual fidelity, would not a revision of the ethical norms, in force up to now, seem to be advisable, especially when it is considered that they cannot be observed without sacrifices, sometimes heroic sacrifices?

1166   And again: by extending to this field the application of the so-called "principle of totality," could it not be admitted that the intention of a less abundant but more rationalized fecundity might transform a materially sterilizing intervention into a licit and wise control of birth? Could it not be admitted, that is, that the finality of procreation pertains to the ensembled of conjugal life, rather than to its single acts? It is also asked whether, in view of the increased sense of responsibility of modern man, the moment has not come for him to entrust to his reason and his will, rather than to the biological rhythms of his organism, the task of regulating birth.

1167   4. Such questions required from the teaching authority of the Church a new and deeper reflection upon the principles of the moral teaching on marriage: a teaching founded on the natural law, illuminated and enriched by divine revelation.

1168   No believer will wish to deny that the teaching authority of the Church is competent to interpret even the natural moral law. It is, in fact, indisputable, as our predecessors have many times declared,[1] that Jesus Christ, when communicating to Peter and to the Apostles His divine authority and sending them to teach all nations His commandments,[2] constituted them as guardians and authentic interpreters of all the moral law, not only, that is, of the law of the Gospel, but also of the natural law, which is also an expression of the will of God, the faithful fulfillment of which is equally necessary for salvation.[3]

Conformably to this mission of hers, the Church has always provided—and even more amply in recent times—a coherent teaching concerning both the nature of marriage and the correct use of conjugal rights and the duties of husband and wife.[4]   1169

5. The consciousness of that same mission induced us to confirm and enlarge the study commission which our predecessor Pope John XXIII of happy memory had instituted in March, 1963. That commission which included, besides several experts in the various pertinent disciplines also married couples, had as its scope the gathering of opinions on the new questions regarding conjugal life, and in particular on the regulation of births, and of furnishing opportune elements of information so that the magisterium could give an adequate reply to the expectation not only of the faithful, but also of world opinion.[5]   1170

The work of these experts, as well as the successive judgments and counsels spontaneously forwarded by or expressly requested from a good number of our brothers in the episcopage, have permitted us to measure more exactly all the aspects of this complex matter. Hence with all our heart we express to each of them our lively gratitude.   1171

6. The conclusions at which the commission arrived could not, nevertheless, be considered by us as definitive, nor dispense us from a personal examination of this serious question; and this also because, within the commission itself, no full concordance of judgments concerning the moral norms to be proposed had been reached, and above all because certain criteria of solutions had emerged which departed from the moral teaching on marriage proposed with constant firmness by the teaching authority of the Church.   1172

Therefore, having attentively sifted the documentation laid before us, after mature reflection and assiduous prayers, we now intend, by virtue of the mandate entrusted to us by Christ, to give our reply to these grave questions.   1173

1174   7. The problem of birth, like every other problem regarding human life, is to be considered, beyond partial perspectives—whether of the biological or psychological demographic or sociological orders—in the light of an integral vision of man and of his vocation, not only his natural and earthly, but also his supernatural and eternal vocation. And since, in the attempt to justify artificial methods of birth control, many have appealed to the demands both of conjugal love and of "responsible parenthood," it is good to state very precisely the true concept of these two great realities of married life, referring principally to what was recently set forth in this regard, and in a highly authoritative form, by the Second Vatican Council in its pastoral constitution *Gaudium et Spes*.

1175   8. Conjugal love reveals its true nature and nobility when it is considered in its supreme origin, God, who is love,[6] "the Father, from whom every family in heaven and on earth is named."[7]

1176   Marriage is not, then, the effect of chance or the product of evolution of unconscious natural forces; it is the wise institution of the Creator to realize in mankind His design of love. By means of the reciprocal personal gift of self, proper and exclusive to them, husband and wife tend towards the communion of their beings in view of mutual personal perfection, to collaborate with God in the generation and education of new lives.

1177   For baptized persons, moreover, marriage invests the dignity of a sacramental sign of grace, inasmuch as it represents the union of Christ and of the Church.

1178   9. Under this light, there clearly appear the characteristic marks and demands of conjugal love, and it is of supreme importance to have an exact idea of these.

1179   This love is first of all fully *human*, that is to say, of the senses and of the spirit at the same time. It is not, then, a simple transport of instinct and sentiment, but also, and principally, an act of the free will, intended to endure and to grow by means of the joys and sorrows of daily life, in such a way that husband and wife become one only heart and one only soul, and together attain their human perfection.

Then, this love is *total*, that is to say, it is a very special 1180
form of personal friendship, in which husband and wife generously share everything, without undue reservations or selfish calculations. Whoever truly loves his marriage partner loves
not only for what he receives, but for the partner's self, re-
joicing that he can enrich his partner with the gift of himself.

Again, this love is *faithful* and *exclusive* until death. Thus 1181
in fact do bride and groom conceive it to be on the day when
they freely and in full awareness assume the duty of the marriage bond. A fidelity, this, which can sometimes be difficult,
but is always possible, always noble and meritorious, as no
one can deny. The example of so many married persons
down through the centuries shows, not only that fidelity is
according to the nature of marriage, but also that it is a source
of profound and lasting happiness.

And finally this love is *fecund* for it is not exhausted by 1182
the communion between husband and wife, but is destined
to continue, raising up new lives. "Marriage and conjugal love
are by their nature ordained toward the begetting and educating of children. Children are really the supreme gift of marriage and contribute very substantially to the welfare of their
parents."[8]

10. Hence conjugal love requires in husband and wife an 1183
awareness of their mission of "responsible parenthood,"
which today is rightly much insisted upon, and which also
must be exactly understood. Consequently it is to be considered under different aspects which are legitimate and connected with one another.

In relation to the biological processes, responsible parent- 1184
hood means the knowledge and respect of their functions;
human intellect discovers in the power of giving life biological laws which are part of the human person.[9]

In relation to the tendencies of instinct or passion, re- 1185
sponsible parenthood means that necessary dominion which
reason and will must exercise over them.

In relation to physical, economic, psychological and social 1186
conditions, responsible parenthood is exercised, either by the
deliberate and generous decision to raise a numerous family,
or by the decision, made for grave motives and with due

respect for the moral law, to avoid for the time being, or even for an indeterminate period, a new birth.

1187   Responsible parenthood also and above all implies a more profound relationship to the objective moral order established by God, of which a right conscience is the faithful interpreter. The responsible exercise of parenthood implies, therefore, that husband and wife recognize fully their own duties towards God, towards themselves, towards the family and towards society, in a correct hierarchy of values.

1188   In the task of transmitting life, therefore, they are not free to proceed completely at will, as if they could determine in a wholly autonomous way the honest path to follow; but they must conform their activity to the creative intention of God, expressed in the very nature of marriage and of its acts, and manifested by the constant teaching of the Church.[10]

1189   11. These acts, by which husband and wife are united in chaste intimacy, and by means of which human life is transmitted, are as the Council recalled, "noble and worthy,"[11] and they do not cease to be lawful if, for causes independent of the will of husband and wife, they are foreseen to be infecund, since they always remain ordained towards expressing and consolidating their union. In fact, as experience bears witness, not every conjugal act is followed by a new life. God has wisely disposed natural laws and rhythms of fecundity which, of themselves, cause a separation in the succession of births. Nonetheless the Church, calling men back to the observance of the norms of the natural law, as interpreted by their constant doctrine, teaches that each and every marriage act (*quilibet matrimonii usus*) must remain open to the transmission of life.[12]

1190   12. That teaching, often set forth by the magisterium, is founded upon the inseparable connection, willed by God and unable to be broken by man on his own initiative, between the two meanings of the conjugal act: the unitive meaning and the procreative meaning. Indeed, by its intimate structure, the conjugal act, while most closely uniting husband and wife, capacitates them for the generation of new lives, according to laws inscribed in the very being of man and of woman. By safeguarding both these essential aspects, the unitive and the

procreative, the conjugal act preserves in its fullness the sense
of true mutal love and its ordination towards man's most
high calling to parenthood. We believe that the men of our
day are particularly capable of seizing the deeply reasonable
and human character of this fundamental principle.

13. It is in fact justly observed that a conjugal act imposed
upon one's partner without regard for his or her condition
and lawful desires is not a true act of love, and therefore
denies an exigency of right moral order in the relationships
between husband and wife. Likewise, if they consider the
matter, they must admit that an act of mutual love, which is
deterimental to the faculty of propagating life, which God
the Creator of all, has implanted in it according to special
laws, is in contradiction to both the divine plan, according
to whose norm matrimony has been instituted, and the will
of the Author of human life. To use this divine gift destroying, even if only partially, its meaning and its purpose is to
contradict the nature both of man of woman and of their
most intimate relationship, and therefore it is to contradict
also the plan of God and His will. On the other hand, to make
use of the gift of conjugal love while respecting the laws of
the generative process means to acknowledge oneself not to
be the arbiter of the sources of human life, but rather the
minister of the design established by the Creator. In fact, just
as man does not have unlimited dominion over his body in
general, so also, with particular reason, he has no such dominion over his generative faculties as such, because of their
intrinsic ordination towards raising up life, of which God is
the principle. "Human life is sacred," Pope John XXIII recalled; "from its very inception it reveals the creating hand
of God."[13]

14. In conformity with these landmarks in the human and
Christian vision of marriage, we must once again declare that
the direct interruption of the generative process already begun,
and, above all, directly willed and procured abortion, even if
for therapeutic reasons, are to be absolutely excluded as licit
means of regulating birth.[14]

Equally to be excluded, as the teaching authority of the
Church has frequently declared, is direct sterilization, whether

1191

1192

1193

perpetual or temporary, whether of the man or of the woman.[15] Similarly excluded is every action which, either in anticipation of the conjugal act, or in its accomplishment, or in the development of its natural consequences, proposes, whether as an end or as a means, to render procreation impossible.[16]

1194   To justify conjugal acts made intentionally infecund, one cannot invoke as valid reasons the lesser evil, or the fact that such acts would constitute a whole together with the fecund acts already performed or to follow later, and hence would share in one and the same moral goodness. In truth, if it is sometimes licit to tolerate a lesser evil in order to avoid a greater evil or to promote a greater good,[17] it is not licit, even for the gravest reasons, to do evil so that good may follow therefrom;[18] that is, to make into the object of a positive act of the will something which is intrinsically disorder, and hence unworthy of the human person, even when the intention is to safeguard or promote individual, family or social well-being. Consequently it is an error to think that a conjugal act which is deliberately made infecund and so is intrinsically dishonest could be made honest and right by the ensemble of a fecund conjugal life.

1195   15. The Church, on the contrary, does not at all consider illicit the use of those therapeutic means truly necessary to cure diseases of the organism, even if an impediment to procreation, which may be foreseen, should result therefrom, provided such impediment is not, for whatever motive, directly willed.[19]

1196   16. To this teaching of the Church on conjugal morals, the objection is made today, as we observed earlier (no. 3), that it is the prerogative of the human intellect to dominate the energies offered by irrational nature and to orientate them towards an end conformable to the good of man. Now, some may ask: in the present case, is it not reasonable in many circumstances to have recourse to artificial birth control if, thereby, we secure the harmony and peace of the family, and better conditions for the education of the children already born? To this question it is necessary to reply with clarity: the Church is the first to praise and recommend the intervention of intelligence in a function which so closely associates the rational creature with his Creator; but she affirms that this must be done with respect for the order established by God.

If, then, there are serious motives to space out births, which derive from the physical or psychological conditions of husband and wife, or from external conditions, the Church teaches that it is then licit to take into account the natural rhythms immanent in the generative functions, for the use of marriage in the infecund periods only, and in this way to regulate birth without offending the moral principles which have been recalled earlier.[20]   1197

The Church is coherent with herself when she considers recourse to the infecund periods to be licit, while at the same time condemning, as being always illicit, the use of means directly contrary to fecundation, even if such use is inspired by reasons which may appear honest and serious. In reality, there are essential differences between the two cases; in the former, the married couple make legitimate use of a natural disposition; in the latter, they impede the development of natural processes. It is true that, in the one and the other case, the married couple are concordant in the positive will of avoiding children for plausible reasons, seeking the certainty that offspring will not arrive; but it is also true that only in the former case are they able to renounce the use of marriage in the fecund periods when, for just motives, procreation is not desirable, while making use of it during infecund periods to manifest their affection and to safeguard their mutual fidelity. By so doing, they give proof of a truly and integrally honest love.   1198

17. Upright men can even better convince themselves of the solid grounds on which the teaching of the Church in this field is based, if they care to reflect upon the consequences of methods of artificial birth control. Let them consider, first of all, how wide and easy a road would thus be opened up towards conjugal infidelity and the general lowering of morality. Not much experience is needed in order to know human weakness, and to understand that men—especially the young, who are so vulnerable on this point—have need of en-   1199

couragement to be faithful to the moral law, so that they must not be offered some easy means of eluding its observance. It is also to be feared that the man, growing used to the employment of anti-conceptive practices, may finally lose respect for the woman and, no longer caring for her physical and psychological equilibrium, may come to the point of considering her as a mere instrument of selfish enjoyment, and no longer as his respected and beloved companion.

1200   Let it be considered also that a dangerous weapon would thus be placed in the hands of those public authorities who take no heed of moral exigencies. Who could blame a government for applying to the solution of the problems of the community those means acknowledged to be licit for married couples in the solution of a family problem? Who will stop rulers from favoring, from even imposing upon their peoples, if they were to consider it necessary, the method of contraception which they judge to be most efficacious? In such a way men, wishing to avoid individual, family, or social difficulties encountered in the observance of the divine law, would reach the point of placing at the mercy of the intervention of public authorities the most personal and most reserved sector of conjugal intimacy.

1201   Consequently, if the mission of generating life is not to be exposed to the arbitrary will of men, one must necessarily recognize insurmountable limits to the possibility of man's domination over his own body and its functions; limits which no man, whether a private individual or one invested with authority, may licitly surpass. And such limits cannot be determined otherwise than by the respect due to the integrity of the human organism and its functions, according to the principles recalled earlier, and also according to the correct understanding of the "principle of totality" illustrated by our predecessor Pope Pius XII.[21]

1202   18. It can be foreseen that this teaching will perhaps not be easily received by all: Too numerous are those voices— amplified by the modern means of propaganda—which are contrary to the voice of the Church. To tell the truth, the Church is not surprised to be made, like her divine Founder, a "sign of contradiction",[22] yet she does not because of this cease to proclaim with humble firmness the entire moral law, both natural and evangelical. Of such laws the Church was not the author, nor consequently can she be their arbiter; she is only their depositary and their interpreter, without ever being able to declare to be licit that which is not so by reason of its intimate and unchangeable opposition to the true good of man.

In defending conjugal morals in their integral wholeness, the Church knows that she contributes towards the establishment of a truly human civilization; she engages man not to abdicate from his own responsibility in order to rely on technical means; by that very fact she defends the dignity of man and wife. Faithful to both the teaching and the example of the Saviour, she shows herself to be the sincere and disinterested friend of men, whom she wishes to help, even during their earthly sojourn, "to share as sons in the life of the living God, the Father of all men."[23]   **1203**

19. Our words would not be an adequate expression of the thought and solicitude of the Church, Mother and Teacher of all peoples, if, after having recalled men to the observance and respect of the divine law regarding matrimony, we did not strengthen them in the path of honest regulation of birth, even amid the difficult conditions which today afflict families and peoples. The Church, in fact, cannot have a different conduct towards men than of the Redeemer: She knows their weaknesses, has compassion on the crowd, receives sinners; but she cannot renounce the teaching of the law which is, in reality, that law proper to a human life restored to its original truth and conducted by the spirit of God.[24]   **1204**

20. The teaching of the Church on the regulation of birth, which promulgates the divine law, will easily appear to many to be difficult or even impossible of actuation. And indeed, like all great beneficent realities, it demands serious engagement and much effort, individual, family and social effort. More than that, it would not be practicable without the help of God, who upholds and strengthens the good will of men. Yet, to anyone who reflects well, it cannot but be clear that such efforts ennoble man and are beneficial to the human community.   **1205**

1206   21. The honest practice of regulation of birth demands
first of all that husband and wife acquire and possess solid
convictions concerning the true values of life and of the
family, and that they tend towards securing perfect self-
mastery. To dominate instinct by means of one's reason
and free will undoubtedly requires ascetical practices, so that
the affective manifestations of conjugal life may observe the
correct order, in particular with regard to the observance of
periodic continence. Yet this discipline which is proper to
the purity of married couples, far from harming conjugal
love, rather confers on it a higher human value. It demands
continual effort yet, thanks to its beneficent influence, husband and wife fully develop their personalities, being enriched
with spiritual values. Such discipline bestows upon family life
fruits of serenity and peace, and facilitates the solution of
other problems; it favors attention for one's partner, helps
both parties to drive out selfishness, the enemy of true love;
and deepens their sense of responsibility. By its means, parents acquire the capacity of having a deeper and more efficacious influence in the education of their offspring; little children and youths grow up with a just appraisal of human
values, and in the serene and harmonious development of their
spiritual and sensitive faculties.

1207   22. On this occasion, we wish to draw the attention of
educators, and of all who perform duties of responsibility in
regard to the common good of human society, to the need of
creating an atmosphere favorable to education in chastity,
that is, to the triumph of healthy liberty over license by
means of respect for the moral order.

1208   Everything in the modern media of social communications
which leads to sense excitation and unbridled customs, as well
as every form of pornography and licentious performances,
must arouse the frank and unanimous reaction of all those
who are solicitous for the progress of civilization and the
defense of the common good of the human spirit. Vainly
would one seek to justify such depravation with the pretext
of artistic or scientific exigencies,[25] or to deduce an argument
from the freedom allowed in this sector by the public authorities.

23. To Rulers, who are those principally responsible for   1209
the common good, and who can do so much to safeguard
moral customs, we say: Do not allow the morality of your
peoples to be degraded; do not permit that by legal means
practices contrary to the natural and divine law be introduced
into that fundamental cell, the family. Quite other is the way
in which public authorities can and must contribute to the
solution of the demographic problem: namely, the way of a
provident policy for the family, of a wise education of peoples
in respect of moral law and the liberty of citizens.

We are well aware of the serious difficulties experienced by   1210
public authorities in this regard, especially in the developing
countries. To their legitimate preoccupations we devoted our
encyclical letter *Populorum Progressio*. But with our predecessor Pope John XXIII, we repeat: no solution to these
difficulties is acceptable "which does violence to man's essential dignity" and is based only on an utterly materialistic
conception of man himself and of his life. The only possible
solution to this question is one which envisages the social and
economic progress both of individuals and of the whole of
human society, and which respects and promotes true human
values.[26] Neither can one, without grave injustice, consider
divine providence to be responsible for what depends, instead,
on a lack of wisdom in government, on an insufficient sense
of social justice, on selfish monopolization, or again on blameworthy indolence in confronting the efforts and the sacrifices
necessary to ensure the raising of living standards of a people
and of all its sons.[27]

May all responsible public authorities—as some are already   1211
doing so laudably—generously revive their efforts. And may
mutual aid between all the members of the great human
family never cease to grow: This is an almost limitless field
which thus opens up to the activity of the great international
organizations.

24. We wish not to express our encouragement to men of   1212
science, who "can considerably advance the welfare of marriage and the family, along with peace of conscience, if by
pooling their efforts they labor to explain more thoroughly the
various conditions favoring a proper regulation of births."[28]

It is particularly desirable that, according to the wish already expressed by Pope Pius XII, medical science succeed in providing a sufficiently secure basis for a regulation of birth, founded on the observance of natural rhythms.[29] In this way, scientists and especially Catholic scientists will contribute to demonstrate in actual fact that, as the Church teaches, "a true contradiction cannot exist between the divine laws pertaining to the transmission of life and those pertaining to the fostering of authentic conjugal love."[30]

1213   25. And now our words more directly address our own children, particularly those whom God calls to serve Him in marriage. The Church, while teaching imprescriptible demands of the divine law, announces the tidings of salvation, and by means of the sacraments opens up the paths of grace, which makes man a new creature, capable of corresponding with love and true freedom to the design of his Creator and Saviour, and of finding the yoke of Christ to be sweet.[31]

1214   Christian married couples, then, docile to her voice, must remember that their Christian vocation, which began at baptism, is further specified and reinforced by the sacrament of matrimony. By it husband and wife are strengthed and as it were consecrated for the faithful accomplishment of their proper duties, for the carrying out of their proper vocation even to perfection, and the Christian witness which is proper to them before the whole world.[32] To them the Lord entrusts the task of making visible to men the holiness and sweetness of the law which unites the mutual love of husband and wife with their cooperation with the love of God the author of human life.

1215   We do not all intend to hide the sometimes serious difficulties inherent in the life of Christian married persons; for them as for everyone else, "the gate is narrow and the way is hard, that leads to life."[33] But the hope of that life must illuminate their way, as with courage they strive to live with wisdom, justice and piety in this present time,[34] knowing that the figure of this world passes away.[35]

1216   Let married couples, then, face up to the efforts needed, supported by the faith and hope which "do not disappoint. . . because God's love has been poured into our hearts through the Holy Spirit, who has been given to us;"[36] let them implore divine assistance by persevering prayer; above all, let them draw from the source of grace and charity in the Eucharist. And if sin should still keep its hold over them, let them not be discouraged, but rather have recourse with humble perseverance to the mercy of God, which is poured forth in the sacrament of Penance. In this way they will be enabled to achieve the fullness of conjugal life described by the Apostle: "husbands, love your wives, as Christ loved the Church. . . husbands should love their wives as their own bodies. He who loves his wife loves himself. For no man ever hates his own flesh, but nourishes and cherishes it, as Christ does the Church. . . this is a great mystery, and I mean in referance to Christ and the Church. However, let each one of you love his wife as himself, and let the wife see that she respects her husband."[37]

26. Among the fruits which ripen forth from a generous   1217
effort of fidelity to the divine law, one of the most precious
is that married couples themselves not infrequently feel the
desire to communicate their experience to others. Thus there
comes to be included in the vast pattern of the vocation of
the laity a new and most noteworthy form of the apostolate
of like to like; it is married couples themselves who become
apostles and guides to other married couples. This is assuredly,
among so many forms of apostolate, one of those which seem
most opportune today.[38]

27. We hold those physicians and medical personnel in the   1218
highest esteem who, in the exercise of their profession, value
above every human interest the superior demands of their
Christian vocation. Let them persevere, therefore, in promoting on every occasion the discovery of solutions inspired by
faith and right reason, let them strive to arouse this conviction and this respect in their associates. Let them also consider as their proper professional duty the task of acquiring all
the knowledge needed in this delicate sector, so as to be able
to give to those married persons who consult them wise counsel and healthy direction, such as they have a right to expect.

28. Beloved priest sons, by vocation you are the counselors   1219
and spiritual guides of individual persons and of families. We

now turn to you with confidence. Your first task—expecially in the case of those who teach moral theology—is to expound the Church's teaching on marriage without ambiguity. Be the first to give, in the exercise of your ministry, the example of loyal internal and external obedience to the teaching authority of the Church. That obedience, as you know well, obliges not only because of the reasons adduced, but rather because of the light of the Holy Spirit, which is given in a particular way to the pastors of the Church in order that they may illustrate the truth.[39] You know, too, that it is of the utmost importance, for peace of consciences and for the unity of the Christian people, that in the field of morals as well as in that of dogma, all should attend to the magisterium of the Church, and all should speak the same language. Hence, with all our heart we renew to you the heartfelt plea of the great Apostle Paul: "I appeal to you, brethren, by the name of Our Lord Jesus Christ, that all of you agree and that there be no dissensions among you, but that you be united in the same mind and the same judgment."[40]

1220   29. To diminish in no way the saving teaching of Christ constitutes an eminent form of charity for souls. But this must ever be accompanied by patience and goodness, such as the Lord himself gave example of in dealing with men. Having come not to condemn but to save,[41] he was indeed intransigent with evil, but merciful towards individuals.

1221   In their difficulties, may married couples always find, in the words and in the heart of a priest, the echo of the voice and the love of the Redeemer.

1222   And then speak with confidence, beloved sons, fully convinced that the spirit of God, while He assists the magisterium in proposing doctrine, illumines internally the hearts of the faithful inviting them to give their assent. Teach married couples that indispensable way of prayer; prepare them to have recourse often and with faith to the sacraments of the Eucharist and of Penance, without ever allowing themselves to be discouraged by their own weakness.

1223   30. Beloved and venerable brothers in the episcopate, with whom we most intimately share the solicitude of the spiritual good of the People of God, at the conclusion of this encyclical our reverent and affectionate thoughts turn to you. To all of you we extend an urgent invitation. At the head of the priests, your collaborators, and of your faithful, work ardently and incessantly for the safeguarding and the holiness of marriage, so that it may always be lived in its entire human and Christian fullness. Consider this mission as one of your most urgent responsibilities at the present time. As you know, it implies concerted pastoral action in all the fields of human activity, economic, cultural and social; for, in fact, only a simultaneous improvement in these various sectors will make it possible to render the life of parents and of children within their families not only tolerable, but easier and more joyous, to render the living together in human society more fraternal and peaceful, in faithfulness to God's design for the world.

31. Venerable brothers, most beloved sons, and all men of good will, great indeed is the work of education, of progress and of love to which we call you, upon the foundation of the Church's teaching, of which the successor of Peter is, together with his brothers in the episcopate, the depositary and interpreter. Truly a great work, as we are deeply convinced, both for the world and for the Church, since man cannot find true happiness—towards which he aspires with all his being—other than in respect of the laws written by God in his very nature, laws which he must observe with intelligence and love. Upon this work, and upon all of you, and especially upon married couples, we invoke the abundant graces of the God of holiness and mercy, and in pledge thereof we impart to you all our apostolic blessing. 1224

Given at Rome, from St. Peter's, this 25th day of July, feast of St. James the Apostle, in the year 1968, the sixth of our pontificate. 1225

Address of Pope Paul VI
to a General Audience
July 31, 1968

Our Words today concern a subject that We must take up because of the encyclical *Humanae Vitae*, dealing with birth control, which We issued this week. We presume that you are acquainted with the text of this papal document, or at least its essential contents. It is not just a declaration about a negative moral law, which forbids any action aimed at making procreation impossible,[1] it is above all a positive presentation of conjugal morality in relation to its mission of love and fruitfulness "within the integral vision of man and of his supernatural and eternal, as well as natural and earthly, vocation."[2] It is a clarification of a basic point in the personal, conjugal, family and social life of man; but it isn't a complete treatment of everything regarding human existence in the sphere of marriage, the family and upright living. This is a vast field, to which the Church's magisterium could and perhaps should return with a ground plan that will be broader, more organized and more systematic.

1227   This encyclical provides the answer to questions, doubts and tendencies that have, as everyone knows, been eagerly discussed on a wide scale in recent times and that have attracted a great deal of interest from Us because of Our pastoral and doctrinal office. We will not speak to you now about this document, partly because the seriousness and delicacy of the subject seem to transcend the ordinary simplicity of this weekly talk, and partly because there are already and will be more publications on the encyclical available to those interested in the subject.

We will say only a few words to you, not on the document itself but on some of the feelings that filled Our mind during the rather lengthy period of its preparation.   1228

The first feeling was that of Our own very grave responsibility. It brought Us into and sustained Us in the heart and core of the question for the four years of study and planning that went into this encyclical. We will confide to you that this feeling caused Us no small measure of mental anguish. We never felt the weight of Our office as much as in this situation. We studied, read and discussed all We could; and We also prayed a great deal.   1229

You are already aware of some of the circumstances surrounding this matter. We had to give an answer to the Church, to the whole of mankind. We had to evaluate a traditional doctrine that was not only age-old but also recent, having been reiterated by Our three immediate predecessors, and We had to do this with all of the sense of obligation and all of the liberty that go with Our apostolic duty. We had to make Our own the Council's teaching, which We Ourself had promulgated. Even though the conclusions of the commission established by Pope John, of venerable memory, and enlarged by Us, were only of a consultative nature, still We felt inclined to accept them, insofar as We thought We could; but at the same time We realized We had to act with all due prudence.   1230

We knew of the heated, passionate and authoritative discussions on this very important subject. We heard the loud voices of public opinion and of the press. We listened to the softer voices that penetrated into Our paternal, pastoral heart—the voices of many people, especially of highly respected women, who were distressed by this difficult problem and by their own even more difficult experience with it. We read the scientific reports on alarming population problems, often supported by the studies of experts and by government programs. We received publications from all directions, some of them based on a study of particular scientific aspects of the problem, others on a realistic consideration of many grave   1231 sociological conditions, and still others on the urgent demands arising from the changes that have burst forth in all areas of modern living.

1232   Many times We felt as if We were being swamped by this wave of documents; and many times, humanly speaking, We felt Our own humble inadequacy in the face of the formidable apostolic task of having to speak out on this matter. Many times We trembled before the dilemma of giving in easily to current opinions, or of making a decision that would be hard for modern society to accept, or that might be arbitrarily too burdensome for married life.

1233   We consulted many people with high moral, scientific and pastoral qualifications. We invoked the enlightenment of the Holy Spirit and put Our mind at the complete disposal of the voice of truth, striving to interpret the divine law that rises from the intrinsic requirements of genuine human love, from the essential structures of the institution of marriage, from the personal dignity of the spouses, from their mission in the service of life and from the holiness of Christian marriage. We reflected on the enduring elements of the traditional doctrine in force in the Church, and then in particular on the teachings of the recent council. We pondered the consequences of one decision and the other; and We had not doubts about Our duty to set forth Our decision in the terms expressed in the present encyclical.

1234   Our encyclical "Humanae Vitae" has caused many reactions. But as far as We recall, the Pope has never received so many spontaneous messages of gratitude and approval for the publication of a document as on this occasion. These messages have poured in from every part of the world and from every class of people. We mention this to express Our cordial thanks to all those who have welcomed Our encyclical letter and assured Us of their support. May the Lord bless them.

1235   We know, of course, that there are many who have not appreciated Our teaching, and not a few have opposed it. We can, in a sense, understand their lack of comprehension and even their opposition. Our decision is not an easy one. It is not in line with a practice unfortunately widespread today which is regarded as convenient and, on the surface, helpful to family harmony and love.

Once again We would remind you that the ruling We have reaffirmed is not Our own. It originates from the very structure of life, love and human dignity, and is thus derived from the law of God. It does not ignore the sociological and demographic conditions of our time. Contrary to what some seem to suppose, it is not in itself opposed to the rational limitation of births. It is not opposed to scientific research and therapeutic treatment, and still less to truly responsible parenthood. It does not even conflict with family peace and harmony. It is just a moral law—demanding and austere—which is still binding today. It forbids the use of means which are directed against procreation and which thus degrade the purity of love and the purpose of married life.   **1236**

The duty of Our office and pastoral charity have led Us to speak out. We therefore send a paternal greeting to all married couples and to all families who seek and find their moral strength and true happiness in the order willed by God. From Our heart We bless them and all of you, wishing you well in building a society based on the Christian way of life.   **1237**

Another feeling that always guided Us in Our labors is that of charity, of pastoral sensitivity toward those who are called upon to integrate their individual personalities into conjugal and family life. We willingly followed the personalistic conception that was characteristic of the Council's teaching on conjugal society, thus giving love—which produces that society and nourishes it—the preeminent position that rightly belongs to it in a subjective evaluation of marriage. Then We accepted all the suggestions formulated within the bounds of what was licit, to facilitate observance of the norm which We reaffirmed. We wanted to add to the doctrinal explanation some practical directions of a pastoral nature.   **1238**

We paid tribute to the role of scientists in pursuing their biological studies on birth, and in rightly applying therapeutic remedies and the moral law inherent in them. We recognized the responsibility and freedom of spouses as ministers of God's plan for human life, which is interpreted by the magisterium of the Church, for their own personal   **1239** good and that of their children. And We stressed the lofty purpose running through the Church's teaching and practice: that of helping men, defending their dignity, understanding them and supporting them in their difficulties, training them to have a keen sense of responsiblity, a strong and calm mastery over themselves, a courageous concept of the great and common duties of life and of the sacrifices inherent in practicing virtue and in building a fruitful and happy home.

1240   Finally, a feeling of hope accompanied the labor of editing this document. We hoped that it would be well received for its own merit and for its human truth, despite the variety of opinions spread far and wide at the present time, and despite the difficulty which the path traced out might present to those who intend to follow it faithfully, and also to those who must teach it frankly, with the help of the God of life, of course. We hoped that scholars in particular would be able to find in this document the genuine thread that connects it with the Christian concept of life, and that authorizes Us to take the words of the Apostle as Our own: *Nos autem sensum Christi habemus.*[3]

1241   Lastly, We hoped that Christian married couples would understand that Our words, however severe and hard they may seem, are intended to express the genuineness of their love, which is called upon to transfigure itself in imitation of Christ's love for His mystical spouse, the Church; and that these couples would be the first to support every practical movement to help families in their needs, to make them flourish in their full integrity, and to infuse into the modern family a spirituality of its own to serve as a source of perfection for its individual members and of moral witness within society.[6]

1242   As you can see, beloved sons, this is a very special question that has to do with an extremely delicate and serious aspect of human life. Just as We have tried to study and present it with the truth and charity that such a subject requires from Our magisterium and from Our ministry, so We ask all of you, whether you are directly concerned with the matter or not, to give it the attention it deserves, within the broad and radiant framework of Christian living.

With Our apostolic blessing.   1243

Human Life in Our Day
Selection from Pastoral Letter
by National Conference of Catholic Bishops of America
November 15, 1968

We honor God when we reverence human life. When human life is served, man is enriched and God is acknowledged. When human life is threatened, man is diminished and God is less manifest in our midst.

1245   A Christian defense of life should seek to clarify in some way the relationship between the love of life and the worship of God. One cannot love life unless he worships God, at least implicitly, nor worship God unless he loves life.

1246   The purpose of this pastoral letter of the United States bishops is precisely the doctrine and defense of life. Our present letter follows the moral principles set forth in the *Pastoral Constitution on the Church in the Modern World* issued by Vatican Council II. It presupposes the general doctrine of the Church which we explored in our pastoral letter *The Church in Our Day.* It responds to the encyclical *Humanae Vitae* in this same context.

1247   We are prompted to speak this year in defense of life for reasons of our pastoral obligation to dialogue within the believing community concerning what faith has to say in response to the threat to life in certain problems of the family and of war and peace.

1248   We also choose to speak of life because of the needed dialogue among all men of faith. This is particulary necessary among Christians and all believers in God, and between believers and all who love life if peace is to be secured and life

is to be served. There is evidence that many men find difficulty in reconciling their love for life with worship of the
Lord of life.

On the other hand, it is becoming clear that the believer   1249
and the humanist have common concerns for both life and
peace. For example, an agnostic philospher, much listened
to by contemporary students, has this to say:

"Why do not those who represent the traditions of reli-   1250
gion and humanism speak up and say that there is no deadlier
sin than love for death and contempt for life? Why not encourage our best brains—scientists, artists, educators—to
make suggestions on how to arouse and stimulate love for
life as opposed to love for gadgets?. . .Maybe it is too late.
Maybe the neutron bomb which leaves entire cities intact,
but without life, is to be the symbol of our civilization"
(Erich Fromm: *The Heart of Man: Its Genius for Good and
Evil*).

The defense of life provides a starting point, then, for posi-   1251
tive dialogue between Christians and humanists. Christians
bring to the dialogue on the defense of life a further motivation. We are convinced that belief in God is intimately bound
up with devotion to life. God is the ultimate source of life,
His Son its Redeemer, so that denial of God undermines the
sanctity of life itself.

Our pastoral letter will emphasize the maturing of life in   1252
the family and the development of life in a peaceful world
order. Threats to life are most effectively confronted by an
appeal to Christian conscience. We pray that our words may
join us in common cause with all who reverence life and seek
peace. We pray further that our efforts may help join all
men in common faith before God Who "gives freely and His
gift is eternal life" (*Rm*. 6, 23).

The attitude man adopts toward life helps determine the   1253
person he becomes. In the family, man and life are first
united. In the family, the person becomes the confident servant of man. The Church must make good her belief in human life and her commitment to its development by active
as well as doctrinal defense of the family and by practical
witness to the values of family life.

1254   The Church thinks of herself as a family, the family of God and, so, is the more solicitous for the human family. She sees Christian marriage as a sign of the union between Christ and the Church (cf. *Eph.* 5, 31-32), a manifestation to history of the "genuine nature of the Church" *(Gaudium et Spes,* 48). Chrsitian married love is "caught up into divine love and is governed and enriched by Christ's redeeming power and the saving activity of the Church" *(Gaudium et Spes,* 48). No institution or community in human history has spoken more insistently and profoundly than the Church of the dignity of marriage.

1255   It is in terms of Christ and of salvation history, never of sociology alone, that the Church thinks of marriage. That is the point of her positive teachings on the sanctity, the rights and the duties of the married state; it is also the point of her occasional strictures, as when Vatican Council II realistically cautions that "married love is too often profaned by excessive self-love, the worship of pleasure, and illicit practices against human generation" *(Gaudium et Spes,* 47).

1256   The family fulfills its promise when it reinforces fidelity to life and hope in its future. The values of fidelity and hope, essential to human life and Christian love, are sometimes weakened even while men continue to think all is well. Such is often the case in our times. Fidelity and hope are especially threatened when the family is considered largely in terms of the pleasures or conveniences it provides for the individual or in terms of its economic or political potential. Christians should be the first to promote material improvement and provide for the family structure, but they must never measure the worth of the family nor the purpose of a family life by these standards alone.

1257   For the believer, the family is the place where God's image is reproduced in His creation. The family is the community within which the person is realized, the place where all our hopes for the future of the person are nourished. The family is a learning experience in which fidelity is fostered, hope imparted and life honored; it thus increases the moral resources of our culture and, more importantly, of the person. The family is a sign to all mankind of fidelity to life and of hope in the future which become possible when persons are in communion with one another, it is a sign to believers of the depth of this fidelity and this hope when these center on God; it is a sign to Christians of the fidelity and hope which Christ communicates as the elder brother of the family of the Church for which He died (cf. *Eph*. 5, 25).

It is the unfortunate fact that in all times some men have acted against life. The forms of the threat have varied, some of these endure to this day. Since the family is the source of life, no act against life is more hostile than one which occurs within the family. By such an act, life is cancelled out within that very community whose essential purposes include the gift of life to the world and the service of life in fidelity and hope.   1258

For all these reasons, the Christian family is called more now than ever to a prophetic mission, a witness to the primacy of life and the importance of whatever preserves life. The Christian family therefore occupies a pre-eminent place in our renewed theology, particularly the theology of marriage and of the vocation of the laity. Christian families are called to confront the world with the full reality of human love and proclaim to the world the mystery of divine love as these are revealed through the family.   1259

The prophetic mission of the family obliges it to fidelity to conjugal love in the face of the compromises and infidelities condoned in our culture. Its prophetic mission obliges the family to valiant hope in life, contradicting whatever forces seek to prevent, destroy or impair life. In its emphasis on the virtues of fidelity and hope, so essential to the prophetic witness of the family, Christian sexual morality derives therefore not from the inviolability of generative biology, but ultimately from the sanctity of life itself and the nobility of human sexuality.   1260

The Christian ascetic of chastity, within and outside marriage, honors the sanctity of life and protects the dignity of human sexuality. Were there no Revelation nor religion, civilization itself would require rational discipline of the sexual instinct. Revelation, however, inspires chastity with more sublime purposes and creative power. In chaste love, the   1261

Christian, whether his vocation be to marriage or to celibacy, expresses love for God Himself. In the case of spouses, marital chastity demands not the contradiction of sexuality but its ordered expression in openness to life and fidelity to love, which means also openness and faithfulness to God.

1262 These considerations enter into the definition of responsible parenthood. The decision to give life to another person is the responsibility, under God, of the spouses who, in effect, ask the Creator to commit to their care the formation of a child (cf. *Gaudium et Spes*, 50). The fact that the decision touches upon human life and the human person is an indication of the reverence in which it must be made; the fact that the decision involves openness to God's creative power and providential love demands that it be unselfish, free from all calculation inconsistent with generosity.

1263 Responsible parenthood, as the Church understands it, places on the properly formed conscience of spouses all the judgments, options and choices which add up to the awesome decision to give, postpone or decline life. The final decision may sometimes involve medical, economic, sociological or psychological considerations, but in no case can it deliberately choose objective moral disorder. If it is to be responsible, it cannot be the result of mere caprice nor of superficial judgments concerning relative values as between persons and things, between life and its conveniences.

1264 Marital love, then, in its deepest meaning relates not only to the birth and rearing of children within the family society, but to the growth and well—being of human society on its every level and in its every aspect. It relates at the same time to the eternal life of those who choose marriage as their way to salvation. It is within this perspective of a total vision of man and not merely of isolated family considerations, narrowly conceived, that Pope Paul, drawing extensively on the content of Vatican Council II, has written his encyclical *Humanae Vitae*.

1265 *The Pastoral Constitution on the Church in the Modern World* provides the thological framework within which Pope Paul works out the teaching set forth in *Humanae Vitae*:

"Therefore when there is question of harmonizing conjugal   1266
love with the responsible transmission of life, the moral aspect
of any procedure does not depend solely on sincere intentions
or on an evaluation of motives. It must be determined by
objective standards. These, based on the nature of the human
person and his acts, preserve the full sense of mutual self-
giving and human procreation in the context of true love.
Such a goal cannot be achieved unless the virtue of conjugal
chastity is sincerely practiced. Relying on these principles,
sons of the Church may not undertake methods of regulating
procreation which are found blameworthy by the teaching
authority of the Church in its unfolding of the divine law.

"Everyone should be persuaded that human life and the   1267
task of transmitting it are not realities bound up with this
world alone. Hence they cannot be measured or perceived
only in terms of it, but always have a bearing on the eternal
destiny of men" *(Gaudium et Spes,* 51).

Pope Paul speaks of conjugal love as "fully human,"   1268
"a very special form of personal friendship," "faithful
and exclusive until death," "a source of profound and lasting
happiness." Such love, however, "is not exhausted by the
communion between husband and wife, but is destined to
continue, raising up new lives." There is an "objective moral
order established by God" which requires that "each and
every marriage act must remain open to the transmission of
life."

Both conciliar and papal teaching, therefore, emphasize   1269
that the interrelation between the unitive meaning and the
procreative meaning of marriage is impaired, even contradicted, when acts expressive of marital union are performed
without love on the one hand and without openness to life
on the other. Consistent with this, the encyclical sees the use
of the periodic rhythms of nature, even though such use
avoids rather than prevents conception, as morally imperfect
if its motivation is primarily refusal of life rather than the
human desire to share love within the spirituality of responsible parenthood.

The encyclical *Humanae Vitae* is not a negative proc-   1270
lamation, seeking only to prohibit artificial methods of con-

traception. In full awareness of population problems and family anxieties, it is a defense of life and of love, a defense which challenges the prevailing spirit of the times. Long-range judgments may well find the moral insights of the encyclical prophetic and its world-view providential. There is already evidence that some peoples in economically under-developed areas may sense this more than those conditioned by the affluence of a privileged way of life.

1271   The encyclical is a positive statement concerning the nature of conjugal love and responsible parenthood, a statement which derives from a global vision of man, an integral view of marriage, and the first principles, at least, of a sound sexuality. It is an obligatory statement, consistent with moral convictions of Eastern and Western Christian faith; it is an authoritative statement solemnly interpreting imperatives which are divine rather than ecclesiastical in origin. It presents without ambiguity, doubt or hesitation the authentic teaching of the Church concerning the objective evil of that contraception which closes the marital act to the transmission of life, deliberately making it unfruitful. United in collegial solidarity with the Successor of Peter, we proclaim this doctrine.

1272   The encyclical reminds us that the use of the natural rhythms never involves a direct positive action against the possibility of life; artificial contraception always involves a direct positive action against the possibility of life. Correspondence with the natural rhythms remains essentially attuned to the unitive and procreative intent of the conjugal act even when the spouses are aware of the silence of nature to life.

1273   There are certain values which may not oblige us always to act on their behalf, but we are prohibited from ever acting directly against them by positive acts. Truth is such a value; life is surely another. It is one thing to say that an action against these values is inculpable, diminished in guilt, or subjectively defensible; it is quite another to defend it as objectively virtuous.

1274   The Church's teaching on the moral means to responsible parenthood presupposes certain positive values. One of these is that Christian marriage involves an ever-maturing mutuality between husband and wife, a constantly increasing awareness of the manner in which the total nuptial relationship parallels and symbolizes the love-sharing and life-giving union between Christ and His Church. The unitive and creative values symbolized by sexual expression permeate marriage in its every aspect. This consideration becomes more important as the years of married life go by, especially when changes in society give couples longer years of leisure together after their children begin to live on their own. This explains the importance that couples be united from the beginning of their love by common interests and shared activities which will intensify their nuptial relationship and insure its unity against disruption because of disappointment in one or another of their hopes.

No one pretends that responsible parenthood or even   **1275** fidelity to the unitive love of marriage, as these are understood by the Church, is easy of attainment without prayerful discipline. Recourse to natural rhythms, for example, presents problems which the Holy Father has asked medical science to help solve. Chastity, as other virtues, is not mastered all at once or without sacrifice. It may involve failures and success, declines and growth, regressions in the midst of progress. A hierarchy of values that reflects a conformity to the example of Christ is neither easily achieved nor insured against loss. Moreover, Christians, however many their failures, will neither expect nor wish the Church to obscure the moral ideal in the light of which they press forward to perfection.

In the pursuit of the ideal of chastity, again as of every   **1276** other virtue to which he is bound, the Christian must never lose heart; least of all can he pretend that compromise is conquest. At all times, his mind and heart will echo St. Paul: "Not that I have become perfect yet; I have not yet won, but I am still running, trying to capture the prize for which Christ Jesus captured me" (*Phil.* 3, 12). In no case, does he suppose that the Church, in proposing such goals, teaches erroneously and needlessly burdens its members.

They are quite right who insist that the Church must labor   **1277** to heal the human condition by more than word and precept alone if it wishes its preaching to be taken seriously. All the moral teaching of the Church proposes objective standards difficult to attain: of honesty, respect for other peoples' property and lives, social justice, integrity in public office, devotion to learning, to service, to God. These standards demand of those to whom they are preached renunciations, frequently against the grain, but creative in their final effect. They also demand of those who preach these ideals that they, too, play their full part in the struggle against the social evils which obstruct their attainment.

1278   We shall consider later in this letter some of our pastoral responsibilities toward the promotion of distributive justice, the rights and stability of the family, and the consequent social climate favorable to marriage morality. In the meantime, the Church, when She fulfills her prophetic role of preaching moral ideals and social reform, must do so with all the patience that the work of teaching requires (cf. 2 *Tim.* 4, 2).

1279   The existence of the Sacrament of Penance in the Church is an indication that Christian ideals are not easy to achieve nor, once achieved, ours forever. The Church cannot, however, compromise the ideal. She is bound to teach it as it is.

1280   Developing last year the teaching of the Council on the nature of the Church, we spoke of the reciprocal claims of conscience and authority in the Christian community as Christ called it into being. We noted that conscience "though it is inviolable is not a law unto itself"; that "the distinction between natural religion and revealed lies in this: that one has a subjective authority, and the other an objective," though both invoke conscience. We recalled that "God does not leave man to himself but has entered history through a Word which is 'the true light that enlightens all men'; that Word speaks to us and still enlightens us in the Church of Jesus Christ which carries the double burden of human conscience and divine authority."

1281   These wider questions of conscience, its nature, witness, aberrations and claims, above all its formation, are presupposed in this encyclical as in any papal or conciliar decisions on moral teaching. We recognize the role of conscience as a "practical dictate," not a teacher of doctrine.

Thomas Aquinas describes conscience as the practical 1282
judgment or dictate of reason, by which we judge what here
and now is to be done as being good, or to be avoided as evil.
Vatican Council II says that a man is not to be forced to act
in a manner contrary to his conscience (cf. *Dignitatis Humanae Personae*, 3). This is certainly true in any conflict between a practical dictate of conscience and a legislative or
administrative decree of any superior.

However, when it is question of the Pope's teaching, as 1283
distinct from a decree or order, on a matter bound up with
life and salvation, the question of conscience and its formation
takes on quite different perspectives and dimensions. Cardinal
Newman puts it in strong terms: ". . .I have to say again, lest
I should be misunderstood, that when I speak of conscience,
I mean conscience truly so called. When it has the right of
opposing the supreme, though not infallible Authority of the
Pope, it must be something more than miserable counterfeit
which, as I have said above, now goes by the name. If in a
particular case it is to be taken as a sacred and sovereign
monitor, its dictate, in order to prevail against the voice of
the Pope, must follow upon serious thought, prayer, and all
available means of arriving at a right judgment on the matter
in question. And further, obedience to the Pope is what is
called 'in possession'; that is, the *onus probandi* (burden of
proof) of establishing a case against him lies, as in all cases of
exception, on the side of conscience. Unless a man is able to
say to himself, as in the Presence of God, that he must not,
and dare not, act upon the Papal injunction, he is bound to
obey it and would commit a great sin in disobeying it. *Prima
facie* it is his bounden duty, even from a sentiment of loyalty,
to believe the Pope is right and to act accordingly . . ." *(A
Letter to the Duke of Norfolk)*.

Humanae Vitae does not discuss the question of the good 1284
faith of those who make practical decisions in conscience
against what the Church considers a divine law and the Will
of God. The encyclical does not undertake to judge the consciences of individuals but to set forth the authentic teaching
of the Church which Catholics believe interprets the divine
law to which conscience should be conformed.

1285   *The Pastoral Constitution on the Church in the Modern World* reminds us that "in their manner of acting, spouses should be aware that they cannot proceed arbitrarily. They must always be governed according to a conscience dutifully conformed to the divine law itself, and should be submissive toward the Church's teaching office, which authentically interprets that law in the light of the Gospel. That divine law reveals and protects the integral meaning of conjugal love and impels it toward a truly human fulfillment" *(Gaudium et Spes,* 50). We must not suppose that there is such conflict between authority and freedom, between objective values and subjective fulfillment, that one can only prevail by the elimination of the other.

1286   Married couples faced with conflicting duties are often caught in agonizing crises of conscience. For example, at times it proves difficult to harmonize the sexual expression of conjugal love with respect for the life-giving power of sexual union and demands of responsible prarenthood. Pope Paul's encyclical and the commentaries of the international episcopates on it are sensitive as are we to these painful situations. Filled with compassion for the human condition the Holy Father offers counsel which we make our own:

1287   "Let married couples, then, face up to the efforts needed, supported by the faith and hope which do not disappoint. . . because God's love has been poured into our hearts through the Holy Spirit, Who has been given to us; let them implore divine assistance by persevering prayer; above all, let them draw from the source of grace and charity in the Eucharist. And if sin should still keep its hold over them, let them not be discouraged, but rather have recourse with humble perseverance to the mercy of God, which is poured forth in the Sacrament of Penance" *(Humanae Vitae,* 25).

1288   We feel bound to remind Catholic married couples, when they are subjected to the pressures which prompt the Holy Father's concern, that however circumstances may reduce moral guilt, no one following the teaching of the Church can deny the objective evil of artificial contraception itself. With pastoral solicitude we urge those who have resorted to artifical contraception never to lose heart but to continue to take full advantage of the strength which comes from the Sacrament of Penance and the grace, healing, and peace in the Eucharist. May we all be mindful of the invitation of Jesus: "The man who comes to me I will never turn away" *(Jn.* 6, 37). Humility, awareness of our pilgrim state, a willingness and determination to grow in the likeness of the Risen Christ will help to restore direction of purpose and spiritual stability.

The position taken by the Holy Father in his encyclical   1289 troubled many. The reasons for this are numerous. Not a few had been led and had led others to believe that a contrary decision might be anticipated. The mass media which largely shape public opinion have, as the Holy Father himself pointed out, at times amplified the voices which are contrary to the voice of the Church. Then, too, doctrine on this point has its effect not only on the intellects of those who hear it but on their deepest emotions; it is hardly surprising that negative reactions have ranged from sincere anguish to angry hurt or bitter disappointment, even among devout believers. Finally, a decision on a point so long uncontroverted and only recently confronted by new questions was bound to meet with mixed reactions.

That tensions such as these should arise within the house-   1290 hold of the faith is not surprising and need not be scandalous. The Holy Father frankly confessed that his teaching would not be easily received by all. Some reactions were regrettable, however, in the light of the explicit teaching of Vatican Council II concerning the obligation of Catholics to assent to papal teaching even when it is not presented with the seal of infallibility. The Council declared:

"In matters of faith and morals, the bishops speak in the   1291 name of Christ and the faithful are to accept their teaching and adhere to it with a religious assent of soul. This religious submission of will and of mind must be shown in a special way to the authentic teaching authority of the Roman Pontiff, even when he is not speaking *excathedra.* That is, it must be shown in such a way that his supreme magisterium is acknowledged with reverence, the judgments made by him are sincerely adhered to, according to his manifest mind and will. His mind and will in the matter may be known chiefly either from the character of the documents, from his frequent repetition of the same doctrine, or from his manner of speaking" (*Lumen Gentium*, 25).

1292 Pope Paul has recalled this obligation several times with respect to his encyclical on the regulation of birth, beginning when he exhorted priests "to be the first to give, in the exercise of your ministry, the example of loyal internal and external obedience to the teaching authority of the Church" (*Humanae Vitae*, 28).

1293 There exist in the Church a lawful freedom of inquiry and of thought and also general norms of licit dissent. This is particularly true in the area of legitimate theological speculation and research. When conclusions reached by such professional theological work prompt a scholar to dissent from non-infallible received teaching the norms of licit dissent come into play. They require of him careful respect for the consciences of those who lack his special competence or opportunity for judicious investigation. These norms also require setting forth his dissent with propriety and with regard for the gravity of the matter and the deference due the authority which has pronounced on it.

1294 The reverence due all sacred matters, particularly questions which touch on salvation, will not necessarily require the responsible scholar to relinquish his opinion but certainly to propose it with prudence born of intellectual grace and a Christian confidence that the truth is great and will prevail.

1295 When there is question of theological dissent from non-infallible doctrine, we must recall that there is always a presumption in favor of the magisterium. Even non-infallible authentic doctrine, though it may admit of development or call for clarification or revision, remains binding and carries with it a moral certitude, especially when it is addressed to the universal Church, without ambiguity, in response to urgent questions bound up with faith and crucial to morals. The expression of theological dissent from the magisterium is in order only if the reasons are serious and well-founded, if the manner of the dissent does not question or impugn the teaching authority of the Church and is such as not to give scandal.

Since our age is characterized by popular interest in theo-   1296
logical debate and given the realities of modern mass media,
the ways in which theological dissent may be effectively
expressed, in a manner consistent with pastoral solicitude,
should become the object of fruitful dialogue between
bishops and theologians. These have their diverse ministries
in the Church, their distinct responsibilities to the faith and
their respective charisms.

Even responsible dissent does not excuse one from faithful   1297
presentation of the authentic doctrine of the Church when
one is performing a pastoral ministry in Her name.

We count on priests, the counsellors of persons and fam-   1298
ilies, to heed the appeal of Pope Paul that they "expound the
Church's teaching on marriage without ambiguity"; that they
"diminish in no way the saving teaching of Christ," but "teach
married couples the indispensable way of prayer. . .without
ever allowing them to be discouraged by their weakness"
(*Humanae Vitae*, 29). We commend to confessors, as does
Pope Paul, the example of the Lord Himself, Who was indeed
intransigent with evil, but merciful towards individuals.

Our concern for family life must extend far beyond the   1299
publication of pastoral letters. We pledge ourselves to cooperate in multiplying ways and means toward the renewal of
the family and the enhancing of its prestige. Specifically, we
shall increase our encouragement in the dioceses and the
nation of programs undertaken by apostolic groups whose
objective is the natural and spiritual strengthening of the
Christian family.

Because of the primacy of the spiritual in all that makes   1300
for renewal, we give top priority to whatever may produce a
sound "family spirituality." Family prayer, above all that
which derives its content and spirt from the liturgy, and other
devotions, particularly the Rosary; family reading of the
Scriptures; family attendance at Mass and reception of
Communion; family retreats, days of recollection and other
special devotions; the observance of occasions of spiritual
significance for members of the household—all these will
increase the awareness of the family that it is the "Church in
miniature."

1301   For these reasons, we welcome the work of those theologians who are preparing a modern and valid ascetical theology of marriage. We recall gratefully the spiritual emphasis in many family-life programs, national and local, whose primary focus of concern has been the theology of the Christian family.

1302   To prepare future spouses more adequately we recommend specialized team-efforts in their behalf on the part of pastors of souls and qualified counsellors, including devout married couples. Such projects will give engaged couples the benefit of human wisdom and of Christian spirituality in the planning of their home, the founding of a family, the education of children, and all that makes for fidelity and hope in their lives together.

1303   We endorse the establishment of diocesan family life centers throughout the country so that Christian couples, physicians, psychologists, sociologists and priests may cooperate in implementing responsible parenthood in accordance with the principles enunciated in *Humanae Vitae*. On the national level, in response to the Holy Father's request for scientific research into effective and moral means of family planning, we bishops in the United States intend to establish an independent, non-denominational, non-profit foundation which will sponsor scientific research resulting in conclusions which will be helpful to doctors, educators and, ultimately, spouses in licit family planning.

1304   The responsibility of our Family Life Division to provide information, educational tools and guidance in the face of the mounting problems of family life will make it an increasing source of service to diocesan family programs. We also hope to see established centers of education in family life under the auspices of local medical schools or doctors' guilds together with collegiate or adult education programs, and the chaplains to students or young-adult groups. We note the Holy Father's tribute to the promising apostolate which brings together married couples who desire to communicate their experiences to other married couples and thus become apostles of fidelity to the divine law and guides to fulfillment in love.

In accord with the *Decree on Christian Education* of Vati-   1305
can Council II we affirm the value and necessity of wisely
planned education of children in human sexuality, adapted to
the maturity and background of our young people. We are
under a grave obligation, in part arising from the new circumstances of modern culture and communications, to assist the
family in its efforts to provide such training. This obligation
can be met either by systematic provision of such education
in the diocesan school curriculum or by the inauguration of
acceptable educational programs under other diocesan auspices, including the Confraternity of Christian Doctrine.
Parents are those primarily responsible for imparting to their
children an awareness of the sacredness of sexuality; this will
ordinarily be best accomplished when both parents discharge
this duty in mutual consultation and shared responsibility.
The necessity for greater communication and cooperation
between parents and teachers is highlighted in this program;
the consequent role of Parent-Teacher Guilds and similar
home-school associations is apparent.

Parents are sometimes fearful that their right to teach the   1306
norms of sexual morality to their children may be usurped
or that programs such as we envision may lead to the sexual
misdirection of their children if the teachers involved are in-
adequately prepared or emotionally immature. In the light
of such legitimate concerns, the careful selection of instruc-
tors for these discussions is a serious responsibility to be
shared by priests, school authorities and parents, perhaps
best under the auspices of parent-teacher associations.

The content of these instructions should provide an   1307
appreciation of "the true values of life and of the family"
(Humanae Vitae, 21), in addition to a healthy inculcation,
from the earliest years of moral and intellectual formation,
of how conjugal love involves a harmonious response from
the emotions, the passions, the body and the mind. At the
same time, healthy Christian attitudes toward life will be
developed in young people if they are given an understanding,
consistent with their years, of why the Council insists that
those "actions within marriage by which the couple are

united intimately and chastely are noble and worthy ones" (*Gaudium et Spes*, 49).

1308   During these early years of physical growth and spiritual formation, especially throughout adolescence, our young people and their neighbors should be taught to appreciate the heroic witness to divine life and the unique service to human life given by those who, with love undivided, dedicate to God and their fellow-men the consecration of their celibacy and virginity for the sake of the Kingdom of God. Our priests, religious brothers and sisters have bound themselves to live in persevering single-hearted commitment as intimate collabora-tors with God Himself, from Whom every family, whether spiritual or natural, takes its name both in heaven and earth (*Eph.* 3, 15). Every family is therefore in their debt: the fam-ilies from which they come, the families to which they bear their special witness of life and love, the national family of the Church. No one knows this more than their bishops; no one is more grateful.

1309   In facing current problems of the American family, we welcome the open approach of the *Pastoral Constitution on the Church in the Modern World* toward marriage and the family. It provides a timely and optimistic overview of the community aspect of marriage, a community that functions best when all its members understand that freedom is their birthright and a developing sense of responsibility their challenge. It sets up balances which provide for the more perfect personal development of each family member and, at the same time, assures the optimum effect of the family unit in the larger family of man. It recognizes the continual and rapid changes which characterize our times.

1310   The style of family living is undoubtedly affected by changing social conditions, yet the family retains a resilience and strength that helps it adapt to change. In fact, the family has always been the witness to change as it passes on the wis-dom, successes and accomplishments of one generation to the next as a patrimony for the pursuance of its dreams.

1311   Commenting on this adaptability to change that is almost inherent in the family, Pope Paul VI notes that "in a world in the midst of change, it would be useless to want to close one's eyes to the adaptations which even the most stable, most traditional institutions must accept. No matter how great the merits of the family of yesterday may have been, it is the one of today and of tomorrow which must attract the attention of men who are really preoccupied with the welfare of humanity. These 'new families' possess many new characteristics, some of which may certainly give rise to legitimate disquietude. But—we say without fear—the Church looks with pleasure upon many of these innovations: the cessation, for example, of certain social or family restrictions, the freer and more conscious choice of a spouse, the greater stress placed upon the development of husband and wife, the more lively interest in the education of children, and still many other traits which it is not possible to enumerate in detail" *(Paul VI to IUFO).*

One of the best examples of this new type of family   1312 structure is the present-day American family. It is a community of individual persons joined by human love, and living a community life that provides for the greatest expression of individualism. At the same time, equalitarian marriage patterns have so developed among Americans as to avoid rigid role assignments within the family and thus make possible a deeper family unity.

The family unit develops apart from the parent-families,   1313 yet not totally isolated. In our technological culture, transportation facilities and communications media provide new systems of mobility and yet fortunately allow for a strengthening of human bonds among families, despite the distances in geographical location.

The educational attainment of women and a new emphasis   1314 on legal and social equality between men and women create further tensions but also opportunities for more effective partnership in marriage. This adds a further reason why a Catholic theology of family life must be spelled out to match the changing patterns of the American family. A relevant theology will reinforce the efforts of spouses to achieve conjugal maturity; it will enable them to realize the more profoundly the difference between romance and love and to understand that only gradually will they achieve the harmony between healthy individualism and mutual self-giving in which Christian personalism consists.

1315   Technological and cultural changes bring with them complexities not easily resolved. Some of these set up pressures on the family from outside, some from within. For example, even the family today finds itself under the necessity to develop new channels of "communication"; this seems a formidable word to describe relations within the intimate community that a human family should be. However, the problem is made real by the profoundly changed circumstances under which each family member now seeks to establish an identity while preserving a warm sense of family unity and pride. Family harmony in our day will depend on just such "communication" as parents attempt to solve the authority-obedience dilemma with their growing children. Moreover, reformed "communication" within the family is needed if the manifold educational resources of family life itself are to complement the formal schooling of children.

1316   The individual family is now challenged to new responsibilities toward the plurality of families which comprises the nation, the human community and the Church. And so Christian families, conscious of their part in the progress of the wider human family, will wish to share not only their spiritual heritage with families less privileged but also their material resources. They will seek by their own initiatives to supplement government action, being painfully aware that in our own country many families are victims of poverty, disease and inadequate living standards.

1317   Informed social critics are asserting that family instability in the urban areas of America is the result, in part at least, of our national failure to adopt comprehensive and realistic family-centered policies during the course of this century. The breakdown of the family has intrinsic causes, some of them moral, but these have been aggravated by the indifference or neglect of society and by the consequences of poverty and racist attitudes. The object of wise social policy is not only the physical well-being of persons but their emotional stability and moral growth, not as individuals but, whenever possible, within family units.

In principle, American social theory has always recognized   1318
that the normal family enjoys a real autonomy; only the
abnormal inadequacy of a particular family places its members
within the competency of our courts. Even then, whenever
possible, it is the disposition of our public agencies to supply
the defects of nature by providing the neglected, delinquent
or homeless child with the nearest possible approach to life
and training in a family setting. Americans have tended to
prefer, particularly recently, the plan of foster homes where
the role of natural parents can be somehow supplied in the
development of the person within a human family. Our
theory in all these respects has been admirable; its implementation in legislation and in practice has not always kept pace
with the problems testing the theory. The present urban crisis
is but one evidence of this.

Though families, like man himself, do not live on bread   1319
alone, without bread they suffer and die. Food programs
still need a family orientation. Poor housing, for further
example, has an adverse effect on family stabilty. We urge an
expansion of home ownership programs for low and moderate-
income families, especially the larger families frequently
neglected in these plans, as well as programs for low-rent
housing and housing rehabilitation.

Programs devised to assist less advantaged families should   1320
at all cost avoid disruption of the family unit. A major
disruption occurs when mothers are required to separate
themselves from their young children for the sake of added
income. Disruption has too often been the result of certain
welfare policies which, whether consciously intended or not,
have destroyed rather than supported family stability; one
such policy we pin-pointed in our reference to the "man in
the house" rule when we spoke in a recent statement on the
national social problem, but others could be documented.
Every member of each family has a right to be cared for, not
as an isolated person but as a person who belongs with and
depends upon a family. We therefore favor the trend to
consider social service programs, domestic relations courts
and child welfare casework as involving family rather than
merely individual dimensions and solutions.

1321   Whenever a family is undermined, society suffers the loss. There are no insignificant families, as there is no insignificant person. If families are to function as the good of society requires, each must have income proportionate to its needs.

1322   Wages in our country are usually based upon the work done, plus productivity. Little or no consideration is given to the family situation of the individual, his marital status, or the number of children in his home. It should not normally be necessary for the father of a family to "moonlight," seeking employment from more than one source to support his wife and children. Single men and the married men with families receive the same rates of pay for the same work. As a result, one sector of the population bears a disproportionately large share of the financial burden of maintaining the child population, which means the future nation, except for income tax benefits, which may unfortunately be cancelled out by consumer taxes. The effective solution we are urging may well require a family allowance system in the United States similar to those adopted by Canada, many European nations, Australia, New Zealand and some governments of South America. We stand ready to support enlightened legislation in this sense.

1323   The challenges and threats to contemporary family life may often seem insuperable. However, the resources of this nation are more than sufficient to enhance the security and prosperity of our families at home while leaving us free to fulfill our duties in charity and justice abroad. The scientific, educational and financial resources of our nation cannot be better utilized than in defense and development of the family. The future of civilization itself depends upon such creative use of our resources.

1324   Our concern with improved social conditions and public policies protective of the family includes recognition of the special merits of some families. We second the tribute of the Council's Pastoral Constitution to parents of large families; we add a further tribute to those parents who, in a tradition that has been the strength of American Catholicism, have provided their children, very often at great sacrifice, with ed-

ucational opportunities under religious auspices from pre-
school years to higher education.

We are mindful of those families which include disadvan-   1325
taged children and of families which by adoption assume full
responsibility for children not born to them. Adoption corresponds with a deeply human instinct; it gives a home to the
homeless and parents to the orphaned while at the same time
rewarding the love with which a family welcomes life not
originally committed to its keeping.

Likewise praiseworthy is the unselfishness which prompts   1326
qualified people to become foster parents to children who
need material, emotional or spiritual assistance at some
point in their lives. Finally, we offer a word of encouragement
to our brothers or sisters in Christ who care for children in
one-parent families. The sacrifices required to provide for the
physical welfare and psychological development of children
under these circumstances are sometimes extraordinary.
Those who thus spend themselves on behalf of life and love
witness to the world and the Church a generosity which cannot fail to inspire others and to sanctify themselves.

At this tense moment in our history when external wars   1327
and internal violence make us so conscious of death, an
affirmation of the sanctity of human life by renewed attention
to the family is imperative. Let society always be on the side
of life. Let it never dictate, directly or indirectly, recourse
to the prevention of life or to its destruction in any of its
phases; neither let it require as a condition of economic
assistance that any family yield conscientious determination
of the number of its children to the decision of persons or
agencies outside the family.

Stepped-up pressures for moral and legal acceptance of   1328
directly procured abortion make necessary pointed reference
to this threat to the right to life. Reverence for life demands
freedom from direct interruption of life once it is conceived.
Conception initiates a process whose purpose is the realization
of human personality. A human person, nothing more and
nothing less, is always at issue once conception has taken
place. We expressly repudiate any contradictory suggestion as

contrary to Judaeo-Christian traditions inspired by love for life, and Anglo-Saxon legal traditions protective of life and the person.

1329   Abortion brings to an end with irreversible finality both the existence and the destiny of the developing human person. Conscious of the inviolability of life, the Vatican Council II teaches:

"God, the Lord of life, has conferred on man the surpassing ministry of safeguarding life, a ministry which must be fulfilled in a manner that is worthy of man. Therefore, from the moment of its conception life must be guarded with the greatest care while abortion and infanticide are unspeakable crimes" *(Gaudium et Spes,* 51).

1330   The judgment of the Church on the evil of terminating life derives from the Christian awareness that men are not the masters but the ministers of life. Hence, the Council declares:

". . .whatever is opposed to life itself, such as any type of murder, genocide, abortion, euthanasia, or wilful self-destruction, whatever violates the integrity of the human person. . . all these things and others of their like are infamies indeed. They poison human society but they do more harm to those who practice them than those who suffer from the injury. Moreover, they are a supreme dishonor to the Creator" *(Gaudium et Spes,* 27).

1331   Pressing concerns of the hour have led us to consider with you many of the problems of family life, together with a Christian appraisal of them. The family is, however, much more than the sum of its problems. It is, as we said earlier, the place where the person occurs, where life begins, where fidelity and hope are nourished, where human love reaches its most intense expression. The family is, indeed, that "school of deeper humanity" of which the Vatican Council II speaks. *(Gaudium et Spes,* 52).

1332   The Christian family is an image of God and a sign of the Church. It is the community wherein Christ is most powerfully preached, where Christians first hear the name of God, first learn to pray, and first express their faith. In the words and example of their believing parents, children come to know what faith is and how it must be lived, what life is and how it must be honored. For this reason, a spirituality which is suitable to the contemporary family and which brings all members of the family together in faith and hope is, we re-repeat, the most urgent need of modern culture.

Since the family is the basic unit of human society, it   1333
should be the object of civilization's most enlightened concern. Since it is the basic unit of their life, parishes should
make the needs of the family and the benefits which the
family brings to the parish controlling norms in the planning
of parish organizations and activities, liturgical, educational,
charitable and social.

As bishops of the Catholic Church in the United States,   1334
concerned for its present well-being and prospects, our first
prayer is for the families who comprise its parishes and
dioceses. Our optimism for the future of the Church, the
family of God, springs largely from optimism for the future
of the family. In turn, our basis for optimism for the future
of family life, despite occasional negative signs, rests upon
the persevering hope of married couples whose responsibility
to life and vocation to live have been the opening theme of
this pastoral letter.

As last year we saluted priests, for their special part in the   1335
work of God, so this year we salute Christian spouses who
"made to the image of the living God and enjoying the
authentic dignity of persons, are joined to one another in
equal affection, harmony of mind and the work of mutual
sanctification. Thus, following Christ Who is the principle of
life, by the sacrifices and joys of their vocation and through
their faithful love, (they have) become witnesses of the
mystery of love which the Lord revealed to the world by His
dying and His rising up to live again." *(Gaudium et Spes,* 52).

Address of Pope Paul VI
to the Teams of Our Lady
May 4, 1970

First of all, We thank you from the bottom of Our heart for your faith-inspired words, for your nightly prayers for Our intentions, and for your efforts on behalf of vocations. We want to express Our joy at welcoming you here this morning and addressing Ourself through you to the 20,000 families of the Teams of Our Lady.

1337   You spoke to Us a moment ago about the spread of your movement throughout the world, your concern to live with Christ, and your desire to weave with Him the day-to-day fabric of your conjugal love. You constitute small groups of Christian couples offering each other mutual spiritual help, supported in your efforts by the presence of a priest. How could We not rejoice over this? Beloved sons and daughters, the Pope warmly encourages you and calls down God's blessing on your work.

1338   All too often the Church has seemed to hold human love suspect, but this impression is erroneous. Today We wish to tell you clearly that God is not the enemy of noble human realities, and that the Church does not deprecate the daily values lived in millions of homes. On the contrary, the good news brought by Christ the Savior is also good news for human love, which is also noble in origin: "And God saw that all he had made was very good."[1] It, too, has been redeemed, so that through grace it has become a means of holiness.

Like all the baptized, you are truly called to holiness. This   1339
teaching of the Church has been solemnly reaffirmed by the
Council.[2] But you are to achieve this in your own proper
way, in and through your home life.[3] It is the Church which
teaches us: "With the help of grace, married people can lead
a holy life,"[4] and can make their home "a domestic extension of the Church's sanctuary."[5]

These thoughts, forgotten with tragic results in our day,   1340
are surely familiar ones to you. We would like to ponder
them with you for a few moments to reconfirm in you, if
necessary, your will to live generously your human and Christian vocation in marriage[6] and to collaborate with God's
loving design for the world, which is to fashion a people
"for the praise of his glory."[7]

As Holy Scripture teaches us, marriage is a great earthly   1341
reality even before it is a sacrament: "God created man to
his own image; to the image of God he created him. Male
and female he created them."[8] We must always return to
this first chapter of the Bible if we wish to know what a
married couple, a family, is and ought to be. Psychological
analyses, psychoanalytic studies, sociological inquiries and
philosophical reflections can certainly shed their own ray of
light on sexuality and human love. But they would delude us
if they neglected this basic lesson that was given to us at the
very start. The duality of the sexes has been willed by God,
so that man and woman together might be the image of
God and, like Him, a source of life: "Be fruitful and multiply, fill the earth and subdue it."[9] Moreover, a careful reading of the Prophets, the Wisdom Books and the New Testament shows us the import of this fundamental reality. They
teach us not to reduce it to physical desire and genital activity, but to discover in it the complementary values of man
and woman, the grandeur and frailty of conjugal love, its
fruitfulness and its openness to the mystery of God's loving
design.

This message retains its full value today, and fortifies   1342
us against the enticements of a ruinous eroticism. The latter
aberration should at least alert us to the sad situation of

a materialistic civilization that is, in an obscure fashion, forcing its way into this mysterious domain, which is the last refuge of a sacred value. Shall we be able to wrest it from the engulfing sensuality? Faced with the cynical encroachments of greedy business interests, let us at least suppress their harmful effects on the young. Without raising obstacles or having recourse to repression, we must foster an education that will help children and adolescents to become gradually aware of the forceful drives awakening in them; to integrate these drives into the development of their personality, to master the intensifying forces, so as to achieve full emotional as well as sexual maturity; and thus to prepare themselves for the gift of self in a love that will give them its authentic dimension in an exclusive and definitive way.

1343   The union of man and woman differs radically from every other human association. It constitutes a truly singular reality, the married couple, grounded on the mutual gift of self to one another: "And they become one flesh."[10] Irrevocable indissolubility is the seal on this unity, stamped on the free, mutual commitment of two free persons who now "are no longer two, but one flesh."[11] They are one flesh, one couple—we could almost say, one being. Their unity takes on social and juridical form through marriage, and is manifested by a community of life which finds fruitful expression in their bodily self-giving.

1344   In other words, when spouses marry, they express a desire to belong to each other for life, and to this end they contract an objective bond whose laws and requirements, far from involving servitude, are a guarantee, a protection and a real support—as you yourselves know from your day-to-day experience.

1345   As a matter of fact, this giving is not a total fusion. Each personality remains distinct, and it is not at all dissolved in the mutual self-giving. On the contrary, it is affirmed and refined. It grows through the course of their conjugal life, following the noble law of love: giving of one another so as to give together. Love is, in effect, the binding force that gives solidity to their communal life, and the impulse that carries it toward ever more complete fullness. The whole being participates in it, in the depths of its personal mystery and of its affective, sensitive, bodily and spiritual components, thus forming ever more perfectly the image of God that the married couple is summoned to incarnate day by day, weaving it out of their joys and their tribulations—so true is it that love is more than love. There is no married love that is not, in its exultation, an impulse toward the infinite, and that does not wish to be, in this impulse, total, faithful, exclusive and fecund.[12]

It is within this perspective that desire finds its full significance. As a means of expression as well as a means of knowledge and communion, the conjugal act supports and fortifies love, and its fecundity leads the couple to their full development. They become a source of life in God's image.

    1346

The Christian knows very well that human love is good in its origins. If it has been blemished and disfigured by sin, like everything else in man, it finds its salvation and redemption in Christ. And do we not also have the lesson taught by 20 centuries of Christian history? How many couples have found the road to holiness in their conjugal life, that communal life which is the only one founded on a sacrament!

    1347

As the work of the Holy Spirit,[13] the rebirth of Baptism makes us new creatures,[14] "so we also may walk in newness of life."[15] In this great work of renewing all things in Christ, marriage too is renewed and purified, it becomes a new reality, a sacrament of the New Covenant. There at the doorway of the New Testament, as at the beginning of the Old, we find a married couple. But while Adam and Eve were the source from which evil burst into the world, Joseph and Mary are the summit from which holiness is lavished on the whole earth. The Savior began the work of salvation through this holy, virginal union, wherein is manifested His omnipotent will to purify and sanctify the family, this sanctuary of love and cradle of life.

    1348

Since then everything is transformed. Two Christians wish to marry, and St. Paul admonishes them: "You are not your own."[16] Both of them are members of Christ, "in the Lord." Their union, too, is made "in the Lord," like that of the

    1349

Church. That is why it is ' a great mystery"[17]—a sign that not only represents the mystery of Christ's union with the Church, but also embodies and radiates it through the grace of the Holy Spirit, who is its life-giving soul. For it is God's own love that He communicates to us, so that we may love Him and also love each other through this divine love: "Even as I have loved you, that you also love one another."[18]

1350 For Christian spouses, the very manifestations of their tenderness are permeated with the love they draw from the heart of God. While its human source runs the risk of drying up, its divine source is as inexhaustible as the unfathomable depths of God's tenderness. This tells us the depth and richness of the intimate communion toward which conjugal love tends. An interior, spiritual reality, it transforms the communal life of the spouses into what might be called, according to the Council's teaching, "the church of the home."[19] It is a veritable "cell of the Church," as Our predecessor John XXIII told your pilgrimage of May 3, 1959.[20] It is a basic, germinal cell the smallest, to be sure, but also the most fundamental one in the ecclesial body.

1351 Such is the mystery in which conjugal love is rooted and which illumines all its manifestations. It is the mystery of the Incarnation, which elevates our human potentialities by penetrating them from within. Far from despising these potentialities, Christian love carries them to their full measure with patience, generosity, fortitude and gentleness, as St. Francis de Sales loved to stress in praising the married life of St. Louis.[21]

1352 For if the fascination of the flesh is dangerous, the temptation to angelism is no less dangerous; and a spurned reality is quick to claim its place. And so, aware that they bear their treasures in earthen vessels,[22] Christian spouses strive with humble fervor to apply in their conjugal lives the admonitions of St. Paul: "Your bodies are members of Christ. . .the temple of the Holy Spirit. . .Glorify God and bear him in your body."[23] "Wedded in the Lord," spouses henceforth cannot but unite in the name of Christ, to whom they belong and for whom they must work as active members. In using their body, particularly insofar as it is a source of procreation, they can only do so in the spirit of Christ and for His work, since they are members of Christ.

"Free and responsible collaborators with the Creator,"[24] Christian spouses thereby see their bodily fertility acquire a new nobility. The impulse which prompts them to unite with each other is a bearer of life, and it permits God to give Himself children. Having become father and mother, the spouses discover with wonder, at the baptismal font, that their child is henceforth a child of God, "born again of water and the Spirit,"[25] and that he has been entrusted to them so that they watch over not only his physical and moral growth, but also over the budding and flowering in him of the "new man."[26]   1353

Their child is no longer simply what they see, but also what they believe—"an infinity of mystery and love that would dazzle us if we saw it face to face."[27] Education thus becomes a veritable service to Christ, as He Himself has said: `As long as you did it for one of these, the least of my brethren, you did it for me."[28] And if it happens that the adolescent closes himself to the educative work of his parents, then they, in their own flesh, participate sorrowfully in Christ's suffering from man's rejection.   1354

Beloved parents, God did not entrust such an important task to you[29] without offering you a wondrous gift—His love as a Father. Through parents who love their child, in whom Christ lives, the Father's love is poured out on His beloved Son.[30] Through their authority, His own authority is exercised. Through their devoted efforts is shown the providence of the Father, "from whom all fatherhood in heaven and on earth receives its name."[31] Through the love of his parents, the baptized child discovers God's paternal love and, as the Council tells us, has his `first experience. . .of the Church."[32]   1355

Of course the child will become aware of this only as he grows up, but through his mother's and father's tender care, God's love is already nurturing and developing in him his life as a child of God. This indicates the splendor of your vocation, which St. Thomas aptly compares to the priestly ministry: `Some propagate and maintain the spiritual life through   1356 a uniquely spiritual ministry, that is the concern of the Sacrament of Orders. Others do it through a ministry that is both corporeal and spiritual. that is carried out in the Sacrament of Marriage, which unites man and woman so that they may beget offspring and rear them to worship God."[33]

1357 Homes that endure the difficult ordeal of not having children are also called to cooperate in the growth of God's People in many ways. This morning We simply wish to focus your attention on hospitality, which is an eminent form of the home's apostolic mission. Consider St. Paul's injunction to the Romans: 'Share the needs of the saints, practicing hospitality.'[34] Is it not directed, first of all, to homes? In formulating it, did he not have in mind the hospitality of Aquila's and Priscilla's home, from which he was the first to benefit and which was afterwards to welcome the Christian assembly?[35]

1358 In our times, which are so hard for many, what a grace it is to be welcomed "into this little church,"[36] as St. John Chrysostom expresses it, to enter its tenderness, to discover its motherliness and experience its mercy. How true it is that a Christian home is the gentle, smiling face of the Church"![37] It is an irreplaceable apostolate, which it is up to you to carry out generously. It is the apostolate of the home, with its privileged domains: the formation of engaged couples, aid to young married couples, help to homes in distress. If you support each other, what tasks will be beyond your capabilities in the Church and the worldly city? We urge you to undertake these tasks with great hope and confidence: "The Christian family loudly proclaims the present virtues of God's kingdom and hope in a blessed life. Thus by its example and its testimony it accuses the world of sin and enlightens those who seek truth."[38]

1359 Dear sons and daughters, you know very well that in living the sacramental graces of marriage, you journey with 'generous, untiring love'[39] toward the holiness to which we are all summoned by grace.[40] This is not prompted by an arbitrary demand but by the love of our Father, who desires the full development and total happiness of His children. And you are not left to yourselves in attaining it because Christ and the Holy Spirit, "the two hands of God,"[41] work incessantly for you.

So do not allow yourselves to be led astray by the temptations, difficulties and trials that arise along the way. When necessary, do not be afraid to go against the currents of what is thought and said in a world of pagan deportment. St. Paul cautions you. "Be not conformed to this world, but be transformed in the newness of your mind."[42] And do not be discouraged in moments of weakness. Our God is a Father full of tenderness and mercy, overflowing with solicitude and love for His children who struggle on their journey. And the Church is a mother who knows how to help you live to the full the ideal of Christian marriage, reminding you of its beauty and its demands.

1360

Dear chaplains of the Teams of Our Lady, your long and rich experience has taught you that your consecrated celibacy renders you particularly qualified to be active witnesses of Christ's love in the Church, to stand beside families as they journey toward holiness. Day after day, you help them to "walk in the light,"[43] to think aright, that is, to direct the will of responsible people toward goodness. You help them to act aright, that is, to harmonize this life with the ideal of Christian marriage that they are pursuing generously through the vicissitudes of existence.

1361

Who is not aware of this? It is only step by step that a human being manages to order and integrate his manifold tendencies, to the point of organizing them harmoniously in this virtue of conjugal chastity, wherein the couple find their full human and Christian development. This work of liberation, for that is what it is, is the fruit of the authentic freedom of God's children. Awareness of this freedom must be respected, formed and developed in a climate of confidence, not of anxiety. In this climate the moral laws, far from having the inhuman coldness of an abstract objectivity, are there to guide the couple on their journey. When married people make the effort—patiently and humbly, not allowing themselves to be discouraged by failures—to truly live the profound demands of a sanctified love, then the moral laws,

1362

present there as a reminder of these demands, are recognized as a powerful aid rather than an obstacle.

1363   The journey of married people, like that of all human lives, has its stages, difficult and sorrowful moments have their place in it, as you know from your experience through the years. But it must be stated clearly that anxiety or fear should never be found in souls of good will. For is not the Gospel also good news for family life? For all the demands it makes, is it not a profoundly liberating message? One naturally reacts with distress when he realizes that he has not yet won his interior liberty, that he is still subject to the impetus of his inclinations. He is distressed when he finds himself apparently incapable of respecting the moral law immediately in such a fundamental domain. But this is a decisive moment for the Christian in his confusion. This is the moment when, instead of giving way to sterile and destructive revolt, he humbly makes his way to the astounding discovery that he is a man before God, a sinner before the love of Christ the Savior.

1364   All progress in the moral life starts with this radical awareness. The spouses thus find themselves "evangelized" in the depths of their being. "With fear and trembling,"[44] but also with wonder and joy, they discover that in their marriage, as in the union of Christ and the Church, the Paschal mystery of death and resurrection is being accomplished. In the bosom of the larger Church, this little church sees itself for what it truly is: a community—fragile, sometimes sinful, penitent and pardoned—on the road to holiness in "the peace of God which surpasses all understanding."[45]

1365   This does not at all mean that the spouses are safe from all weakness: "Let him who thinks he stands take heed lest he fall."[46] They are not excused from persevering effort, sometimes in cruel circumstances that are bearable only by the realization that they are participating in Christ's Passion.[47] Nonetheless they know that the demands of conjugal morality which the Church brings to their attention are not intolerable or impracticable. They know that these laws are a gift from God, meant to help them to move through and beyond their frailties to the riches of a fully human and Christian love.

So the spouses do not have the anguished feeling that they   1366
are driven to an impasse. They do not sink into sensuality,
abandoning reception of the sacraments or revolting against a
seemingly inhuman Church. Nor do they grow hardened in an
impossible effort that destroys harmony and equilibrium. Instead they open up to hope, certain that the Church's resources of grace are there to help them journey toward the
perfection of their love.

It is within these perspectives that Christian families live   1367
the good news of Christ's salvation in the midst of the world.
It is within these perspectives that they progress on the road
to holiness in and through their marriage, with the Savior's
light, strength and joy. And these are also the dominant perspectives of the apostolate of the Teams of Our Lady, wherein married couples offer the witness of their own life, whose
persuasive power is so great.

Restless and feverish, our world vacillates between fear and   1368
hope. Many young people stumble along the road that opens
before them. May this serve as a stimulus and a summons to
you. With the power of Christ, you can and should accomplish
great things. Ponder His word. Receive His grace in prayer
and in the Sacraments of Penance and the Eucharist. Comfort
one another, bearing witness to your joy with simplicity and
discretion. A man and woman who love each other, the smile
of a child, the peace of a home: it is a sermon without words,
but astonishingly effective. In it every human being can
glimpse quite transparently the reflection of another love and
its infinite appeal.

Dear children, you are the living cells of the Church.   1369
Through your homes the Church gives experiential proof of
the power of redeeming love, and bears its fruit of holiness.
Happy, faithful and tested, your homes are preparing a new
springtime for the Church and the world, and its first buds
already fill us with joy. Seeing you here and contemplating
the millions of Christian homes spread throughout the world,
We are filled with irrepressible hope. In the name of the Lord,
We say to you with confidence: ' Let your light shine before
men, in order that they may see your good works and give
glory to your Father in heaven.' [48] In His name We call down

an abundance of divine graces on you and your beloved children, on your chaplains, and particularly on Father Caffarel. May Our apostolic blessing be a pledge of the graces.

1370   Before We give you this blessing, We should like to say an *Our Father* with you for the intentions of your movement:

—For all the homes of the Teams of Our Lady, and also for the widows and widowers who belong to the movement;

—For their children, that God may protect them and inspire vocations among them;

—For homes undergoing times of trial;

-Finally, that an ever increasing number of married people may discover the riches of Christian marriage.

1371   Our Father. . .

Address of Pope Paul VI
to the Society of Italian Catholic Jurists
December 9, 1972

I t is with paternal sentiments of affection and esteem that We greet all of you who are participating in the 23rd national convention of the Society of Italian Catholic Jurists. Your visit offers Us a welcome opportunity to reestablish contact once more with your worthy organization and to congratulate you. For in your national convention and your local chapter meetings, in your periodical *Justitia* and your monthly newsletter, you follow and examine contemporary problems with a Christian spirit and with great professional competence.

You have manifested a desire to receive from Us some word that might guide and enlighten you in your labors and activities. This confirms your vivid awareness of the obligations imposed upon you by your profession as jurists, and even more, your awareness of the obligations stemming from our Christian faith.   1373

We are all the more happy to heed your request because the topic of abortion, which you have chosen as the main theme of your national convention, is one of great interest and timeliness. It is a topic which is much discussed today, but which is very often poorly formulated and handled. You have spoken correctly of *defending* the right to birth.   1374

As you well know, the Church has always condemned abortion. So the teachings of Our predecessor Pius XII[1] and of Vatican II[2] merely serve to confirm its ever un-   1375

changed and immutable moral doctrine. You also know
that the episcopate of the whole world has raised its voice
against recent laws or draft proposals in various States which
implement, or seek to implement, the so-called "liberalization
of abortion." The bishops have proposed more suitable remedies to eliminate this widespread *social calamity* or to contain
it as much as possible.

1376   Vatican II reiterated the point: "Abortion and infanticide are abominable crimes."[3] The theological reason is
spelled out clearly in the aforementioned teaching of Pius
XII: "Every human being, even the baby in its mother's
womb, has the right to life *immediately* from God—not
from its parents or from any human society or authority.
Hence there is no human being, no human authority, no
science, no 'indication'—medical, eugenic, social, economic,
moral—which could possibly offer or give a valid juridical
title for a *direct,* deliberate disposition over an innocent
human life: that is to say, a disposition which aims at its
destruction, either as an end in itself or as a means to another
end which may be not at all illicit in itself."

1377   In its Constitution on the Church in the World of Today,
the Council, addressing itself to all human beings and not just
to Christians, offers reasons from natural and social law as
well. First of all, there is the dignity of the human person,
which is offended not only in the innocent victim of the killing, but also in the mother who voluntarily exerts herself to
this end and in those people—doctors or hospital personnel—
who cooperate in a voluntary abortion.

1378   Next and no less serious are the reasons connected with
social law, which are particularly valid today and more
strictly within your competence as jurists. Vatican II ad-
vises us as follows: "God, the Lord of life, committed to man
the high responsibility to be carried out in a way worthy of
man."[4] This being the case, it is a mission which rests upon
every human being, every intermediary community (starting
with the family) and, above all, on the political community.
It is a mission which we can and *must* carry out. If the contemporary social State is more and more shouldering this task
of protecting and promoting human life in a way worthy of

man, thereby acting in conformity with the Universal Declarations of the Rights of Man and of the Child, then there is no doubt that this protection should start from conception—not with birth or with the attainment of adulthood. For conception is the beginning of a single, univocal vital process which ends with the birth of a new human being.

In Western civilization this protection of the unborn child   1379
began very early, although for particular reasons. Just as his interests were favored by the ancient institutions of the *curator ventris*,[5] the change in successions and the revocation of gifts, so present-day ordinances regarding privileged treatment for pregnant women in cases of arrest or penal sentence demonstrate not only that there is public concern for the life of the conceived child, but also that positive law itself reserves certain *rights* to him. How then can one deny that the conceived child, from the first instant of life, has a lawful claim to rights—a claim which is quite distinct from the mere capacity to act and which now coincides with the juridical concept of the person?

Now the first and most fundamental right of man is the   1380
right to life, that is, to the protection of his life. And no one can have a contrary right where an innocent person is concerned. The weaker the subject is, the more he needs protection, and the more all have a duty to protect him. The mother is particularly accountable as long as she has the baby in her womb.

The present-day cause of women's liberation is, in itself,   1381
just. But some distorted features of this cause, and of so-called sexual freedom, are false and disaffected in their aim. Such, for example, are those which run contrary not only to Catholic morality but also to universal human ethics. The problem of abortion, as it is called, cannot be formulated solely in terms of an individualistic consideration of the woman; it must also be formulated in terms of the common good and, above all, in terms of the personality of the unborn child. In like manner, woman's authentic liberation does not consist in a formalistic or materialistic equality with the other sex, but in recognizing what the female personality has that is essentially specific to it: woman's vocation to be a mother.

1382 Implicit in this vocation, and destined to assume concrete form, is the first and most fundamental of those relationships that make up the human personality: the relationship between this one new human being and this one woman who is its mother. Now to say *relationship* is to say *right*. To talk about a fundamental relationship is to talk about *a correlation between a right and a duty that are equally fundamental.* And to talk about a fundamental human relationship is to talk about *a universal human value* which deserves to be protected as part of the equally universal common good, since every individual is first of all and constitutively *born of woman.*

1383 Along these lines, therefore, jurists have no higher task than defending this universal human value in society, for it is at the very roots of life and civilization—not just Christian but all human civilization. We congratulate you for such efforts, and We hope that the conclusions of your convention will be able to provide satisfactory, well balanced and enlightening answers to the questions posed. For such are the answers being sought today by honest people who are concerned about the real welfare of nations. We confidently call down God's assistance on your work, praying that the Lord's grace will make it richly fruitful. And We bestow Our apostolic blessing on all of you and on those you represent.

Declaration of the Belgian Bishops on Abortion
April 6, 1973

Difficult questions are now agitating public opinion: procured abortion, certain tragic consequences of its clandestineness, its eventual legalization or even its liberalization. From everywhere voices arise taking sides. Moved by the ruin and suffering of all those who are facing real dramas, many are those who try to relieve their misfortunes by giving help. This emotion and these worries are certainly legitimate in themselves and we share them wholeheartedly. But are all the means proposed acceptable? On the other hand —we feel obliged to say for truth's sake—it is also possible to discern in this controversy the influence (often unconsciously borne) of motives not really concerned with the elimination of these dramas by which we are moved so deeply. No wonder, therefore, that these controversies are characterized by a real confusion—so much the more so because, despite their delcate nature, they are passionately made public and sometimes accompanied by slanted information and excessive simplification.

Christians cannot avoid the lively controversies of the moment. Some are bewildered; others feel guilty, for they see themselves accused of inhumanity if they do not support the legalization of abortion. For this reason many people are asking us to state our position publicly. **1385**

Repression alone cannot overcome the social evil constituted by abortion: there's no difficulty to admit it. In fact, **1386** this does not suppress its remote or immediate causes, nor does it remove the painful situations in which conscience is confronted with difficult decisions.

1387   These situations demand of all both benevolent understanding and efficacious help. However, neither the different instances nor the levels of solutions should be confused. It is the duty of legislators to prevent the evil as far as possible and then to find a remedy for it in the best way possible with laws that promote the good of society and of all its members. On their part, magistrates are obliged to take all the circumstances into account, for a fair judgment on individual cases.

1388   The Church is respectful of the field peculiar to the legislative and judicial authorities. But she is not indifferent to their pronouncements and the repercussions involved, when they concern people and their fundamental rights.

1389   Already in a declaration issued on December 14, 1970, we dealt with this grievous problem; then in January, 1973. The present circumstances impel us to return to the subject, answering the problems brought out by troubled consciences. By virtue of our pastoral responsibility, while fully sharing the emotion and respect of all in the face of human suffering, we are moved by the most ardent desire of contributing to the common effort to alleviate this suffering and seek a true solution to this human and social evil.

1390   Christian revelation stresses the inviolable dignity of the human person. Created in the likeness of God and sharing in the life of Jesus Christ, man is called to arise with our Lord Jesus, to participate eternally as a son in the fullness of life and love of God, in fellowship with Him and with men, his brothers.

1391   Human life is, therefore, something sacred. It is identified in some way with man himself on the way toward this supreme and definitive fellowship in which "God will be everything in everyone." Earthly existence is the time of maturation of a human being. To deprive a human being of life means preventing him from fulfilling himself and answering his divine vocation. It is a radical injustice to the victim and a serious offense against God, whose love is thus despised.

The respect of the life of others is, therefore, the first and   1392
fundamental requirement of justice and charity, the supreme
norm of action in the fellowship of persons. "God is love,"
and we must love as He loves us. To love, for God, is to call
to life. The "You shall not kill" is, without doubt, neither
the heart nor the apex of the Gospel. Yet this commandment
is made by God Himself as an indispensable condition and
primary duty of love.

Certainly, the very logic of this charity can drive us, in the   1393
footsteps of Jesus, to give up our own life for others; in fact,
"There is no greater love than this: to lay down one's life
for one's friend" (Jn. 15:13).

Nevertheless, it is one thing to sacrifice one's life out of   1394
love, and another to presume to dispose of life for very
different motives, especially when one chooses to dispose of
the life of his neighbor, whatever be the motive.

Faithful to the teaching of the Gospel and never con-   1395
tradicting itself, the ecclesiastical magisterium has always
affirmed that "from the moment of conception, life must
be guarded with the greatest care, while abortion and infanticide are unspeakable crimes" *(Gaudium et Spes,* n. 51).
Shortly before Vatican II, Pius XII had recalled the supreme
principle which must inspire the decisions of those who have
to solve difficult and distressing cases: "For the one and for
the other, the requirement can be only one: to make any
effort to save the life of both the mother and the child"
(Address to the Family Front Congress, November 27, 1951).

In the cases—today fortunately more rare, thanks to the   1396
progress of the sciences—in which the lives of the mother and
of the child are really in danger, the Church, in her concern
to face up to the situation, has always recognized the legitimacy of intervention, even if it implies the loss of one of the
two lives. In medical practice it is sometimes difficult to
establish whether this loss of life derives directly or indirectly
from the intervention itself. The latter, from a moral point of
view, can be considered as a whole. Its supporting moral
principle can be expressed thus: when two lives are in danger,
although the utmost is done to save both, every effort is
made to save one rather than let both go lost.

1397   If therefore, one is not allowed to suppress an innocent life directly and intentionally, even if another life be in danger, far less still may one presume to authorize or justify an abortion for motives of health, of physical balance, of mutual understanding between the spouses, of family preservation, of prosperity or of economic and social advancement.

1398   However, Christians are far from being the only ones to share this conviction. Even mere human reflection suffices to give a foundation to it. Through a long process, morality and law, each discipline on its own level, have developed without ambiguity their supreme criterion, which is founded on the very nature of human beings and their activity.

1399   What is this criterion? It is respect for persons, that is, for individuals who are, or one day will be, capable of reflecting and directing themselves toward their destiny. The human person is a value in himself and for himself, an end and never a means. No one can decide in his place about the course of his life, far less his death; no one can suppress him under the pretext that he is a nuisance or useless.

1400   In many fields our age reveals splendid progress; we rejoice sincerely over every human advance. But more insistently we denounce what alienates man, threatening or destroying his dignity as a person: the abominations of war, inhuman violence, euthanasia, genocide, undevelopment, prostitution, etc. Therefore, we pose this question: at the moment when progress has reached the point of calling for the abolition of all unjust discrimination between sexes, races, people, and social classes, can another, even more scandalous discrimination be legally admitted, based on the stage reached in the development of life?

1401   For its part, the United Nations rejects this view. The U.N. has unanimously accepted the humanity of the child, who, "because of his physical and intellectual immaturity, needs special protection and special care, above all an appropriate juridical protection both before and after his birth" (*Declaration of the Rights of the Child*, November 20, 1959, approved by the General Assembly of the United Nations and confirmed at the international conference on the rights of man held at Teheran, May, 1968).

To escape this demand of morality and law, some would   1402
question the humanity of the fetus, of the embryo, of the
fertilized ovum, or would refuse to deal with this point under
the pretext that the question is merely philosophical.

Is it necessary to recall that a doubtful case is to be resolved   1403
in favor of those who might suffer damage? If anyone should
remain in doubt and consider the embryo (the fertilized
ovum) only a probable human being, he should remember
that even in this case it is not lawful to run the risk of taking
its life.

But we cannot see any real basis for denying to the con-   1404
ceived child the nature of a man and a person. Those who do
so are the first ones to disagree as to the moment at which
"humanization" begins. And not without reason.

Before conception, there are two cells, egg and sperm,   1405
certainly alive with the life of the man and the woman, but
destined to die shortly, like many others, unless they fuse.
From their fusion originates a unique cell endowed with a
dynamism all its own that will sustain the individual until his
death, even if this is to occur in extreme old age. Right from
the first moment, the fertilized ovum contains the entire,
original program of the new being.

Remaining within the limits of their own competence,   1406
biologists are not called to give their own opinion on personality, however, they can and must recognize that the mature person is connected without a break in continuity with
the primitive cell, whose structure differs greatly from that of
the cells of the father and mother. The only moment that can
be determined to assign a beginning to human life, is therefore,
that of fertilization. This affirmation is valid both from the
scientific and from the philosophical point of view. In the
collective work *Abortus provocatus*, published by the center
of demographic and family studies of the Minister of Public
Health and the Family, it is clearly stated that: "No objective
criterion exists to establish in this process of gradual development a limit between 'non-human' and 'human life.' In this
process each state is a necessary condition for the next one,
and no state is 'more important.' 'more decisive' or 'more
essential' than another." The different stages of the develop-

ment of a human being: the nestling of the ovum: the formation of the brain; the possibility of survival outside the uterus; birth, the different periods of infancy, school age, puberty, etc., are actually only different steps in the same process. It can certainly happen, either before or after birth, that this process might be interrupted by natural and unforeseeable causes. This does not authorize man to intervene by putting an end to life himself.

1407   Stressing the important role of interpersonal relationship in the process of "personalization," others ask whether the embryo becomes a person, "is humanized" before being recognized, accepted into social relations. Or they appeal to pretexts that are logical consequences of "responsible parenthood" to justify the refusal of such "recognition." But is not this a sophism? For a person will give a name to a sub-human being, fondle it and treat it as a person; yet this creature will never become capable of reflection or of responsible commitment. In spite of the stupefying progress that it will be able to make on account of its friendship with man, it will ever lack the structure that will make it capable of personal life.

1408   Such a structure, instead, is present in a human being even before that being's acceptance by others. Surely the love of parents for the child they expect creates within them new ties with this child and a climate favorable to his acceptance. Undoubtedly this is very important for his further development. But such a relationship is the source neither of the child about to be born nor of his fundamental rights. On the contrary, it is the embryo's personality-in-becoming that constitutes the basis of the duties of the parents and society toward this baby. Parents refusing their child nourishment and education would be judged unfit. If they refuse him affection they do him incalculable harm. If, under the pretext of not having wanted him, they refuse him recognition and life, they commit an act of homicide.

1409   This imprescriptible right of the human embryo to recognition places an impassable limit on the exercise of responsible parenthood. However desirable its development may be, this latter never suppresses its duties toward a life already present, even if conceived contrary to all expectation. In the hypothesis that the parents were incapable of loving and bringing up a child, there would be others ready to receive him. Many childless couples actually desire children passionately. Contrary to the scandalous formula hurled by public opinion, both for the child and the parents, adoption is infinitely less shocking than abortion, which does not allow the former to live and renders the latter guilty of a crime.

Morality and right demand respect for persons. But what is present in an individual to motivate the duty of others and require the protection of the law is not merely the exercise of personal activity but rather the fundamental capacity for such activity. An infant neither reflects nor makes responsible decisions. The same can be said of the fertilized ovum: it is a person-in-becoming, and in this lies the basis of its rights. Moreover, the weakness of the unborn child and his inability to defend himself demand additional attention from his parents and those members of society who have a responsibility toward him.   1410

If society and the legislator fail to guarantee this right to life right from its immediate beginning, many other human lives are endangered. Once accepted, the arguments brought out in the attempt to justify abortion will pave the way for others which will imperil the lives of the disabled, the incurable, the old—outcasts of every kind. Once the principle of respect due equally to every human being has been violated, who would be able to stem the flood of its consequences?   1411

But, it will be objected, some accept and defend the legitimacy of abortion. This would be, therefore, a matter of freedom of opinion. The pluralistic society cannot allow a portion of its citizens to impose views upon the others, restricting their freedom unduly.   1412

This view could be accepted whenever dealing with a legitimate liberty. But this is not the case! Actually there are different kinds of opinions. On a theoretical level it should also be asked whether a pluralistic society should admit the propaganda of even the most subversive ideas. Whatever the question, when ideas imply practical consequences, it is necessary to begin accurately distinguishing between the profess-   1413 ing of opinions and the presumption of translating them into action or incarnating them in institutions.

1414   Real pluralism implies in the first place respect for persons, whatever their ideas may be. Then it demands that people should be left absolutely free to express their opinions and act accordingly, only so far as their way of seeing things does not contradict the real common good and respects the rights of others. The freedom and rights of each person end where those of others begin. If someone willed to appropriate his neighbor's goods, could we demand that society authorize him to act according to such convictions? Even more, if one's opinions led him to contradict the essential rights of persons —especially the right to life—and presumed to act accordingly, society, the guardian and protector of the rights of all its members, could neither let him do it nor allow such an opinion to be approved and institutionalized. And since the embryo is a real human being in the formation stage, respect for his rights is not a question of opinion but of elementary justice. In the name of a well-understood pluralism, therefore, abortion must be repelled.

1415   We have risen up against abortion and whatever could facilitate it on a legal level, above all because it is—as the legal classics tell us—"an attempt on the life of the person-in-becoming who is the conceived child" (Rigaux Trosse, *Les crimes et les delits du Code penal*, V, 1968, pp. 138-139; 144). It also is necessary to recognize that abortion, even legalized, harms woman seriously in her biological, psychological and moral being. For propagandistic purposes this truth is undermined and masked. Medical inquiries of an unquestionable seriousness and objectivity, especially from such very different countries as Japan, Hungary and England, concerning legal abortions carried out in specialized clinics, show numerous consequences regarding the woman's health, her further pregnancies, and the children born from these pregnancies. Psychologists and psychiatrists, who in general and from their own standpoint admit no valid motives to cause an abortion, point out tragic consequences sometimes hidden in the subconscious but later manifested in periods of crisis. Moral life is deeply disturbed, not only because the so-called social taboos or legal interdictions are violated, but because an attempt against life has been accomplished, an attempt which moreover contrasts with the vocation proper to woman. The real and genuine advancement of woman is not to be found in means that disregard her physical integrity and personal dignity. The great majority of the women who have to face this terrible possibilty shows aversion to a dehumanizing solution.

In reality, the alleged "right of woman" to abortion is an 1416 expression that merely consecrates her slavery. Wouldn't the liberation advocated by some women in the name of their own freedom perhaps allow selfish males to use their mate without any respect for her biological rhythms and her power of consequences? Wouldn't a solution that mutilates woman and suppresses the fruit of her womb lead her to a terrible regression in her gradual ascent to autonomy and maturity?

Actually, doesn't this degradation proceed from a wrong 1417 conception of sexuality? According to some, the satisfaction of sexual desires is such a value as to unconditionally legitimize the search for it in all its forms and manifestations. Especially in the intimacy of the conjugal life, the couple should have the right to show their reciprocal love without having to worry about its orientation toward fecundity and the gift of life.

In reality, sexuality, like everything else, is good only to 1418 the extent that it fosters the real promotion and fellowship of persons—promotion and fellowship understood not arbitrarily according to individual desire, but according to the objective norms of morality and the demands of charity. Sexuality becomes aberrant and harmful when it encourages selfishness, degrades the couple, refuses to be open to procreation, and even worse leads to the suppression of the fruit of the union.

The real freedom of woman, implying full responsibility, 1419 must be exercised with a choice before conception. This liberty demands reciprocal respect, self-mastery, commitment and loyalty, that is, true love. Privileged guardian of life, woman will find her genuine freedom only when she carries out fully her task as mother and educator of love.

1420   Recalling thus the conditions and requirements of a real liberation of woman in this field, let us not forget that her mate also has duties and responsibilities. In spite of all the difficulties confronting him, man also has the duty of doing his utmost to protect the life of which he, too, is author.

1421   Generally it is admitted that abortion is the worst solution, a failure. Nevertheless, some see it as a solution for other problems. Is it a real solution? And if it can be seen as such in some cases, is it an acceptable solution? Does it solve the problems of mothers of large families, of distressed mothers, of unmarried mothers?

1422   No! Their situation calls for a more demanding and elaborate social arrangement than the legalization or liberalization of abortion. The latter would bring them merely the illusion of a passing relief, leaving them once more at grips with their original problems. And society, having silenced its remorse with the granting of abortion, might feel less committed to efforts to improve the fate of women in difficulty, to help those who wish to keep their baby in spite of all difficulties. Rather than fighting for pro-abortion legislation, as some do, let us commit ourselves to the achievement of better living and working conditions for women, to half-time organizations; to the provision of maternity homes, nurseries and kindergartens; to the revision of the laws concerning family and social aid.

1423   We have repeatedly recalled the right and duty of society to protect the lives of all its members, especially the weakest. We have also stressed the dangers to which abortion, once approved and made widespread, would expose society as such. Isnt't it perhaps the legislator's duty to take care of these grave problems?

1424   Petitions, questions and varied notions have been increasing in these last months with very objectionable considerations, while arguments unable to stand a critical examination have been aired. We take the liberty of expressing our own opinions on some controversial points. We would fail to do our duty and face our responsibilities, if we were to remain silent.

1425   Law cannot limit itself to the reflection of common opinion or a compromise between opposing viewpoints. Law is a technique of social organization which has the task of promoting, even against egoistic interests, the good of all and the protection of each. Even though it is not a school of morality, law cannot nevertheless lead consciences astray. But in actual fact many persons in good faith are induced to identify what is legal with what is moral, what is permitted by law with what is legitimate in itself.

A law striking at the fundamental principle of the respect due to persons would doubtless be guilty of countless transgressions and individual and social abuses.   1426

The legalization and even more the liberalization of abortion would end up by conditioning attitudes and behavior, because many people would conclude that abortion is morally permissible and socially harmless.   1427

It is up to penal law to define the actions harmful to persons and society and to establish the penalty. If penalties are considered inadequate, the technique of their application must be revised, but the principle cannot be suppressed. Since in law what is not forbidden is permitted, the suppression of penalties for abortion would necessarily imply the right to practice it and would challenge some essential foundations of the civilization of the country and of the rights of man: the respect for life in all its forms.   1428

For persons confronted with particularly difficult cases, both physical and moral, the legislator can appeal to the judicial authority on which it devolves to apply the law to particular cases. Thus, both rest on their own legal level.   1429

According to law, magistrates have three means at their own disposal: they have the power to recognize "the state of necessity." to admit "justifying causes" on the legal plane, to gauge "attenuating circumstances" and even to suspend the prosecution of clearly dramatic cases, in which understanding and indulgence are called for more than repression.   1430

It seems preferable to keep the distinction between the powers and competences: law ratifies the fundamental principle of the respect of persons, punishing every attempt against it; the magistrate examines the behavior of persons in the concrete circumstances in which they acted.   1431

1432   If ever, in spite of all, the legislator were to think of introducing into the law the cases already resolved by jurisprudence —a solution to which we never could give our consent—he should at any rate study and choose the formulas with the greatest care to prevent the abuses that are found in other countries.

1433   Would legal authorization suppress clandestine abortions? Relying on the present statistics, the experience of foreign countries give negative results. Unless a total liberalization is granted, on account of which some countries pay the consequences tragically, clandestinity exists for all the cases that lie on the fringe of the norms. Statistics indicate that in most countries clandestine abortions are by no means decreasing because of the abortive frame of mind fostered by the law, while the number of legal abortions increases in an alarming way.

1434   The evils resulting from clandestinity, however grievous and real they be—and no one can remain insensible about them—are secondary in comparison with the fundamental evil of abortion as such. One does not remedy the symptoms of a disease by aggravating the disease itself.

1435   Would the legalization of abortion eliminate a glaring social inequality? Undoubtedly inequality exists, but not in the sense that, because of their greater financial means, some benefit from an opening of the juridical organization to commit a crime without paying the penalty. The true remedy would consist in completing the dispositions of law to prevent this horrible crime from being committed with impunity outside national boundaries.

1436   Real social injustice springs from unjustly depriving some members of society of goods or advantages granted to others. But is inequality abolished in offering the less well-to-do the possibility of doing something that is wrong for everyone?

1437   The comparison with neighboring countries, where abortion is legal under certain conditions, certainly strikes the imagination. But does the objection stand up to examination?

1438   As we have already stated, the experience of these countries shows how a permissive and ambiguous law considerably increases the number of abortions without suppressing the clandestine abortions which are intended to be abolished. If my neighbor behaves badly and I can do the same with impunity in his house, that is no reason to authorize a bad action in my house. An error shared never becomes a truth.

In ancient times, slavery was widespread and some philos-   1439
phers and magistrates were ready to justify it. In the age of the great discoveries and the slave-trade, as well as in the nineteenth century, some economists justified it to explain the necessity of insufficient salaries. For these reasons are unjust salaries justified? Many countries have legalized apartheid and racial discrimination. Is that a reason for us to legalize them here?

Finally: should our country lag behind the errors of others?   1440
It has tried to build up an ever more just social order; it has committed and is committing itself to work out a legislation protecting and promoting social values and rights. Among them aren't life and its protection essential? Should we exclude from the protection of the law the weakest among us? Shouldn't we rather devote ourselves to the organization of an ever more human society that guarantees to all its members the respect of life and assures the necessary aid to the future mother and her child?

In any case, legislation for abortion can never be con-   1441
sidered a valid remedy for social evils or an admissible way of regulating births or means of promoting the rights of woman.

Abortion on demand, resulting from an ambiguous law,   1442
would not bring any real solution to the problem of abortion itself and to its causes. On the contrary, it would risk rooting abortion in custom and neutralizing the efforts that could be made in behalf of sound education in the sexual, conjugal and family spheres, especially for the development of responsible and generous parenthood.

In a positive way, the common good demands of the legis-   1443
lator the commitment to guarantee jointly and effectively:
-the rights of woman and of the child, offering the former moral and material assistance in the face of the problem of maternity, with recognition of the right to just improvement of her legal, economic and social status; and offering the child effective legal protection from the moment of conception;

-the efforts of those responsible for information and education with regard to sexuality and responsible parenthood, in spirit of formation to the true love and respect for the person;

-a renewed social, cultural and family policy, to assist the disabled, the illegitimate, unmarried mothers, families in difficulties;

-a revision of legislation in order to facilitate and encourage adoption.

1444   The common good also demands that scientific, political, moral, jurisdictional and social authorities should seek together, in an atmosphere of serene objectivity, the positive solutions best suited to eliminate the causes of abortion.

1445   Finally, it is necessary to hope that the whole population will become aware of the imperious necessity of working in a spirit of solidarity and responsibility, with all the means at the disposal of an advanced society, to solve a problem that concerns it in the person of each of its members. Technical progress will daily make it easier to destroy at an early stage life already conceived. It is very important in the presentation of abortion, to revive with an intense education the sense of human life and to strengthen in consciences and in customs a deeply respectful attitude toward it. A serious common task is laid upon morality and law: especially that of assuring the necessary protection to every human life.

1446   Once more we must repeat: abortion is not the solution to the varied problems. Certainly we understand that for those who are in a difficult situation, it may appear to be the only possibility still available. With all the concern within our power, we would like to sustain those who would be tempted to have recourse to it, helping them and leading them to understand that this possiblity is not even a solution of desperation. No situation, however tragic it may be, can justify merely and simply as a remedy the suppression of a person, and particularly of this weak and defenseless person-in-becoming which is the human embryo before birth.

1447   With deep anguish because of the apparent mockery that words and formulas can have in the face of the suffering and confusion of one who carries an unwanted child in her womb, we wish to make ourselves understood by her above all. We are aware that our stand—sometimes difficult to maintain against our own sensitivity—will be labeled in inhuman position. Nevertheless, we sincerely believe that, if all that is at stake is taken into consideration, it is the most human one, because it alone saves man, defending the very principle of his existence and dignity.

The position we have publicily stated seems to us the only one worthy of man's civilization. It is oriented towards an original effort rather than the imitation of what is happening elsewhere. Nor does it amount to surrender in the face of difficulties. It promotes the respect of all persons, especially the weakest. **1448**

But it is absolutely necessary to recall that if we are obliged to reprove certain immoral and illegitimate ways of behaving, neither we nor others have the right to judge consciences or moral responsibilities. And if the demands of social life lay or justify measures upon persons, the situation of the latter and their anguish can be such as to suggest understanding more than intransigence. **1449**

It will never be emphasized enough that a social community must first of all apply itself to the elimination of the conditions that drive women to abortion, working on the ground of personal assistance, moral education, social order and legislation. It is a duty concerning all, according to their own possibilities and competence. **1450**

This duty must be carried out in a special and exemplary way by all those—physicians, nurses, social assistants, educators and many more (we cannot mention all)—who consecrate their hearts, time and resources to encourage mothers in difficulty or anguish, helping them to bring forth life. They have the right to the esteem and gratitude of the entire community. **1451**

Our admiration also goes out, together with a special love, to the parents of the severely handicapped, whose trial gives rise to an ever-increasing love. **1452**

It goes finally to those women who, despite all the difficulties, contempt and mockery of their environment, refuse to deny life to the child they carry in their womb and feed with their vital lymph and love. Their example is a lesson, and God looks on them with love. Let us also show the same charity. **1453**

Declaration on Abortion
Issued by the Sacred Congregation for the Doctrine
of the Faith
November 18, 1974

The problem of abortion and its possible legalization has been almost everywhere the subject of intense debate. The debate would be less important if it did not concern human life, which is the most basic of all goods for man and must therefore be protected and fostered. Everyone agrees on this in principle, even though many people are now looking for reasons which will prove, in the face of the evidence, that abortion can serve the cause of life. It is indeed amazing that there should be, on the one hand, a widespread outcry against captial punishment and against war in any form and, on the other, a growing demand for the freedom to have abortions, whether the freedom demanded be unrestricted or subject to certain ever lessening limitations.

1455 Vividly aware as it is of its obligation to defend man against whatever destroys or degrades him, the Church cannot remain silent on this question. Since the Son of God became a man, every man, possessing as he does the same human nature, is a brother of the Lord and is called to become a Christian and share in the salvation Christ offers.

1456 In many countries, when public authority refuses to legalize abortion, it is bombarded with vehement appeals to change its position. The practice of abortion, it is argued, does not do violence to anyone's conscience, since each person is left free to follow his own judgment while being enjoined from imposing his own view on others. The right of "ethical pluralism" is asserted as though it flowed with inner logic from ideological pluralism. But the two things are in fact very different, since actions impinge upon the rights of others far more quickly than simple opinions do, and since no one may invoke freedom of thought as justification for attacking the rights of others, especially the right to life.

Many of the Christian laity—especially doctors, but also as-   1457
sociations of parents, men of political experience or now holding high office—have offered strong resistance to this carefully organized propaganda campaign. Most notably, however, many episcopal conferences as well as individual bishops in their own names have considered it opportune to remind the faithful in unambiguous terms of the traditional teaching of the Church.[1] In a remarkably similar way these statements expound the respect due to human life in the light both of human nature itself and of Christian teaching. Yet these statements have been received in various places with less than enthusiasm or have even been rejected outright.

In keeping, therefore, with its duty of protecting and   1458
fostering faith and morals in the universal Church,[2] this Sacred Congregation for the Doctrine of the Faith has decided to issue to all the faithful a reminder of the essential points of that doctrine as it concerns human life. By doing so the Congregation will emphasize the unity of the Church and confirm with the authority of the Apostolic See the teaching which the bishops have already so auspiciously proposed. We hope that all the faithful, including those who have been confused by current controversies and new views, will clearly understand that there is no question here of simply defending one opinion against others but of declaring the constant teaching of the supreme doctrinal authority, whose function it is to expound the laws of morality in the light of faith.[3] Clearly, then the present Declaration lays a serious obligation on the consciences of the faithful.[4] God grant that it may also bring light to all who seek "to do the truth" with a sincere heart (see *Jn.* 3, 21).

"God did not make death, nor does he rejoice in the   1459
destruction of the living" (*Wis.* 1, 13). It is true, of course, that God created certain living beings which live only for a

limited time and that death is inescapable in the world of living corporeal things. Yet God's primary purpose is life. Everything in our visible world has been created for the sake of man, who is the image of God and the crown of creation (*Gn.* 1, 26-28). As far as man is concerned, it was "by the envy of the devil" that "death entered the world" *(Wis.* 2, 24). Death was introduced by sin and continues to be inseparable from sin, of which it is both the sign and the consequence; yet death cannot finally prevail. For Christ the Lord, in arguing to the reality of resurrection, asserts in the Gospel that God is the God not of the dead but of the living *(Mt.* 22, 32) and that death, along with sin, will be overcome by resurrection in Christ (see 1 *Cor.* 15, 20-27). It follows that human life, even in this world, is a precious thing. The Creator gives it to man and the Creator takes it back again (see *Gn.* 2, 7; *Wis.* 15, 11).

1460   Human life is constantly under God's protection; the blood of man cries out to Him (see *Gn.* 4, 10) and He will demand an accounting for it: "For in the image of God has man been made" *(Gn.* 9, 5-6). "You shall not kill" *(Ex.* 20, 13) is God's commandment. Life is a gift but it brings obligations with it; for it is not simply received as a "talent" put at our disposition (see *Mt* 25, 14-30) but must be made to yield a profit. In order that his life may bear its proper fruits, many duties which he may not refuse are laid upon man in this world. The Christian has a deeper understanding than other men of this truth, for he is well aware that his eternal life depends on what he does during his earthly life with the help of God's grace.

1461   In her Tradition the Church has always taught that human life is to be protected and fostered, both in its beginnings and at every stage of its course. From earliest times when the Church was forced to raise her voice against the degenerate morals of the Greeks and Romans, she has strongly insisted on the difference between Christian and pagan morality in this matter of human life. We find her teaching already clearly stated in the *Didache*: "You shall not kill a fetus by abortion nor commit infanticide." Athenagoras emphasizes that Christians regarded as murderers, women who resorted to drugs in order to induce an abortion; he condemns those who kill children, even if these be still in their mother's womb, for there, he claims, they are already "the object of God's concern." Tertullian's statements on the subject are perhaps not always consistent, but he does lay down the essential principle with all desirable clairty: "To prevent a child being born is to accelerate its death and commit murder. It makes no difference whether one kills a child already born or a child about to be born, for he will be a human being is already a human being."[8]

Over the centuries the Church's holy Fathers, pastors and   1462
Doctors have all taught the same doctrine. Differences of opinion as to the precise moment when the spiritual soul is infused into the body never caused any doubt in their minds about the illiceity of abortion. It is true that in the Middle Ages, when the spiritual soul was commonly thought to be present in the fetus only after the first weeks of life, there were divergent views concerning the degree of sin and the severity of the punishments for it. In other words, even excellent authors, in handling cases that dealt with these early weeks of life, accepted milder views which they rejected for later period of pregnancy. But in no case did they deny that abortion, even in the first days of pregnancy, was an objectively serious sin. All agree in thus condemning it.

It will be enough here to mention but a few of the numer-   1463
ous statements that have come down to us. The first Council of Mainz (A.D. 847) makes its own the penalties prescribed for abortion by earlier councils, and levies very severe penances on women who "kill their children or deliberately cause themselves to abort."[9] The Decree of Gratian quotes these words of Pope Stephen V: "Anyone who kills an infant in the womb by abortion is a murderer."[10] St. Thomas, the Common Doctor of the Church, teaches that abortion is a serious sin against the natural law.[11] During the Renaissance, Sixtus V condemns abortion in the following harshest terms.[12] In the following century Innocent XI rejects the propositions of certain canonists, inclined to laxism, who wanted to deny that abortion was sinful if it occured before the point

when, according to one view, the spiritual soul was first infused into the new living being.[13]

1464 In our own times the Roman Pontiffs have restated the same teaching in very precise terms. Pius XI expressly answered the weightier objections to the teachings.[14] Pius XII clearly condemned direct abortion, that is, abortion which is an end in itself or a means to an end.[15] John XXIII echoes the teachings of the holy Fathers when he asserts the sacredness of human life which "from its very inception. . .reveals the creating hand of God."[16] The recent Second Vatican Ecumenical Council, over which Paul VI presided, issued a stern condemnation of abortion: "Life must from its conception be guarded with the greatest care. Abortion and infanticide are abominable crimes."[17] Finally, Paul VI himself, who has frequently dealt with this matter, has not hesitated to say that this teaching of the Church is "unchanged and immutable."[18]

1465 Due respect for human life is not solely a Christian commandment. Reason itself requires such respect once it asks what a human person is and ought to be. Possessing a rational nature, man is a personal subject, capable of reflection on himself and determining his own actions and therefore his own destiny. He is free. Consequently, he is master of himself, or rather (since he develops through time) he has at his disposal the means of becoming master of himself. In fact, such mastery is his proper task since his soul, being immediately created by God, is spiritual and therefore immortal. He is open to God and only in God will he find his completion and fulfillment. He lives his life in close connection with his fellows and is, as it were, nourished by reciprocal personal communion with them amid an intimate co-existence in society. Over against society and other men, every human person has the right to possess himself, his life and the various things that contribute to it; all others have a strict obligation in justice to respect this right.

1466 The person is not limited, however, to a temporal life in this world, for he has a higher kind of life that can know no end. Bodily life must indeed be regarded as a fundamental good which on earth is the condition of all others. But there

are more excellent goods for the sake of which it is allowable
—and may even be necessary—to risk bodily life. In the society
made up of persons the common good is an end which each
person must pursue and to which he is bound to subordinate
his private interests. But the good of society is not the ultimate end of the human person, and from this point of view
it is rather society that must serve the person, since only in
God can the latter reach his supreme goal. This is why it is
never permitted to treat a man as a mere tool that can be
used at whim in achieving some higher purpose.

With regard to the reciprocal rights and obligations of the   1467
person and society, it is the role of moral theology to enlighten consciences, define rights and determine the order of
obligations. There are a number of rights of which society
itself cannot be the source because they exist prior to society,
but which society is obliged nonetheless to protect and render
effective. The rights in question are for the most part those
which nowadays are called "rights of man" and which our
age may claim to have clearly formulated.

The right to life is the primordial right of the human per-   1468
son. The person has other goods, some of them even more
precious to him than life, but the right to life is the foundation
and condition of all others. It is not within the competence
of society or public authority, whatever its form, to give that
right to some and take it away from others. Any such discrimination on grounds of race or sex, skin color or religion, is
always unjust. The right to life does not derive from the
favor of other human beings but exists prior to any such
favor and must therefore be acknowledged as such. The denial
of it is an injustice in the strict sense of the word.

Discrimination based on the various stages of human life   1469
is no less inexcusable than discrimination on any other
grounds. The right to life belongs intact to the elderly person,
no matter how poor his health. It is not lost by the incurably
ill. It belongs no less to the newborn child than to the mature
adult. In fact, every human life must be respected from the
moment the process of generation begins. For, as soon as the
egg is fertilized, a life begins that belongs not to the father
or mother but to the new living human being who now de-

velops on his own account. He will never become human if he is not already human.

1470   Contemporary genetic science affords valuable confirmation of this point, which has indeed always been evident and does not depend in any way on solving the problem of the precise time of animation.[19] Science has shown that from the very first moment this living being possesses a stable structure or genetic program; it is a human being, an individual human being with all its characteristic traits already fixed. At the moment of fertilization the marvelous course of human life begins, even if each of the great powers by which that life is exercised requires time to become properly disposed and readied for action. The least that can be said, then, is that contemporary science, no matter how highly developed, can provide no effective help to those who favor abortion.

1471   In any case, it is not for the biological sciences to pass a definitive judgment in properly philosophical and moral questions, such as that of the moment when the human person first exists or the liceity of abortion. From the moral viewpoint, on the other hand, it is clear that, even if there be some doubt whether the entity conceived is already a human person, it is an objectively serious sin to expose oneself to the danger of committing murder: "He who will be a human being is already a human being."[20]

1472   Neither divine law nor human reason, then, admit any right of directly killing an innocent person. On the other hand, if the reasons offered in defense of abortion were always evidently evil or worthless, the whole question would not be the subject of such passionate debate. What makes the problem such a troublesome one is the fact that in some cases, perhaps even in very many, the decision not to have an abortion endangers other important goods which men are likewise to protect and which at times may even seem to take priority over all others.

1473   We must face up to these very serious difficulties: for example, the mother's health, or even her life, may be endangered; a new addition to the family may be a heavy burden, especially if there is good reason to believe that the child will be abnormal or permanently defective in some way; in some parts of the world, considerations of honor and shame, or even the forfeiture of civil rights and social standing, can exercise great influence; and so on.

Nonetheless we must assert without qualification that none of these reasons justifies disposing of the life of another human being, even in its earliest stages. As far as the future unhappiness of the child is concerned, no one, not even its father or mother, can claim to represent the child—even if it be still in the early embryonic state—and in its name choose death over life.   1474

When the child itself reaches maturity, it will never have the right to commit suicide; much less, then, do its parents have the right to choose death in its behalf while it is still incapable of deciding for itself. Human life is too basic a good to be compared with and offset by even the greatest disadvantages.[21]   1475

Insofar as the women's liberation movement is chiefly concerned with freeing women from every kind of unjust discrimination, it can only meet with full approval.[22] In this respect society undoubtedly has a long way to go in various areas. But nature itself cannot be changed; nor can woman, any more than man, be exempted from the obligations nature places upon her. Moreover, the freedoms granted by civil law are always limited by the indisputable rights of others.   1476

The same must be said of the claim to sexual freedom. If "sexual freedom" means the gradual mastery of natural drives by reason and true love, so that sexual pleasure, while not being rejected, is assigned its proper place, there can be no objection to the phrase. Such mastery represents, after all, an authentic freedom, and a freedom that will always avoid violating the rights of others. But if men and women are considered "free" to enjoy sexual pleasure to the point of satiety without any regard for law or the essential ordination of sexual life to offspring,[23] then there is nothing Christian about such an attitude. In fact, the attitude is even unworthy of a human being. In any case, it does not justify disposing of the life of another, even an embryo, or destroying it on the grounds that it represents a burden.   1477

1478   Scientific progress now makes it possible—and will continue to do so in an ever increasing measure—for the skilled technician to interfere in subtle ways with human life, and the good or bad consequences of such interference may be very serious. These discoveries of the human mind are of themselves quite admirable. But technology is subject to the scrutiny of moral teaching, for its function is to serve man and it must therefore respect the finality proper to man. Just as no one may use atomic energy for any purpose he pleases, neither may anyone manipulate human life as he chooses or usurp authority over it. Technology may only be used in the service of man: to enable him to apply his natural powers more effectively, to prevent or cure diseases, to foster man's fuller development. It is evident that superior techniques make abortion easier near the beginning of pregnancy, but this fact does not change the moral judgment on abortion.

1479   We are fully aware of how important it is for some families and nations to check the birth rate. That is why the recent Ecumenical Council and, later, the encyclical *Humanae Vitae* (July 25, 1968) spoke of "responsible parenthood."[24] Therefore we must once again unwaveringly assert what the Council's Constitution on the Church in the World of Today, the encyclical *Populorum Progressio* and other pontifical statements have all taught; that no reason can justify the use of abortion, by family or political authority, as a means of lowering the birth rate.[25] The violation of moral principles always does more serious damage to the common good than does any economic or demographic distress.

1480   The debate on the liceity of abortion is almost always linked with a dispute over the scope of law. There is not a nation on earth that does not forbid and punish murder; many countries include the practice of abortion in this prohibition and prescribe the same punishments for it. But in our own day public opinion on a broad front has been calling for a softening of the prohibition, while there has existed for some time a very widespread tendency to do away with coercive laws as much as possible, especially such as seem to invade personal privacy. "Pluralism" provides yet another argument. Many citizens (it is argued), especially Catholics,

condemn abortion, but many others approve of it, at least
as a lesser evil. Why should the latter be forced to act according to a view they do not accept, especially in countries where
they are in the majority?

On the other hand, where laws against abortion are still on   1481
the books, it is difficult to apply them. Violations of the law
have become far too frequent for punishment to be possible
in every case. Public authority therefore thinks it wiser to
wink at the violations. But if an unenforced law is kept on
the books, it can only lessen the authority of other laws.
It must be added that clandestine abortions expose the
women who seek them to very great risks as far as their future
fertility and often even their lives are concerned. Therefore,
while continuing to regard abortion as an evil, can legislators
not try to limit the harm clandestine abortions do?

The above reasons, and others which various people allege,   1482
cannot justify the legalization of abortion. It is undeniable,
of course, that civil law cannot embrace the whole field of
morality or punish every crime, but then no one expects it
to do so. Often, too, civil law must tolerate what is in the last
analysis a lesser evil so that a greater evil may be avoided. At
the same time, however, we must guard against what may happen if the laws are changed: many people will interpret a
simple decision not to punish as a license for action. In the
case of abortion, indeed, the very refusal to punish seems to
signify at least that the legislator no longer considers abortion
a crime against human life, for he continues to levy severe
penalties against murder.

It is also true that the law's function is not to decide be-   1483
tween opinions and to impose one rather than the other. But
the life of the child is to be preferred to any opinion, nor can
an appeal to freedom of thought justify taking that life.

Whatever the civil law may decree in this matter, it must   1484
be taken as absolutely certain that a man may never obey an
intrinsically unjust law, such as a law approving abortion in
principle. He may not take part in any movement to sway
public opinion in favor of such a law, nor may he vote for
that law. He cannot take part in applying such a law. Doctors
and nurses, for example, must not be forced into the position

of cooperating proximately in abortion and thus of having to choose between the law of God and the pursuit of their profession.

1485   The true purpose of human law is to promote the reform of society and to see to it that conditions in all ranks of the citizenry (especially those less fortunate in wordly terms) are such that every child born into the world may always and everywhere be welcomed in a truly human fashion. Well thought out, fruitful policies—such as subsidies to families and unwed mothers, help for children, laws protecting children born out of wedlock, and a well ordered system of adoption—must be promoted so that there will always be a really possible and honorable alternative to abortion.

1486   It is not always easy to follow conscience and obey the divine law, for the latter imposes inconveniences and burdens which must not be minimized. Sometimes it even requires heroic virtue if its moral demands are to be met. At the same time, however, we need to assert without hesitation that constant fidelity of this kind to a true and correct conscience is the way to the authentic fulfillment of the human person. But we must also exhort all who have the means of doing so to lighten the burdens of a great many men and women and come to the aid of the many families and children who live in extremely difficult, almost unbearable conditions.

1487   The Christian evaluation of any situation cannot be made solely in terms of this limited earthly life, for Christians are well aware that during this present life we are readying ourselves for another life so far superior that it must provide the standard for all our judgments.[26] According to this standard no earthly misfortune may be regarded as unqualified, not even the bitter sorrow of having to raise a child that is defective in mind or body. Here we have the revaluation preached by Christ the Lord: "Blest too are the sorrowing; they shall be consoled" (*Mt.* 5, 4). To measure man's happiness in this world by the absence of sorrows and trials is therefore to reject the Gospel.

1488   This is not to say, of course, that we may be indifferent to these sorrows and trials. On the contrary, any man of sensitive heart, certainly any Christian, must be ready to do all he can to alleviate these evils. The law of charity requires this, for its first concern must be to establish genuine justice. Abortion may never be approved, but we must certainly remove the causes that lead to it. Such a goal requires political action, and that takes us above all into the realm of legislation. But morality is also to be fostered and effective aid of every kind given to families, mothers and children. Medical science has already made great progress in the service of human life and even greater progress may yet be expected, for it is the proper function of medicine to support and promote life to the greatest possible extent, not to destroy it in any way. It is also desirable that all types of aid be given in an ever more effective way, either through institutions set up for the purpose or, if these are unavailable, through the fervent generous love of Christians.

The effective promotion of morality is impossible without effective action in the area of ideas. We must not passively allow the spread of that frame of mind—or rather, cast of soul—that looks on fertility as an evil. It is a fact, of course, that not all types of civilization are equally favorable to the large family and that there are especially serious obstacles to the latter in urban life and in an industrial society based on the profit motive. For this reason the Church in recent years has repeatedly spoken of "responsible parenthood," that is, the exercise of a truly human Christian prudence.   1489

But such prudence cannot in fact be authentic unless it is paired with generosity. It must, moreover, always be accompanied by an awareness of the great responsibility of cooperating with the creator in the transmission of life, whereby the human community is enriched with new members and the Church with new sons and daughters. The chief concern of Christ's Church is the protection and promotion of life. "Life" here undoubtedly means first and foremost the life Christ brought to the world: "I came that they might have life and have it to the full" (*Jn* 10, 10). But all kinds of life come from God and; as far as man is concerned, bodily life is the necessary starting-point.   1490

Sin introduced suffering and death into earthly life, spread them abroad and made them even more difficult to bear; but   1491

Jesus took these burdens on Himself and transformed them. For those who believe in Him suffering and death have become the way to resurrection. Therefore St. Paul can rightly say: "I consider the sufferings of the present to be as nothing compared with the glory to be revealed in us" (*Rom.* 8, 18). And for those who wish to pursue the comparison we may add with St. Paul: "The present burden of our trial is light enough, and earns for us an eternal weight of glory beyond all comparison" (2 *Cor.* 4, 17).

1492   Paul VI, by divine providence our Pope, in an audience granted to the undersigned Secretary of the Sacred Congregation for the Doctrine of the Faith on June 28, 1974, has approved and confirmed this Declaration on Abortion and ordered it to be promulgated.

1493   Published at Rome, by the Sacred Congregation for the Doctrine of the Faith, on November 18, 1974, feast of the Dedication of the Basilicas of Sts. Peter and Paul.

Franjo Cardinal Seper
Perfect
Jerome Hamer
Tit. Archbishop of Lorium
Secretary

Address of Pope Paul VI
to the Convention of the Union of Italian Catholic Jurists
December 8, 1974

Dear and distinguished Italian Catholic Jurists, as We attend this final meeting of your Convention with its theme "Woman in Contemporary Italian Society," happy memories, old and new, of your association and, even more, of your individual members, fill Our mind. We welcome you, therefore, most cordially. The theme you have been discussing is so important that it requires much more extensive study and a much fuller development than We can give it in a short talk. Nonetheless, We would like to offer you a few reflections—though nothing that will be new to you— as Our contribution to a comprehensive grasp of a problem that is all the more topical now that the United Nations has proclaimed 1975 International Women's Year.

The Church, as you know, is also, and indeed more than anyone else, vitally concerned with the question of the place and role of women at all levels of contemporary society. This concern has even led Us to set up a special Commission for the study of problems relating to women.

1495

Neither We nor any other observer of the contemporary scene are unaware of the sociocultural transformation that has caused, among other things, a remarkable change in the position and roles of women. A rather rapid transition has brought us from a primarily agricultural society to a new type of society characterized by industrialization and its satellite phenomena: urbanization, population mobility and insta-

1496

bility, and a revolution in domestic life and social relationships.

1497 One effect of this shift has been to put woman at the center
of an as yet unresolved crisis in institutions and culture. The
crisis has affected especially her relationships within the family, her educational mission, her very identity as woman and
her entire specific way of sharing in the life of society through
work, friendships and the help and comfort she gives to
others. Even her religious outlook and practice have been affected. Today, then, we are faced with developments of enormous importance: first and foremost, the equal rights given
to women, along with their increasing emancipation from the
control of men; a new conception and interpretation of their
roles as wives, mothers, daughters and sisters; the ever greater
availability to them of a vast and expanding range of specialized professional occupations, their growing tendency to
prefer jobs outside the home, with its effects on the marital
relationship and, above all, on the education of the children,
who are prematurely freed from the authority of the parents
and especially of the mother.

1498 The new situation is evidently not wholly negative in its
impact. In these new circumstances the woman of today
and tomorrow will perhaps be able more easily to develop her
full potential. Even the misguided experiments of the present
time can be useful, if the sound universal principles of conscience take firmer root in society and lead to a new balance
in family and social life.

1499 The real problem is to bring about a recognition, respect
and, where necessary, recovery of these principles, which are
also irreplaceable values proper to the civilization of a highly
developed people. Let us call them briefly to mind. We are
referring, above all, to the functional differentiation of
woman from man within the nature they share; furthermore,
the uniqueness of her nature, her psychology, and her vocation as a human being and a Christian, her dignity, which
must not be degraded as it so often is today in the spheres
of morality, work, advertising and entertainment, and
through promiscuity, finally, the primordial place of woman
in all those areas of human existence where we confront

more directly the problems of life itself, suffering, and help to our fellow men, and especially in the area of motherhood.

If we were to reduce to a few essentials these brief indications concerning the place women should have in a renewed society, we might say: Let us willingly vote for: 1500

1) the recognition of the civil rights of women as the full equals of men, wherever these rights have not yet been acknowledged;

2) laws that will make it really possible for women to fill the same professional, social and political roles as men, according to the individual capacities of the person;

3) the acknowledgement, respect and protection of the special prerogatives of women in marriage, family, education and society;

4) the maintenance and defense of the dignity of women as persons, unmarried women, wives and widows; and the help they need, especially when the husband is absent, disabled or imprisoned, that is, when he cannot fulfill his function in the family.

If these principles and values are respected, they will assure   1501
women of their authentic, unique, and incomparable dignity. As We said on another occasion: "As We see her, Woman is a reflection of transcendent beauty, a symbol of limitless goodness, a mirror of the ideal human being as God conceived it in his own image and likeness. As We see her, Woman is a vision of virginal purity that revitalizes the highest affective and moral sentiments of the human heart. As We see her, she is, for man in his loneliness, the companion whose life is one of unreserved loving dedication, resourceful collaboration and help, courageous fidelity and toil, and habitual heroic sacrifice. As We see her, she is the Mother—let us bow in reverence before her!—the mysterious wellspring of life, through whom nature still receives the breath of God, creator of the immortal soul. . . .As We See her, she symbolizes mankind itself when it is most receptive to the drawing power of religion, when mankind wisely follows that attraction and thus reaches its highest fulfillment in an attitude of spirit that reflects the very essence of the woman-

ly; when mankind, therefore, in its singing and praying, its sighing and weeping, seems to be striving to fuse, as it were, into a single, ideal person, immaculate and sorrow-filled, which one privileged Woman, blessed beyond all others, was alone destined to embody. Mary, the Virgin Mother of Christ."[1]

1502   In the exercise of Our apostolic ministry. We move beyond sociological situations and problems and adopt a theological and spiritual viewpoint. We call the attention of all to that creature whom Christ, her Son, frequently addressed as "Woman," for she can serve as a point of departure in the attempt to answer many questions even of the temporal order, the family and society. We wish to encourage the woman of today, in her quest for authentic development as a woman, to look to Mary as a model, for Mary is radiant with genuine beauty and spotless holiness, as the feast we celebrate tomorrow reminds us.

1503   Along with these heartfelt wishes We give you Our blessing.

Address of Pope Paul VI
to the Committee for the International Women's Year
April 18, 1975

Welcome, dear daughters, and, with you, all members of the Committee for the International Women's Year, as well as all those who represent, on the larger Commission of which you are a part, the tribunals of the Holy See or other international organizations.

November 17, 1973, We defined the task of the Study Commission on Women in Society and in the Church. The task was concerned with documentation and with reflection on the ways of effectively promoting the dignity and responsibility of women. These purposes are certainly present in your minds. The fulfillment of the task of promotion must be gradual and none of the stages in the process may be bypassed. Prudent discernment is needed, for the questions with which you deal require tact. Nothing is accomplished by talking of equalization of rights, since the problem goes far deeper. The aim must be a complementarity in which men and women contribute their respective resources and energies to the building of a world which is not leveled into uniformity but is harmoniously organized and unified in accordance with the plan of the Creator, or, to use terms associated with the Holy Year, a world which is renewed and reconciled.

Moreover, you must know what you are about. You must not excogitate utopian programs which are conceived at the summit by and for an elite but must meet the true needs of the people and enable them to advance together by timely

1505

1506

and realistic stages. How much needs to be done in this area! Need We say that there are still millions of women who do not enjoy basic rights or receive elementary consideration?

1507   The inauguration of the Study Commission's work coincided very fortunately with the worldwide preparation for the International Women's Year which the United Nations proclaimed for 1975.

1508   We have already pointed out (November 6, 1974) how very much in agreement the Church was with the purposes of the International Women's Year. The Holy See is happy to accept the invitation extended by the United Nations to cooperate at its own level. But the whole Church is also involved in the task, for it is at the level of the local communities that there must be an examination of conscience. The examination has to do with the manner in which the rights and duties of both men and women are respected and fostered and also with the participation of women in the life of society, on the one hand, and in the life and mission of the Church, on the other.

1509   Let us speak first of the last mentioned area, although you must not limit your goals to that. The life of society and the life of the Church cannot be separated! Vatican II solemnly reminded us of the right and duty of all the baptized—men and women alike—to share as responsible members of God's people in the mission of the Church. The Council then noted specifically: "Further, in our times women have an increasingly larger role in the life of society; it is then quite important that they participate more intensively also in the various areas of the apostolate."[1]

1510   Many groups today are looking to the word of God for inspiration in this effort at renewal. How can we help but rejoice in this fact, provided the word of God is interpreted correctly and dispassionately, in continuity with the living tradition of the Church?

1511   People like to point to the example of Jesus and to the novelty, so daring in relation to the customs of his day, of his behavior toward women. If women do not receive the same call to the apostolate that was given to the Twelve and thereby to ordained ministers, they are nonetheless invited to follow Christ as disciples and co-workers. The women who accompanied Jesus ever since his days in Galilee were with him under the cross[2]; they saw him buried and were again present on the morning of the Resurrection.[3] We can say with all justice that the witness of the Apostles was the foundation of the Church but that the witness of the women contributed greatly to feeding and strengthening the faith of the Christian communities.

We cannot change either our Lord's actions or his call to women. Our duty is rather to acknowledge and help develop the role of women in the mission of evangelization and in the life of the Christian community. To do so will not be to introduce novelty into the Church, for we find traces of such participation, in various forms, even in the original communities and, later on, in many a page of Church history. Today, however, the cause is being more clearly advanced.   1512

For several decades now, a very large number of Christian communities have in fact been profiting from the apostolic involvement of women, especially in the important area of pastoral care of the family. At present, some women are even called to take part in the work of authoritative reflection on the pastoral scene, at the level of diocese, parish, or deanery. It is clear that these new experiments must be allowed time to mature. The Apostolic See itself, as you know, has called on some specially qualified women to take positions in some of its working bodies.   1513

The most pressing need at the moment, quite clearly, is the immense task of awakening women and advancing their cause at the grass-roots level, both in civil society and in the Church. This is the task We strongly emphasized in Our address to the Italian jurists last December 7: to endeavor everywhere to bring about the discovery of, respect for, and protection of the rights and prerogatives of every woman, single or married, in education, in the professions, and in civil, social, and religious life.   1514

The International Women's Year does not, however, aim simply at winning equal rights for women. It aims also at guaranteeing the full participation of women in the worldwide effort at development and their ever larger contribution   1515 to the strengthening of peace between individuals and peoples. This last named purpose has a very special relevance during the present Holy Year. In the family, in the educational field, and in all sectors of society, women have an irreplaceable contribution to make to world peace and to the formation of a society characterized by greater justice and brotherhood. We are convinced, and the experience of nations is there to confirm, that without their special contribution any progress made will not be fully human in character.

1516   Yes, Christian women, civil society and the ecclesial community expect much in the future from your sensitivity and capacity for understanding, your gentleness and perseverance, your generosity and humility. These virtues, which harmonize so well with the psychological makeup of women and were so splendidly developed in the Blessed Virgin, are also the fruits of the Holy Spirit. This Holy Spirit will guide you safely to the full flowering and advancement that you and all of us wish.

1517   With our Apostolic Blessing.

Declaration on Certain Questions Concerning Sexual Ethics
Issued by Sacred Congregation for the Doctrine of the Faith
December 29, 1975

According to contemporary scientific research, the human person is so profoundly affected by sexuality that it must be considered as one of the factors which give to each individual's life the principle traits that distinguish it. In fact it is from sex that the human person receives the characteristics which, on the biological, psychological and spiritual levels, make that person a man or a woman, and thereby largely condition his or her progress towards maturity and insertion into society. Hence sexual matters, as is obvious to everyone, today constitute a theme frequently and openly dealt with in books, reviews, magazines and other means of social communication.

In the present period, the corruption of morals has in-   1519
creased, and one of the most serious indications of this corruption is the unbridled exaltation of sex. Morever, through the means of social communication and through public entertainment this corruption has reached the point of invading the field of education and of infecting the general mentality.

In this context certain educators, teachers and moralists   1520
have been able to contribute to a better understanding and integration into life of the values proper to each of the sexes; on the other hand there are those who have put forward concepts and modes of behavior which are contrary to the true moral exigencies of the human person. Some members

of the latter group have even gone so far as to favor a licentious hedonism.

1521　As a result, in the course of a few years, teachings, moral criteria and modes of living higherto faithfully preserved have been very much unsettled, even among Christians. There are many people today who, being confronted with so many widespread opinions opposed to the teaching which they received from the Church, have come to wonder what they must still hold as true.

1522　2. The Church cannot remain indifferent to this confusion of minds and relaxation of morals. It is a question, in fact, of a matter which is of the utmost importance both for the personal lives of Christians and for the social life of our time.[1]

1523　The Bishops are daily led to note the growing difficulties experienced by the faithful in obtaining knowledge of wholesome moral teaching, especially in sexual matters, and of the growing difficulties experienced by pastors in expounding this teaching effectively. The Bishops know that by their pastoral charge they are called upon to meet the needs of their faithful in this very serious matter, and important documents dealing with it have already been published by some of them or by Episcopal Conferences. Nevertheless, since the erroneous opinions and resulting deviations are continuing to spread everywhere, the sacred Congregation for the Doctrine of the Faith, by virtue of its function in the universal Church[2] and by a mandate of the Supreme Pontiff, has judged it necessary to publish the present Declaration.

1524　3. The people of our time are more and more convinced that the human person's dignity and vocation demand that they should discover, by the light of their own intelligence, the values innate in their nature, that they should ceaselessly develop these values and realize them in their lives, in order to achieve an ever greater development.

1525　In moral matters man cannot make value judgments according to his personal whim: "In the depths of his conscience, man detects a law which he does not impose on himself, but which holds him to obedience. . . .For man has in his heart a law written by God. To obey it is the very dignity of man; according to it he will be judged."[3]

Moreover, through his revelation God has made known to us Christians his plan of salvation, and he has held up to us Christ, the Saviour and Sanctifier, in his teaching and example, as the supreme and immutable Law of life: "I am the light of the world; anyone who follows me will not be walking in the dark, he will have the light of life."[4]

1526

Therefore there can be no true promotion of man's dignity unless the essential order of his nature is respected. Of course, in the history of civilization many of the concrete conditions and needs of human life have changed and will continue to change. But all evolution of morals and every type of life must be kept within the limits imposed by the immutable principles based upon every human person's constitutive elements and essential relations—elements and relations which transcent historical contingency.

1527

These fundamental principles, which can be grasped by reason, are contained in "the divine law—eternal, objective and universal—whereby God orders, directs and governs the entire universe and all the ways of the human community, by a plan conceived in wisdom and love. Man has been made by God to participate in this law, with the result that, under the gentle disposition of divine Providence, he can come to perceive ever increasingly the unchanging truth."[5] This divine law is accessible to our minds.

1528

4. Hence, those many people are in error who today assert that one can find neither in human nature nor in the revealed law any absolute and immutable norm to serve for particular actions other than the one which expresses itself in the general law of charity and respect for human dignity. As a proof of their assertion they put forward the view that so-called norms of the natural law or precepts of Sacred Scripture are to be regarded only as given expressions of a form of particular culture at a certain moment of history.

1529

But in fact, divine Revelation and, in its own proper order, philosophical wisdom, emphasize the authentic exigencies of human nature. They thereby necessarily manifest the existence

1530

of immutable laws inscribed in the constitutive elements of human nature and which are revealed to be identical in all beings endowed with reason.

1531   Furthermore, Christ instituted his Church as "the pillar and bulwark of truth."[6] With the Holy Spirit's assistance, she ceaselessly preserves and transmits without error the truths of the moral order, and she authentically interprets not only the revealed positive law but "also...those principles of the moral order which have their origin in human nature itself"[7] and which concern man's full development and sanctification. Now in fact the Church throughout her history has always considered a certain number of precepts of the natural law as having an absolute and immutable value, and in their transgression she has seen a contradiction of the teaching and spirit of the Gospel.

1532   5. Since sexual ethics concern certain fundamental values of human and Christian life, this general teaching equally applies to sexual ethics. In this domain there exist principles and norms which the Church has already unhesitatingly transmitted as part of her teachings, however much the opinions and morals of the world may have been opposed to them. These principles and norms in no way owe their origin to a certain type of culture, but rather to knowledge of the divine law and of human nature. They therefore cannot be considered as having become out of date or doubtful under the pretext tha a new cultural situation has arisen.

1533   It is these principles which inspired the exhortations and directives given by the Second Vatican Council for an education and an organization of social life taking account of the equal dignity of man and woman while respecting their difference.[8]

1534   Speaking of "the sexual nature of man and the human faculty of procreation," the Council noted that they "wonderfully exceed the dispositions of lower forms of life."[9] It then took particular care to expound the principles and criteria which concern human sexuality in marriage, and which are based upon the finality of the specific function of sexuality.

In this regard the Council declares that the moral goodness   1535
of the acts proper to conjugal life, acts which are ordered
according to true human dignity, "does not depend solely on
sincere intentions or on an evaluation of motives. It must be
determined by objective standards. These, based on the nature
of the human person and his acts, preserve the full sense of
mutual self-giving and human procreation in the context of
true love."[10]

These final words briefly sum up the Council's teaching—   1536
more fully expounded in an earlier part of the same Constitution"—on the finality of the sexual act and on the principle
criterion of its morality: it is respect for its finality that en-
sures the moral goodness of this act.

This same principle, which the Church holds from divine   1537
Revelation and from her authentic interpretation of the
natural law, is also the basis of her traditional doctrine, which
states that the use of the sexual function has its true meaning
and moral rectitude only in true marriage.[12]

6. It is not the purpose of the present Declaration to deal   1538
with all the abuses of the sexual faculty, nor with all the elements involved in the practice of chastity. Its object is rather
to repeat the Church's doctrine on certain particular points,
in view of the urgent need to oppose serious errors and
widespread aberrant modes of behavior.

7. Today there are many who vindicate the right to sexual   1539
union before marrriage, at least in those cases where a firm
intention to marry and an affection which is already in some
way conjugal in the psychology of the subjects require this
completion, which they judge to be connatural. This is especially the case when the celebration of the marriage is impeded
by circumstances or when this intimate relationship seems
necessary in order for love to be preserved.

This opinion is contrary to Christian doctrine, which states   1540
that every genital act must be within the framework of marriage. However firm the intention of those who practice such
premature sexual relations may be, the fact remains that these
relations cannot ensure, in sincerity and fidelity, the interpersonal relationship between a man and a woman, nor espe-

cially can they protect this relationship from whims and caprices. Now it is a stable union that Jesus willed, and he restored its original requirement, beginning with the sexual difference. "Have you not read that the creator from the beginning made them male and female and that he said: This is why a man must leave father and mother, and cling to his wife, and the two become one body? They are no longer two, therefore, but one body. So then, what God has united, man must not divide."[13] Saint Paul will be even more explicit when he shows that if unmarried people or widows cannot live chastely they have no other alternative than the stable union of marriage: ". . .it is better to marry than to be aflame with passion."[14] Through marriage, in fact, the love of married people is taken up into that love which Christ irrevocably has for the Church,[15] while dissolute sexual union[16] defiles the temple of the Holy Spirit which the Christian has become. Sexual union therefore is only legitimate if a definitive community of life has been established between the man and the woman.

1541   This is what the Church has always understood and taught,[17] and she finds a profound agreement with her doctrine in men's reflection and in the lessons of history.

1542   Experience teaches us that love must find its safeguard in the stability of marriage, if sexual intercourse is truly to respond to the requirements of its own finality and to those of human dignity. These requirements call for a conjugal contract sanctioned and guaranteed by society—a contract which establishes a state of life of capital importance both for the exclusive union of the man and the woman and for the good of their family and of the human community. Most often, in fact, premarital relations exclude the possibility of children. What is represented to be conjugal love is not able, as it absolutely should be, to develop into paternal and maternal love. Or, if it does happen to do so, this will be to the detriment of the children, who will be deprived of the stable environment in which they ought to develop in order to find in it the way and the means of their insertion into society as a whole.

The consent given by people who wish to be united in   1543
marriage must therefore be manifested externally and in a
manner which makes it valid in the eyes of society. As far as
the faithful are concerned, their consent to the setting up of
a community of conjugal life must be expressed according to
the laws of the Church. It is a consent which makes their
marriage a Sacrament of Christ.

8. At the present time there are those who, basing them-   1544
selves on observations in the psychological order have begun
to judge indulgently, and even to excuse completely, homosexual relations between certain people. This they do in
opposition to the constant teaching of the Magisterium and
to the moral sense of the Christian people.

A distinction is drawn, and it seems with some reason, be-   1545
tween homosexuals whose tendency comes from a false
education, from a lack of normal sexual development, from
habit, from bad example, or from other similar causes, and
is transitory or at least not incurable; and homosexuals who
are definitively such because of some kind of innate instinct
or a pathological constitution judged to be incurable.

In regard to this second category of subjects, some people   1546
conclude that their tendency is so natural that it justifies in
their case homosexual relations within a sincere communion
of life and love analogous to marriage, in so far as such
homosexuals feel incapable of enduring a solitary life.

In the pastoral field, these homosexuals must certainly be   1547
treated with understanding and sustained in the hope of
overcoming their personal difficulties and their inability to
fit into society. Their culpability will be judged with prudence.
But no pastoral method can be employed which would give
moral justification to these acts on the grounds that they
would be consonant with the condition of such people. For
according to the objective moral order, homosexual relations
are acts which lack an essential and indispensable finality. In
Sacred Scripture they are condemned as a serious depravity
and even presented as the sad consequence of rejecting God.[18]
This judgment of Scripture does not of course permit us to
conclude that all those who suffer from this anomaly are

personally responsible for it, but it does attest to the fact that homosexual acts are intrinsically disordered and can in no case be approved.

1548   9. The traditional Catholic doctrine that masturbation constitutes a grave moral disorder is often called into doubt or expressly denied today. It is said that psychology and sociology shows that it is a normal phenomenon of sexual develop-ment, especially among the young. It is stated that there is real and serious fault only in the measure that the subject deliberately indulges in solitary pleasure closed in on self ("ipsation"), because in this case the act would indeed be radically opposed to the loving communion between persons of different sex which some hold is what is principally sought in the use of the sexual faculty.

1549   This opinion is contradictory to the teachings and pastoral practice of the Catholic Church. Whatever the force of certain arguments of a biological and philosphical nature, which have sometimes been used the theologians, in fact both the Magisterium of the Church—in the course of a constant tradition— and the moral sense of the faithful have declared without hesitation that masturbation is an intrinsically and seriously disordered act.[19] The main reason is that, whatever the motive for acting in this way, the deliberate use of the sexual faculty outside normal conjugal relations essentially contradicts the finality of the faculty. For it lacks the sexual relationship called for by the moral order, namely the relationship which realizes "the full sense of mutual self-giving and human procreation in the context of true love."[20] All deliberate exercise of sexuality must be reserved to this regular relationship. Even if it cannot be proved that Scripture condemns this sin by name, the tradition of the Church has rightly understood it to be condemned in the New Testament when the latter speaks of "impurity," "unchasteness" and other vices contrary to chastity and continence.

1550   Sociological surveys are able to show the frequency of this disorder according to the places, populations or circumstances studies. In this way facts are discovered, but facts do not constitute a criterion for judging the moral value of human acts.[21] The frequency of the phenomenon in question is certainly to be linked with man's innate weakness following original sin; but it is also to be linked with the loss of a sense of God, with the corruption of morals engendered by the commercialization of vice, with the unrestrained licentiousness of so many public entertainments and publications, as well as with the neglect of modesty, which is the guardian of chastity.

On the subject of masturbation modern psychology pro-   1551
vides much valid and useful information for formulating a more equitable judgment on moral responsibility and for orienting pastoral action. Psychology helps one to see how the immaturity of adolescence (which can sometimes persist after that age), psychological imbalance or habit can influence behavior, diminishing the deliberate character of the act and bringing about a situation whereby subjectively there may not always be serious fault. But in general, the absence of serious responsibility must not be presumed; this would be to misunderstand people's moral capacity.

In the pastoral ministry, in order to form an adequate judg-   1552
ment in concrete cases, the habitual behavior of people will be considered in its totality, not only with regard to the individual's practice of charity and of justice but also with regard to the individual's care in observing the particular percepts of chastity. In particular, one will have to examine whether the individual is using the necessary means, both natural and supernatural, which Christian asceticism from its long experience recommends for overcoming the passions and progressing in virtue.

10. The observance of the moral law in the field of sexuality   1553
and the practice of chastity have been considerably endangered, especially among less fervent Christians, by the current tendency to minimize as far as possible, when not denying outright, the reality of grave sin, at least in people's actual lives.

There are those who go as far as to affirm that mortal sin,   1554
which causes separation from God, only exists in the formal refusal directly opposed to God's call, or in that selfishness which completely and deliberately closes itself to the love of neighbor. They say that it is only then that there comes into play the fundamental option, that is to say the decision

which totally commits the person and which is necessary if
mortal sin is to exist; by this option the person, from the
depths of the personality, takes up or ratifies a fundamental
attitude towards God or people. On the contrary, so-called
"peripheral" actions (which it is said, usually do not involve
decisive choice), do not go so far as to change the fundamental option, the less so since they often come, as is observed, from habit. Thus such actions can weaken the fundamental option, but not to such a degree as to change it completely. Now according to these authors, a change of the
fundamental option towards God less easily comes about in
the field of sexual activity, where a person generally does not
transgress the moral order in a fully deliberate and responsible
manner but rather under the influence of passion, weakness,
immaturity, sometimes even through the illusion of thus
showing love for someone else. To these causes there is often
added the pressure of the social environment.

1555   In reality, it is precisely the fundamental option which in
the last resort defines a person's moral disposition. But it can
be completely changed by particular acts, especially when, as
often happens, there have been prepared for by previous
more superficial acts. Whatever the case, it is wrong to say
that particular acts are not enough to constitute mortal sin.

1556   According to the Church's teaching, mortal sin, which is
opposed to God, does not consist only in formal and direct
resistance to the commandment of charity. It is equally to be
found in this opposition to authentic love which is included
in every deliberate transgression, in serious matter, of each of
the moral laws.

1557   Christ himself has indicated the double commandment of
love as the basis of the moral life. But on this commandment
depends "the whole Law, and the Prophets also."[22] It therefore includes the other particular percepts. In fact, to the
young man who asked, ". . .what good deed must I do to
possess eternal life?" Jesus replied: ". . .if you wish to enter
into life, keep the commandments. . . .You must not kill.
You must not commit adultery. You must not steal. You
must not bring false witness. Honor your father and mother,
and: you must love your neighbor as yourself."[23]

A person therefore sins mortally not only when his action   1558
comes from direct contempt for love of God and neighbor,
but also when he consciously and freely for whatever reason,
chooses something which is serously disordered. For in this
choice, as has been said above, there is already included contempt for the divine commandment: the person turns himself
away from God and loses charity. Now according to Christian
tradition and the Church's teaching, and as right reason also
recognized, the moral order of sexuality involves such high
values of human life that every direct violation of this order
is objectively serious.[24]

It is true that in sins of the sexual order, in view of their   1559
kind and their causes, it more easily happens that free consent
is not fully give; this is a fact which calls for caution in all
judgment as to the subject's responsibility. In this matter it
is particularly opportune to recall the following words of
Scripture: "Man looks at appearances but God looks at the
heart."[25] However, although prudence is recommended in
judging the subjective seriousness of a particular sinful act,
it in no way follows that one can hold the view that in the
sexual field mortal sins are not committed.

Pastors of souls must therefore exercise patience and good-   1560
ness, but they are not allowed to render God's commandments null, nor to reduce unreasonably people's responsibility.
"To diminish in no way the saving teaching of Christ constitutes an eminent form of charity for souls. But this must
ever be accompanied by patience and goodness, such as the
Lord himself gave example of in dealing with people. Having
come not to condemn but to save, he was indeed intransigent
with evil, but merciful towards individuals."[26]

11. As has been said above, the purpose of this Declaration   1561
is to draw the attention of the faithful in present-day circumstances to certain errors and modes of behavior which they
must guard against. The virtue of chastity, however, is in no
way confined solely to avoiding the faults already listed. It is
aimed at attaining higher and more positive goals. It is a virtue
which concerns the whole personality, as regards both interior
and outward behavior.

1562   Individuals should be endowed with this virtue according to their state in life: for some it will mean virginity or celibacy consecrated to God, which is an eminent way of giving oneself more easily to God alone with an undivided heart.[27] For others it will take the form determined by the moral law, according to whether they are married or single. But whatever the state of life, chastity is not simply an external state; it must make a person's heart pure in accordance with Christ's words: "You have learned how it was said: You must not commit adultery. But I say this to you: if a man looks at a woman lustfully, he has already committed adultery with her in his heart."[28]

1563   Chastity is included in that continence which Saint Paul numbers among the gifts of the Holy Spirit, while he condemns sensuality as a vice particularly unworthy of the Christian and one which precludes entry into the kingdom of heaven.[29] "What God wants is for all to be holy. He wants you to keep away from fornication, and each one of you to know how to use the body that belongs to him in a way that is holy and honorable, not giving way to selfish lust like the pagans who do not know God. He wants nobody at all ever to sin by taking advantage of a brother in these matters. . . . We have been called by God to be holy, not to be immoral. In other word, anyone who objects is not objecting to a human authority, but to God, who gives you his Holy Spirit."[30] Among you there must not be even a mention of fornication or impurity in any of its forms, or promiscuity: this would hardly become the saints! For you can be quite certain that nobody who actually indulges in fornication or impurity or promiscuity—which is worshipping a false god—can inherit anything of the kingdom of God. Do not let anyone deceive you with empty arguments: it is for this loose living that God's anger comes down on those who rebel against him. Make sure that you are not included with them. You were darkness once, but now you are light in the Lord, be like children of light, for the effects of the light are seen in complete goodness and right living and truth."[31]

1564   In addition, the Apostle points out the specifically Christian motive for practicing chastity when he condemns the sin of fornication not only in the measure that this action is injurious to one's neighbor or to the social order but because the fornicator offends against Christ who has redeemed him with his blood and of whom he is a member, and against the Holy Spirit of whom he is the temple. "You know, surely, that your bodies are members making up the body of Christ. . . . All the other sins are committed outside the body; but to fornicate is to sin against your own body. Your body, you know, is the temple of the Holy Spirit, who is in you since you received him from God. You are not your own property, you have been bought and paid for. That is why you should use your body for the glory of God."[32]

The more the faithful appreciate the value of chastity and　　**1565**
its necessary role in the lives as men and women, the better they will understand, by a kind of spiritual instinct, its moral requirements and counsels. In the same way they will know better how to accept and carry out, in a spirit of docility to the Church's teaching, what an upright conscience dictates in concrete cases.

12. The Apostle Saint Paul describes in vivid terms the　　**1566**
painful interior conflict of the person enslaved to sin: the conflict between "the law of his mind" and the "law of sin which dwells in his members" and which holds him captive.[33] But man can achieve liberation from his "body doomed to death" through the grace of Jesus Christ.[34] This grace is enjoyed by those who have been justified by it and whom "the law of the spirit of life in Christ Jesus has set free from the law of sin and death."[35] It is for this reason that the Apostle adjures them: "That is why you must not let sin reign in your mortal bodies or command your obedience to bodily passions."[36]

This liberation, which fits one to serve God in newness of　　**1567**
life, does not however suppress the concupiscence deriving from original sin, nor the promptings to evil in this world, which is "in the power of the evil one."[37] This is why the Apostle exorts the faithful to overcome temptations by the power of God[38] and to "stand against the wiles of the devil"[39] by faith, watchful prayer[40] and an austerity of life that brings the body into subjection to the Spirit.[41]

1568   Living the Chrisitan life by following in the footsteps of
Christ requires that everyone should "deny himself and take
up his cross daily,"[42] sustained by the hope of reward, for
"if we have died with him, we shall also reign with him."[43]

1569   In accordance with these pressing exhortations, the faithful
of the present time, and indeed today more than ever, must
use the means which have always been recommended by the
Church for living a chaste life. These means are: discipline of
the senses and the mind, watchfulness and prudence in
avoiding occasions of sin, the observance of modesty, moderation in recreation, wholesome pursuits, assiduous prayer and
frequent reception of the Sacraments of Penance and the
Eucharist. Young people especially should earnestly foster
devotion to the Immaculate Mother of God, and takes as
examples the lives of the Saints and other faithful people,
especially young ones, who excelled in the practice of chastity.

1570   It is important in particular that everyone should have a
high esteem for the virtue of chastity, its beauty and its power
of attraction. This virtue increases the human person's dignity
and enables him to love truly, disinterestedly, unselfishly and
with respect for others.

1571   13. It is up to the Bishops to instruct the faithful in the
moral teaching concerning sexual morality, however great
may be the difficulties in carrying out this work in the face
of ideas and practices generally prevailing today. This traditional doctrine must be studied more deeply. It must be handed on in a way capable of properly enlightening the consciences of those confronted with new situations and it must
be enriched with a discernment of all the elements that can
truthfully and usefully be brought forward about the meaning
and value of human sexuality. But the principles and norms
of moral living reaffirmed in this Delcaration must be faithfully held and taught. It will especially be necessary to bring
the faithful to understand that the Church holds these
principles not as old and inviolable superstitions, nor out of
some Manichaean prejudice, as is often alleged, but rather
because she knows with certainty that they are in complete
harmony with the divine order of creation and with the spirit
of Christ, and therefore also with human dignity.

It is likewise the Bishops' mission to see that a sound 1572
doctrine enlightened by faith and directed by the Magisterium
of the Church is taught in Faculties of Theology and in
Seminaries. Bishops must also ensure that confessors enlighten
people's consciences and that catechetical instruction is given
in perfect fidelity to Catholic doctrine.

It rests with Bishops, the priests and their collaborators to 1573
alert the faithful against the erroneous opinions often expressed in books, reviews and public meetings.

Parents, in the first place, and also teachers for the young 1574
must endeavor to lead their children and their pupils, by way
of a complete education, to the psychological, emotional
and moral maturity befitting their age. They will therefore
prudently give them information suited to their age; and they
will assiduously form their wills in accordance with Christian
morals, not only by advice but above all by the example of
their own lives, relying on God's help, which they will obtain
in prayer. They will likewise protect the young from the
many dangers of which they are quite unaware.

Artists, writers and all those who use the means of social 1575
communication should exercise their profession in accordance
with their Christian faith and with a clear awareness of the
enormous influence which they can have. They should remember that "the primacy of the objective moral order must
be regarded as absolute by all,"[44] and that it is wrong for
them to give priority above it to any so-called aesthetic
purpose, or to material advantage or to success. Whether it be
a question or artistic or literary works, public entertainment
or providing information, each individual in his or her own
domain must show tact, discretion, moderation and a true
sense of values. In this way, far from adding to the growing
permissiveness of behavior, each individual will contribute
towards controlling it and even towards making the moral
climate of society more wholesome.

All lay people, for their part, by virtue of their rights and 1576
duties in the work of the apostolate, should endeavor to act
in the same way.

Finally, it is necesssary to remind everyone of the words 1577
of the Second Vatican Council: "This Holy Synod likewise

affirms that children and young people have a right to be encouraged to weigh moral values with an upright conscience, and to embrace them by personal choice, to know and love God more adequately. Hence, it earnestly entreats all who exercise government over people or preside over the work of education to see that youth is never deprived of this sacred right."[45]

1578   At the audience granted on November 7, 1975 to the undersigned Perfect of the Sacred Congregation for the Doctrine of the Faith, the Sovereign Pontiff by divine providence Pope Paul VI approved this Declaration "On certain questions concerning sexual ethics." confirmed it and ordered its publication.

1579   Given in Rome, at th Sacred Congregation for the Doctrine of the Faith, on December 29, 1975.

Address of Pope Paul VI
to the Study Commission on Women
January 31, 1976

Dear Sons and Daughters. After more than two years of intense and arduous work you have at last reached the end of the sixth and final plenary session of your commission. As you look back over the road traveled, you can feel a legitimate pride and a sense of gratitude to the Lord. For Our part, We must tell you today how happy and satisfied We are with the work you have accomplished.

The Synod of Bishops at their 1971 meeting took note of the widespread movement for the advancement of women in the secular sphere and urged that "women have their own share of responsibility and participation in the community life of society and also of the Church."[1] It was in response to this wish that your Study Commission on the Role of Women in Society and the Church was established. As We reminded the Committee for the International Women's Year. April 18, 1975, the task of the Commission was to study the ways and means of "effectively promoting the dignity and responsibility of women."[2] We added that "there must be an examination of conscience" concerning "the participation of women in the life of society, on the one hand, and in the life and mission of the Church, on the other."[3]

We are glad to know that in two years of work the commission has compiled on these matters a rich dossier which will be most serviceable to the universal Church and the local

1581

1582

churches. You have been wise to recall at the beginning the place of human beings, men and women alike, in God's plan, so that all in the Church work in any fashion for the advancement for women, may always do so within an authentically Christian framework. Furthermore, you have gathered an important set of documents on the participation of women in the pastoral responsibilities of the Church. You have also offered concrete suggestions on how women may take a greater part in the Church's activities. Finally, at the Synod of Bishops in 1974 you presented resolutions for giving women a larger share in the work of evangelization. We must tell you how grateful We are for these intense labors which testify to your heartfelt love of the Church.

1583   The International Women's Year is now over and the work of your commission is at an end. Yet, we should speak of a new beginning rather than an end. The program you developed in these final months must now be implemented step by step. As We told you April 18, 1975, the most pressing need is "to endeavor everywhere to bring about the discovery of, respect for and protection of the rights and prerogatives of every woman, single or married, in education, in the professions, and in civil, social and religious life."[4] That is the task which needs doing and to which each of you will be trying to contribute according to your abilities. We want to take this occasion to point out some principles which can guide you in this effort.

1584   Let us recall, first of all, this basic Christian principle: God has created the human person—man and woman both—as part of a unified divine plan, and in his own image. Men and women are therefore equals before God: equal as persons, equal as children of God, equal in dignity and equal in rights.

1585   This fundamental equality must be acknowledged at different levels. It must be acknowledged, first and foremost, at the personal level. That is, women have an inalienable right to respect, their dignity must be recognized and safeguarded both in private and in public. There is need of strong action in this area, because contemporary society has developed new ways of enslaving and degrading women. There is also an urgent need of changing the climate of public life and making it more moral, healthy and respectful of the dignity of women.

The equality of men and women must also be respected   1586
in professional and social life.[5] In many countries, of course,
men and women have already acquired, at least in theory,
the same basic rights. Yet, discriminations of various kinds
persist. We are thinking of the situation of the wives of migrant workers, and of migrant working women, too. We
are thinking of women in rural and working-class areas who
cannot acquire the formation they need if they are to develop
fully as human beings and who must work for wages which
are often inadequate.

We must repeat here the pressing appeal which the delega-   1587
tion from the Holy See to the World Conference in Mexico
issued on behalf of women who are poor or in distress. We
ask you all to read the text of this resolution and make it
known to those around you, and to do all in your power
to help impoverished women everywhere in the world. But
We cannot fail also to call attention here to the fact that in
more developed countries a prudent realism must mark the
accession of women to positions of policy making and decision which influence all areas of social life.

We also want to see women encouraged and helped in ful-   1588
filling their primordial role in the family. We are well aware,
of course, that some feminist groups suspect Us of trying to
tie women down to grinding, narrow domestic tasks and,
thus, to prevent them from developing their potentialities in
other sectors of society. For this reason, these groups reject
any and every reminder of the role of women in the home.
But is it realistic or a mark of wisdom to exchange one extreme for another? We think that in this very important
area Christians should show both wisdom and courage in
sticking to their convictions and commitment.

To be quite specific, it is desirable that both father and   1589
mother collaborate in raising and educating the children,
and there is certainly room for men to make a greater contribution. Yet, the woman's role is evidently essential. Or is it
but a paltry thing to contribute to the formation of human
personalities and to prepare the generations which tomorrow
will make up society? The society of tomorrow will require

an account from the homes of today concerning the quality of the love and education given to children and adolescents.

1590   Women must also, however, invest in the Church and her work of evangelization an ever great share of the human and spiritual riches which are theirs. Such is the wish clearly expressed by the recent council.[6] It is also the desire your commission expressed to the members of the 1974 Synod of Bishops.

1591   Women are already engaged in an impressive range of apostolic activities wherever the effort has been made to give them access to the responsibilities they are capable of exercising. The very important field of religious education and spiritual formation, preparation for the sacraments, overtures to those baptized persons who are almost completely ignorant of the faith, the approach to non-Christians, the acceptance of and association with the poor and those on the margins of society, the leadership of Catholic Action, the discernment and fostering of vocations, participation in Catholic socio-professional movements—these are some of the many areas of activity that are everywhere open to Christian women.

1592   As for yourselves, while you should continue to be very alert to needs as they appear, it would prove useless and illusory for you to become involved in an endless variety of experiments. The need, rather, is to enter fully into the responsibilities you have accepted, not in a spirit of competition or vanity but in a spirit of cooperation and evangelical humility.

1593   Dear sons and daughters, We wish also to put you on guard against some deviations which can affect the contemporary movement for the advancement of women. Equalization of rights must not be allowed to degenerate into an egalitarian and impersonal elimination of differences. The egalitarianism blindly sought by our materialistic society has but little care for the specific good of persons, contrary to appearances it is unconcerned with what is suitable or unsuitable to women. There is, thus, a danger of unduly masculinizing women or else simply depersonalizing them. In either case, the deepest things in women suffer. Egalitarianism can even favor forms of a hedonism which is a real threat not only to the spiritual and moral integrity of women but even to their basic human dignity.

The genuinely Christian advancement of women will not be limited to a vindication of their rights. The Christian spirit obliges all of us, men and women alike, to keep ever in mind our duties and responsibilities. The chief need today is to bring about a closer and more extensive collaboration between men and women, both in society at large and in the Church, so that all may "contribute their respective resources and energies to the building of a world which is not leveled into uniformity but is harmoniously organized and unified."[7] When thus understood, the advancement of women can help greatly in deepening the unity of mankind and establishing peace in the world. **1594**

The Church expects women to contribute much to her mission of evangelization. In the present critical period the part they play can be decisive for the humanization of civil society as well as for the deepening of faith within the family and the ecclesial community and for the more effective spread of the Christian message. **1595**

Upon all of you and all who will help women find their rightful place and role We ask the Holy Spirit to bestow his graces of light and love so that this important work may be carried forward in the best possible way. We ask the help of Mary who responded so completely to the Holy Spirit in every phase of the work of salvation. We assure you once more of Our gratitude for your invaluable collaboration and give you Our fatherly Apostolic Blessing. **1596**

Address of Pope Paul VI
to the Sacred Roman Rota
February 9, 1976

Dear Sons, members of the Tribunal of the Sacred Roman Rota, it is with deep pleasure that We greet you on your annual visit to Us. We have listened carefully and respectfully to the words of your dean, Boleslaus Filipiak, for whom We have such affection and esteem. He has spoken eloquently and movingly in expressing the thoughts of all of you. In his speech he voice ideas certainly deserving of Our attention on questions of the exercise of judicial power in the Church and on the circumstances which affect this exercise.

Your visit is especially meaningful and important since you enjoy a privileged position. Whenever, esteemed brothers, We have the opportunity of meeting you or observing you in the exercise of your office, We are always struck by the seriousness of your task and the paramount importance of the ministry you carry out on behalf of the Church as you issue judgments in the name and by the authority of the Apostolic See. To this ministry a high dignity attaches because of the splendid traditions of your tribunal. Moreover, your energetic labors and especially your priestly apostolic spirit lend weight to your judgments and show the preparation you give to your task as well as the great zeal you bring to the daily duties which the Apostolic See has entrusted to you in the confidence that justice will indeed be done.

1598

1599   The solemn opening of the judicial year offers a welcome opportunity for bestowing well-deserved public praise on this illustrious tribunal, for telling you of Our gratitude and for encouraging you in the fulfillment of the difficult task you carry on unnoticed by men. We express Our sentiments the more willingly because in our day the exercise of judicial power and, in fact, everything connected with the juridical order, is under extensive attack in the Church as being a structure which cramps the spiritual power and freedom proper to the Gospel message. But this is a criticism We have dealt with elsewhere.

1600   As We turn to the more important questions which call for canonical judgments, We must not neglect to call your attention to the area in which both your concern for justice and your tribunal's moral and doctrinal effectiveness, so worthy of its great past, must be most in evidence. We are speaking of marriage cases. The notable increase in the number of such cases is a sad proof of the dangers by which contemporary society is beset as far as the stability, vigor and happiness of the family are concerned.

1601   We are glad, of course, that the concern of the Second Vatican Council to foster the spiritual side of marriage and to open new doors for the pastoral action of the Church has been echoed by this tribunal. The tribunal has become more aware of its serious obligations and has come to understand the full importance of the personalist approach which the council emphasizes in its teaching and which consists in rightly esteeming conjugal love and the mutual perfection of the spouses. But this emphasis cannot be allowed to lessen the dignity and stability of the family or to detract from the immense importance of the conjugal duty of procreation.[1] The extensive and varied experience of your tribunal enables you, today as in the past, to provide very useful and, indeed, unparalleled material for the new canonical legislation now being drawn up.

1602   We wish to insist once more on the trust the Church places in you and the salutary, indispensable help you give in protecting and lending stability to the institution of marriage. For, the judgments you reach show clearly that you take into account such findings of jurisprudence, biology, psychology and the social sciences as contribute to a better knowledge and appreciation of the true nature of marriage as a community of love. At the same time, however, you adhere firmly to the basic principles which have always been followed in the teaching and practice of the Church, whether in resisting errors about and corruptions of the institution of marriage or in helping to bring out ever more completely and aptly the nature of marriage as conjugal community and sacrament.

At this point We must call your attention to certain opin- 1603 ions which originate in views widespread today and which also appeal to lines of thought opened up by the council. Promoters of the opinions in question at times lay undue emphasis on conjugal love and the perfection of the spouses. They go so far as to neglect or even completely eliminate children as a basic value of marriage. They consider conjugal love to be so important as to make the validity of the marriage depend on it. Thus, almost without taking anything else into consideration, they open the door to divorce. In their view, once love—or, more accurately, the original feeling of love—ceases, with it goes the validity of the irrevocable conjugal pact which a free and loving consent had brought into existence.

It will be enough for Us to dwell on this one point. You 1604 are already aware of it, of course, but it certainly deserves to be recalled on this occasion.

There can be no doubt that the council set a high impor- 1605 tance on conjugal love, for it speaks of it as representing the perfection of marriage and the great goal to which spouses are urged always to be directing their life together. The point, however, which in the present context We wish to see once again emphasized, is this: that the Christian teaching on the family, as you are well aware, cannot admit any concept of conjugal love which will lead to the abandonment or lessening of the force and meaningfulness of the well-known principle, "consent makes a marriage." This principle is of paramount importance in the whole traditional canonical and theological teaching and has frequently been restated by the Church's magisterium as one of the chief bases of both the natural and the evangelical law on marriage.[2]

1606   In virtue of this well-known principle, a marriage exists at the moment when the spouses express a juridically valid matrimonial consent. This consent is a will-act which establishes a contract (or a conjugal convenant, to use the phrase preferred today). In an indivisible moment of time it produces a juridical effect, namely, an existing marriage as a state of life. Once the moment is past, of wills of the consenting partners have no power to affect the juridical reality they have brought into being. Consequently, once the consent has produced its juridical effect, it automatically becomes irrevocable and lacks power to destroy what it created.

1607   Despite its pastoral character, the *Constitution on the Church in the World of Today* clearly teaches the doctrine We have just summarized. Listen to this passage, for example: "The intimate community character of married life and love, established by the Creator and deriving its structure from His laws, is based on the conjugal pact, an irrevocable personal consent. From this human act, by which the parties give and receive each other, there arises an institution which by divine ordinance is stable, even in the eyes of society. This bond, which is sacred for the good of the married parties, the children and society itself, does not depend on men's choice."[3]

1608   We must, therefore, reject without qualification the idea that if a subjective element (conjugal love especially) is lacking in a marriage, the marriage ceases to exist as a juridical reality which originated in a consent once and for all efficacious. No, the juridical reality continues to exist in complete independence of love, it remains even though love may have totally disappeared. For, when spouses give their free consent, they are entering into and making themselves part of an objective order or "institution" which transcends them and does not in the slightest depend on them as far as its nature and special laws are concerned. The institution of marriage does not originate in the free will of men but in God who willed it to have its own laws. Spouses, for the most part, spontaneously and freely acknowledge these laws and praise them; in any event they must accept them for their own good and that of their children and society. Love ceases to be a purely voluntary affection and becomes a binding duty.[4]

What We have been saying is not to be understood as in any way lessening the importance and dignity of conjugal love, since the rich blessings proper to the institution of marriage are not limited to those which have juridical standing. Although conjugal love does not enter into the purview of law, it nonetheless plays a lofty and necessary role in marrige. It is a force of the psychological order and God has set as its goals the ends of marriage itself. In fact, when love is wanting, spouses lack a powerful stimulus for carrying out with mutual sincerity all the duties and functions proper to conjugal life. On the other hand, where genuine conjugal love is strong, that is a love that is "human...total...faithful and exclusive of all other, and this until death,"[5] a marriage can reach the full perfection meant for it.   1609

Esteemed and dear sons, it is Our hope in making these self-evident observations that your judical activity will always be guided by strict observance of canon law and by an unwearying concern for its effective pastoral interpretation. You must proceed thus especially since, in view of contemporary permissiveness which often militates against the true moral law, there is need, as the recent Council insisted, of prudently defending the higher values of life.   1610

We are well aware of your tribunal's laudable and diligent fidelity to the norms set down for canonical processes. It is Our wish that all ecclesiastical judges would model themselves on you, so as neither too readily nor without legitimate cause to allow dispensations from these norms.   1611

Such are Our heartfelt wishes. We pray for a constant outpouring of heavenly Wisdom on you and your work during the new judicial year. May God's grace be with you always! May the perfect service of the Church be ever before your eyes as the highest goal of your work and sustain you in the difficulties you will certainly meet! Finally, may the noble traditions of your tribunal spur you on to exercise in an ever more generous spirit your outstanding powers of mind and heart!   1612

We ratify Our wishes and prayers with the Apostolic Blessing.   1613

To Live in Christ Jesus
Selection from A Pastoral Reflection
on the Moral Life
by National Conference of Catholic Bishops
November 11, 1976

II. Moral Life in the Family, the Nation and the Community of Nations

We turn now to three social clusters, three concentric communities, which provide the setting for human life and fulfillment in Christ:
- the family,
- the nation,
- and the community of nations.

1615   In speaking of matters which bear upon these three communities today, we treat them as moral issues in light of the values given us by Jesus Christ and His Church, in whose name we proclaim them. We cannot here discuss every important issue. Moreover, we admit that in some cases the complexity of the problems does not permit ready, concrete solutions. Nevertheless, as teachers of morality we insist that even such complex problems must be resolved ultimately in terms of objective principles if the solutions are to be valid.[44]

Our point of focus is the human person. "The progress of the human person and the advance of society itself hinge on each other."[45] Every human being is of priceless value: made in God's image, redeemed by Christ, and called to an eternal destiny. That is why we are to recognize all human beings as our neighbors and love them with the love of Christ.   1616

This love of neighbor, inseparably linked to love of God and indeed an expression and measure of it, is summoned forth first in regard to those closest to us—the members of our own families.   1617

The Family

Every human being has a need and right to be loved, to have a home where he or she can put down roots and grow. The family is the first and indispensable community in which this need is met. Today, when productivity, prestige or even physical attractiveness are regarded as the gauge of personal worth, the family has a special vocation to be a place where people are loved not for what they do or what they have but simply because they are.   1618

A family begins when a man and woman publicly proclaim before the community their mutual commitment so that it is possible to speak of them as one body.[46] Christ teaches that God wills the union of man and woman in marriage to be lifelong, a sharing of life for the length of life itself.   1619

The Old Testament takes the love between husband and wife as one of the most powerful symbols of God's love for His people: "I will espouse you to Me forever: I will espouse you in right and in justice, in love and in mercy: I will espouse you in fidelity, and you shall know the Lord."[47] So husband and wife espouse themselves, joined in a holy and loving covenant.   1620

The New Testament continues this imagery: only now the union between husband and wife rises to the likeness of the union between Christ and His Church.[48] Jesus teaches that in marriage men and women are to pledge steadfast uncon-   1621 ditional faithfulness which mirrors the faithfulness of the Son of God. Their marriages make His fidelity and love visible to the world. Christ raised marriage in the Lord to the level of a sacrament, whereby this union symbolizes and effects God's special love for the couple in their total domestic and social situation.

1622   Jesus tells us that the Father can and will grant people the greatness of heart to keep such pledges of loving faithfulness.[49] The Church has always believed that in making and keeping noble promises of this sort people can through the grace of God grow beyond themselves—grow to the point of being able to love beyond their merely human capacity. Yet contemporary culture makes it difficult for many people to accept this view of marriage. Even some who admire it as an ideal doubt whether it is possible and consider it too risky to attempt. They believe it better to promise less at the start and so be able to escape from marital tragedy in order to promise once again.

1623   But this outlook itself has increased marital tragedy. Only men and women bold enough to make promises for life, believing that with God's help they can be true to their word as He is to His, have the love and strength to surmount the inevitable challenges of marriage. Such unselfish love, rooted in faith, is ready to forgive when need arises and to make the sacrifices demanded if something as precious and holy as marriage is to be preserved. For the family to be a place where human beings can grow with security, the love pledged by husband and wife must have as its model the selfless and enduring love of Christ for the Church. "Husbands, love your wives, as Christ loved the Church. He gave Himself up for her."[50]

1624   Some say even a sacramental marriages can deteriorate to such an extent that the marital union dies and the spouses are no longer obliged to keep their promise of lifelong fidelity. Some would even urge the Church to acknowledge such dissolution and allow the parties to enter new, more promising unions. We reject this view.[51] In reality it amounts to a proposal to forego Christian marriage at the outset and substitute something entirely different. It would weaken marriage further, while paying too little heed to Jesus' call to identify ourselves with His redeeming love, which endures all things. Its fundamental difficulty is that it cannot be reconciled with the Church's mission to be faithful to the word entrusted to it. The covenant between a man and woman joined in Christian marriage is as indissoluble and irrevocable as God's love for His people and Christ's love for His Church.

Since the following of Christ calls for so much dedication   1625
and sacrifice in the face of strong, contrary social pressures, Christ's Church has a serious obligation to help His followers live up to the challenge. In worship, pastoral care, education, and counseling we must assist husbands and wives who are striving to realize the ideal of Christ's love in their lives together and with their children. Young people and engaged couples must be taught the meaning of Christian marriage. Married couples must have the support and encouragement of the Christian community in their efforts to honor their commitments.

It remains a tragic fact that some marriages fail. We must   1626
approach those who suffer this agonizing experience with the compassion of Jesus Himself. In some cases romanticism or immaturity may have prevented them from entering into real Christian marriages.

But often enough 'broken marriages' are sacramental, in-   1627
dissoluble unions. In this sensitive area the pastoral response of the Church is especially needed and especially difficult to formulate. We must seek ways by which the Church can mediate Christ's compassion to those who have suffered marital tragedy, but at the same time we may do nothing to undermine His teaching concerning the beauty and meaning of marriage and in particular His prophetic demands concerning the indissolubility of the unions of those who marry in the Lord. The Church must ever be faithful to the command to serve the truth in love.[52]

Children

The love of husband and wife finds its ideal fulfillment in   1628 their children, with whom they share their life and love. Children are really the supreme gift of marriage who in turn substantially enrich the lives of their parents.[53]

1629   Openness to children is vitally linked to growth in marital and family love. Couples have a right to determine responsibly, in accord with God's law, how many children they should have, and they may also have valid reasons for not seeking children immediately. But in marrying with the intention of postponing children indefinitely, some appear simply to wish to enjoy one another's company without distraction or to achieve an arbitrary level of material comfort. This can mark a selfish entry into what should be an experience of generous giving. Even worse, children may come to be regarded as an intrusion and a burden instead of a gift. This may lead to a rejection of the children, particularly those who are disadvantaged, either before or after birth.

1630   In order to reflect seriously upon the value they assign children, couples should begin by reflecting upon their understanding of marriage itself. Do they believe God is with them in this adventure to which they have committed themselves? If so, their love will reach confidently toward the future and provide a setting in which new life can be generously accepted, take root and grow. Openness to new life, founded on faith, in turn will strengthen their love. They will come to see how the love-giving and life-giving meanings of their love are joined in loving acts of marital intercourse, linked by a necessary relationship which exists not only on the biological level but on all levels of personality.

1631   One need not always act to realize both of these values, but one may never deliberately suppress either of them. The love-giving and life-giving meanings of marital intercourse are real human values and aspects of human personhood. Because they are, it is wrong to act deliberately against either. In contraceptive intercourse the procreative or life-giving meaning of intercourse is deliberately separated from its love-giving meaning and rejected; the wrongness of such an act lies in the rejection of this value.[54]

1632   Some distinguish between a so-called contraceptive mentality—a deep-seated attitude of selfish refusal to communicate life and love to a future generation—and particular contraceptive acts during a marriage otherwise generally open to the transmission of life. Though there is a difference, even in the latter case an act of contraceptive intercourse is wrong because it severs the link between the meanings of marital intercourse and rejects one of them.

We ask Catholics to reflect on the value at stake here. The   1633
Church is not engaged in a mere quibble over means of birth regulation; it is proclaiming the value of the life-giving meaning of marital intercourse, a value attacked, though in different ways, by both the ideology of contraception and by contraceptive acts.

Pastoral sensitivity requires that we be understanding to-   1634
ward those who find it hard to accept this teaching, but it does not permit us to change or suppress it. We recognize that couples face increasing pressures in family planning. Contraceptive birth control results not only from selfishness and improperly formed conscience but also from conflicts and pressures which can mitigate moral culpability. Therefore, we ask our people not to lose heart or turn away from the community of faith when they find themselves caught in these conflicts. We urge them to seek appropriate and understanding pastoral counsel, to make use of God's help in constant prayer and recourse to the sacraments, and to investigate honestly such legitimate methods of birth limitation as natural family planning.[55] At the same time we urge those who dissent from this teaching of the Church to a prayerful and studied reconsideration of their position.

Our Christian tradition holds the sexual union between   1635
husband and wife in high honor, regarding it as a special expression of their covenanted love which mirrors God's love for His people and Christ's love for the Church. But like many things human, sex is ambivalent. It can be either creative or destructive. Sexual intercourse is a moral and human good only within marriage; outside marriage it is wrong.[56]

Our society gives considerable encouragement to premarital   1636
and extramarital sexual relations as long as, it is said, 'no one gets hurt.' Such relations are not worthy of beings created in God's image and made God's adopted children nor are they

according to God's will. The unconditional love of Christian marriage is absent, for such relations are hedged around with many conditions. Though tenderness and concern may sometimes be present, there is an underlying tendency toward exploitation and self-deception. Such relations trivialize sexuality and can erode the possibility of making deep, life-long commitments.

1637   Some persons find themselves through no fault of their own to have a homosexual orientation. Homosexuals, like everyone else, should not suffer from prejudice against their basic human rights. They have a right to respect, friendship and justice. They should have an active role in the Christian community. Homosexual activity, however, as distinguished from homosexual orientation, is morally wrong. Like heterosexual persons, homosexuals are called to give witness to chastity, avoiding, with God's grace, behavior which is wrong for them, just as non-marital sexual relations are wrong for heterosexuals. Nonetheless, because heterosexuals can usually look forward to marriage, and homosexuals, while their orientation continues, might not, the Christian community should provide them a special degree of pastoral understanding and care.

1638   Though most people have two families, the one in which they are born and the one they help bring into being, the single and celibate have only the first. But from this experience they, too, know family values. Love and sacrifice, generosity and service have a real place in their lives. They are as much tempted as the married—sometimes more—to selfishness. They have as great a need for understanding and consolation. Family values may be expressed in different terms in their lives, but they are expressed.

The Aged

1639   The adventure of marriage and family is a continuing one in which elderly people have important lessons to teach and learn. Contemporary American society tends to separate the aging from their families, isolating kin in ways that are more than physical, with the result that the wisdom of experience is often neither sought, imparted nor further developed.[5 8]

Families should see the story of loving reciprocity through   1640
life's closing chapters. Where possible, the elderly should be
welcomed into their own families. Moreover, children have an
obligation of human and Christian justice and love to keep
closely in touch with aging parents and to do what lies in
their power to take care for them in their old age. "If anyone
does not provide for his own relatives and especially for
members of his immediate family, he has denied the faith; he
is worse than an unbeliever."[5 9] The community should provide for those who lack families and, in doing so, attend to all
their needs, not just physical ones. Here the Church has played
and continues to play a special role. The elderly must be
cherished, not merely tolerated, and the Church community,
through parishes and other agencies, should seek to mediate
to them the loving concern of Jesus and the Father.

Euthanasia or mercy killing is much discussed and increas-   1641
ingly advocated today, though the discussion is often confused
by ambiguous use of the slogan 'death and dignity.' Whatever
the word or term, it is a grave moral evil deliberately to kill
persons who are terminally ill or deeply impaired. Such
killing is incompatible with respect for human dignity and
reverence for the sacredness of life.

Something different is involved, however, when the ques-   1642
tion is whether hopelessly ill and painfully afflicted people
must be kept alive at all costs and with the use of every
available medical technique.

Some seem to make no distinction between respecting the   1643
dying process and engaging in direct killing of the innocent.
Morally there is all the difference in the world. While euthanasia or direct killing is gravely wrong, it does not follow that
there is an obligation to prolong the life of a dying person
by extraordinary means. At times the effort to do so is of no
help to the dying and may even be contrary to the compassion
due them. People have a right to refuse treatment which offers
no reasonable hope of recovery and imposes excessive burdens
on them and perhaps also their families. At times it may even
be morally imperative to discontinue particular medical
treatments in order to give the dying the personal care and

attention they really need as life ebbs. Since life is a gift of God we treat it with awesome respect. Since death is part and parcel of human life, indeed the gateway to eternal life and the return to the Father, it, too, we treat with awesome respect.

The Family and Society

1644   Marriage and the family are deeply affected by social patterns and cultural values. How we structure society, its approach to education and work, the roles of men and women, public policy toward health care and care of the young and old, the tone and cast of our literature, arts and media—all these affect the family. The test of how we value the family is whether we are willing to foster, in government and business, in urban planning and farm policy, in education and health care, in the arts and sciences, in our total social and cultural environment, moral values which nourish the primary relationships of husbands, wives and children and make authentic family life possible.

The Nation

1645   Our nation is committed in principle to the inviolable dignity of the human person, to respect for religious faith and the free exercise of religion, to social and legal structures by which citizens can participate freely in the governmental process, and to procedures by which grievances can be adjudicated and wrongs can be righted. This commitment is a constant challenge, and at times we have failed to live up to its demands. Nevertheless, it remains possible to develop here a social order "founded on truth, built on justice, and animated by love."[60]

The Individual and the Nation

1646   While the ultimate and most substantive values inhere in individuals, individuality and community are inseparable elements of the moral life. So, for instance, honesty, courage and hope, which abide only in individuals, can be fostered by freedom to learn, protection from violence, adequate income, and the availability of health care.

As followers of Jesus we are called to express love of neighbor in deeds which help others realize their human potential. This, too, has consequences for the structures of society. Law and public policy do not substitute for the personal acts by which we express love of neighbor; but love of neighbor impels us to work for laws, policies and social structures which foster human goods in the lives of all persons.   1647

Respect for the Unborn

It is therefore as ironic as it is tragic that, in a nation committed to human rights and dignity, the practice of legalized abortion is now widespread. Every human life is inviolable from its very beginning. While the unborn child may not be aware of itself and its rights, it is a human entity, a human being with potential, not a potential human being. Like the newborn, the unborn depend on others for life and the opportunity to share in human goods. Their dependence and vulnerability remind us of the social character of all human life: to live and thrive as a human being, each of us needs the help and support of others.[61]   1648

To destroy these innocent unborn children is an unspeakable crime, a crime which subordinates weaker members of the human community to the interests of the stronger. God who calls us to Himself loves the helpless and weak; like Him we should affirm the unborn in their being, not close our eyes to their humanity so that we may more easily destroy them. Their right to life must be recognized and fully protected by the law.   1649

While many today seek abortion for frivolous and selfish reasons, there are women who see it as a tragic solution to agnoizing problems. They deserve society's help in meeting and resolving these problems so that they will not feel a need to resort to the inhuman expedient of abortion. Recognition of the incomparable dignity of all human beings, including the unborn, obliges us to assume loving responsibility for all   1650 who are in need. The Church must take appropriate initiatives in providing support to women with problems during pregnancy or after, and in doing so bear witness to its belief in human dignity.[62]

Women in Society

1651   As society has grown more sensitive to some new or newly recognized issues and needs (while at the same time growing tragically less sensitive to others), the movement to claim equal rights for women makes it clear that they must now assume their rightful place as partners in family, institutional, and public life. The development of these roles can and should be enriching for both women and men.

1652   Even today some still consider women to be men's inferiors, almost their property. It is un-Christian and inhuman for husbands to regard their wives this way; they ought instead to "love (them) as Christ loved the Church."[63] Such un-Christian and inhuman attitudes are expressed in a truly degraded manner when they take the form of exploiting women for pleasure and financial profit through prostitution and pornography.

1653   Efforts to win recognition that women have the same dignity and fundamental rights as men are praiseworthy and good. But the same cannot be said of views which would ignore or deny significant differences between the sexes, undermine marriage and motherhood, and erode family life and the bases of society itself. Liberation does not lie in espousing new modes of dehumanization, nor in enslavement to an ideology which ignores the facts of human sexuality and the requirements of human dignity.

1654   There is much to be done in the Church in identifying appropriate ways of recognizing women's equality and dignity. We have every reason and precedent for doing so, since our tradition has always honored the Mother of God and recognized Mary as the one in whom, next to Jesus Himself, human nature is expressed most perfectly. In canonizing so many women over the centuries, including our own country's St. Frances Xavier Cabrini and St. Elizabeth Seton, the

Church has proposed them to both women and men as models of what it means to live the life of Christ. Thus we fully support constructive efforts to remove demeaning attitudes and customs with respect to women, however subtle and unconscious in origin they may be.

Address of Pope Paul VI
to the Congress of the Italian Women's Center
December 6, 1976

Dear daughters in Christ, You have come in great numbers to Rome as delegates of your various regions and provinces to the National Congress of the Italian Women's Center and in order to elect a National Council which will hold office for the next three years.

1656   The theme of your discussion is "The Condition of Women." A vast and many faceted theme, indeed, but surely a highly topical and compelling one as well. With it you enter in an authoritative way—being representatives of a very important organization—into the worldwide debate on the status and advancement of women. It is a debate which, in various and often quite lively forms, is a characteristic of contemporary society.

1657   The entire Church is following with great interest and concern the various movements in behalf of women's rights, the aim of which is to win "legal and practical quality with men."[1] For in Christianity more than in any other religion, women have from the very beginning been accorded an especially high dignity. The New Testament bears witness to various important aspects of this dignity.

1658   The New Testament tells us of "Mary the mother of Jesus,"[2] whose extraordinary and holy role makes her the most revered of women. It tells us of the women who followed and assisted the Lord during the time of his public ministry[3] and who later were graced by the early appearances of the risen

Christ.[4] It tells us of the women who were with the 12 in the upper room on Pentecost[5] and of the many women whom Paul mentions by name in his letters because of the numerous roles they had in the first churches.[6] From all this it is clear that women have an important place in the living, dynamic structure of Christianity—so much so that all the implications and possibilities of their role have perhaps not yet come to light. If to the valuable information provided by the New Testament we add all the texts which urge respect for every woman and a special love of husband for wife,[7] we have further confirmation that in this area the Church has shown a creative originality ever since her first appearance in the world.

Like the Church of the first age, the Church of today cannot but be on the side of women, especially where, instead of being treated as active, responsible subjects, they are reduced to the status of passive, insignificant objects, as happens in some work situations, in degenerate exploitation of the mass media, in social relations and in the family. It might be said that for some men women are the easiest tool to use in expressing their impulses to outrageous violence. This explains and to some extent makes intelligible the bitterness and vehemence with which various feminist movements seek to retaliate.   **1659**

We are entirely convinced that the participation of women at the various levels of social life must not only be recognized but promoted and, above all, sincerely valued. In this respect, much progress undoubtedly has yet to be made.   **1660**

At the same time, let us remember that, according to the statement of the Second Vatican Council, "women . . . should assume their proper role in accordance with their own nature."[8] This special nature women must not surrender. In fact, the very "image and likeness" of God[9] that makes her fully like and equal to man is realized in her in a special way which distinguishes her from man, just as man is distinct from woman. The difference is not in dignity of nature but in diversity of function. Woman must be on guard against an insidious kind of depreciation of the womanly state, which she can fall into today where there is an attempt being made   **1661** to misconceive the differentiating characteristics which are determined by nature itself in the two sexes.

1662   It is in keeping with the very order of creation, then, that woman should seek her fulfillment as woman. She should seek it, that is, not by an effort to win the upper hand in a confrontation with man but by a harmonious, fruitful integration with man, based on a respectful recognition of the roles proper to each. For that reason it is most desirable that to the various spheres of life in society in which she works woman should bring that unmistakably human quality and concern which is uniquely hers.

1663   In particular, We very much encourage you, the women of the Italian Women's Center, to pursue with enthusiasm, fidelity and joy your commitment to giving witness as citizens and Christians in contemporary Italian life. We also take the liberty of inviting you to extend the activity of your organization, and to make it ever more responsive to the changing needs of the times by not only directing it to specific social services which promote the good of mankind generally but also applying yourselves with unwearying concern to the specific problems of the world of women. The task of promoting a feminist movement on a mass scale could stimulate and concentrate your powers of generous understanding in a very profitable manner. You would, thus, achieve a greater presence and influence both in the world of women in particular and in society at large, so as to make the latter more sensitive to the problems of women and to a more satisfactory and honorable way of facing these problems and solving them.

1664   What is being asked of you, then, is to evolve a prudent overall strategy and opportune ways of implementing it, not in a partisan and polemical spirit but with serene, unyielding dedication to an ideal which, being based on faith, is destined to make its way by reason of its radiant beauty and beneficent value.

1665   Because of the special charism you possess as individuals and as a group, the entire community expects of you a selfless energetic witness to the Christian presence of woman in the world, a witness of which you alone are capable and which you certainly know how to give. To you, then, members of the Italian Women's Center, We entrust this mission, in the name of the Lord. You represent in Italy a well-organized and experienced Catholic feminist movement and you are called on to accept this responsibility which is surely worthy of your best efforts; to dedicate yourselves, that is, to a task for which you are uniquely fitted and in which your best selves can shine forth resplendent.

As a pledge of future success We bestow on you Our   1666 fatherly Apostolic Blessing, in order that the Lord may be always with you, sustaining you and strengthening you with his energizing inspiration.

References

CASTI CONNUBII, Encyclical Letter of Pope Pius XI on Christian Marriage, December 31, 1930.

1   Encycl. *Arcanum divianae sapientiae*, 10 Febr. 1880.

2   *Gen.*, I, 27-28; II, 22-23; *Matth.*, XIX, 3 sqq.; *Eph.*, V, 23. sqq.

3   Conc. Trid., Sess XXIV.

4   Cod. iur. can., c. 1081 § 2.

5   Cod. iur. can., c. 1081 § 1.

6   S. THOM. AQUIN., *Summa theol.*, p. III, Supplem. 9, XLIX, rt. 3.

7   Encycl. *Rerum novarum*, 15 May 1891.

8   *Gen.*, I, 28.

9   Encycl. *Ad salutem*, 20 April 1930.

10   ST. AUGUST., *De bono coniug.*, cap. 24, n. 32.

11   ST. AUGUST., *De Gen. ad litt.*, IX, cap. 7, n. 12.

12   *Gen.*, I, 28.

13   I *Tim.*, V. 14.

14   ST. AUGUST., *De bono coniug.*, cap. 24, n. 32.

15   I *Cor.*, II, 9.

16   *Eph.*, II, 19.

17   *John* XVI, 21.

18   Encycl. *Divini illius Magistri*, 31, Dec. 1929.

19   ST. AUGUST., *De Gen. ad litt*, lib. IX, cap. 7, n. 12.

20   Cod. iur. can., c. 1013 § 7.

21   Conc. Trid., Sess. XXIV.

22   *Matth.*, V. 28.

23   Decr. S. Officii, 2 March 1679, propos. 50.

24   *Eph.*, V. 25; *Col.*, III, 19.

25   *Catech. Rom.*, II, cap. VIII, q. 24.

26   ST. GREG. THE GREAT, *Homil. XXX in Evang.* (John XIV, 23-31), n. 1.

27   *Matth.*, XXII, 40.

28   I *Cor.*, VII, 3.

29   *Eph.*, V. 22-23.

30   Encycl. *Arcanum divinae sapientiae*, 10 Febr. 1880.

31   *Matth.*, XIX, 6.

32   *Luke*, XVI, 18.

33   ST. AUGUST., *De Gen. ad litt*, IX, cap. 7, n. 12.

34   Pius VI, *Rescript. ad. Episc. Agriens.*, 11 July 1789.

35   *Eph.*, V. 32.

36   ST. AUGUST., *De nupt. et. concup.*, lib. I, cap. 10.

37   I *Cor.*, XIII, 8.

38   Conc. Trid., Sess XXIV.

39   Conc. Trid., Sess. XXIV.

40   Cod. iur. can., c. 1012.

41   ST. AUGUST., *De nupt. et concup.*, lib. I, cap. 10.

42   *Matth.*, XIII, 25.

43   II *Tim.*, IV, 2-5.

44   *Eph.*, V. 3.

45   ST. AUGUST., *De coniug. adult.*, lib. II, n. 12; *Gen.*, XXXVIII, 8-10.

46   *Matth.*, XV, 14.

47   *Luke*, VI, 38.

48   Conc. Trid., Sess. VI, cap. 11.

49   Const. Apost. *Cum occasione*, 31 May 1653, prop. 1.

50   *Exod.*, XX, 13; cfr. Decr. S. Offic. 4 May 1897, 24 July 1895; 31 May 1884.

51   ST. AUGUST., *De nupt. et concupisc.*, cap. XV.

52   *Rom.*, III, 8.

53   *Gen.*, IV, 10.

54   *Summ. theol.*, 2a 2ae, q. 108 a4 ad2 um.

55   *Exod.*, XX, 14.

56   *Matth.*, V. 28.

57   *Hebr.*, XIII, 8.

58   *Matth.*, v. 18.

59   *Matth.*, VII, 27.

60   Leo XII, Encycl. *Arcanum*, 10 Febr. 1880.

61   *Eph.*, V. 32: *Hebr.*, XIII, 4.

62   Cod. iur. can., c. 1060.

63   MODESTINUS, in Dig. (Lib. XXIII, *De ritu nuptiarum*), lib. I, Regularum.

64   *Matth.*, XIX, 6.

65   *Luke*, XVI, 18.

66   Conc. Trid., Sess XXIV, cap. 5.

67   Conc. Trid., Sess. XXIV, cap. 7.

68   Cod. iur. can., c. 1128 sqq.

69   *Leo XIII*, Encycl. Arcanum divinae sapientiae, 10 Febr. 1880.

70   Encycl. *Arcanum*, 10 Febr. 1880.

71   Encycl. *Arcanum*, 10 Febr. 1880.

72   ST. THOM. OF AQUIN. *Summ. Theolog.*, 1a 2ae, q, 91, a. 1-2.

73   Encycl. *Arcanum divinae sapientiae*, 10 Febr. 1880.

74   ST. AUGUST., *Enarrat. in Ps.* 143.

75   *Rom.* I, 24, 26.

76   *James* IV, 6.

77   *Rom.*, VII, VIII.

78   Conc. Vat., Sess. III, cap. 2.

79   Conc. Vat., Sess. III, cap. 4; Cod. iur. can., c 1324.

80   *Acts*, XX, 28.

81   *John*, VIII, 32 sqq.; *Gal.*, V. 13.

82   Encycl. *Arcanum*. 10 Febr. 1880.

83   ST. ROB. BELLARMIN., *De controversis, tom. III, De Matr.*, controvers. II, cap. 6.

84   I *Tim.*, IV, 14.

85   I *Tim.*, I. 6-7.

86   *Gal.*, VI. 9.

87   *Eph.*, IV, 13.

88   Encycl. *Divini illius Magistri*, 31 Dec. 1929.

89   *Eph.*, VI, 2-3; *Exod.*, XX, 12.

90   Encycl. *Rerum novarum*, 15 May 1891.

91   *Luke*, X, 7.

92   *Deut.* XXIV, 14, 15.

93   Leo XIII, Encycl. *Rerum novarum*, 15, May 1891.

94   *Matth.*, XXV, 34 sqq.

95   I *John*, III, 17.

96   Encycl. *Arcanum divinae sapientiae*, 10 Febr. 1880.

97   Concord., art. 34; *Act. Apost. Sed.*, XXI (1929), pag. 290.

98   *Tit.*, II, 12-13.

99   *Eph.*, III, 15.

100   Conc. Trid., Sess. XXIV.

101   *Phil.*, II, 13.

Address of Pope Pius XII to the Italian Medical-biological Union of St. Luke, November 12, 1944.

1   Cf. 1 *Cor.* 1:21 ff.

2   A. de Musset, *La nuit d'doctobre*.

3   Cf. *Luke* 24:26-46.

4   *In Joan.*, tr. VIII, ch. IV, 4-8. ML 35, 2033.

5   *Matt.* 25:36.

6   Cf. 1 *Cor.* 13:4-7.

7   *Exodus* 20:13.

8   *Col.* 4:14.

9   *Luke* 4:40.

Address of Pope Pius XII to Midwives, October 29, 1951.

1   *Gen.* 1:26-27.

2   *2 Mach.* 7:22.

3   Decree of the Holy Office, December 2nd, 1940, Acta Apostolicae Sedis, Vo. 32, 1940, pp. 553-554.

4   *Exod.* 20:13.

5   *Ps.* 126:3-4.

6   *Ps.* 127:3-4.

7   *Ps.* 108:13.

8   *Matt.* 25:21.

9   *John* 16:21.

10   1 *Tim.* 2:15.

11   *Matt.* 5:7.

12   *Luke* 1:38.

13   *Gal.* 4:4.

14   *John* 1:14.

15   *Luke* 1:31.

16   Can. 1013, par. 1.

17   Holy Office, April 1, 1944. AAS. vo. 36, 1944, p. 10.

18   *Gen.* 1:27.

19   *Gen.* 2:24; *Matt.* 19:5; *Eph.* 5:31.

20   *Matt.* 19:11.

SACRA VIRGINITAS, Encyclical Letter of Pope Pius XII on Holy Virginity, March 25, 1954.

1   Cfr. S. AMBROS., *De virginibus.*, lib. I, c. 4, n. 15; *De virginitate*, c. 3, n. 13; P.L. XVI, 193, 269.

2   Cfr. Ex. XXII, 16-17; *Deut.* XXII, 23-29, *Eccli.* XLII, 9.

3   S. AMBROS., *De virginibus*, lib. I. c. 3, n. 12; P.L. XVI, 192.

4   I *Cor.* X, 11.

5   *Act.* XXI, 9.

6   Cfr. S. IGNAT. ANTIOCH., *Ep. ad Smyrn.*, c. 13; ed. Funk-Diekamp, *Patres Apostolici*, vol. I, p. 286.

7   S' IUSTIN., *Apol.* I *pro christ.*, c. 15; P.G. VI, 349.

8   Cfr. CONST' APOST. *Sponsa Christi*, A. A. S. XLII, 1951, pp. 5-8.

9   Cfr. C. I. C., can. 487.

10   Cfr. C. I. C., can. 132, section 1.

11   Cfr. CONST. APOST. *Provida Mater*, art. III, section 2; A. A. S. XXXIX, 1947, p. 121.

12   MATTH. XIX, 10.

13   *Ibid.*, XIX, 11-12.

14   *Ibid.*, XIX, 12.

15   S. AUGUSTIN., *De sancta virginitate*, c. 22; P.L. XL, 407.

16   Cfr. can. 9; MANSI, *Coll. concil.*, II, 1096.

17   I *Cor.* VII, 32, 34.

18   S. CYPR., *De habitu virginum*, 4; P.L. IV, 443.

19   S. AUGUSTIN., *De Sancta virginitate*, cc. 8, 11; P.L. XL, 400, 401.

20   S. THOM., *Summa Th.*, II-II, q. 152, a. 3, ad 4.

21   S. BONAV., *De perfectione evangelica*, q. 3, a. 3, sol. 5.

22   Cfr. S. CYPR.. *De habitu virginum*, c. 20; P.L. IV, 459.

23   Cfr. S. ATHANAS., *Apol. ad Constant.*, 33; P.G. XXV, 640.

24   S. AMBROS., *De virginibus*, lib. I, c. 8; n. 52; P.L. XVI, 202.

25   Cfr. Ibid., lib III, cc. 1-3, nn. 1-14; *De institutione virginis*, c. 17, nn. 104-114; P.L. XVI, 219-224, 333-336.

26   Cfr. *Sacramentarium Leonianum*, XXX; P.L. LV, 129; *Pontificale Romanum:* De benedictione et consecratione virginum.

27   Cfr. S. CYPR., *De habitu virginum*, 4 et 22; P.L. IV, 443-444 et 462; S. AMBROS., *De virginibus*, lib. I, c. 7, 37; P.L. XVI, 199.

28   S. AUGUSTIN., *De sancta virginitate*, cc. 54-55; P.L. XL, 428.

29   *Pontificale Romanum*: De benedictione et consecratione virginum.

30   S. METHODIUS OLYMPI, *Convivium decem virginum*, orat. XI, c. 2; P.G. XVIII, 209.

31 *Apoc.* XIV, 4.

32 *Ibid.*

33 I *Petr.* II, 21; S. AUGUSTIN., *De sancta virginitate,* c. 27; P.L. XL, 411.

34 S. BONAV., *De perfectione evangelica,* q. 3, a. 3.

35 S. FULGENT., *Epist.* 3, c. 4, n. 6, P.L. LXV, 326.

36 I *Cor.* VII, 32-33.

37 *Gen.* II, 24; Cfr. MATTH, XIX, 5.

38 Cfr. I *Cor.,* VII, 39.

39 S. THOM, *Summa Th.,* II-II, q. 186, a. 4.

40 Cfr. C. I. C., can. 132, section 1.

41 Cfr. Litt. Enc. *Ad catholici sacerdotii fastigium,* A.A.S. XXVIII, 1936, pp. 24-25.

42 Cfr. *Lev.* XV, 16-17; XXII, 4; I *Sam.* XXI, 5-7; cfr. S. SIRIC. PAPA, *Ep. ad Himer.* 7; P.L. LVI, 558-559.

43 S. PETRUS DAM., *De coelibatu sacerdotum,* c. 3; elibatu sacerdotum, P.L. CLXV, 384.

44 Cfr. MATTH. XIX, 10-11.

45 I *Cor.,* VII, 38.

46 *Ibid.,* VII 7-8; Cfr. 1 et 26.

47 Cfr. S. THOM., *Summa Th.,* II-II, q. 152, aa. 3-4.

48 Cfr. I *Cor.,* VII, 33.

49 MATTH. XII, 33.

50 MATTH. XXV, 35-36, 40.

51 A.A.S. XLII, 1950, p. 663.

52 S. CYPR., *De habitu virginum,* 22; P.L. IV, 462; cfr. S. AMBROS.; *De virginibus,* lib. I, c. 8, n. 52; P.L. XVI, 202.

53 Matth. XIII, 46.

54 S. THOM., *Summa Th.,* II-II, q. 152, a. 5.

55 *Pontificale Romanum:* De benedictione et consecratione virginum.

56 S. CYPR., *De habitu virginum,* 3; P.L. IV, 443.

57 SESS. XXIV, can 10.

58 Cfr. S. THOM., *Summa Th.,* I-II, q. 94, a. 2.

59 Cfr. *Gal.* V. 25; I *Cor.* IX, 27.

60   Cfr. Allocutio ad Moderatrices supremas Ordinum et Institutorum Religiosarum, d. 15 septembris 1952; A.A.S. XLIV, 1952, p. 824.

61   Cfr. Decretum S. Officii, *De matrimonii finibus*, d. 1 aprilis 1944; A.A.S. XXXVI, 1944, p. 103.

62   Cfr. I *Cor*. VII, 5.

63   Cfr. C.I.C., can. 1013, section 1.

64   *Gal.* II, 20.

65   S. AMBROS., *De virginitate*, c. 5, n. 26; P.L. XVI, 272.

66   Cfr. Io. X, 14; X, 3.

67   Cfr. A.A.S., XLIII, 1951, p. 20.

68   I *Cor*. VII, 25.

69   MATTH. XIX, 11.

70   S. SMBROS., *De viduis*, c. 12, n. 71; P.L. XVI 256; cfr. S. CYPR., *De habitu virginum*, c. 23; P.L. IV, 463.

71   Cfr. I *Cor*. VII, 7.

72   MATTH. XIX, 11, 12.

73   S. HIERONYM, *Comment. in Matth.*, XIX, 12; P.L. XXVI, 136.

74   S. IOANN. CHRYSOST., *De virginitate*, 80; P.G. XLVIII, 592.

75   S. AMBROS, *De virginitate*, lib. I, c. 11, n. 65; P.L. XVI, 206.

76   Cfr. S. METHODIUS OLYMPI, *Convivium decem virginum*, Orat. VII, c. 3; P.G. XVIII, 128-129.

77   S. GREGOR. M., *Hom. in Evang.*, lib. I, hom. 3, n. 4; P.L. LXXVI, 1089.

78   MATTH. XIX, 12.

79   I *Cor*. VII, 9.

80   Cfr. *Conc. Trid.*, sess. XXIV, can. 9.

81   Cfr. S. AUGUSTIN., *De natura et gratia*, c. 43, n. 50; P.L. XLIV, 271.

82   *Conc. Trid.*, sess. VI, c. 11.

83   I *Cor*. X, 13.

84   MATTH. XXVI, 41.

85   *Gal.* V, 17.

86   Cfr. *Ibid.* 19-21.

87   *Ibid.* 24.

88   I *Cor*. IX, 27.

89 MATTH. V, 28-29.

90 Cfr. S. CAESAR. ARELAT., *Sermo* 41; ed. G. Morin, Maredsous, 1937, vol. I, p. 172.

91 Cfr. S. THOMAS, *In Ep. I ad Cor.* VI, lect. 3; S. FRANCISCUS SALES. *Introduction a la vie devote*, part. IV, c. 7; S. SLPHONSUS A LIGUORI, *La vera sposa di Gesu Cristo*, c. 1, n. 16; c. 15, n. 10.

92 S. HIERONYM., *Contra Vigilant.*, 16; P.L. XXIII, 352.

93 S. AUGUSTIN., *De sancta virginitate*, c. 54; P.L. XL, 428.

94 *Eccli.*, III, 27.

95 S. AUGUSTIN., *Epist.*, 211; n. 10; P.L. XXXIII, 961.

96 Io. XVII, 18.

97 *Ibid.* 16.

98 *Ibid.* 15.

99 Cfr. C.I.C., can. 124-142. Cfr. B. PIUS PP. X, Exhort. ad cler. cath. *Haerent animo*, A.A.S., XLI, 1908, pp. 565-573; PIUS PP. XI, Litt. enc. *Ad catholici sacerdotii fastigium*, A.A.S., XXVIII, 1936, pp. 23-30; PIUS XII, Adhort. Apost. *Menti Nostrae*, A.A.S., XLII, 1950, pp. 692-694.

100 Cfr. A.A.S. XLII, 1950, pp. 690-691.

101 Cfr. I *Cor.* VI, 15.

102 *Ibid.* 19.

103 Alloc. *Magis guma mentis*, d. 23 Sept., a. 1951; A.A.S. XLIII, 1951, p. 736.

104 S. CLEMENS ROM., *Ad Corinthios*, XXXVIII, 2; ed. Funk-Diekamp. *Patres Apostolici*, vol. I, p. 148.

105 I IOANN., IV, 8.

106 S. AUGUSTIN., *De sancta virginitate*, cc. 33, 51; P.L. XL, 415, 426; cfr. cc. 31-32, 38; 412-415, 419.

107 Cfr. MATTH. XIX, 11.

108 Cfr. Ibid. VII, 8; S. HIERON., *Comm. in Matth.* XIX, 11; P.L. XXVI, 135.

109 Cfr. S. AMBROS., *De virginibus*, lib. III, c 4, nn. 18-20; P.L. XVI, 225.

110 Cfr. S. ALPHONSUS A LIGUORI, *Practica di amar Gesu Cristo*, c. 17, nn. 7-16.

111 LEO XIII, Encyclica *Mirae caritatis*, d. 28 Maii, a. 1902; A.L. XXII, pp. 1902-1903.

112 IO. VI, 57.

113   S. AMBROS., *De institutione virginis,* c. 6, n. 46; P.L. XVI, 320.

114   Cfr. S. ATHANAS., *De virginitate,* ed. Th. Lefort, *Museon,* XLII, 1929, p. 247.

115   S. AUGUSTIN., *Serm.* 51, c. 16, n. 26; P.L. XXXVIII, 348.

116   Cfr. S. ATHANAS. *Ibid.* p. 244.

117   S. AMBROS., *De institutione virginis,* c. 14, n. 87; P.L. XVI, 328.

118   S. AMBROS., *De virginibus,* lib. II, c. 2, n. 6, 15; P.L. XVI, 208, 210.

119   *Ibid.,* c. 3, n. 19; P.L. XVI, 211.

120   S. AMBROS., *De institut. virginis,* c. 7, n. 50; P.L. XVI, 319.

121   *Ibid.,* c. 13, n. 81, P.L. XVI, 339.

122   S. BERNARD., *In nativitate B. Mariae Virginis,* Sermo de aquaeductu, n. 8; P.L. 183, 441-442.

123   S. HERONYM., *Epist.* 22, n. 18; P.L. XXII, 405.

124   S. AMBROS., *De virginibus,* lib. I, c. 10, n. 58; P.L. XVI, 205.

125   *Ibid.,* c. 7, n. 32; P.L. XVI, 198.

126   Cfr. S. Ambros., *De virginibus,* lib. II, c. 4, n. 32; P.L. XVI, 215-216.

127   *Phil.,* II, 8.

128   *Apoc.* XIV, 4.

129   *Ibid.,* 3.

130   MATTH. V, 10.

Address of Pope Pius XII to the Second World Congress on Fertility and Sterility, May 19, 1956.

1   The Holy Father here spoke for several minutes in Latin.

Address of Pope Pius XII to a Pilgrimage Sponsored by the Federation of Italian Women, October 14, 1956.

1   *Discorsi e Radiomessaggi,* v. 7, p. 240.

Address of Pope Pius XII to the Seventh International Hematological Congress in Rome, September 12, 1958.

1   *Discorsi e Radiomessaggi* XI, pp. 223-25.

2   Cf. *Denzinger* n. 1151-1216; 1221-1228.

3   *Discorsi e Radiomessaggi* XIII, p. 342.

4   *Ibid.* XV, pp. 373-379.

5   *AAS* 22 (1930) 559-560.

6   *AAS* 22 (1930) 561.

7   Cf. *AAS* 22 (1930) 564-565.

Explosion or Backfire? The 1959 Statement on Birth Control by National Conference of Catholic Bishops, November 19, 1959.

1   After the signatures of the Administrative Board there is appended a lengthy quotation from "An Address to the Association for Large Families of Rome and Italy" by Pius XII, January 20, 1958.

Address of Pope John XXIII to the Sacred Roman Rota, October 25, 1960.

1   *Discorsi e Radiomessaggi*, IV, 45.

2   *Eph.* 3, 15.

3   *Wisd.* 9, 4, and 10-11.

Address of Pope John XXIII to the Italian Center for Women, December 7, 1960

1   "And there shall come forth a rod out of the root of Jesse, and a flower shall rise up out of his root." (*Isa.* 11, 1).

2   *Discorsi, Messaggi, Colloqui* I, 172. A digest of this talk appeared in TPS v. 5, no. 3, 290.

3   *Ibid.*

4   *Deut.* 30, 19-20.

5   *Phil.* 2, 13.

6   "She hath opened her mouth to wisdom, and the law of clemency is on her tongue." (*Prov.* 31, 26).

Address of Pope Paul VI to the Special Papal Commission Examining the Problems of Population Growth, Family Planning, and Birth Regulation   March 27, 1965.

1   New things and old things.

Address of Pope Paul VI to Participants in the 13th National Congress of the Italian Women's Center, February 12, 1966.

1   *Pastoral Constitution on the Church in the Modern World,* n. 50.

2   I *Cor* 13, 5.

3   *Pastoral Constitution on the Church in the Modern World,* n. 48.

4   *Mt.* 5, 1.

5   *Mt.* 7, 13-14.

6   *Eph.* 5, 27.

7   I *Tim.* 2, 15.

SACERDOTALIS CAELIBATUS, Encyclical Letter of Pope Paul VI on Priestly Celibacy, June 24, 1967.

1   Letter of Oct. 10, 1965 to H.E. Card. E. Tisserant, read in the 146th General Congregation on Oct. 11.

2   Second Vatican Ecumenical Council, Decree *Christus Dominus,* n. 35; *Apostolicam actuositatem,* n. 1; *Presbyterorum Ordinis,* nn. 10, 11; *Ad Gentes,* nn. 19, 38.

3   Second Vatican Ecumenical Counctil, Constitution *Gaudium et Spes,* n. 62.

4   Decree *Presbyter. Ordinis,* n. 16.

5   Second Vatican Ecumenical Council, Dogmatic Constitution *Dei Verbum,* n. 8.

6   Second Vatican Ecumenical Council, Dogmatic Constitution *Lumen Gentium,* n. 28; Decree *Presbyter. Ordinis,* n. 2.

7   Decree *Presbyter. Ordinis,* n. 16.

8   Decree *Presbyter. Ordinis,* n. 16.

9   Constitition *Lumen Gentium,* n. 42.

10   Cf. Dogmatic Constitution *Lumen Gentium,* n. 42; Decree *Presbyter. Ordinis,* n. 16.

HUMANAE VITAE, Encyclical Letter of Pope Paul VI on the Regulation of Birth, July 25, 1968.

1   Cf. Pius IX, encyclical *Qui Pluribus,* Nov. 9, 1846; in PII IX P. M. Acta, I, pp. 9-10; St. Pius X, encyc. *Singulari Quadam,* Sept. 24, 1912; in AAS IV (1912), p. 658; Pius XI, encyc. *Casti Connubii,* Dec. 31, 1930; in AAS XXII (1930), pp. 579-581; Pius XII, allocution *Magnificate Dominum* to the episcopate of the Catholic world, Nov. 2, 1954; in AAS XLVI (19540, pp. 671-672; John XXIII, ency. *Mater et Magistra,* May 19, 1961; in AAS LIII (1961), p. 457.

2   Cf. Matt. 28:18-19.

3   Cf. Matt. 7:21.

4   Cf. *Catechismus Romanus Concilii Tridentini,* part II, ch. VIII; Leo XIII, encyc. *Arcanum,* Feb. 19, 1880; in *Acta Leonis* XIII, II (1881), pp. 26-29; Pius XI, encyc. *Divini Illius Magistri,* Dec. 31, 1929, in AAS XXII (1930), pp. 58-61; encyc. *Casti Connubii,* in AAS XXII (1930), pp. 545-546; Pius XII, alloc. to the Italian medico-biological union of St. Luke, Nov. 12, 1944, in *Discorsi e Radiomessaggi,* VI, pp. 191-192; to the Italian Catholic union of midwives, Oct. 29, 1951, in AAS XLIII (1951), pp. 857-859; to the seventh Congress of the International Society of Haematology, Sept. 12, 1958, in AAS L (1958), pp. 734-735; John XXIII, encyc. *Mater et Magistra,* in AAS LIII (1961), pp. 446-447; *Codex Iuris Canonici,* Canon 1067; Can. 1968, S 1, Can. 1066 S 1-2; Second Vatican Council, Pastoral constitution *Gaudium et Spes,* nos. 47-52.

5   Cf. Paul VI, allocution to the Sacred College, June 23, 1964, in AAS LVI (1964), p. 588; to the Commission for Study of Problems of Population, Family and Birth, March 27, 1965, in AAS LVII (1965), p. 388, to the National Congress of the Italian Society of Obstetrics and Gynaecology, Oct. 29, 1966, in AAS LVIII (1966), p. 1168.

6   Cf. I John 4:8.

7   Cf. Eph. 3:15.

8   Cf. II Vat. Council, Pastoral const. *Gaudium et Spes,* No. 50

9   Cf. St. Thomas, *Summa Theologica*, I-II, q. 94, art. 2.

10   Cf. Pastoral Const. *Gaudium et Spes*, nos. 50, 51.

11   *Ibid.*, no. 49.

12   Cf. Pius XI, encyc. *Casti Connubii*, in AAS XXII (1930), p. 560; Pius XII, in AAS XLIII (1951), p. 843.

13   Cf. John XXIII, encyc. *Mater et Magistra*, in AAS LIII (1961), p. 447.

14   Cf. *Catechismus Romanus Concilii Tridentini*, part. II, Ch. VIII; Pius XI, encyc. *Casti Connubii*, in AAS XXII (1930), pp. 562-564; Pius XII, *Discorsi e Radiomessaggi*, VI (1944), pp. 191-192; AAS XLIII (1951), pp. 842-843; pp. 857-859; John XXIII, encyc. *Pacem in Terris*, Apr. 11, 1963, in AAS LV (1963), pp. 259-260; *Gaudium et Spes*, no. 51.

15   Cf. Pius XI, encyc. *Casti Connubii*, in AAS XXII (1930) p. 565; decree of the Holy Office, Feb. 22, 1940, in AAS L (1958), pp. 734-735.

16   Cf. *Catechismus Romanus Concilii Tridentini*, part. II, Ch. VIII; Pius XI, encyc. *Casti Connubii*, in AAS XXII (1930), pp. 559-561; Pius XII, AAS XLIII (1951), p. 843; AAS L. (1958), pp. 734-735; John XXIII, encyc. *Mater et Magistra*, in AAS LIII (1961), p. 447.

17   Cf. Pius XII, alloc. to the National Congress of the Union of Catholic Jurists, Dec. 6, 1953, in AAS XLV (1953), pp. 798-799.

18   Cf. Rom. 3:8.

19   Cf. Pius XII, alloc. to Congress of the Italian Association of Urology, Oct. 8, 1953, in AAS XLV (1953), pp. 674-675; AAS L (1958) pp. 734-735.

20   Cf. Pius XII, AAS XLIII (1951), p. 846.

21   Cf. AAS XLV (1953), pp. 674-675; AAS XLVIII (1956), pp. 461-462.

22   Cf. Luke 2:34.

23   Cf. Paul VI, encyc. *Populorum Progressio*, March 26, 1967, No. 21.

24   Cf. Rom. 8.

25   Cf. II Vatican Council, decree *Inter Mirifica*, On the Media of Social Communication, nos. 6-7.

26   Cf. encyc. *Mater et Magistra*, in AAS LIII (1961), p. 447.

27   Cf. encyc. *Populorum Progressio*, nos. 48-55.

28   Cf. Pastoral Const. *Gaudium et Spes*, n. 52.

29   Cf. AAS XLIII (1951), p. 859.

30   Cf. Pastoral Const. *Gaudium et Spes*, no. 51.

31   Cf. Matt. 11:30.

32   Cf. Pastoral Const. *Gaudium et Spes*, no. 48; II Vatican Council, Dogmatic Const. *Lumen Gentium*, no. 35.

33   Matt. 7:14; cf. Heb. 11:12.

34   Cf. Tit. 2:12.

35   Cf. 1 Cor. 7:31.

36   Cf. Rom. 5:5.

37   Eph. 5:25, 28-29, 32-33.

38   Cf. Dogmatic Const. *Lumen Gentium*, nos. 35 and 41; Pastoral Const. *Gaudium et Spes*, nos. 48-49; II Vatican Council, Decree *Apostolicam Actuositatem*, no. 11.

39   Cf. Dogmatic Const. *Lumen Gentium*, no. 25.

40   Cf. I Cor. 1:10.

41   Cf. John 3:17.

Address of Pope Paul VI to a General Audience, July 31, 1968.

1   *Humanae Vitae*, no. 14.

2   *Ibid.*, no. 7.

3   I *Cor.* 2, 16.

Address of Pope Paul VI to the Teams of our Lady, May 4, 1970.

1   *Gn.* 1, 31.

2   Vat. Coun. II, *Dogmatic Constitution on the Church*, no. 11.

3   *Ibid.*, no. 41.

4   Vat. Coun. II, *Pastoral Constitution on the Church in the World of Today*, no. 49.

5   Vat. Coun. II, *Decree on the Apostolate of the Laity*, no. 11.

6   See *Pastoral Constitution on the Church in the World of Today*, nos. 1, 47-52.

7   *Eph.* 1, 14.

8   *Gn.* 1, 27.

9   *Gn.* 1, 28.

10   *Gn.* 2, 24.

11   *Mt.* 19, 6.

12   See Paul VI, *Humanae Vitae*, no. 9.

13   See *Ti.* 3, 5.

14   See *Gal.* 6, 15.

15   *Rom.* 6, 4.

16   I *Cor.* 6, 19.

17   *Eph.* 5, 32.

18   *Jn.* 13, 34.

19   *Dogmatic Constitution on the Church*, no. 11.

20   *Discorsi, messaggi, colloqui del Santo Padre Giovanni* XXIII, I: Vatican Polyglot Press, p. 298.

21   *Introduction to the Devout Life*, Part III, chap. 38.

22   See 2 *Cor.* 4, 7.

23   I *Cor.* 6, 15-20.

24   Paul VI, *Humanae Vitae*, no. 1.

25   *Jn.* 3, 5.

26   *Eph.* 4, 24.

27   Emmanuel Mounier to his wife Paulette, Mar. 20, 1940, *Oeuvres*, Paris: Seuil (1963), vol. IV, p. 662.

28   *Mt.* 25, 40.

29   See Vat. Coun. II, *Declaration on Christian Education*.

30   See I, *Jn.* 4, 7-11.

31   *Eph.* 3, 15.

32   *Declaration on Christian Education*, no. 3.

33   St. Thomas, *Contra Gentes*, IV, 58.

34   *Rom* 12, 13.

35   See Acts 18, 23; Rom 16, 3-4; I Cor. 16, 19.

36   Homily 20 on Ephesians 5, 22-24, N. 6: *PG* 62, 135-140.

37   Phrase coined by a member-home of the Teams of Our lady, cited by H. Caffarel, in *l'Anneau d'Or*, no. 111-112; *Le mariage, ce grand sacrement*, Paris: Feu nouveau (1963), p. 282.

38   *Dogmatic Constitution on the Church*, no. 35.

39   *Ibid.*, no. 41.

40   See *Mt.* 5, 48; I *Thes.* 4, 3; *Eph.* 1, 4.

41   St. Irenaeus, *Adversus Haeresses* IV, 28, 4: *PG* 7, 1, 200.

42   *Rom.* 12, 2.

43   See I *Jn.* 1, 7.

44   *Phil.* 2, 12.

45   *Phil.* 4, 7.

46   I *Cor.* 10, 12.

47   See *Col.* 1, 24.

48   *Mt.* 5, 16.

Address of Pope Paul VI to the Society of Italian Catholic Jurists, December 9, 1972.

1   Address of Oct. 29, 1951.

2   *Pastoral Constitution on the Church in the World of Today*, nos. 27 and 51.

3   *Ibid.*, no. 51.

4   *Ibid.*

5   See *Dig.*, 26, 27, 42. "Guardian of the womb."

Declaration on Abortion Issued by the Sacred Congregation for the Doctrine of the Faith, November 18, 1974.

1   A number of bishops' statements are to be found in G. Caprile, *Non uccidere. Il Magistero della Chiesa sull'aborto*, Part II, pp. 47-300, Rome, 1973.

2   *Regiminis Ecclesiae Universae* III, 1, no. 29. See ibid., no. 31: *AAS* 59 (1967), 897 [*TPS* XII, 401] : "All matters concerning the doc-

trine of faith and morals, or connected with the faith, pertain to this congregation."

3   *Dogmatic Constitiution on the Church*, no. 12: *AAS* 57 (1965), 16-17 [*TPS* X, 369-370]. The present Declaration does not heal with all questions pertaining to abortion; it is up to theologians to examine and discuss these. Only certain basic principles are recalled here; these will be a guide and rule for the theologians and help all Christians deepen their certainty concerning some important points of Catholic teaching.

4   *Dogmatic Constitution on the Church*, no. 25: *AAS* 57 (1965), 29-31 [*TPS* X, 380-31].

5   The authors of Scripture do not make any philosophical observations about when the soul is infused, but they do speak of the period of life, preceding birth as being the object of God's attention: God creates and forms man, shaping him as it were with His own hands. The first expression of this theme seems to be in *Jer.* 1, 5, but it appears in many other texts as well: see (*Is.* 49, 13; 46, 3; *Jb.* 10, 8-12; *Ps.* 22, 10; 71, 6; 139, 13. In *Lk.* 1, 44 we read: "The moment your greeting sounded in may ears, the baby leapt in my womb for joy."

6   *Didache Apostolorum*, V, 2, ed. Funk, *Patres Apostolici*, I, 17; *Epistola Barnabae*, XIX, 5, expresses the same idea (Funk, op. mem. I, 91-93).

7   Athenagoras, *Legatio pro christianis*, 35: *PG* 6, 970; SC 3, pp. 166-167. See also *Ep. ad Diognetum*, V, 6 (Funk, op. mem. I, 399; *SC* 63), where it says of Christians: "They procreate children, but they do not reject the fetus."

8   Tertullian, *Apologeticum* IX, 8: PL I, 314-320: *Corp. Christ.* I, p. 103, l, 31-36.

9   Canon 21 (Mansi, 14, col. 909). See Council of Elvira, canon 63 (Mansi, 2, col. 16) and the Council of Ancyra, canon 21 (ibid., 519). See also the decree of Gregory III regarding the penance to be imposed upon those guilty of this crime (Mansi, 12, p. 292, canon 17).

10   Gratian, *Concordia discordiantium canonum*, chap. 2, canon 20, q. 5. During the Middle Ages appeal was often made to the authority of St. Augustine, who wrote as follows regarding this matter in *De nuptiis et concupiscentiis*, chap. 15: "Sometimes this sexually indulgent cruelty or this cruel sexual indulgence goes so far as to procure potions which produce sterility. If the desired result is not achieved, the mother terminates the life and expels the fetus which was in her womb, so that the child dies before having lived or, if the baby was living already in its mother's womb, it is killed before being born" (*PL* 44, 423-424; *CSEL* 42, p. 230; see the Decree of Gratian, chap. 32, q. 2, c. 7).

11   *In IV Sententiarum* dist. 31, exposition of the text.

12   Constitution *Effraenatum*, 1588 (*Bullarium Romanum*, V, 1, pp. 25-27; *Fontes Iuris Canonici*, I, no. 165, pp. 308-311).

13   DS 2134 (1184). See also the constitution *Apostolicae Sedis* of Pius IX; *Acta Pii* IX, V, 55-72: ASS 5 (1869), pp. 287-312; *Fontes Iuris Canonici*, III, no. 552, pp. 24-31.

14   Encyc. *Casti Connubii*: *AAS* 22 (1930), 562-565; DS 3719-21 (2242-2244).

15 The statements of Pius XII are definite, precise and numerous; they would require a whole study on their own. We quote only this one from the discourse to the St. Luke Union of Italian Doctors of Nov. 12, 1944: "As long as a man is not guilty, his life is untouchable, and therefore any act directly tending to destroy it is illicit, whether such destruction is intended as an end in itself or only as a means to an end; whether it is a question of life in the embryonic state, in a stage of full development or already in its final stages" (*Discorsi e Radiomessaggi*, VI, p. 191).

16   Encyc. *Mater et Magistra*: *AAS* 53 (1961), 557 [TPS VII, 331].

17   *Constitution on the Church in the World of Today*, II, chap. 1, no. 51: *AAS* 58 (1966), 1072 [*TPS* XI, 293]; see no. 27: ibid., 1047 [*TPS* XI, 275-276].

18   Allocution *Salutiamo con paterna effusione*, Dec. 9, 1972: *AAS* 64 (1972) 777 [*TPS* XVII, 333]. Among the statements on this unchangeable teaching the declaration of the Holy Office condemning direct abortion is especially important: AAS 17 (1884), 555-556; 22 (1888-1890), 748; DS 3258 (1890).

19   The present Declaration deliberately leaves untouched the question of the moment when the spiritual soul is infused. The tradition is not unanimous in its answer and authors hold different views: some think animation occurs in the first moment of life, others that it occurs only after implantation. But science really cannot decide the question, since the very existence of an immortal soul is not a subject for scientific inquiry; the question is a philosophical one. For two reasons the moral position taken here on abortion does not depend on the answer to that question: 1) even if it is assumed that animation comes at a later point, the life of the fetus is nonetheless incipiently *human* (as the biological sciences make clear); it prepares the way for and requires the infusion of the soul, which will complete the nature received from the parents; 2) if the infusion of the soul at the very first moment is at least *probable* (and the contrary will in fact never be established with certainty), then to take the life of the fetus is at least to run the *risk* of killing a human being who is not merely awaiting but is already in possession of a human soul.

20   Tertullian, cited in footnote 8.

21   Cardinal Jean Villot, Secretary of State, wrote on October 10, 1973, to Cardinal Julius Döpfner regarding the protection of human life: "[The Church] cannot however approve the use of contraceptives, much less abortion, as morally acceptable soulutions to these difficult problems" (*L'Oss. Rom.*, German edition, Oct. 25, 1973, p. 3).

22   Encyc. *Pacem in Terris: AAS* 55 (1963), 267 ff. [*TPS* IX, 211].

23   *Constitution on the Church in the World of Today*, no. 48: *AAS* 58 (1966), 1068 [*TPS* XI, 290]: "By their natural character the institution of marriage and married love are ordained for the procreation and bringing up of children." Likewise no. 50: *AAS* 58 (1966), 1070 [*TPS* XI, 292]: "Marriage and conjugal love are by their nature ordained toward the procreation and education of children."

24   *Constitution on the Church in the World of Today*, nos. 50-51: *AAS* 58 (1966), 1070-1073 [*TPS* XI, 292-293]. Paul VI, encyc. *Humanae Vitae*, no. 10: *AAS* 60 (1968), 487 [*TPS* XIII, 334-335]. Responsible parenthood implies that only licit means will be used in determining the number of children. See *Humanae Vitae*, no. 14: *AAS* 60 (1968), 490 [*TPS* XIII, 336-337].

25   *Constitution on the Church in the World of Today*, no. 87: *AAS* 58 (1966), 1110-1111 [*TPS* XI, 319-320]. Paul VI, encyc. *Populorium Progressio*, no. 31: *AAS* 59 (1967), 272 [*TPS* XII, 154]; address to the United Nations: *AAS* 57 (1965), 883 [*TPS* XI, 55-56]. John XXIII, *Mater et Magistra: AAS* 53 (1961), 445-448 [TPS VII, 330-332].

26   Cardinal Jean Villot, Secretary of State, wrote to the World Congress of Catholic Doctors at Barcelona, May 26, 1974: "Human life is certainly not a one-dimensional reality but may rather be likened to a bundle of lives. The levels of its being, connected as they are by relations of dependence and interaction, cannot be reduced to some one elementary kind of life without doing them serious harm. There are the bodily, affective, and rational levels, as well as that depth of the soul wherein the divine life, received through grace, can unfold by means of the gifts of the Holy Spirit" (*L'Oss. Rom.*, May 29, 1974).

Address of Pope Paul VI to the Convention of the Union of Italian Catholic Jurists, December 8, 1974.

1   Pope Paul VI, *La vostra visita: Address to the Italian Society of Obstetricians and Gynecologists*, October 29, 1966; *AAS* (1966), 1168.

Declaration on Certain Questions Concerning Sexual Ethics, December 29, 1975.

1   *Decree on the Apostolate of Laity*, no. 9.

2   *Lk.* 23, 49.

3   *Lk.* 24, 1-10.

Address of Pope Paul VI to the Study Commission on Women, January 31, 1976.

1   Cf. Second Vatican Ecumenical Council, Constitiution on the Church in the Modern World *Gaudium et Spes*, 47: AAS 58 (1966), p. 1067.

2   Cf. Apostolic Constitution Regimini Ecclesiae Universae, 29 (August 15, 1967): AAS 59 (1967), p. 897.

3   Gaudium et Spes, 16: AAS 58 (1966), p. 1037.

4   Jn 8:12.

5   Second Vatican Ecumenical Council, Declaration *Dignitatis Humanae*, 3: AAS 58 (1966), p. 931.

6   Tim 3:15.

7   Dignitatis Humanae, 14: AAS 58 (1966), p. 940; cf. Pius XI, Encyclical Letter *Casti Connubii*, December 31, 1930: AAS 22 (1930), pp. 579-580; Pius XII, Allocution of November 2, 1954: AAS 46 (1954), pp. 671-672; John XXIII, Encyclical Letter *Mater et Magistra*, May 15, 1961: AAS 53 (1961), p. 457; Paul VI, Encyclical Letter *Humanae Vitae*, 4, July 25, 1968: AAS 60 (1968), p. 483.

8   Cf. Second Vatican Ecumenical Council, Declaration *Gravissimum Educationis*, 1, 8: AAS 58 (1966), pp. 729-730; 734-736. *Gaudium et Spes*, 29, 60, 67: AAS 58 (1966), pp. 1048-1049, 1080-1081, 1088-1089.

9   *Gaudium et Spes*, 51: AAS 58 (1966), p. 1072.

10   Ibid,; cf. also 49: loc. cit, pp. 1069-1070.

11   Ibid., 49, 50: loc. cit., pp. 1069-1072.

12   The present Declaration does not go into further detail regarding the norms of sexual life within marriage; these norms have been clearly taught in the Encyclical Letters *Casti Connubii* and *Humanae Vitae*.

13   Cf. Mt 19:4-6.

14   1 Cor 7:9.

15   Cf. Eph 5:25-32.

16   Sexual intercourse outside marriage is formally condemned: 1 Cor 5:1; 6:9; 7:2; 10:8; Eph 5:5; 1 Tim 1:10; Heb 13:4; and with explicit reasons: 1 Cor 6:12-20.

17   Cf. Innocent IV, Letter *Sub catholica professione*, March 6, 1254, DS 835; Pius II, *Propos. damn. in Ep. Cum sicut accepimus*, November 14, 1459. DS 1367; Decrees of the Holy Office, September 24, 1665, DS 2045; March 2, 1679, DS 2148. Pius XI, Encyclical Letter *Casti Connubii*, December 31, 1930: AAS 22 (1930) pp. 558-559.

18   Rom 1:24-27; "That is why God left them to their filthy enjoyments and the practices with which they dishonor their own bodies, since they have given up divine truth for a lie and have worshipped and served creatures instead of the creator, who is blessed for ever. Amen! That is why God has abandoned them to degrading passions: why their women have turned from natural intercourse to unnatural practices and why their menfolk have given up natural intercourse to be consumed with passion for each other, men doing shameless things with men and getting an appropriate reward for their perversion" See also what Saint Paul says of masculorum concubitores in 1 Cor 6:10; 1 Tim 1:10.

19   Cf. Leo IX, Letter *Ad splendidum nitentis*, in the year 1054: DS 687-688, Decree of the Holy Office, March 2, 1679: DS 2149; Pius XII, *Allocutio*, October 8, 1953: AAS 45 (1953), pp. 667-678; May 19, 1956: AAS 48 (1956), pp. 472-473.

20   Gaudium et Spes, 51: AAS 58 (1966), p. 1072.

21   ". . .if sociological surveys are useful for better discovering the thought patterns of the people of a particular place, the axnieties and needs of those to whom we proclaim the word of God, and also the opposition made to it by modern reasoning through the widespread notion that outside science there exists no legitimate form of knowledge, still the conclusions draw from such surveys could not of themselves constitute a determining criterion of truth," Paul VI, Apostolic Exhortation *Quinque iam anni*, December 8, 1970, AAS 63 (1971), p. 102.

22   Mt 22:38, 40.

23   Mt 19:16-19.

24   Cf. note 17 and 19 above: Decree of the Holy Office, March 18, 1666, DS 2060; Paul VI, Encyclical Letter *Humanae Vitae*, 13, 14: AAS 60 (1968), pp. 489-496.

25   1 Sam 16:7.

26   Paul VI, Encyclical Letter *Humanae Vitae*, 29: AAS 60 (1968), p. 501.

27   Cf. 1 Cor 7:7, 34; Council of Trent, Session XXIV, can. 10: DS 1810; Second Vatican Council, Constitution Lumen Gentium, 42, 43, 44: AAS 57 (1965), pp. 47-51; Synod of Bishops, De Sacerdotio Ministeriali, part II,4, b: AAS 63 (1971), pp. 915-916.

28   Mt 5:28.

29   Cf. Gal 5:19-23; 1 Cor 6:9-11.

30   1 Thess 4:3-8; cf. Col 3:5-7; 1 Tim 1:10.

31   Eph 5:3-8; cf. 4:18-19.

32   1 Cor 6:15, 18-20.

33   Cf. Rom 7;23.

34   Cf. Rom 7:24-25.

35   Cf. Rom 8:2.

36   Rom 6:12.

37   1 Jn 5:19.

38   Cf. 1 Cor 10:13.

39   Eph 6:11.

40   Cf. Eph 6:15, 18.

41   Cf. 1 Cor 9:27.

Address of Pope Paul VI to the Sacred Roman Rota, February 9, 1976.

1   See the *Pastoral Constitution on the Church in the World of Today*, nos. 47-48.

2   See *Mt.* 19, 4-6; H. Denzinger and A. Schönmetzer; *Enchiridion Symbolorum* (32nd ed.; Freiburg, 1963), nos. 643, 756, 1497, 1813, 3701, 3713.

3   *Pastoral Constitution on the Church in the World of Today*, no. 48.

4   See *Eph.* 5, 25.

5   Pope Paul VI, Encyclical Letter *Humanae Vitae*, no. 9.

To Live in Christ Jesus, Selection from A Pastoral Reflection on the Moral Life, by National Conference of Catholic Bishops, November 11, 1976.

44 Many of the matters treated here have been discussed in detail in papal and conciliar documents, documents of the Holy See and the Synods of Bishops, and statements of national episcopal conferences. The references which follow note a few of the sources.

45 Vatican Council II, *The Church in the Modern World*, 25.

46 Cf. *Gn.* 2:24.

47 *Ho.* 2:21-29.

48 Cf. *Eph.* 5:25-32.

49 Cf. *Mt.* 19:10-12.

50 *Eph.* 5:25.

51 Cf. Vatical Council II, *The Church in the Modern World*, 48.

52 *Eph.* 4:15.

53 Vatican Council II, *The Church in the Modern World*, 50.

54 Cf. *Humanae Vitae*, 12, 13.

55 Cf. Vatican Council II, *The Church in the Modern World*, 52; *Humanae Vitae*, 24.

56 Cf. Sacred Congregation for the Doctrine of the Faith, *Declaration on Certain Questions Concerning Sexual Ethics*, Dec. 29, 1975.

57 Cf. 1 *Cor.* 6:9-10, 18.

58 Cf. United States Catholic Conference, *Society and the Aged: Toward Reconciliation*, May 5, 1976.

59 1 *Tim.* 5:8.

60 Vatican Council II, *The Church in the Modern World*, 26.

61 Cf. Vatican Council II, *The Church in the Modern World*, 51.

62 National Conference of Catholic Bishops, *Pastoral Plan for Pro-Life Activities*, November 20, 1975.

63 *Eph.* 5:25.

Address of Pope Paul VI to the Congress of the Italian Women's Center, December 6, 1976.

    1   *Pastoral Constitution on the Church in the World of Today,* no. 9.

    2   *Acts* 1, 14.

    3   See *Lk.* 8, 2-3.

    4   *Mt.* 28, 1-10; *Mk* 16, 1-8; *Lk* 24, 1-11, 22-23; *Jn.* 20; 1-2, 11-18.

    5   *Acts* 1, 14.

    6   *Rom.* 16, 1-2, 12; *Phil* 4, 2-3; *Col* 4, 15; see 1 *Cor* 11, 5a; 1 *Tim.* 5, 16.

    7   *Eph.* 5, 25.

    8   *Pastoral Constitution on the Church in the World of Today,* no. 60.

    9   See *Gn.* 1, 26-27.